Disorienting Neoliberalism

Disorienting Neoliberalism

Global Justice and the Outer Limit of Freedom

BENJAMIN L. MCKEAN

OXFORD
UNIVERSITY PRESS

OXFORD
UNIVERSITY PRESS

Oxford University Press is a department of the University of Oxford. It furthers
the University's objective of excellence in research, scholarship, and education
by publishing worldwide. Oxford is a registered trade mark of Oxford University
Press in the UK and certain other countries.

Published in the United States of America by Oxford University Press
198 Madison Avenue, New York, NY 10016, United States of America.

First issued as an Oxford University Press paperback, 2022

Library of Congress Cataloging-in-Publication Data
Names: McKean, Benjamin Laing, 1980– author.
Title: Disorienting neoliberalism : global justice and the outer limit of freedom / Benjamin McKean.
Description: New York : Oxford University Press, 2020. |
Includes bibliographical references and index.
Identifiers: LCCN 2020018719 (print) | LCCN 2020018720 (ebook) |
ISBN 9780190087807 (hardback) | ISBN 9780190087821 (epub) |
ISBN 9780190087814 | ISBN 9780190087838 |
ISBN 9780197674192 (paperback)
Subjects: LCSH: Neoliberalism. | Free enterprise. | Social problems. | Social justice. | Globalization.
Classification: LCC HB95 .M384 2020 (print) | LCC HB95 (ebook) | DDC 330.01—dc23
LC record available at https://lccn.loc.gov/2020018719
LC ebook record available at https://lccn.loc.gov/2020018720

3 5 7 9 8 6 4 2

Paperback printed by Marquis, Canada

Contents

Introduction

Injustice in a Disorienting World

In December 2012, just north of Dhaka, Bangladesh, a fire started on the ground floor of a garment factory named Tazreen Fashions. Even though it was late on a Saturday night, hundreds of workers were in the factory, making clothes for US corporations like Walmart, Disney, and Sears. When smoke began to drift up through the factory, managers ordered workers to stay at their sewing machines. One survivor later testified, "Our production manager . . . pulled down the collapsible gate on the third floor, forcing us to continue working. We pleaded with him to let us out, but [he] assured us that nothing was wrong and we should keep working. He told us not to listen to any rumors. He said again, 'Nothing has happened, just keep working.'"[1] Workers who disobeyed and tried to leave found that there were no emergency exits and even the regular exit was locked during business hours. To escape the flames, workers jumped out of windows from five floors up, breaking their legs and spines. At least 125 people died, with more than 200 injured.[2] Seeking compensation from the US corporations whose products he sewed, another survivor who leaped from the building testified, "I was the only earning member [in my family]. My brother stopped studying because of my accident and now works as a daily wage laborer. I have not done any work since the accident because the doctor told me not to do any heavy work. I still have to spend money on medicines. I cannot sit on the floor anymore."[3] In the end, after years of pressure from worker activists, Walmart finally contributed just $250,000 to the fund set up to compensate the hundreds of survivors and families of those died.[4]

The fire at Tazreen Fashions was not only a tragedy but an injustice. Such avoidable catastrophes are a normal part of the global economy as it is currently structured; the International Labour Organization estimates that more than 2.3 million people die from occupational accidents or work-related diseases every year.[5] Indeed, just a few months later, an even worse disaster occurred nine miles away when Rana Plaza, an eight-story commercial

Disorienting Neoliberalism. Benjamin L. McKean, Oxford University Press (2020). © Oxford University Press.
DOI: 10.1093/oso/9780190087807.001.0001.

building with multiple garment factories, collapsed. This disaster took place around 9 a.m., after most workers had already arrived, and killed 1,132 while injuring more than 2,500; workers had pointed out ominous cracks in the building to their managers the previous day but were told to come to work or be fired. While the Tazreen fire drew comparisons with New York City's infamous Triangle Shirtwaist Factory fire of 1911, which killed 146 people, the Rana Plaza collapse was worse by an order of magnitude, the deadliest accident in the history of the global garment industry.[6]

The Rana Plaza collapse is a paradigmatic global injustice not only because the humanitarian scale of the disaster was immense, but also because Bangladesh's garment industry is fully integrated into and dependent on the global economy. Employing more than four million people, Bangaldesh's garment industry is, in turn, a linchpin of the national economy; in defending their industry in the wake of these disasters, manufacturers argued that garments represented 80 percent of Bangladesh's total exports and more than 12 percent of the country's entire GDP for FY 2016.[7] Politicians and factory owners see the industry's success in the global economy as dependent on low costs, so when workers have gone on strike to demand better wages and working conditions, garment manufacturers have collaborated with the government of Bangladesh to violently repress them—killing some workers, imprisoning hundreds more, and firing thousands.[8]

If you're like me, you probably find thinking about this unsettling. The injustice of the situation is not only obvious but urgent and ongoing; while circumstances have improved since 2013, workers in Bangladesh still struggle for safe working conditions and better wages while the garment industry continues to resist even modest reform efforts.[9] I want to do my part to stop this injustice. But what can I do? The problem seems far away and the solutions unclear. Workers are dying making clothes for US corporations to sell in the United States. As a US citizen and as an apparel consumer, I feel connected to the injustice, but the nature of that connection seems complicated and difficult to grasp. I have my own problems to attend to and my own work to do—none of it as urgent as these daily injustices, of course, but pressing enough for me to wonder if I really have a responsibility to do anything, especially when I feel largely powerless in relation to the social, political, and economic structures that I inhabit. Even when I have had the opportunity to take some action—for example, signing a petition to Walmart executives or leafleting in front of a Disney store—I sometimes have to wonder if what I did was meaningful. I'm left uneasy, with a bad conscience about living my life amid injustice and unsure not only about what I should do but about how I should think about my circumstances.

Questions about what global justice requires have been a hot topic in political theory for quite some time, yet these particular practical questions about what global justice means for individuals in our unjust world still lack satisfactory answers. This is not entirely surprising. For one thing, globalization is complicated, making it difficult to understand what is happening, much less what to do about it. Economists, political scientists, sociologists, and others debate almost every claim about the global economy, from the effect of trade agreements like the North American Free Trade Agreement (NAFTA) to the employment impact of immigration. Many political theorists and philosophers respond by trying to bracket the global economy's complexity. Some offer works of ideal theory that consider what fully just institutions would look like, putting aside questions about how we get there from here; others suggest this complexity is largely irrelevant to our urgent, humanitarian duty to meet the needs of the world's poorest.

When theorists and philosophers do evaluate the justice of the global economy, their standard approach takes as its starting point the fact that most residents of the developed world have more resources and better life chances than residents of the developing world and asks if this inequality can be justified. This standard approach to global justice, which I aim to critique and transform in this book, owes its structure to the egalitarian liberal political philosophy of John Rawls. Rawls self-consciously saw himself as extending and updating the liberal social contract tradition and one of his major contributions is formulating the "difference principle," which requires that social and economic inequalities be to the greatest benefit of the least advantaged members of society. Consequently, political theorists have often debated whether or not post-Rawlsian egalitarian convictions about social justice should be extended by analogy to the world as a whole or defended as normatively best when confined to domestic politics. Those who defend global egalitarianism debate whether distributive justice is always owed to humanity as a whole or required only on account of contemporary international political institutions and economic interdependence; those who defend limiting distributive justice to the state argue about whether that is due to the nature of sovereignty or national culture or some other unique feature of domestic politics. As a result, much egalitarian political theory about global justice remains structured by its origin in the challenge Charles Beitz first posed in 1975: Is it morally permissible to ensure a fair domestic distribution of wealth while ignoring glaring international inequalities?[10] As critics like Raymond Geuss have pointed out, though, the ascendance of distributive justice within political theory has coincided with its retreat in the actual politics of the Global North.[11] Arguably, we are further than ever from realizing the difference principle on any scale.

This standard approach is plainly inadequate for answering the questions I want to ask about injustice in the global economy. Looking at the general level of inequality is important but insufficient for understanding my particular relation to garment workers in Bangladesh. It doesn't capture the specific injustices done in the production of garments so it doesn't help me think about my own relation to those particular wrongs. What's more, focusing entirely on the ways in which Americans are better off than Bangladeshis overlooks the fact that many Americans also experience the contemporary global economy as unjust.[12] For forty years, American income inequality increased while median wages stagnated.[13] At the same time, much manufacturing that had been done in the United States was either automated or moved abroad—a process that only intensified in the wake of permanent normal trade relations with China. US manufacturing employment declined by nearly one-fifth between 2001 and 2007.[14] Workers and their communities scarcely had time to recover before the 2008 global financial crisis hit, raising the national unemployment rate to 10 percent and causing the net worth of Americans to drop by a third; on average, an American worker could expect to earn $150,000 less over their lifetime as a result of the crisis.[15] European workers also suffered significantly in the years after the crisis. Eurozone GDP per capita declined from 2007 to 2015. The unemployment rate in the Eurozone as a whole stood at 13 percent in 2014 while countries like Spain and Greece saw their unemployment rates spike over twice that.[16] The causes of this crisis were intimately tied to a global economy increasingly reliant on financial markets and products like mortgage-backed securities and derivative options; products like these ultimately bankrupted the investment bank Bear Stearns, dramatically heralding the global crisis.[17] Even as millions of American homeowners were forced out of their homes by foreclosure, political elites authorized massive state spending and intervention to save the financial industry, all justified by appeals to the necessity of sustaining markets and liquidity.[18] Any account of global justice that overlooks these developments ignores the experiences of workers across the globe and will have a hard time guiding action. This book is an effort to show that we can do better if we take as our starting point the recognition that many people in both Bangladesh and the United States have an interest in changing the institutions that govern the global economy.

Within contemporary American politics, globalization is often framed as though we face a choice between the existing global economy and autarky. This false choice disguises the fact that the contemporary terms of global economic integration are shaped by *neoliberalism*, an influential political theory that defines freedom as choice in the market and asserts the creation and sustaining of markets as the primary value of politics. Beginning in earnest in the 1970s, just as Rawls was publishing his *Theory of Justice*, neoliberal thinkers and their followers became key policymakers in domestic and international political institutions, from the US Federal Reserve to the International Monetary Fund (IMF) and World Trade Organization (WTO).[19] Legitimated by their shared, market-centered vision of freedom and politics, they pursued policies that made capital mobility and transnational supply chains centerpieces of the global economy, giving rise to injustices like the Tazreen fire and the Rana Plaza collapse. Meanwhile, following neoliberal prescriptions, states shifted their domestic policies from a Keynesian consensus on public spending aimed at softening economic turmoil and hardship to austerity policies that cut welfare spending in order to minimize budget deficits. Consumers in the developed world faced increasing precarity even as they were able to buy ever cheaper t-shirts.

The global economy does not need to be conducted on these terms. Seeing economic inequalities in the United States as related to injustices in Bangladesh through these neoliberal policies and institutions opens up possibilities for theorizing that many theorists of global justice have passed over. Grasping the transnational connections between these injustices doesn't add a layer of complexity to otherwise comprehensible domestic problems, but is essential for properly understanding both the injustices themselves and how to combat them. Appreciating these complicated political and economic relations need not lead to practical paralysis. On the contrary, people want to understand the forces that shape their lives and constrain their freedom. Theories of global justice can satisfy this desire by giving an account of how people should *orient* themselves to the most important features of the global economy, helping us to identify shared interests and build coalitions that can actually achieve global justice. However, little of the existing literature on global justice addresses this need.[20] The standard approach provides little immediate guidance for responding to current catastrophe; meanwhile, those who urge a humanitarian approach to global suffering overlook the political nature of our relations, framing my motivation as altruistic concern unrelated to how the global economy touches my own interests. Meanwhile, the robust literature on neoliberalism is essential for understanding the institutions of the contemporary global economy, but it lacks a normative framework for understanding our political responsibilities to combat their injustice.

My aim in this book is to bring these literatures together in order to provide an *orientation* to the neoliberal global economy that can facilitate actions to resist and replace it with the aim of better realizing egalitarian justice. Being effectively oriented to one's political circumstances requires accounting for three features:

1. how social and political arrangements operate;
2. how those operations are generally made intelligible and legitimate to those subject to them; and
3. the normative values that one's actions should promote in the context of (1) and (2).

When effectively oriented, individuals can undertake actions that they believe meaningfully contribute to realizing their values in light of their actual circumstances. In this book, I aim to provide accounts of these three features so that readers can better orient themselves to their own role in the global economy. These features are interrelated. Understanding my circumstances is not a matter of being acquainted with bare facts, but requires some judgment of their meaning. Interpretive work separating significant from peripheral aspects of our circumstances invariably employs normative concepts—not just whether we think something is good or bad, freeing or oppressive, but whether it is appropriately described as a matter of politics at all.

On the account of orientation I offer, the operations of the global economy today are (2) made intelligible and legitimate to those subject to them by neoliberalism, which asserts the primacy of the economy as a realm of life. For neoliberalism, political institutions are legitimate to the extent that they contribute to the creation and functioning of markets, but largely illegitimate when they pursue other aims. The paradigm of individual freedom is choice in the market; guided by this value, individuals can navigate even traditionally non-economic realms of life thinking of themselves as consumers or entrepreneurs. Within political institutions, neoliberal theory has served to justify policies creating and sustaining pervasive domestic austerity, capital mobility, and transnational supply chains. However, if we attend carefully to (1) the actual operations of the global economy, we can see that they diverge from neoliberal theory in important ways that reveal other political possibilities. I look specifically at transnational supply chains and show how they are better described as political institutions that govern the workers and consumers subject to them rather than the free exchanges of neoliberal theory.

Those who want to contest the authority of these institutions and resist global injustice can be guided by (3) an account of freedom as the capacity of individuals to affirm the institutions that have shaped us as those we could have freely chosen. Such freedom is denied to those who developed under and are habituated by unjust institutions, but it can serve as a critical ideal to orient efforts to resist them. For example, many people in Bangladesh and the United States can see each other as partners in a movement to resist an unjust global economy because of the way it impairs their freedom, in diverse ways. Such resistance will not be in the interest of everyone; some people are not subject to unjust institutions, but rather claim authority within them. But for those who experience their freedom as constrained, their shared interest in transforming the global economy should lead them to be disposed to solidarity with the others who are also subject to those unjust institutions and practices, even when those relations cross state borders.

Social change requires coalitions of people of diverse social and political statuses working together. My conception of freedom reflects this, both in its applications and in its sources, by drawing from the work of G. W. F. Hegel, John Rawls, W. E. B. Du Bois, Gloria Anzaldúa, Theodor Adorno, Iris Marion Young, and others. Most individuals lack the power to influence institutions on their own and can only take effective political action as part of a movement; consequently, an account of orientation also has to be one that can be adopted widely enough to facilitate the participation of many different people. My account accordingly offers a significant rereading of the egalitarian liberal tradition that frames much contemporary writing on global justice in order to develop a view that can be supported by the multiple political traditions that share an interest in resisting neoliberalism, including egalitarian liberalism, Marxism, critical race theory, and feminist theory.

Such a coalition of egalitarian views is both possible and necessary in light of how neoliberalism orients us to existing inequality. Earlier laissez faire justifications of economic inequality treated politics and the economy as independent realms, holding that great material inequality was compatible with political equality. Because of this presumption of independence, Marx could position himself as unmasking a hidden truth about the relationship between liberalism and capitalism by revealing the unfreedom of real economic inequality concealed by formally equal citizenship rights.[21] Such an unmasking presumes the political sphere to at least appear to be a place for robust expressions of freedom. But unlike laissez faire views, neoliberalism already proclaims that politics is determined by economic motives because all activity is understood as fundamentally economic; there is thus nothing to unmask and the space for *internal* critique of neoliberal freedom is accordingly limited.

Because it explicitly subordinates the political to the economic, neoliberalism no longer pits the liberal defense of rights against the Marxist unmasking of the limits of formal rights.[22] When consumer choice is exalted as a superior expression of freedom to political action, the limits of formal rights in the face of economic power prevail as common knowledge that liberals and Marxists alike can lament. Egalitarian critics of neoliberalism share an interest in *reorienting* our view and inverting the normative valence of this common sense, so that the contemporary impotence of public collective action relative to the market becomes a critique of the status quo rather than its validation. Under neoliberalism, all those concerned with economic inequality have a reason to want to repoliticize the economy, to show that it is not best understood as a realm characterized by private individuals making free choices but one where some people claim authority over others and where we can and should collectively decide to organize our relations to each other differently.

Now is an especially auspicious time to propose an alternative orientation. In the long wake of the 2008 financial crisis, many of the institutions and individuals who were responsible for enacting neoliberal policies have begun to question the efficacy of their own prescriptions. Two years before the crisis, Larry Summers, the former Chief Economist of the World Bank and US Treasury Secretary, commemorated the passing of Milton Friedman, the great popularizer of neoliberalism, by writing, "We are all Friedmanites now"—avowing neoliberalism's political hegemony by explicitly contrasting this state of affairs with Richard Nixon's 1971 description of himself as a Keynesian when that allegiance was de rigueur. Neoliberalism's crumbling self-evidence a decade later can be measured by Summers's shift to arguing— in the pages of the *Financial Times*, no less—that populists were actually right to see globalization as "a project carried out by elites for elites with little consideration for the interests of ordinary people."[23] Two months later, the June 2016 issue of the IMF's own quarterly magazine ran an article by three members of its research department titled "Neoliberalism: Oversold?" that critiqued the inequality and instability caused by austerity and capital mobility.[24]

The futility of discussing global justice in isolation from real world developments was made abundantly clear by the election of Donald Trump to the US presidency in 2016. Explicitly running against globalization, Trump won the electoral college on the strength of better-than-expected performance in Wisconsin, Michigan, and Pennsylvania—states where many believe Trump's promises to bring jobs "back" from Mexico and China made the difference. Once in office, Trump withdrew the United States from the Trans-Pacific Partnership and renegotiated NAFTA on terms that he sees as more favorable.[25] While the Trump administration's other policies largely offer clear continuities with neoliberal agendas, the discursive break with elite consensus about global economic integration makes proceeding as though globalization unambiguously benefits Americans and the victims of global injustice reside entirely in the developing world seem more blinkered than ever.[26] Even neoliberalism's defenders have lost their confidence in Margaret Thatcher's slogan "There is No Alternative"; no one can take for granted the stability of neoliberal institutions if people who grow up under them do not reliably develop into subjects willing to identify their freedom with the market.

Critique as Reorientation

To many worried about really existing global injustice, the development of an alternative orientation may seem like an unnecessary detour. Who needs political theory to know that Bangladeshi garment workers shouldn't have to risk their lives to make as little as $68 a month?[27] In this section, I aim to address such skepticism by showing how political theory can be of use here. Both those who doubt the utility of normative theorizing and those who doubt the importance of empirical developments for understanding justice overlook the role that political theory can play as a source of *orientation* to the world. The need for orientation is especially clear when we consider the difference between the scale of the global economy and our everyday experiences. As Samuel Scheffler points out, "An emphasis on the significance for human affairs of various large-scale global developments and dynamics—economic, political, technological, and environmental—does not translate in any obvious way into a determinate picture of how ordinary individuals should conduct their lives."[28] Trillions of dollars of global trade flows can feel like too much for our understanding to get a grip on; the numbers are too different from those that we encounter in our everyday lives. An orientation addresses this experience by identifying the features of our world that we should regard as the most salient for judgments about how to act within it. When properly oriented, individuals find the institutional context of their action comprehensible and can act accordingly, confident that their actions are meaningful and appropriate (though, of course, their success cannot be guaranteed).

When I suggest that political theory can and should guide action, I don't mean that political theory can or should provide a "to do" list for political action or a set of rules that, if followed, would put one beyond reproach. The kind of guidance it can provide is different. Explaining his view of what political theory can do, Geuss writes, "My interest is in the practical coherence of a certain general framework for orienting political action in the contemporary world."[29] Geuss, an acid critic of Rawlsian liberalism, thinks this interest separates his "political realism" from other approaches to political theory, but in *Justice as Fairness: A Restatement*, Rawls himself calls orientation one of the primary practical aims of political philosophy. Geuss is right that egalitarian liberals have rarely centered this practical aim in their theorizing, but Rawls's avowal of orientation as a central aim suggests that this failure is better understood not as the result of an error with their philosophical methodology, as Geuss and others argue, but as a political shortcoming by their own lights.[30]

The shortcomings of egalitarian liberalism as a source of orientation are nicely illustrated by a 2013 op-ed by conservative Senator Ted Cruz, which asserted that "We should assess policy with a Rawlsian lens, asking how it affects those least well-off among us."[31] Yet Cruz's orientation was explicitly anti-egalitarian and he concluded, "Conservative policies help those struggling to climb the economic ladder, and liberal policies hurt them." Taking the difference principle as a way of seeing, Cruz nevertheless argued against the redistribution Rawls supported and in favor of neoliberal policies that interpret entrepreneurship as the highest form of citizenship. Cruz's argument shows how, taken as a normative principle in isolation, the difference principle may fail to orient us to even great inequality as an injustice; it needs to be connected to some particular understanding of existing institutions in order to serve a critical function. Rawls recognized this need in his call for orientation, but he failed to meet it; by providing (3) a guiding normative value without properly accounting for (1) how political and social institutions operate and (2) are legitimated, the actions that follow from his theory are importantly undetermined.[32]

The account of orientation that I offer here, in part by rectifying Rawls's view, thus begins the book's work of developing an account that can be endorsed by multiple egalitarian traditions in political theory. Rawls writes, "The members of any civilized society need a conception that enables them to understand themselves as members having a certain political status—in a democracy, that of equal citizenship—and how this status affects their relation to their social world. This need political philosophy may try to answer, and this role I call that of orientation."[33] Given the daunting complexity of modern society, it is very difficult to judge what those arrangements require of me; internationally but also domestically, I take part in a system of cooperative interdependence in which I am not able to understand all the details of the social functions I rely on and contribute to. An orientation can help us comprehend our relation to existing institutions by giving an account of our political status and the typical relationships between our status and the political status of others. This can make the complex interdependence of society comprehensible by describing a role that it is feasible for individuals to play and which helps them meet their obligations. In Rawls's example, in a modern democracy, each person contributes something different to the functioning of social institutions, but it is understood that they share the political status of citizen and this shapes how people perceive each other and how they understand themselves. An orientation thus helps individuals navigate their world by giving them a general picture of where they stand and how they ought to see the others who share their world. Ideally, in a well-ordered society, orientation would come easily; most people would not need to make any special efforts to see themselves and others as citizens with equal political status, for example.

Notably, though, an orientation is not meant to work only in ideal societies, but is meant to help us understand how to act today. An orientation does not provide a road map to a society where equality is fully realized, but it puts existing inequality in perspective, enabling us to identify and act against injustice more effectively. When oriented by our role as citizens, we perceive and treat others as the political equals they ought to be, even though many Americans do not enjoy descriptively equal political status due to factors like their race, gender, and sexuality. Though it may not be easily acquired in a society that reinforces racial hierarchy in many subtle and unsubtle ways, an orientation to equal status is appropriate: it promotes values that are embedded in our political institutions but imperfectly realized and, by leading us to treat others as they deserve to be treated, promotes the fuller realization of political equality.[34]

In order to facilitate effective action that promotes genuine equality, an orientation cannot simply lead people to act as though such equality already exists; formally equal treatment can allow persistent racial disadvantage to remain unaddressed so an effective orientation must acknowledge these real inequalities. Consequently, one must be oriented to (1) the factual existence of entrenched hierarchy, (2) its legitimation, and (3) the normatively equal status others ought to enjoy. In the United States, an effective orientation considers (3) the normative value of political equality in the context of (1) the actual operation of the United States' inegalitarian and hierarchical political and social institutions that, for example, reproduce the racial wealth gap, and (2) the legitimation of those institutions by appeals to formal equality; this facilitates the promotion of political equality in ways that do not legitimate and entrench existing inequality. For white people, this may require developing an alienation from the habitual attitudes that they have developed in the course of their experiences of social institutions that have largely treated them as equals. In such circumstances, those who experience oppression are in a better epistemic position to perceive how institutions operate while those who are privileged with respect to that oppression may be easily oriented to overlook the obstacles to equality that remain for others; W. E. B. Du Bois's conceptions of "second sight" and "the veil" provide an important account of this, as I discuss in chapter 4. When it comes to neoliberalism and global justice, we likewise need to understand (1) the global economy's most important empirical features; (2) the orientations which most readily arise from our interactions with those features and which tend to legitimate them; and the institutions' relationship with (3) the values we want to realize.

A shared orientation does not replace the need to exercise judgment about strategy and tactics, but prepares the way for such judgments to be shared by ensuring people attend to the same features of the political landscape. Thus a widespread orientation to equal status will make some potential political actions seems obviously incoherent or inappropriate without leading everyone to converge on precisely the same actions as best; political movements, after all, do not require internal unanimity to succeed, though they do need their disagreements to be mutually intelligible against a shared background of empirical and normative assumptions. Because of these practical uses, a political theory is not only a collection of arguments which can be judged sound or unsound but also a kind of practice to be judged more pragmatically—one that facilitates particular forms of action by describing a way of understanding our political status. Such descriptions can transform our self-understanding in a way that disposes us to act in certain manners and to see and treat others in a particular fashion as a result. Political theories need not consciously aim at orienting us in order to do so; they can (and often do) provide material for our self-conceptions without themselves offering a theory of self-conceptions. However, making such material explicit can be illuminating. Evidence that a theory has the resources to describe and promote an effective orientation to our social world should weigh in favor of adopting it. I hope that the account I give in what follows passes this test.

Overview of the Book

So, how should I be oriented to the Bangladeshi workers in garment factories struggling for better wages and working conditions? Because egalitarian liberal theorists of global justice have largely overlooked the neoliberal transformation of the world economy that has taken place since Rawls published *A Theory of Justice* in 1971, they have not met the need for an orientation to contemporary international politics.[35] Many theorists of global justice offer persuasive arguments that existing global institutions are sufficiently consequential that distributive justice requires some concern for relative equality beyond state borders.[36] But these arguments focus on institutional rules and omit any guidance for individuals, aside from a general exhortation to bring about more just institutions. As Scheffler puts it, we still lack "a set of clear, action-guiding, and psychologically feasible principles which would enable individuals to orient themselves in relation to the larger [global] processes, and general conformity to which would serve to regulate those processes and their effects in a morally satisfactory way"—and he proclaims himself doubtful that anything is forthcoming to meet this need.[37] One reason why such concepts are both needed and hard to find is the apparent complexity of my international political statuses. For example, simply being a citizen of the United States means that I have some political status in relation to many important international issues; the United States plays a key role in sustaining the international trade regime that makes it possible for me to buy garments made elsewhere, for example. Beyond that, the United States is also a member of many international organizations and some, like the IMF, influence the governance of other countries. Sometimes individuals are even given standing directly by these arrangements; trade agreements now standardly include investor–state dispute settlement, for example, which permits investors of signatory nations to sue the states party to it for laws that affect the profitability of their investments.[38] Each of these features affects my political status, since it makes me subject to some institutions and even grants me some share of authority over others.

Equal citizenship doesn't seem to readily orient us to these circumstances. Some egalitarian liberals conclude from this that the global economy isn't properly a political domain. But it is equally clear that purely economic roles, like that of the consumer, are insufficient to orient us; the choices that many want—for example, to buy clothes made in safe conditions by workers who enjoy a living wage and freedom of association—aren't available while the choices that are available are often contrary to one's own economic interests as a worker. In such circumstances, consumer choice hardly feels like an expression of freedom, as neoliberalism claims. Understanding how we ought to act in the global economy requires a new set of orienting roles which are rooted in people's current experiences but incorporate different self-understandings that more readily dispose people to resist injustice.

With that larger aim of the book in mind, I'd like to explain its structure and provide a brief chapter-by-chapter overview of its contents, with an eye to the multiple theoretical traditions I hope to address. Chapter 1 substantiates my interpretation of the neoliberal theory of political legitimacy through a reconstruction of the views of Friedrich Hayek and Milton Friedman, whose works were key to popularizing neoliberalism and its attendant orientation. Even people who have not read Hayek or Friedman live in conditions and institutions that were shaped by them and, as a result, have been habituated to their way of seeing. As the economy has increasingly adopted neoliberal policies and employment has become experienced as correspondingly precarious, it makes more and more practical sense for individuals to adopt the neoliberal conception of themselves as entrepreneurs who experience freedom in the market. The task for those who want to resist neoliberalism is to provide people in such circumstances with another way of attending to their situation. I begin this work by considering neoliberal theory's own account of what leads individuals to adopt a neoliberal orientation and show

how it relies on an understanding of power that troubles their efforts to separate an economic realm of freedom from a political realm of coercion.

It is in this context that I undertake a detailed look at transnational supply chains in chapter 2 to make visible their actual operation, which diverge from that neoliberal way of dividing up and legitimating the political and economic realms. Focusing on the impressive mobility of multinational corporations and the extensive dispersal of their supply chains across the globe often leads analysts to assume that supply chains exemplify neoliberal market exchange. In practice, supply chains diverge significantly from the vision of spontaneous, self-organizing market activity and more closely resemble the kind of economic planning neoliberal theorists ostensibly decry. When pressed to explain these prevalent economic forms, even neoliberals concede that economic activity is not only dependent on extraeconomic coercion from the political realm, but itself shot through with claims to authority. Workers and consumers who are subject to supply chains can contest these claims to authority—in the first place, by insisting on their right to freedom of association with each other—and thus begin to repoliticize the economic realm that neoliberals seek to encase. The appropriate metaphor here is not an unmasking, but a reorientation—reinterpreting features of our lives that are already visible so that we understand them differently and attend to them in a different way, noticing new things about them as we approach from different angles. The supply chain is especially useful in this regard because supply chain products are omnipresent in our daily lives. We literally wear the products of supply chains on our backs every day, which helps anchor critique of a global economy that can otherwise be profoundly disorienting.[39]

Sustaining this critique requires a deeper explanation of how freedom can reorient us and so, in chapter 3, I offer an account of freedom that shows how many people can see themselves as having an interest in reforming or replacing unjust institutions. The injustices of the global economy vary around the world, from the physical and sexual abuse of workers in the factories of global supply chains to diminishing the value of political liberties by limiting the ability of states to effectively regulate corporations. Egalitarian liberal theorists have often overlooked these other forms of injustice, which are not well captured by Rawls's difference principle, in favor of debates about the appropriate scope of distributive justice. While diverse, I argue that a common thread among these injustices is that they violate the freedom of individuals. Against the neoliberal understanding of freedom as paradigmatically individual choice in the market, I place individuals' dispositions and habits at the heart of freedom. Taking seriously the effects that social and political institutions have on us before we could ever choose them means that freedom has an essentially retrospective element; a key experience of freedom is the recognition that the institutions which have shaped us are ones we could have freely chosen. Rawls calls this "the outer limit of freedom" and says it is expressed in the habitual attitudes or dispositions that we acquire from just institutions. In a well-ordered society that people perceive as one they can affirm, citizens both meet their political obligations and express their freedom when they are disposed to reciprocity with each other.

This dispositional conception of freedom is one that a range of theoretical traditions can endorse, as I highlight by developing this conception through a reading of both Hegel and Rawls. The egalitarian liberalism to which Rawls gave philosophical voice commands considerable public political support—as indicated by Senator Cruz's effort to lay claim to it—but has not been usefully developed as a source of resistance to neoliberalism. Disentangling the parts of egalitarian liberalism that have served to support a neoliberal status quo from those which have the potential to undermine it is nevertheless worthwhile; as Katrina Forrester observes, "even though parts of liberal philosophy seem to be bound up in the political structure that lay behind the crisis of 2008, others seem well suited to provide solutions to this moment of dramatic inequality, with its longing for universalizing principles."[40] Yet even Rawls partisans may doubt the utility of his work for addressing the questions I've posed; Rawls's most extended work of international political theory describes a world of self-sufficient societies—a vision that he calls a "realistic utopia" and concedes is very different from the world of interdependence and injustice that we face.[41] Against the prevailing understanding of Rawls's work as fundamentally Kantian, I show how an appreciation of the crucial Hegelian dimensions of his thought better helps us understand and act within our own unjust world. By systematically elaborating Rawls's dispositional conception of freedom, egalitarian liberalism can more readily contribute to productive conversations with the wide range of theoretical traditions with roots in Hegel.

Employing this dispositional conception of freedom to repoliticize the economic realm requires more than simply invoking ideal justice or bare assertions of the priority of the political. In order to provide an account of orientation to our unjust circumstances, this account of freedom must confront a tension within it: What is the value of this ideal to those of us who have grown up under unjust institutions and who consequently have not developed freely but instead have been profoundly habituated by unjustified inequality and oppressive hierarchy? In chapter 4, I show how thinkers like Du Bois, Anzaldúa, and Adorno transform the dispositional conception of freedom to navigate unjust circumstances. Those of us alive today will never be able to enjoy the kind of free development possible for people growing up in a just society, but we can still use such an ideal critically to orient ourselves to both constraints on our freedom and opportunities to express the freedom we have. My account can thus be accepted even by those who believe the outer limit of freedom to be a pious wish but concede its diagnostic utility, especially as a way of dislodging neoliberal assumptions that have become widely shared.

Where Hegel considers the influence of political institutions on individuals within just and rational states in which the smooth functioning of political institutions effortlessly produces a patriotic disposition, Du Bois's concept of double consciousness provides tools for extending Hegel's framework to a nonideal world in which institutions have more disparate effects and dispose us to misperceive the normative status of others. By showing how the dispositional conception of freedom could lead whites and blacks to regard each other as partners in efforts to remove the veil of racial injustice, Du Bois illuminates both the role of race in the maintenance of global injustice and the importance of people who stand in different relations to injustice seeing each other rightly. Existing institutions constrain people's freedom in intersecting ways: some are constrained by racism that others benefit from; some who benefit from racism are constrained by sexism; and so on. As I've emphasized, reforming unjust institutions requires forming coalitions across these lines, including across national lines; resisting supply chains requires forming coalitions between factory workers in the developing world and Americans who purchase the goods those workers produce, even though the latter materially benefit from the former's exploitation.

This is why I argue in chapter 5 that bringing about egalitarian justice under neoliberal circumstances first and foremost requires being *disposed to solidarity* with others who are also subject to unjust institutions. When unjust institutions that I am subject to cross state borders, I should regard others who are subject to those institutions as potential partners in efforts to reform or replace those institutions. Seeing them as partners means that I should be alert to appeals to act from those I rely on, open to hearing out claims that I have misperceived their political status, and ready to understand the robustness of my freedom as partly dependent upon theirs. Such solidarity is mutually beneficial because we have a common interest in the removal of some shared obstacle to freedom, such as an exploitative economic system that crosses borders or an international organization that imposes austerity policies on member states without a real possibility of exit. This is grounded in the recognition that reforming or replacing political institutions requires the work of many people. Disposing ourselves in this way thus both shows the appropriate attitude toward others and facilitates the achievement of justice. This may seem to make it difficult to know if one is doing one's duty. However, dispositions maintain an essential connection to action; in an unjust world filled with calls for solidarity, a person who never acts in response to them isn't really disposed appropriately. Practically, this entails participating in and supporting transnational social movements that arise in response to calls for solidarity. Such participation also facilitates the further development of the disposition to solidarity, providing opportunities to become habituated to political action and to accountability to one's political partners, as I detail in the conclusion.

However, given the inadequacies in the global justice literature that I have highlighted, many who embrace egalitarian views are skeptical about transnational social movements and seek instead to promote social justice within domestic politics alone. We can see this in the widespread view that reasserting unconstrained sovereignty is essential to resisting neoliberalism; that view is expressed in politics in the arguments for so-called Lexit (that is, self-described left-wing arguments for the United Kingdom to leave the European Union) and within political theory by those who endorse egalitarian liberalism but who deny international institutions like supply chains give rise to duties of justice. Consequently, in chapter 6, I look at how skeptics of global justice depoliticize the market by associating coercion constitutively with the state. Contemporary philosophers like Thomas Nagel and Michael Blake develop views that suggest state coercion and distributive justice are necessarily coextensive; they argue that distributive justice is only possible thanks to state coercion and that distributive justice is necessary to legitimate state coercion. Ultimately, by appealing to unconstrained state sovereignty as necessary for politics, this approach homogenizes state power and consequently overlooks the different ways people experience its force, such as racial disparities in the use of force by police. Such a theory is ill-suited for understanding what equal political status actually requires, even domestically.

In the book's conclusion, I consider widespread dispositions to resentment and pity that can appear to motivate resistance to neoliberalism and show why they too fall short and shore up unjustified hierarchies. While political theory and philosophy can help with understanding and critiquing dispositions to resentment and pity that reinforce inequality, dislodging them is not work for philosophy alone. But individuals are not on their own when they cultivate more just dispositions. I close by arguing that the disposition to solidarity can become prevalent by looking at the crucial role that social movements play in making it possible to call for solidarity and to respond to such calls. Participating in social movements can be an attractive expression of freedom for both workers and consumers governed by supply chains and, by repoliticizing neoliberalism, can create additional political possibilities that we cannot yet anticipate. These social movements are a crucial form of political power undertheorized by egalitarian liberals and neoliberals alike. But these groups are an essential part of how social change occurs and justice may be achieved and a theory of dispositional freedom helps account for their importance. If they want to realize their vision, egalitarians should follow the lead of feminist theories of global justice, which self-reflexively consider their relationship to the social movements that spur their theorizing.[42]

As should be abundantly clear to those familiar with her work, my account is particularly indebted to Iris Marion Young and her approach to global justice, which also addresses how consumers should relate to sweatshop workers.[43] Her engaged theorizing, which draws from egalitarian liberalism even while critiquing it, serves as an intellectual model for me. Like egalitarian liberals, Young avowed that "justice is the primary subject of political philosophy," but she argued that they lacked the conceptual tools to realize their ideals.[44] Her critique of the "distributive paradigm" underlying Rawls's difference principle is especially important for this project, which likewise argues that we need to think about the process of production in order to understand the demands of justice.[45] Throughout her career, she was attentive to the importance of social norms and the role that individuals in their everyday life played in reproducing social structures. As a result, Young's concept of politics gives pride of place to the social movements and associational groups that egalitarian liberals too often ignore. She writes, "My aim is to express rigorously and reflectively some of the claims about justice and injustice implicit in the politics of these movements, and to explore their meaning and implications."[46] Considering such movements in our theorizing is essential because it is through them that the values we promote will actually be realized. Sadly, Young was not able to develop her view of global justice completely before her passing, but I draw on her insights throughout this work and further elaborate on the relationship between my view and hers in chapter 5.

1

Neoliberal Theory as a Source of Orientation

In the introduction, I identified neoliberalism as an urgent impediment to global justice. In this chapter, I substantiate this claim by explaining the nature of neoliberal hegemony and showing how the widespread acceptance of neoliberalism as common sense poses a problem for those concerned about injustices like the Rana Plaza collapse. Neoliberalism has been an influential political theory in part because it offers a complete orientation. In the face of a bewildering global economy where money and goods can come from seemingly anywhere, neoliberalism offers a plausible way of understanding the world it has helped to make. Recall that being effectively oriented to one's political circumstances requires accounting for three features: (1) how social and political arrangements actually operate; (2) how those operations are generally made intelligible and legitimate to those subject to them; and (3) the normative values that one's actions should promote. With its vision of (2) efficient markets operating to general material benefit in the long run, neoliberalism suggests that (1) the actual operation of capital mobility and transnational supply chains exemplify free market exchanges while the importance of (3) the individual freedom to choose means an unpredictable market is both a worthwhile price to pay and an entrepreneurial opportunity to be exploited. Through its account of political legitimacy as well as its conception of individual freedom, neoliberalism makes it harder to discern possibilities for resistance—for example, by making injustice appear to be the responsibility of its victims or by making competition seem more natural than cooperation.

In this chapter, my primary aim is to explain how neoliberal theory habituates us to see the institutions of our world as legitimate. Neoliberal theory divides the world up into the economic realm of freedom and the political realm of coercion, but in order to get people to see the world this way, it relies on the techniques of power that Michel Foucault dubbed "governmentality," which escape this neat dichotomy. Neoliberalism's

Disorienting Neoliberalism. Benjamin L. McKean, Oxford University Press (2020). © Oxford University Press.
DOI: 10.1093/oso/9780190087807.001.0001.

tacit acknowledgment of its reliance on these forms of power, which preserve freedom of choice but nevertheless reliably guide people to particular
perceptions and actions, lays the groundwork for an emancipatory reorientation that recognizes the inherently political nature of the economic realm.
Egalitarians of all stripes have reason to resist the neoliberal legitimation of
economic inequality as beyond political contestation. Where Ellen Meiksins
Wood observes in a Marxist register, "the differentiation of the economic is
in fact a differentiation within the political sphere," John Rawls makes the
same point for egalitarian liberals by writing, "the spheres of the political and
public, of the nonpublic and the private, fall out from the content and application of the conception of justice and its principles. If the so-called private
sphere is alleged to be a space exempt from justice, there is no such thing."[1]
Recovering the common sense that the economic realm is ultimately political, rather than vice versa, is indispensable for effectively challenging neoliberal policies. In the next chapter, I pursue that repoliticization by detailing
the operation of transnational supply chains in order to redescribe the neoliberal economic order with an eye on developing an alternative conception of freedom so that people subject to injustice can perceive their shared
interests more readily.

   In pursuing this aim, I should acknowledge that some doubt the analytic
utility of neoliberalism as a term. Originally used by an organized group of
influential economists and social theorists to describe their own market-
oriented views, neoliberalism has become a highly contested term in both
academic and popular discourse. Some have argued that its use has become
so promiscuous as to render the term almost meaningless as anything other
than a pejorative label.[2] And it's true that neoliberalism is a multivalent term,
referring to both a particular historical form of capitalism and a political
theory that offers a new means of justifying capitalism. Because it names
both theory and practice, which often diverge, the term has understandably
generated confusion and skepticism about its utility. However, recent work
tracing neoliberalism's intellectual history has produced a clear and focused
account of its content that is indispensable for orientation to the contemporary global economy.[3] Without some sense of how neoliberalism has shaped
and justified its operations, we will be badly oriented to our circumstances
and less able to act effectively within them.

   Neoliberalism's roots are typically traced to the 1930s, when classical
liberals from the United States and Europe began developing an alternative to the rising popularity of economic planning in the face of the global

economic crisis. Neoliberalism was conceived from the beginning as both a political movement and a school of thought; it was not merely a diffuse trend in thinking, but an organized effort to promulgate particular economic views and policies. In 1938, leading corporate managers, civil servants, and economists gathered at a colloquium in Paris to discuss the popular American columnist Walter Lippmann's widely read 1937 book *An Inquiry into the Principles of the Good Society*, which critiqued economic planning. Among the attendees were economists who would go on to shape the global economic order, including Friedrich Hayek, Ludwig von Mises, Wilhelm Röpke, and Alexander Rüstow.[4] It was at this gathering that the group first began to describe their views as "neoliberal" in opposition to the laissez-faire liberalism that was perceived to have failed and been discredited by the world economic crisis. After the war, Hayek reconvened many members of the group, with notable additions including the economist Milton Friedman, in the Swiss resort town of Mont Pelerin in 1947. There, they continued their efforts to reformulate classical liberalism so that it would be adequate to the complexity of the modern economy and offer a more compelling alternative to the social liberalism that undergirded the New Deal. The Mont Pelerin Society founded at that meeting became one of the most important forums for the development and circulation of neoliberal ideas in the decades to come.[5]

Neoliberalism is thus a self-consciously political project with the aim of putting politics in its place; because it rests on a theory of political legitimacy grounded on factors it deems nonpolitical, it offers the perplexing spectacle of a global political transformation enacted through decisions that are often understood to be technocratic and apolitical.[6] As critics like Wendy Brown have noted, justifications of neoliberal policies typically depoliticize significant areas of policymaking; the expansion of the market is portrayed as necessary while political action is understood to constitute inefficient interference virtually by definition.[7] Unelected, technocratic bodies like central banks derive legitimacy precisely from their *lack* of popular accountability, which purportedly enhances their capacity to exercise objective expertise and resist partisan motives.[8] Yet these neoliberal government actions remain thoroughly political, though we are often oriented to them otherwise. Free trade agreements exemplify this tendency. Popularly understood as technical documents that reduce tariffs, multilateral trade agreements are actually complex political documents that create new enforceable rights—rights to intellectual property, political standing to sue governments, and penalties for domestic regulations that international bodies determine are obstacles to trade.

Neoliberalism's way of seeing the political and economic realms underwrites the pervasive understanding of globalization as an apolitical, technical, even inevitable process outside of our collective control. As the historian of neoliberalism Quinn Slobodian puts it, for neoliberals, the division between the realms of politics and economics is "more fundamental than the purely political distinction of foreign and domestic."[9] On the one hand, neoliberals see state power as necessary for the operation of the market in order to enforce contracts and prevent extralegal violence; on the other hand, neoliberalism does not require states to be authorized by a *demos* in order to be legitimate and the internal logic of markets calls for them to grow beyond state borders to in order to be more efficient and beneficial. Neoliberalism thus endorses a kind of cosmopolitanism about markets—for example, Hayek remarked, "It is neither necessary nor desirable that national boundaries should mark sharp differences in standards of living"—even as it embraces the continued legitimacy of state coercion.[10] Neoliberalism's ambiguous relation to state borders enables its adherents to pursue multiple political strategies to advance their aims. For example, some neoliberals advocate for the European Union (EU) on the grounds that it enables an efficient common market while others were among the leaders of the "Brexit" campaign to leave the EU on the grounds that it constrains the United Kingdom's ability to implement even more market-friendly policies on its own. As I discuss at greater length in chapter 6, for those who wish to resist neoliberalism, it is insufficient to declare oneself for or against the EU or Brexit since neoliberals also seek to advance their own policies on both sides—and given their institutional power, they are in position to do so. Anyone concerned to effectively resist economic exploitation and inequality needs to provide alternatives to the neoliberal way of dividing up and describing the political and economic realms by engaging in what Nancy Fraser calls "boundary struggles" to redraw this organizing distinction.[11]

Neoliberal Transformations

For the purposes of my account, three neoliberal transformations have been especially significant for thinking about global justice: increased domestic austerity, greater capital mobility, and the prevalence of supply chains.

First, the shift from Keynesian government spending to austerity policies prioritizes reducing public debt as a means of promoting growth. As a result of this strong opposition to certain kinds of government spending, social safety nets are cut and public programs are often privatized.[12] For example, the welfare reform signed by President Bill Clinton cut the number of people receiving federal welfare benefits in half within four years; today just one-quarter of American families with children living in poverty receive welfare in the form of cash assistance.[13] These cuts were justified in part by the idea that it would be easy to find work in the growing US economy of the 1990s. But austerity can also be justified by appeal to the idea that it's important for the government to tighten its belt during lean times; for example, in the wake of 2008 financial crisis, the United Kingdom passed budgets that cut its annual social welfare spending by $36 billion from 2010 to 2020.[14] Notably, from the perspective of global justice, this means that gains from trade are generally not redistributed to those who lose out.[15]

Second, the widespread elimination of capital controls has increased capital mobility without a concomitant change in labor mobility. Both de jure and de facto capital mobility increased significantly from 1980 until the 2008 financial crisis, with foreign ownership growing by an order of magnitude from 1980 to 1984 to 2000 to 2004.[16] The resultant viability of offshoring through foreign investment has made it increasingly difficult to sustain effective national-level regulations while the enhanced ability to engage in speculative investment has also increased the frequency of financial crises.[17] From the neoliberal perspective, constraints on capital mobility are much more serious impediments to freedom than constraints on the movement of persons. Immigration restrictions are compatible with an efficient international division of labor while capital controls are seen as a direct violation of the right to freely engage in economic exchange.[18] Given the size of labor markets within states, neoliberals typically identify trade unions as much more significant obstacles to efficient labor markets than national borders; as we'll see, neoliberal theory has a place for state coercion but no grounds to legitimate collective bargaining or any other kind of collective action by workers.

Finally, we are now long past the time when one could plausibly speak of international trade as "the simple act of exchanging goods," as Michael Blake and Patrick Taylor Smith put it in their survey of the philosophical literature on global justice.[19] Politics has always played a significant role in creating and shaping international markets and making private property rights effective between states. As noted earlier, bilateral and multilateral agreements have now removed many tariffs and other trade barriers while the investor–state dispute settlement systems built into the WTO and other institutions created quasi-judiciary bodies to levy sanctions on countries that enact restrictive policies. Indeed, sometimes geographical areas are literally "depoliticized" to facilitate trade; the Export Processing Zones (EPZs) where supply chain goods are often manufactured generally have separate, business-friendly laws, including severe restrictions on freedom of association and freedom of speech. For example, EPZs in Bangladesh provide foreign investors with specially developed, government-maintained infrastructure along with incentives like decade-long tax holidays and a complete prohibition of trade union activity.[20] The Bangladesh Export Processing Zone Authority (BEPZA) reports directly to the office of the prime minister, who also serves as chair of the BEPZA board; the current executive in charge of BEPZA is also a lieutenant general in the Bangladesh Army, exemplifying the entanglement of state coercion and free trade.[21] By providing special expedited customs processing literally at the factory gate, these EPZs effectively relocate the state border to facilitate business—intensive political activity with the aim of creating a space outside the political realm.[22] Zones that relocate the border to facilitate trade are not unique to the developing world; the United States has 195 active free trade zones that promote the manufacture of cars, electronics, and pharmaceuticals as well as oil refining, among other industries.[23] The remarkable result of all this is that an estimated 80 percent of global trade now consists of supply chains coordinated by multinational corporations.[24] Unlike the image of trade as a fleeting act limited to the moment of transaction, the practice of supply chains sustains much more durable connections.

Taken together, the rise of capital mobility, national austerity, and global supply chains have dramatically reshaped the lives of people throughout the world over the past forty years. Partly as a result of the foregoing, income inequality within developed countries has increased significantly as most workers no longer receive the returns from their improving productivity. In the United States, for example, wages now make up a record low share of GDP.[25] The twenty richest Americans now have as much wealth as the poorest 152 million.[26] The gap continues to widen. In 1965, the CEOs of the 350 largest firms in the United States earned twenty times as much as an average worker; in 2017, CEOs earned 312 times as much.[27] Similar patterns are observed around the world; since 1980, income inequality has increased in every region of the world, varying only by the speed at which it has grown.[28]

These changes in the material conditions of people's lives have contributed to changes in how they understand themselves. As the power of capital has grown and public safety nets have receded, most people have become increasingly exposed to the volatility of the global market. Left to manage their circumstances with less national public assistance, workers have become more tightly linked through international institutions and policies. Yet despite a shared interest in resisting the policies that have disproportionately benefited the very wealthy, these workers are as likely to perceive each other as competitors as potential sources of support and solidarity. Citizens across the political spectrum see that they are increasingly on their own and come to understand themselves as strategic economic actors. It is now entirely unsurprising to come across a liberal *New York Times* columnist despairing about politics because "Whatever your politics, there are activities your tax money supports that I'm sure you find troublesome, if not deplorable" while encouraging readers to act conscientiously in their consumption because "You can vote with your fork . . . and you can do it three times a day."[29] In light of the way that neoliberal policies and institutions have exacerbated inequality and advanced the interests of the wealthy, how have they been able to appear as common sense even to many who have not reaped the benefits?

Market-Based Political Legitimacy

Neoliberalism is sometimes described as a kind of market fundamentalism, but this obscures the fact that it has a theory of politics as a realm subordinate to the economic but necessary for its functions; critics who simply point to the role of government in economic affairs—for example, in sustaining transnational supply chains—as a critique of neoliberalism's assumptions have misunderstood their opponent. For neoliberalism, politics is precisely about coercive institutions that keep order by imprisoning frauds, thieves, and other lawbreakers—not a realm of freedom at all, but ugly, dangerous work that is tolerated because it is unfortunately needed for the economy's functioning. Neoliberals recognize this is not work the market can do itself. In his 1951 article "Neoliberalism and Its Prospects," Milton Friedman explained that classical liberal supporters of laïssez-faire policies "failed to see that there were some functions the price system could not perform and that unless these other functions were somehow provided for, the price system could not discharge effectively the tasks for which it is admirably fitted." The state's task is to provide "a framework within which free competition could flourish and the price system operate effectively."[30] The market is where we enjoy free choice unencumbered by coercion, thanks to the state's dirty work, which must be carefully contained and kept to a minimum using economic tools like cost-benefit analysis. As Thomas Biebricher writes, "What all neoliberals share is the problem of how to identify factors indispensable to the maintenance of functioning markets, since the option of simply leaving them to themselves is no longer on the table."[31] Debates within neoliberalism are organized around the question of how best to accómplish that aim. This too contributes to slippage in the term's use; neoliberalism is defined more by the problem it constructs and tries to solve than by particular solutions to it.

Elevating the protection and sustaining of markets as the highest political aim invariably shapes one's view of what legitimates political institutions.[32] This entails both a negative task of fencing off what state action is illegitimate and a positive account justifying some forceful interventions. We can see the positive side of state action in the definition of neoliberalism offered by the geographer David Harvey, who influentially defines it as "in the first instance a theory of political economic practices that proposes that human well-being can best be advanced by liberating individual entrepreneurial freedoms and skills within an institutional framework characterized by strong private property rights, free markets, and free trade."[33] Economists like Ronald Coase and Gary Becker were key to the development of the policies that defined neoliberalism's institutional framework, but as Harvey's references to "liberating" and "rights" makes clear, neoliberal thinkers did not merely advance particular economic policies, but offered normative and conceptual arguments about freedom and justice to support that agenda. Leading theorists of neoliberalism like Hayek and Friedman argued not only that markets naturally produce efficient, Pareto-optimal outcomes unobtainable through other means, but that the legitimacy of political institutions depended upon their capacity to sustain such markets rather than on political criteria like the consent of the governed.[34]

Having licensed the state in the name of individual freedom to do whatever is necessary to sustain markets, however, neoliberals then must constrain the state's power lest it metastasize. To guard the economic order's apolitical appearance and to strictly delimit the sphere of legitimate political activity, neoliberals portray the economic realm as a space of spontaneous order that needs to be cultivated and protected but not directed or commanded in order to function appropriately. They do this in part by marking that realm as being necessarily beyond human understanding and thus beyond effective control. As Quinn Slobodian puts it, "To disavow the existence or visibility of 'economies' themselves intentionally makes projects of social justice, equality, or redistribution unthinkable. But it does not make power disappear ... Indeed, the invocation of complexity and unknowability is a useful practice of government."[35] We cannot know in advance who wants what or who is willing to supply it at what price; the only way to know what the market wants is to allow it to operate efficiently, trusting that everyone will benefit in the long run. It is thus not entirely surprising to find Milton Friedman promoting neoliberalism in 1951 by announcing, "We have a new faith to offer; it behooves us to make it clear to one and all what that faith is."[36]

After decades of development within neoliberal networks, this combination of economic policies and their justifying normative framework emerged as a key tool to address the legitimacy crisis that arose in the developed world in the 1970s. The postwar order of "embedded liberalism" was under stress from the economic changes wrought by the oil crisis, the end of the gold standard, and high inflation combined with low growth. The terms of global economic integration were in flux as newly decolonized nations contested their subordinate position.[37] In addition, the perceived legitimacy of political institutions had been forcefully questioned by the social movements of the 1960s and 1970s; Nancy Fraser even suggests a "subterranean elective affinity" between neoliberalism and the feminism of the period because they both engaged in "the critique of traditional authority."[38] In the United States, the war in Vietnam and Watergate further eroded the legitimacy of political institutions, but the problem of a legitimation crisis was discussed more widely.[39] In this context, there was a political opportunity for neoliberals to provide a new account of political legitimacy that foregrounded the state's work to maintain markets but did so in the name of individual freedom. Neoliberalism could accordingly position itself as emancipatory even as it provided a new justification for existing hierarchies.

The neoliberal account of individual freedom thus plays a significant political role today and understanding it is crucial to contemporary efforts to achieve global justice. Neoliberal freedom is conceived with a particular view of the individual in mind. Again, neoliberalism offers a different picture of economic life than earlier liberal thinkers; rather than merely being *homo economicus* while in the marketplace and *homo politicus* or *homo familius* the rest of the time, neoliberal thinkers found that all of social and political life, including criminal activity, could be interpreted as a matter of choices made based on expected future returns: voting is not fundamentally different from selecting one's favorite detergent; education is an investment in a child's human capital; families are efforts to reduce the transaction acts of human relations; and so on.[40] Developing a term from Michel Foucault, Wendy Brown calls this neoliberalism's "political rationality...the field of normative reason from which governing is forged."[41] Once one accepts neoliberalism's vision of what constitutes society, then the particular arguments about how society should be governed can be readily accepted.

This way of seeing is facilitated by neoliberalism's epistemological assertion of our necessary ignorance of the market as a whole; not only does this offer a powerful justification for neoliberal economic prescriptions but it also disposes individuals to perceive themselves as wielding economic power when they create demand through their consumption choices while confronting profound uncertainty when supplying their labor to the market. On this view, understanding oneself primarily as a laborer is to identify with the activity where one has the least power; to the extent you want to feel like you are exerting some control over your life, it is more natural to identify primarily as a consumer or entrepreneur. Neoliberalism thus offers a complete orientation to social life, one that explains how institutions work, what legitimates them, and the values one's actions ought to promote.

This way of seeing has had an influence far beyond the circle of those who have read any neoliberal theory. Members of the Mont Pelerin Society would eventually reject the label neoliberal, but others took it up; for example, *Washington Monthly* magazine editor Charles Peters used the label to describe approvingly the liberal movement to accommodate itself to the elections of Ronald Reagan and Margaret Thatcher, though that effort became better known as "Third Way" politics when practiced by Bill Clinton and Tony Blair.[42] Politicians like Gary Hart or Clinton weren't thoroughgoing Hayekians, of course, but they did believe the political ascension of neoliberal policies made it a necessity to limit and reformulate New Deal programs in the terms of the market, thereby accepting the account of political legitimacy endorsed by the Mont Pelerin group and converging on some of the same policies.[43]

Now, as we've seen, the neoliberal legitimation story is itself showing signs of wear and tear, which presents new political opportunities. But those who want to achieve global justice can only take advantage of them if they understand what made neoliberalism appealing in the first place and see how it has transformed the world. In the rest of this chapter, I reconstruct the political theories of Hayek and Friedman and show how they seek to orient people to a market they concede is disorienting by its nature. After laying out their view, I show how and why individuals subject to neoliberal institutions would take up their way of seeing even when those institutions disadvantage them—and how understanding this process can help reorient us.

Becoming Oriented to Neoliberal Institutions

If it ever seemed plausible that—in the famous phrase associated with Thatcher—"there is no alternative" to neoliberalism, this is in part because neoliberalism provides a consistent way of understanding the world it has helped to make. Neoliberalism contains several schools of thought, but Friedrich Hayek and Milton Friedman are undoubtedly its great popularizers.[44] Hayek's book *The Road to Serfdom* became a bestseller shortly after its US publication in 1944, as companies like General Motors bought tens of thousands of copies to distribute to their employees; a condensed summary of the book published in *Reader's Digest* was also widely circulated.[45] The book's US popularity is enduring; more than 100,000 copies were sold in 2010 after the right-wing pundit Glenn Beck devoted an hour of his TV show to praising it.[46] Friedman's 1962 book *Capitalism and Freedom* has similarly sold hundreds of thousands of copies and his profile as a public intellectual was further boosted by the success of his 1980 TV series *Free to Choose*, which was produced with hundreds of thousands of dollars in funding from the Getty Oil Company and the Reader's Digest Association, among others (and telecast on PBS, ironically); the accompanying book was also a bestseller.[47]

Taken together, the work of Hayek and Friedman provides a fully developed orientation that makes sense of the world; within that perspective, neoliberal policies appear freedom-enhancing rather than unjust. This is no easy feat, since a neoliberal orientation has the burden of making people feel that their actions are taking place in a meaningful context while also finding the very unpredictability of the market to be its source of value. Erich Hoppmann, the neoliberal economist appointed to Hayek's chair in Freiburg on his retirement, described the challenge pithily when he wrote, "Uncertainty is the prerequisite of freedom."[48] Writing in the 1940s, Hayek was acutely aware that getting people to take up this perspective was a perpetual project because of their understandable resistance to putting their life

prospects in the hands of forces that they could not influence and that, by definition, had no concern for their well-being. In *The Road to Serfdom*, Hayek
bemoans this "unwillingness to submit to any rule or necessity the *rationale*
of which man does not understand . . . there are fields where this craving for
intelligibility cannot be fully satisfied and where at the same time a refusal to
submit to anything we cannot understand must lead to the destruction of our
civilisation."[49] Though he sees capitalism as the motor of human progress, he
also sees that the experience of capitalism seems only to stoke the desire for
orientation by thwarting it.

How can this popular desire for orientation be met in an inherently
disorienting system? The stakes for resolving this paradox are high, according to Hayek: "It was men's submission to the impersonal forces of the
market that in the past has made possible the growth of a civilisation which
without this could not have developed; it is by thus submitting that we are
every day helping to build something that is greater than anyone of us can
fully comprehend."[50] As this suggests, a neoliberal orientation sets itself two
tasks: on the level of the individual, it reconceives submission to the market as
the archetype of freedom; on the level of the institution, it offers a "sociodicy"
which explains why market forces necessarily produce the best possible
results, despite the fact that no particular outcome can ever be predicted.[51]
The result is a highly effective orientation because it identifies real features of
the world, explains them, and makes it possible to endow one's actions in that
context with meaning. Critics of neoliberalism too often weaken their analysis by failing to grapple with its effectiveness and appeal as an orientation in
favor of polemical denunciation.

Neoliberal freedom is, to echo the title of Friedman's most famous work,
the freedom to choose. But to choose what? Not public goods like clean
air and water or the fraternity that comes from social equality. Rather, it is,
as Hayek puts it, "the possibility of a person's acting according to his own
decisions and plans."[52] This is what Eric MacGilvray aptly calls market
freedom, "freedom to do what you want with what is yours and to enjoy
the rewards or suffer the consequences."[53] The resources you have to enact
a plan; how you came to have the interests and desires that your plan is
meant to satisfy; whatever training you may have received in planning and
decision-making; the outcome of your plan; whether or not you belong to a
class of people who routinely have their plans frustrated while other social
groups typically succeed—all are irrelevant to your freedom. What remains
is a largely formal, negative definition of freedom; the quality and quantity of

the choices available to you make no difference to your freedom so long as no other individual is trying to coerce you into choosing something particular.[54]

Such freedom is deeply individual; Friedman refers to society as "a collection of Robinson Crusoes, as it were."[55] The plans such Crusoes devise are always solo projects; Hayek and Friedman never discuss groups negotiating a plan or devising one together. As Hayek puts it, his view does not "exclude the recognition of social ends," but redescribes them as "a coincidence of individual ends."[56] Though not formally excluded, these accounts clearly orient adherents away from compromise or collaboration in developing a plan and suggest that individuals come to each other with plans and preferences fully formed. In this view, other people figure primarily as threats to freedom because of their potential to coerce us. Hayek defines coercion as "such control of the environment or circumstances of a person by another that, in order to avoid a greater evil, he is forced to act not according to a coherent plan of his own but to serve the ends of another."[57] Freedom is nothing other than the minimization of such coercion; if you are so marginal to society that no one ever formulates the intention to make use of you, you are quite free. As Hayek puts it, "Even if the threat of starvation to me and perhaps to my family impels me to accept a distasteful job at a very low wage . . . I am not coerced."[58] That's because the person offering the low wage did not intentionally impoverish anyone in order to induce him to take the job; the existence of desperately poor people is instead due to the impersonal forces of the market.

From the perspective of neoliberal freedom, all action is either involuntary and coerced by another individual or the voluntary execution of one's own plan, which may include the acceptance of an offer from another individual. A functioning market is, by definition, not a space of coercion because it is a place where individuals voluntarily accept offers from others. In doing so, they give rise to the spontaneous order of the economy, which produces valuable information like prices unobtainable any other way.[59] Neoliberal freedom thus makes individuals responsible for their choices even as it also holds that they cannot control the outcome of the market and that attempts to do are illegitimate.[60] Hayek writes, "The returns of the efforts of each player act as the signs which enable him to contribute to the satisfaction of needs of which he does not know, and to do so by taking advantage of conditions of which he also learns only indirectly through their being reflected in the prices of the factors of production which they use."[61] That means our plans fit together in ways we can never predict and therefore, Hayek argues, the result is beyond judgments of their justice. He writes, "Since only situations which have been created by human will can be called just or unjust, the particulars of a spontaneous order cannot be just or unjust."[62] But such order can be more or less beneficial, depending upon how free they are; the more individuals are free to go through with their plans, the more they can exchange with others on voluntary terms, contributing to the creation of "an overall order so superior to any deliberate organization."[63] This is a key element of neoliberal sociodicy; while the ways of the market are mysterious, its results are nevertheless assuredly good. Recall John Rawls's proposed egalitarian liberal orientation discussed in the introduction, which simplifies the complexity of society by suggesting that our interdependence can be made comprehensible through a focus on equal citizenship. By contrast, a neoliberal orientation reconciles us to an ultimately incomprehensible complexity through an acceptance of its outputs as both the cost of individual freedom and necessary for the advancement of the common good.[64]

In contrast to the bewildering market, neoliberalism sees politics as a realm that is potentially dangerous but capable of being mastered because it is not a spontaneous order like the market but deliberately constituted. Rather than being defined as a space of collective decision-making about a common life, neoliberals are oriented to government in a quasi-Weberian fashion defined by its relation to violence. Conceptually, government is the entity that aspires to a monopoly on coercion; normatively, it is legitimate only when it intentionally uses its coercive power to reduce the threat of coercion from other sources. Hayek writes, "Government is indispensable for the formation of such [social] order only to protect all against coercion and violence from others. But as soon as, to achieve this, government successfully claims the monopoly of coercion and violence, it becomes also the chief threat to individual freedom."[65] Government is never itself an expression of freedom, but at best a tool for the realization of market freedom. Political action is likewise not an expression of freedom but, at best, a form of harm reduction; because it necessarily employs coercion, it is best to engage in it as little as possible.

Because political institutions are, unlike the market, deliberate creations, they are thus evaluable from the perspective of justice—which is determined essentially by compatibility with the market, the locus of freedom. Consequently, political legitimacy derives from successful economic ordering. Employing his distinctive terminology for the study of the market, Hayek writes, "The truth is that catallactics is the science which describes the only overall order that comprehends nearly all mankind, and that the economist is therefore entitled to insist that conduciveness to that order be accepted as a standard by which all particular institutions are judged."[66] A legitimate government does whatever is required to keep the spontaneous order of society operating—like bailing out banks in a liquidity crisis, for example. Of course, all such action must itself be evaluated economically. As Friedman puts it, "In any particular case of proposed intervention, we must make up a balance sheet, listing separately the advantages and disadvantages."[67] This accounting metaphor suggests the pervasiveness of the economic grid for neoliberal orientation, imagining the political actor engaging in calculation like a business executive. Unsurprisingly, neoliberals drawing up such balance sheets tend to find state functions other than coercion to be unnecessary. Hayek distinguishes government's coercive function from "its service functions in which it need merely administer resources placed at its disposal" and, in keeping with neoliberal austerity policies, suggests that many of these could be privatized.[68] Moreover, even though they concede in theory that calculating government coercion should be a matter of carefully weighing specific situations, they argue that in practice, hard limits are required since government is a standing threat to freedom and cannot be trusted. Friedman thus proposes what he calls "package deals . . . self-denying ordinances that limit the objectives we try to pursue through political channels. We should not consider each case on its merits, but lay down broad rules limiting what government may do."[69] But such broad rules can always be bent when the market requires; while Hayek generally praises the rule of law as essential for limiting government action and helping individuals to make plans, he goes so far as to suggest that judges may legitimately depart from the plain meaning of a law when doing so would help to keep the spontaneous order working.[70]

For neoliberals, economics is primary in a deep sense; Friedman calls capitalism "a necessary condition for political freedom" and Hayek similarly says, "only within this system is democracy possible."[71] On their views, economic freedom is the best guarantee that government doesn't overstep its proper function because the concentration of economic power can serve as a counterweight to government power. Inverting the view of government as an institution for organizing collective decision-making about, for example, how to structure economic relations, neoliberals see functioning economic relations as the condition of possibility for free government. Democracy is not, however, necessary for freedom in the neoliberal sense. Hayek specifically contrasts his conception of freedom with "political freedom" and asserts that "it can scarcely be contended that the inhabitants of the District of Columbia . . . do not enjoy full personal liberty" simply because they lack the right to vote for president or Congress; for his part, Friedman simply defines political freedom as "the absence of coercion of a man by his fellow men"—that is, utterly indistinct from market freedom.[72] Indeed, the tumult and unpredictability of democracy can often impede freedom by making it hard to plan whereas a government insulated from the ballot box can sometimes more credibly commit to unpopular economic policies that protect market freedom.[73] Writing in the 1980s, Friedman held out Hong Kong as "the modern exemplar of free markets and limited government," finding it only "somewhat ironic" that there were no elections of any kind there at the time he wrote, since it was ruled directly by a colony governor appointed by the British monarch.[74]

The dispensability—even undesirability—of popular authorization combined with the view that certain kinds of force are not contrary to freedom but rather make freedom possible produces an orientation that normalizes obvious injustices.[75] For example, overthrowing democratically elected governments that refuse to endorse neoliberal conceptions of property rights can appear not as violating important political freedoms, but as making possible the preconditions for markets in which freedom can finally be enjoyed.[76] Even when an injustice is acknowledged, the neoliberal view rules out action to end it. Friedman was just one of many neoliberals who publicly opposed the demand for universal suffrage in apartheid South Africa; both Friedman and Hayek saw sanctions on Rhodesia and South Africa as much graver threats to freedom than apartheid itself. On their view, the state employing unjustified coercion to enforce segregation is regrettable but unsurprising; excessive force is only to be expected from the state and so apartheid is, in principle, no different than enforcing "equal pay for equal work" laws.[77] Hayek accordingly saw criticism of apartheid South Africa as "international character assassination" and worried that "arbitrary measures" like economic sanctions to protest apartheid "have begun to destroy the international economic order" because they represented the politicization of the economy—a line not to be crossed under any circumstances.[78]

Once one accepts the fundamental neoliberal division between economic action as expressive of freedom and political action as necessary coercion, then it becomes implausible to orient oneself to others primarily through the lens of equal citizenship, even as the state remains an essential institution. Friedman frames political participation as less free than consumerism, writing, "When you enter the voting booth once a year, you almost always vote for a package rather than for specific items . . . you will at best get both the items you favored and the ones you opposed but regarded as on balance less important. Generally, you end up with something different from what you thought you voted for." Market freedom, by contrast, can be exercised all the time with much more success: "When you vote daily in the supermarket, you get precisely what you voted for, and so does everyone else."[79] Even during World War II, Hayek went so far as to write, "We have no intention of making a fetish of democracy" since "there has often been much more cultural and spiritual freedom under an autocratic rule than under some democracies."[80] In short, the effectiveness and predictability of government coercion in ordering the economy is more important to freedom than the popular authorization of that coercion. What might lead those subject to political institutions to adopt a view that minimizes the importance of their authorization? And how might they now come to see those institutions otherwise?

Becoming Oriented to Neoliberal Individuals

For people accustomed to think of democracy and political equality as obviously good things, the appeal of this neoliberal orientation may seem puzzling, especially since the material benefits of neoliberal policies largely accrue to the already wealthy. What would lead ordinary people to identify their freedom with the market? At the heart of this appeal is a conception of freedom that allows almost everyone to avoid the ignominy of oppression by saying they are free. Most people do not feel politically empowered; governments' unresponsiveness to the interests and demands of working people has only been exacerbated by the growth of inequality in recent decades.[81] The worry for egalitarians is that inequality can become self-reinforcing as people who feel politically impotent find it better fits their experience to identify their agency with choices in the market, making neoliberal views into common sense. Neoliberals are as aware of this as anyone. Neoliberalism needs people to see the world in a particular way and accept its self-description as freedom-promoting in order for its policies and institutions to function stably. Such self-understanding is easily facilitated for people like supply chain managers who are empowered to make consequential market choices, but for people who more frequently experience themselves as subject to economic institutions rather than exercising authority within them, this may not be the case. Subjects that refuse to identify their freedom with entrepreneurial endeavor and instead associate freedom with democratic decision-making will find the neoliberalism insulation of market rights from majority rule a limit on freedom. Even if they do not actively resist neoliberal policies, such subjects may perform their market functions poorly by being "bad" workers or consumers—a serious problem from the perspective of a theory that identifies maximizing the common good with market efficiencies.

Though they see coercion as the central tool of politics, neoliberals recognize that you cannot directly coerce individuals to adopt an orientation. Friedman notes, "In both games and society also, no set of rules can prevail unless most participants most of the time conform to them without external sanctions."[82] So how can individuals be induced to take up this way of seeing? Hayek argues, essentially, that the experience of living under neoliberal institutions can make one into a properly oriented neoliberal subject who will submit to the market. As he pithily puts it, "Competition is as much a method for breeding certain types of mind as anything else."[83] Competition shapes the mind because of what it forces people to focus on and how it forces them to act or suffer the consequences of losing—though the necessity that prompts people to act does not count as coercion. Hayek acknowledges an element of bait and switch here; people seek freedom and get discipline along with it. Hayek says, "It may well be that the benefits we receive from the liberty of all do not derive from what most people recognize as its effects; it may even be that liberty exercises its beneficial effects as much through the discipline it imposes on us as through the more visible opportunities it offers."[84] That means it is essential to neoliberalism that people be free without a safety net; otherwise, there will be insufficient self-discipline. As Friedman writes, "Indeed, it is important to preserve freedom only for people who are willing to practice self-denial, for otherwise freedom degenerates into license and irresponsibility."[85] A social safety net allows people to avoid the consequences of their decisions.

While the market is the ideal source of discipline and might even be a sufficient source of discipline in an fully neoliberal society, neoliberals also need an account of how to acquire the political power needed to bring that society about—as well as how to encourage self-discipline in a society where the safety net is not yet fully dismantled.[86] Neoliberalism is thus necessarily concerned with social norms, which cannot simply be coerced into being but must be inculcated. As Melinda Cooper has argued, this has led neoliberals to form a political coalition with social conservatives, who are likewise committed to supporting social norms that forbid "license" and reinforce social hierarchies. Neoliberals are generally skeptical about noncoercive state functions, but they enthusiastically embraced state spending to promote marriage precisely on the grounds that it was the most cost-effective means to promote the kind of responsibility that the market requires.[87]

We can reconcile this role for disciplining social norms with the emancipatory spirit of neoliberalism's emphasis on individual freedom by turning to Michel Foucault's concept of governmentality. As Foucault, an early and significant analyst of neoliberalism, puts it, "'governmentality' implies the relationship of the self to itself, and I intend this concept of 'governmentality' to cover the whole range of practices that constitute, define, organize, and instrumentalize the strategies that individuals in their freedom can use in dealing with each other."[88] Governmentality thus takes us beyond the use of coercion and force into less obvious techniques for conducting the actions of subjects by shaping their self-understanding, their orientation, and the habits they adopt. By setting up institutions in particular ways, providing certain incentives, and so on, behavior can be governed and particular outcomes produced without commanding individuals to choose a particular course of action. As Cooper writes, "Neoliberals may well be in favor of the decriminalization of drugs, sodomy, bathhouses, and prostitution . . . Yet, their apparent moral indifference comes with the proviso that the costs of such behavior must be fully borne in private."[89] In other words, state coercion to prohibit certain kinds of markets is unjustified in principle, but political and social institutions can be arranged so that the costs of certain behaviors are prohibitive to the individuals who engage in them, bringing freedom and discipline together. For example, you are free to be gay, but if your family kicks you out of the house for it, there will be no safety net to catch you; once you're homeless, you're free to make money by engaging in sex work, but if you are infected with a disease as a result, there will be no public health insurance to treat you; and so on.

These ways of directing behavior are of particular interest to neoliberals because they are means of governing people that are formally compatible with free choice and so can be disavowed as exercises of political power understood as state coercion. In his 1978–1979 lectures at the Collège de France, Foucault draws a helpful contrast with earlier laissez-faire thinkers, for whom "from the point of view of a theory of government, *homo oeconomicus* is the person who must be let alone." By contrast, for neoliberals, "*homo oeconomicus*, that is to say, the person who accepts reality or who responds systematically to modifications in the variables of the environment, appears precisely as someone manageable, someone who responds systematically to systematic modifications artificially introduced into the environment. *Homo oeconomicus* is someone who is eminently governable."[90] Just as we earlier saw that neoliberalism could shape political institutions and claim the result to be outside politics, here we see neoliberalism reckon with the need to shape the individuals who are subject to it so that they act predictably and comply—and, because their vision of freedom narrowly focuses on the freedom to choose, institutional influence on their character and choice-making capacities does not appear as a constraint on freedom or an exercise of political power.

By using techniques for governing behavior that go beyond the coercion that formally defines political power for them, neoliberals believe that a market system can be both free and stable because people living under properly operating market institutions will internalize their norms and come to find complying with them congenial, even though it involves self-denial. Being constantly subject to the competitive order shapes one's view of life outside the market as well, as one employs its political rationality to understand society as a whole. Foucault described how, for neoliberalism, "the economic grid . . . involves anchoring and justifying a permanent political criticism of political and governmental action."[91] Neoliberals see only one realm of human life; they employ "the generalization of the economic form of the market beyond monetary exchanges . . . as a principle of intelligibility and a principle of decipherment of social relationships and individual behavior."[92] The economic grid interposes itself as a new kind of veil between all relations; Hayek notes, "The ultimate ends of the activities of reasonable beings are never economic. Strictly speaking there is no 'economic motive' but only economic factors conditioning our striving for other ends."[93] Once we recognize this, we will orient our behavior in a similar fashion throughout our lives, understanding freedom as choosing among the options we are presented with rather than changing them. We are free to navigate our circumstances, but powerless to change them.[94] Thus, we can and should conduct our choosing without considering anything other than our preferences and the need to submit to the market and the law. Friedman says, "The participant in a competitive market has no appreciable power to alter terms of exchange; he is hardly visible as a separate entity; hence it is hard to argue that he has any 'social responsibility' except that which is shared by all citizens to obey the law of the land and to live according to his lights."[95]

By seeking to redefine responsibility to others as the imperative to be above all a responsible market actor, neoliberalism changes the self-understanding of those subject to its institutions. I've already argued a neoliberal orientation disposes us to identify with the role of the consumer, which we can more readily identify with the exercise of power and control, rather than the role of worker, where we face a disorienting market and uncertain demand for our labor. However, an effective neoliberal orientation cannot entirely bracket that experience since people who need to sell their labor for income need some way to understand it. Here, Gary Becker's theory of "human capital" provides the resources to reinterpret it in a consistent way.[96] Like supply chains, references to human capital are now nearly ubiquitous, but in his 1978–1979 lectures, Foucault pointed out how significant a shift in understanding one's relationship to the economy it is when the distinction between capital and labor becomes simply the omnipresence of capital. Labor is no longer a uniquely human factor in the economy, but simply one more input that can produce a return. As Foucault explains, to identify oneself directly as a form of capital "is not a conception of labor power; it is a conception of capital-ability which, according to diverse variables, receives a certain income that is a wage, an income-wage, so that the worker himself appears as a sort of enterprise for himself."[97] In other words, every individual is first and foremost a firm of one—a natural entrepreneur who engages above all not in exchanges but in investments.

Why would workers come to identify as, in effect, bosses of themselves? Again, one should not discount the appeal of the theory itself.[98] When taken as a way of understanding the world, human capital theory offers a picture in which individuals can define their own interests and choose to pursue them. Moreover, conceiving of one's daily labor as a form of entrepreneurship can lend an air of potentiality to what might otherwise be drudgery. The business management guru Tom Peters exhorts, "a janitor does not need a 'flashy website.' But a janitor's attention to craft and distinction will always be the key to her/his personal brand, and ensure employment long-term, whether with one employer or a string of them."[99] To be a brand rather than a laborer expands the amount of life interpretable through an economic grid, but in a world where one is forced to compete, it can also imbue actions that might otherwise be understood as undertaken out of necessity with a different kind of meaning and import. My activity's meaning is not determined by the present, but by its future returns, which always remain mine to imagine; it may look like I'm just trying to earn a black belt in Six Sigma quality assurance or working as a janitor, but I know what I'm doing is saving up to get an education and then a higher paying job, or getting by while I work on promoting my personal brand on Twitter—or even just working on my own individual brand *qua* janitor.

This ability to renarrate our lives to make ourselves the protagonist no matter what happens can have a deep appeal—one that is not diminished but rather enhanced by personal, social, and economic crises.[100] This enables neoliberal theory and practice to reinforce each other. As social safety nets in many developed countries were removed over the course of the 1970s, 1980s, and 1990s, individuals were in fact forced to act more and more on their own. Employment relations themselves have become increasingly precarious, as larger and larger portions of the US workforce are treated as independent contractors and forced to cobble together employment from part-time jobs and task-based payment in the "gig economy."[101] In an exemplary instance of economic governmentality, apps now routinely require customers to rate the independent contractor who performed the task they requested, such as giving a ride, and if the driver's rating gets too low, they will kicked off the system and out of work.[102] As Peters's comment suggests, developing a personal brand has effectively become a requirement for many jobs, from high status positions to those typically classed as unskilled labor; for example, while nannies and babysitters used to find work through word of mouth, they now must maintain sophisticated online presences to get jobs as a result of online marketplaces like Care.com.[103] In short, workers really are increasingly treated as entrepreneurs and held individually responsible for the economic outcome of their labor.[104] Consequently, as policies became increasingly neoliberal, human capital theory became a more plausible and even attractive way of understanding how one actually needs to behave in the world. Education has also increasingly reinforced this view, as children become habituated to standardized assessment and are instructed from an early age to see schoolwork as an investment in their future income—a view further naturalized by the staggering amount of debt they're likely to take on to pay for college.[105]

Such neoliberal reorientations are not limited to the developed world. As Bangladesh, China, Vietnam, and other countries developed large export-oriented manufacturing sectors, workers driven from the countryside into the city for employment have also come to regard themselves as neoliberal free agents. Newspapers and magazines aimed at migrants tell lurid stories with the moral that, in the city, no one is looking out for anyone but themselves; exploitative Ponzi schemes provide apparent opportunities for entrepreneurship while preaching that wealth is a sign of virtue; to get ahead in both the job market and the marriage market, they pay for special classes aimed at developing their human capital and are taught that "We are all in the sales business . . . We are selling ourselves."[106] This sense that everyone must act as an entrepreneur to get by is intensified by the incredible turnover in the factories of transnational supply chains. Studies suggest that turnover in factories owned by Foxconn Technology Group, the world's leading personal electronics manufacturer, is roughly 5 percent *per week*, with a majority of workers employed in the same factory for less than six months at a time.[107] Similarly, a majority of workers in the factories that produce electronics for Hewlett-Packard are contract or "agency" workers, hired as temporary employees for a month or two at a time.[108] Factories show little loyalty to workers and workers show little loyalty in return. As a result, workers are frequently in a position where they must demonstrate their exceptional human capital to human resources professionals so they can be hired again. Adopting a neoliberal orientation is an understandable—and readily available—means of navigating these circumstances.

Collectively Reorienting Ourselves

To recap, neoliberalism offers a complete orientation to society that explains (1) how social and political arrangements actually operate; (2) how those operations are generally made intelligible and legitimate to those subject to them; and (3) the normative values that one's actions should promote. From this perspective, (1) social life is fundamentally a competitive order maintained by a coercive government, an arrangement that (2) produces the best possible material outcomes in the long run, however unpredictable it is in the short run, and which protects (3) individual freedom, exemplified by consumer choice and entrepreneurial activity. As societies become increasingly competitive, this orientation becomes correspondingly plausible. Part of why it can be difficult to resist neoliberalism is that this view orients us most effectively to individuals and coercive institutions, leaving other forms of social organization marginal; there are no intermediate associations, except occasionally the family, no way of combining and exercising strength in numbers, except perhaps as consumers who share similar tastes. Hayek says, "A Great Society has nothing to do with, and is in fact irreconcilable with 'solidarity' in the true sense of unitedness in the pursuit of known common goals. If we all occasionally feel that it is a good thing to have a common purpose with our fellows, and enjoy a sense of elation when we can act as members of a group aiming at common ends, this is an instinct which we have inherited from tribal society."[109] Instead of changing the principles that govern our social institutions, we should submit and be grateful for them: "It is precisely because in the cosmos of the market we all constantly receive benefits which we have not deserved in any moral sense that we are under an obligation also to accept equally undeserved diminutions of our incomes. Our only moral title to what the market gives us we have earned by submitting to those rules which makes the formation of the market order possible."[110] For neoliberals, we simply have no standing to object to the global economy; complaints about injustice are not only out of place but reveal our ingratitude.

For those who believe existing inequality is unjust and the neoliberal conception of freedom is inadequate, the task is to reorient ourselves to a world that does in fact increasingly resemble a competitive order in a way that instead disposes us to solidarity, recognizing opportunities to cooperate in the promotion of a shared interest in resisting neoliberalism. In concluding this chapter, my suggestion is that the neoliberal acknowledgment of politically important of forms of power other than state coercion points to elements of social life that can be redescribed to highlight opportunities for cooperation and free association. In other words, the awkward fit between neoliberalism's political rationality and its governmentality creates opportunities for reorientation and resistance. While the neoliberal orientation centers on economic individuals and a coercive state, acknowledging the significance of social norms and governmentality can also orient us to other social actors, like social movements, and that recognition can be used to redraw the boundaries of the political.

We can see this in Milton Friedman's 1962 description of segregated institutions and his opposition to civil rights legislation in *Capitalism and Freedom*. Friedman's account here is strikingly individualizing and suggests that the primary actors are individual consumers and the coercive state. When Friedman writes about "grocery stores serving a neighborhood inhabited by people who have a strong aversion to being waited on by Negro clerks," he sees only the freedom of white people to choose in conformity with their "preference" or "taste" for segregation and the potential for government coercion in the form of fair employment legislation to in-terfere with the exercise of such market freedom.[111] Friedman does not at-tend to how or why white people may have developed such a "taste," since that is regarded as irrelevant to questions of justice. Nor does he consider the forms of nonstate coercion that whites exercised both on blacks and whites to maintain social norms of segregation even where it was not legally enforced. Nor, finally, does he mention the forms of direct political action that the civil rights movement engaged in like sit-ins and boycotts that targeted businesses without appealing to government.

Recognizing that noncoercive forms of power, including social norms, are essential to the market but are not themselves market activity implies three things that are inconvenient for a neoliberal orientation: first, the realm of politics extends beyond state coercion; second, cooperation can be a way to achieve a common aim, as with collective action to change norms; and third, nonstate actors may appropriately exercise authority over others, making claims about how they have a responsibility to act. These features of social life do not necessarily contradict neoliberalism's political rationality but Friedman minimizes them in his description of Jim Crow precisely because centering them in one's orientation readily lends itself to seeing things like ac-cess to businesses as a political matter of public accommodation, not private taste. This is not an internal critique of neoliberalism; reorienting ourselves to these features effectively will require breaking with the neoliberal concep-tion of freedom and offering a different account of freedom's value. But it does suggest elements of social life that people experience and that can be revalued. These are features where the neoliberal orientation is least effective at guiding action—where the operations of society least resemble the com-petitive order of market exchange and where, consequently, neoliberalism's legitimating story and normative values are less obviously relevant. When neoliberals argue that certain forms of governmentality are justified or that certain social norms should be collectively promoted, they are acknowl-edging places where their view of the legitimacy of existing social and polit-ical institutions can most readily be contested. In the next chapter, I pursue this strategy specifically with regard to transnational supply chains and show how a look at their actual operation comes apart from their neoliberal justi-fication precisely where supply chains rely on governmentality, cooperation, and weakly justified claims to authority; as I will argue, contesting supply chains on these grounds can be used to repoliticize the neoliberal economic realm more broadly.

2
Seeing (Like) Supply Chain Managers

Today, though man is born free, he is everywhere in supply chains. Commodities have long been traded internationally, but the particular distributed form of production known as the global supply chains can be traced to the late 1970s, the period of neoliberalism's ascendance; they became common enough that the term "supply chain management" was coined in 1982.[1] Nike offers an exemplary case study: the Nike brand was launched in 1972 in Oregon and already by 1982, 86 percent of Nike's athletic footwear was produced in South Korea and Taiwan; its last American factory closed in 1985.[2] Today, roughly one million workers in around 750 factories around the world make Nike products, but Nike owns none of the factories where its products are assembled.[3] This is a striking development in the history of manufacturing. In 1928, Henry Ford opened the River Rouge plant which took raw materials and turned out Model A cars—a "dream of continuous, integrated manufacturing" that employed 75,000 people in everything from milling steel and glass to its own powerhouse.[4] While River Rouge represented an apex of aspirations to centrally control manufacturing, such "vertical integration," in which a corporation actually owns the facilities that manufacture its products, is now such an exception that when the clothing company American Apparel owned its own factory in Los Angeles, it advertised this fact as evidence that it "considers its workers family."[5] It's a fitting symbol of the ascendance of global supply chains that after American Apparel declared bankruptcy a few years later, the new owners closed the Los Angeles factory and moved production to Honduras, where reports of sweatshop conditions quickly emerged.[6] Today roughly half a billion people are employed in jobs that are part of or depend on transnational supply chains like these.[7]

Transnational supply chains are not only the predominant form of international trade today; they are inseparable from the texture of daily life. As I write this, I'm wearing pants made in Bangladesh and a shirt made in Haiti while communicating with friends and coworkers through a phone assembled in China. These ubiquitous products are an important material

Disorienting Neoliberalism. Benjamin L. McKean, Oxford University Press (2020). © Oxford University Press.
DOI: 10.1093/oso/9780190087807.001.0001.

manifestation of how the global economy intimately shapes my life, but their significance is far from obvious. How should I think about my entanglement in these chains? How should an effective orientation to the global economy account for these physical objects which are a practical precondition to so many of my actions? Consider some infamous facts about the iPhone. Its inner components make use of metals and minerals like tantalum, mined amid armed conflict in the Democratic Republic of Congo. Miners there are lucky to make $2 a day and mining profits are sometimes a source of revenue for militias that prolong violent conflict.[8] The iPhones themselves are assembled in China largely by Foxconn Technology Group, the world's largest electronics manufacturer. Foxconn produces not only for Apple but also Sony, Nintendo, Amazon, and many others, and employs as many as 1.3 million workers when operating at peak capacity. To put that in perspective, that's about as many people as Walmart employs in the United States; Apple itself has about 66,000 employees.[9] With $60 billion in net income in 2018, Apple is one of the most profitable companies in the world, second only to Aramco, Saudi Arabia's national oil company.[10] Notoriously, workers at Foxconn factories in Shenzen found the wages and working conditions there so oppressive that in 2010, fourteen of them jumped to their deaths off the roof of a factory rather than continue working; the company then installed nets on the side of the building to catch falling workers, only to have another worker reportedly die of overwork.[11] The collapse of the garment factories at Rana Plaza occurred not long after the Foxconn suicides—all this in facilities that two supply chain management experts call "textbook cases for highly efficient global supply chains."[12] While Apple keeps most information about the manufacturing process confidential, estimates for the iPod suggest that all assembly, including labor, make up about 3 percent of input costs while Apple makes a gross profit of 40 percent of the wholesale price per device.[13]

These transnational supply chains make the question of how I should be oriented to the global economy concrete and practical when it might otherwise seem abstract. As Jennifer Bair puts it, the study of supply chains "permits one to analyze globalization in situ, directing our attention to the specific locations where particular production processes occur, while simultaneously illuminating how these discrete locations and activities are connected to each other as constituent links that collectively comprise the commodity chain."[14] Yet the standard approach to global justice in political theory offers arguments about justice in the economy without offering a picture of how the economy actually functions, making it hard to provide an orientation and consequently to guide action.[15] As I argued in the introduction, an effective orientation provides an account of (1) how social and political arrangements operate; (2) how those operations are generally made intelligible and legitimate to those subject to them; and (3) the normative values that one's actions should promote, given (1) and (2). In the previous chapter, I provided an account of how neoliberalism orients its subjects through an economic grid that sees the market as the foundation of social life generally and political legitimacy specifically. From a neoliberal perspective, supply chains appear as a natural expression of market logic; the replacement of vertically integrated firms that build products from scratch with multiple firms specializing in distinct steps of the production process is an obvious improvement in efficiency. The decomposition of firms into smaller units brings us another step closer to the complete realization of the neoliberal vision of an economy in which every individual acts as an entrepreneur, a firm of one.

However, as I argued in chapter 1, neoliberalism's own account of why individuals would come to see the world on its terms appeals to features of social life that fit awkwardly with its vision of the world. This provides critics of neoliberalism with an opportunity to reorient our perspective on society; in Foucault's terms, the very techniques of governmentality by which people come to adopt a neoliberal orientation can themselves become the source of an alternative orientation because of their poor fit with neoliberal political rationality. In this chapter, I show how transnational supply chains provide a focal point for this reorientation. I argue that an examination of the mechanisms that habituate workers and consumers to this view show that supply chains are better understood as political entities that claim the authority to govern us rather than as approximations of free exchanges between individual entrepreneurs. What makes the supply chain form so politically potent is the way that the rationality of the chain itself effectively conceives of workers and consumers as linked cooperating enterprises while the governing practices of the chain train workers and consumer in understandings of their role that obscure their links to each other. Reorienting ourselves to supply chains as political entities helps us contest their authority; defending the freedom of association for workers and consumers so that they can cooperate becomes an opportunity to repoliticize the neoliberal economy more broadly.

In the rest of this chapter, I will first look at how neoliberalism manages the popular disorientation produced by transnational supply chains through its account of the consumer's necessary ignorance of commodity production, which it narrates as a kind of sacred mystery. However, supply chain managers need a way of making sense of their own role in production; their expert discourse reveals a political rationality of the supply chain that differs from the perspectives of customers and workers shaped by supply chain governmentality. Third, I exploit this mismatch between political rationality and practices of governmentality and argue that we should reorient our view of supply chains to see them as political institutions; I accomplish this in part by turning to Ronald Coase's theory of the corporation and show how even neoliberal theory acknowledges that corporate power rests on a contestable claim to legitimate authority. Fourth, I show how that authority can be challenged and conclude by illustrating how this reorientation facilitates resisting neoliberalism more broadly.

The Logic of Supply Chains

Consider what it takes to get a Nike shoe into a consumer's hands. The process begins with designers in Nike's headquarters in Oregon sending shoe specifications to a design firm in Taiwan, which in turn sends its design to engineers in South Korea, which in turn sends its plans to a factory in Indonesia. At that factory, workers will assemble shoes out of leather made of skins from cows slaughtered in Texas and tanned in South Korea; foam derived from Saudi Arabian petroleum; and rubber soles refined in South Korea, among other components; the assembled shoes then end up in boxes from a paper mill in New Mexico with tissue paper made from Indonesian trees.[16] Then, of course, there's the matter of getting those boxed shoes to stores in the United States. This logistics process requires the infrastructure to get the shoes from the factory to a port, then loaded onto a boat full of containers that will sail to Long Beach or another West Coast port, where it will be unloaded and put onto a truck which will drive it to a nearby distribution center, where they will be unloaded again as the company figures out their final destination.[17]

I began the book by highlighting injustices in production, but each stage of the process offers new possibilities for exploitation. In the United States, ports are behind only mines in the number of workplace deaths and injuries annually.[18] What's more, port ownership is consolidating worldwide—the UAE-based corporation DP World now owns and operates ports in forty countries, for example—and firms are using the resultant monopoly power to refuse to recognize port worker unions, demanding increasing hours for lower pay.[19] Workers on the container ships that transport all these goods are at sea for months under the authority of a captain with no possibility to leave in cases of abuse; even with a respectful captain, they risk being held hostage by pirates or abandoned in foreign ports.[20] In exchange, the International Labour Organization (ILO) recommends a minimum monthly wage of $614 for seafarers, but enforcement is uneven; many workers pay thousands in bribes just to get the job and unscrupulous employers sometimes simply refuse to pay at the end of a voyage.[21] Meanwhile, the truck drivers that bring the goods from West Coast ports to retailers' nearby distribution centers are sometimes indentured servants, forced to take out exorbitant loans from their employers to pay for their own trucks, leaving them working twenty hours a day while taking home less than a dollar a week.[22]

Trying to keep all this in view at once feels almost impossible, but this dizzying geographic dispersal is the norm in global supply chains. For consumers, contemplating the origins of the everyday goods that constitute the practical context of our daily lives thus predictably produces a profound disorientation. One effect of this disorientation is the compulsion to renarrate these stunning yet banal facts, often as a story of unmasking. I've already done this myself in the way that I've described the activities of Foxconn and Nike; "behind the labels lurk great injustice" is a genre with a long, proud history. There *is* great injustice and many people are genuinely unaware of it. But I expect many readers *do* know about these cases—and yet that doesn't diminish the uncanny magic of how we can't quite grasp these remarkable networks. The gesture of unmasking is ineffectual, but nevertheless feels inescapable.

Neoliberal theory offers a strategy for containing this unsettling feeling by transforming incomprehension into grateful wonder. Rather than muckraking exposure, neoliberals recast the story of production as one of miraculous creation through spontaneous order beyond human control. In the book that precipitated the first convening of neoliberals, Walter Lippmann argued for accepting our necessary ignorance of the production process, writing, "The thinker, as he sits in his study drawing plans for the direction of society, will do no thinking if his breakfast has not been produced for him by a social process which is beyond his detailed comprehension." Similar to the process

I narrated earlier, Lippmann explains that "his breakfast depends upon workers on the coffee plantations of Brazil, the citrus groves of Florida, the sugar fields of Cuba, the wheat farms of the Dakotas, the dairies of New York; that it has been assembled by ships, railroads, and trucks, has been cooked with coal from Pennsylvania in utensils made of aluminum, china, steel, and glass."[23] However, the lesson that Lippmann draws from this is not that the thinker has reason to be concerned with the just treatment of workers in all these places, but rather that the entire process is beyond conscious human control, limiting the potential for its regulation. Because "the human mind must take a partial and simplified view of existence," an effective orientation to action accepts its reliance on these processes with gratitude and without undue reflection.

In the context of this assertion of necessary ignorance, the creation of any product appears as a kind of miracle and the retelling of its creation can approximate the genre of religious revelation. In his television show *Free to Choose*, Milton Friedman famously narrates the incredible geographic dispersal of the production process of a single pencil as a fable about the virtues of the free market. Friedman drew this story from a short 1958 essay called "I, Pencil" by Leonard Read, founder of the libertarian Foundation for Economic Education.[24] Read's story foregrounds the limits of human understanding of the economy by having the pencil itself narrate the story. The commodity testifies to its own unknowability and announces "I am a mystery—more so than a tree or a sunset or even a flash of lightning." The very existence of the pencil itself—bringing together trees from Oregon, graphite from Sri Lanka, clay from Mississippi, rape seed oil from Indonesia, and so on—is presented as evidence of neoliberal sociodicy and a revelation of the market's goodness. The story concludes with the pencil asserting, "I, Pencil, seemingly simple though I am, offer the miracle of my creation as testimony that this is a practical faith, as practical as the sun, the rain, a cedar tree, the good earth." The neoliberal legitimating story thus embraces the uncanniness of mundane objects, turning their unsettling nature into a reason to accept the market's bounty, whose origin is as natural and wholesome as the earth.

This legitimating story fits well with a neoliberal account of supply chain operations as the product of independent individuals producing an economic outcome inadvertently by pursuing their own aims. As Foucault puts it, for neoliberalism, "the basic element to be deciphered by economic analysis is not so much the individual, or processes and mechanisms, but enterprises. An economy made up of enterprise-units, a society made up of enterprise-units, is at once the principle of decipherment linked to liberalism and its programming for the rationalization of a society and an economy."[25] Supply chains can be interpreted as the apotheosis of the enterprise form. Apple and Nike appear as pure enterprise, corporations no longer tied to any location but calling forth commodities from wherever appears most efficient; freed from vertical integration, they coordinate enterprises that become smaller and more focused as they efficiently manage just one link in the chain. The geographic reach of supply chains seems to exemplify the neoliberal commitment to make markets ever bigger and faster.[26] Since, for neoliberalism, an increase in efficiency is by definition an improvement in collective well-being, supply chains' emphasis on the twin virtues of "cost efficiency and supply assurance" can appear to be a contribution to the common good no matter what its other consequences.[27]

In one of the most famous gestures of unmasking in *Capital*, Marx wrote of the need to enter the "hidden abode of production," but it turns out the meaning of what you see there isn't self-evident.[28] From the perspective of neoliberal thinkers, who explicitly avow the primacy of the economic realm which Marx sought to uncover, supply chain production doesn't look all that different from the sphere of commodity circulation which purportedly concealed it. Where Hobbes's Leviathan and Ford's River Rouge plant were composed of many individuals at the direction of one leader, global supply chains can be understood as enterprises all the way down; at each level, one finds an enterprise that is itself composed of enterprises until we reach the level of the individual entrepreneurs of human capital who work in the factories, who buy the commodities produced, and, of course, who manage the sourcing process itself, using their investment in their own human capital to get income returns for the service of making efficient investments of the human capital of others. From this perspective, supply chains embody a neoliberal view of the corporation as, in the words of economists Michael Jensen and William Meckling, "simply legal fictions which serve as a nexus for a set of contracting relationships among individuals."[29] On their face, corporations pose a difficulty for a neoliberal orientation similar to the social movements that Milton Friedman notably omitted from his account of Jim Crow, noted in chapter 1; they both appear to embody consequential cases of group action rather than the independently-choosing individuals that are the paradigm of neoliberal freedom. But on this view, corporations are nevertheless effectively reducible to contracts between individuals; their organizational form simplifies, but does not change, the fundamentally individual nature of the market. Supply chains can thus be understood simply as corporations that have been even further disaggregated, making their nature as enterprises made up of enterprises even clearer.

This picture of ever-mobile and disruptive capital turning the world into a fluid and homogenous space of functionally identical units is tempting for both champions and critics of neoliberalism. Sweatshops in transnational supply chains came to public consciousness in the 1990s and when critics tried to articulate why consumers should be concerned about them, they often cited anxieties about how globalization was "pressing nations into one homogenous global theme park."[30] The way supply chains decompose the corporation served as a convenient synecdoche for neoliberalism as a corrosive force, dissolving a world of diverse cultures and solidarities into a single market. Defenders of globalization often responded by valorizing such homogenizing force. Thomas Friedman not only praised global supply chains for making it possible for "work to be broken apart, reassembled, and made to flow, without friction, back and forth between the most efficient producers," but described their value in aesthetic terms, comparing an efficiently run supply chain to a symphony.[31] Nor did defenders shy away from Read's theological framing of their power. In ranking the work flow software employed by supply chain managers alongside the fall of the Berlin Wall as chief contributors to the creation of a flat world of frictionless flows, Friedman overtly embraced an evangelical register, writing, "The Bible tells us that God created the world in six days and on the seventh day he rested. Flattening the world took a little longer."[32] The work of supply chain managers may be slower than God's, but they're on the same continuum.

The persistence of the theological framing of supply chains as analogous to divine power suggests what remains enduringly useful in Marx's account of commodity fetishism. As Marx explains, a table, despite being the product of human labor, is "changed into something transcendent" when it becomes a commodity. Though it remains nothing more than wood, the table as commodity is endowed with a "mystical," "enigmatic" character because its price seems an objective but immaterial feature of it—an expression of *its* value—when its commodity character is, in reality, a product of social relations. What's important about Marx's analysis for my purposes here is that learning the secret of the commodity's agency doesn't break its power over us. The knowledge we get from reading *Capital* on its own isn't enough to alter the phenomenological character of our encounter with commodities. Marx begins the section on "The Fetishism of Commodities and the Secret

Thereof" by writing that "so soon as it steps forth as a commodity," the table becomes "far more wonderful than 'table-turning' ever was"—that is, commodity fetishism is even more remarkable than séances that purport to speak with the dead.[33] Yet after thoroughly demystifying the commodity, Marx still ends this section by having commodities speak for themselves, saying, "Our use value may be a thing that interests men. It is no part of us as objects. What, however, does belong to us as objects, is our value." Unlike séances, where the dead fall silent when their trickery is revealed, commodities continue to speak to us even when we know they are nothing more than wood, because we cannot "strip off its mystical veil until it is treated as production by freely associated men."[34] But only a real change in social relations can do that; social criticism alone cannot make it the case that existing garment factories like Rana Plaza are genuinely free associations, for example.

This explains why unmaskings of global supply chains always have to be repeated because they never quite take hold; because of the way we experience them, workers and consumers isolated from each other, these complicated and ever shifting institutional connections always feel a bit unreal. In that respect, a neoliberal orientation can feel like a more natural orientation to adopt in our circumstances; where Marx has to explain the persistence of a feeling that we know to be false, neoliberalism can valorize and embrace its persistence. Even though they're intended as exposés, stories of unmasking typically echo "I, Pencil" and turn commodities themselves into anthropomorphized protagonists while people become bit players in "Your T-shirt's life story (before it met you)."[35] Nor is this experience limited to consumers; workers too report the experience of finding it laughably hard to comprehend the "journey" that the products they assemble undertake.[36] This has important implications for an effective orientation to the global economy. It is not enough to identify the injustice hidden in supply chains; absent the creation of new social relations among people at different sites along the chain, such unmasking can be neurotically repeated as the felt unreality of supply chains continues. Consequently, we need an orientation that accounts for the human agency in the production process and that facilitates practical action to change the social relations between workers and consumers. In the next section, I argue that the mismatch between the political rationality of supply chains, which relies on workers and consumers being linked, and their governmentality, which produces their experience of separation, presents an opportunity to reorient workers and consumers to each other as subjects governed by the supply chain.

Rationality and Governmentality in Supply Chains

To see how workers and consumers might develop another orientation to supply chains that better identifies opportunities to promote their shared interests and values, I turn to the perspective of supply chain managers. If ignorance of production can be valorized and even sanctified for consumers, supply chain managers require a somewhat different orientation to perform their duties; the process can remain transcendental but supply chain managers need to understand how to oversee the transubstantiation, as it were. Theirs remains a neoliberal orientation and their job readily lends itself to associating freedom with choice in the market. But beyond the general orientation to economic activity, the perspective of supply chain managers offers a clear view of the specific *political rationality* of the supply chain—that is, what Wendy Brown calls "not an instrument of governmental practice, but rather the condition of possibility and legitimacy of its instruments, the field of normative reason from which governing is forged."[37] As I explained in chapter 1, the political rationality of a practice is the conceptual framework in which the practice makes sense, though the reality of the practice may depart significantly from how the political rationality imagines it. While the term is generally used to refer to the logic of neoliberalism as a whole, I use it here to tease out how those in a particular institutional role make sense of the practice they help to manage. This provides a perspective that those whom they seek to manage can repurpose to understand their own circumstances.

One can readily understand the political rationality of supply chains by looking at how supply chain managers describe their work to each other. As Peter Gibbon and Stefano Ponte note, "Even the briefest glance at the trade press over the last thirty years shows that [supply chain] governance has existed not simply as a type of relation between firms but also as an expert discourse which includes, among other things, paradigms of suppliers' ideal roles and capacities and of how these may be measured and shaped."[38] This expert discourse reveals the logic that makes supply chains comprehensible and self-evidently legitimate practices to those who govern them. The Council of Supply Chain Management Professionals (CSCMP) provides an exemplary source of this expert discourse in the form of a glossary for its work that, in explaining how they understand their jobs, also offers a kind of official version of the political rationality of supply chains. Notably, the CSCMP defines the task of its member as

the planning and management of all activities involved in sourcing and pro-
curement, conversion, and all logistics management activities. Importantly,
it also includes coordination and collaboration with channel partners,
which can be suppliers, intermediaries, third-party service providers, and
customers. In essence, supply chain management integrates supply and demand management *within and across* companies.[39]

On the level of its own political rationality, supply chain management
changes the nature of the boundary of the corporation itself. No longer
is the firm's legal boundary of primary practical importance; instead, the
logics of supply chains operate "within and across companies," traversing
corporate lines and incorporating multiple actors, including consumers
and workers employed by other firms. The CSCMP glossary defines supply
chains themselves as "the material and informational interchanges in the
logistical process stretching from acquisition of raw materials to delivery
of finished products to the end user. All vendors, service providers and
customers are links in the supply chain." I want to note three things about
how this definition illuminates the political rationality of supply chains.
First, by making "interchanges" the heart of supply chains, the definition
indicates clearly that relevant identities are relational; the central unit is
never a single firm.[40] While supply chains do decompose firms into constituent parts, supply chain managers do not see this process as creating isolated enterprise units but rather as a process of constituting connections.
Second, it is an expansive definition that assimilates the customer, whether
the retailer or the individual end user, into just another link in the chain;
if supply chains have a *telos*, it is neither consumption nor production but
the creation of value through movement along the chain. Often, the act
of consumption does not extinguish value but can also augment it further (as the prevalence of iPhones creates more reasons for others to start
using iPhones so they can enjoy shared features like FaceTime and so on).
Supply chains thus became a grid for interpreting the behavior of many
actors who may not even be aware that they belong to the chain and are
themselves a relay connected to others. Third, the distinctive contribution
of the production performed by workers in factories has receded completely from view; material and information interchanges are treated as
equivalent and production itself becomes virtually a black box at the heart
of a process that foregrounds logistics rather than manufacturing.[41] In the
supply chain manager's "logistical gaze," circulation rather than creation is

explicitly the source of value.[42] After all, that is what's complicated about supply chains and makes it possible to imagine them as symphonies; the physical assembly of products can be simple and mind-numbingly repetitive while the process of efficiently determining how to get precisely the right number of components to arrive at precisely the right time so that no inventory ever wastefully sits idle requires the creative interpretation and application of vast quantities of data.[43]

From this perspective, supply chains are not what a critic might see: a way of engaging in regulatory arbitrage, sourcing production from whichever country has the lowest labor and environmental standards, producing a race to the bottom in an increasingly homogenous global market. Rather, they are means of increasing value through large networks that can disaggregate the division of labor at an unprecedented scale that allows for enormous gains in reliability and efficiency, which benefits everyone in the long run. In practice, however, these gains have not been widely distributed but instead contributed to the growth of inequality. While transnational supply chains have improved firms' productivity and profitability, they have not brought improved wages to the developing world but rather contributed to the depression of wages in participating industries.[44] The academic study of supply chains arose partly out of the effort to explain this. The sociologist Gary Gereffi and his colleagues have offered the most influential approach. They defined "global commodity chains" as "sets of interorganizational networks clustered around one commodity or product, linking households, enterprises, and states to one another within the world-economy."[45] They identified four main dimensions of these chains that determine its character: (i) its inputs and outputs, including products, services, and resources; (ii) its geographic scope; (iii) "relationships between firms that determine how financial, material, and human resources are allocated and flow within a chain," which they call its governance structure; and (iv) its local, national, and international institutional context.[46] This definition usefully disaggregates some of the factors that define the field in which supply chain managers operate. In particular, isolating the relations between firms helps to identify a key cause of the unequal distribution of the chain's benefits. Lead brands like Apple and Nike are, ironically, the least fungible part of the chain since their contribution is the most immaterial and thus hardest to duplicate.[47] Their position in the market gives them the ability to pit suppliers against each other and to externalize the risk of the actual production process, giving them the capacity to capture a disproportionate share of gains.[48] Recent estimates suggest Apple earns a gross profit of $283 on the retail sale of a $649 iPhone, while Foxconn and other Taiwan-based firms receive roughly $48—with only about $8.46 going to workers and their bosses in China.[49]

This analysis crucially introduces the question of power into an account of supply chain operations, which is not explicit in the supply chain manager's expert discourse. The rationality of the chain is formally egalitarian, understanding relations as interchanges rather than hierarchies. But hierarchies pervasively structure the chain's operations: not only hierarchy between the lead brand and suppliers but also economic hierarchies between workers and their employers and political hierarchies between the developed countries that have largely determined the terms of trade and the developing countries that have had to accept them. Unfortunately, Gereffi's definition of supply chains occludes many of these important power relations by defining the chain's governance exclusively in terms of relations among firms; the perspective, agency, and governance of workers and consumers, for example, is defined as part of the chain's context rather than internal to the chain itself. In that way, this definition stays too close to the lead firm and its supply chain managers, who remain the paradigmatic agent whose perspective authoritatively defines the chain's operations and boundaries.[50] We can expand on Gereffi's account and reorient our view in a way that better facilitates action by workers and consumers by looking more specifically at the power relations that relate them to supply chains. By distinguishing between supply chain's political rationality and governmentality, we can see the practices that relate workers and consumers to supply chains as techniques aimed at governing them, in part by structuring their experience of the chain to conceal their status as enduring links. While supply managers describe their work as apolitical and technocratic, facilitating connections with others who equally participate in the marketplace, their relationship to consumers and workers is better understood as a hierarchical relation of governance, making claims to authority and subjecting others to power derived from asymmetries of information and resources with the aim of determining their conduct. As is true of neoliberalism generally, this mismatch between political rationality and techniques of governmentality provides an opportunity to contest the legitimacy of existing practices.

Consider first how consumers are related to supply chains. As we've already seen, supply chain managers regard consumers as integral links in the chain, yet most consumers do not experience supply chains that way. Rather than seeing themselves as permanent links in the chain, they imagine that they only intersect with the supply chain at the actual moment of exchange. But such an impression is carefully produced by brands, who in fact intensively track and surveil consumers so that their actions can be anticipated and directed. The concept of governmentality helps us see why it's appropriate to describe consumers as subjects of the supply chain, since their actions are uncoerced but nevertheless shaped by a power that seeks to govern them, nonconsensually leading them to "freely" act in particular ways. Nikolas Rose describes "a whole array of strategies and tactics that have been developed, over the course of the twentieth century, to 'assemble the subject of consumption': to render the consumer knowable and calculable . . . the commercial surveillance aspects of banking, insurance, credit card checking, the datachecking entailed in consumer credit agreements, automatic credit checking at EFTPOS, the strategic use of data on purchasing preferences for targeted marketing on the one hand and retail strategies on the other," and so on.[51] At this point, virtually everything we do can be digitally tracked, which has vastly increased the capacity to anticipate consumer action and produce goods accordingly.[52] This has consequences for the freedom of consumers and supply chain workers alike; as I discuss in the next section, the use that supply chains make of this information leads directly to the increased exploitation of workers who are employed on the increasingly erratic schedules required for just-in-time production.

Of course, brands are not content to merely anticipate consumer actions, but actively seek to shape them—even as they work hard to disguise how much information about individuals they have. And the amount of information they have is staggering. I have so far largely focused on the iPhone as an example of a good produced by supply chains, but the role that it plays once it is in the hands of consumers is also essential. Pew Research Center estimates that more than 75 percent of all US adults have a smartphone while over 90 percent of US adults between eighteen and twenty-nine years old have one.[53] Retailers have a staggering number of tools to track smartphone users not only on the web but also in physical space. Phones that scan for wifi networks announce their location whenever their user approaches physical stores. But retailers can get even more fine-grained information about a customer's location through placing Bluetooth beacons throughout their stores or by using the phone's camera to identify the particular lights installed in that store location, enabling them to see how a consumer proceeds through the store and even how long she stands in front of a particular display.[54] Retailers combine this with other data they purchase, including

GPS data about our other movements, from largely anonymous data brokers—companies like Acxiom, Experian, BlueKai, and eXelate that track your internet use with cookies and correlate it with publicly available information as well as data they purchase from still other retailers.[55] All this is done with an eye toward discerning the most effective ways of intervening in customer behavior—for example, sending a push alert to my phone around 4 p.m. letting me know that the store I usually pass on the commute home from work is offering a discount on the item that I was idly Googling on my work desktop.

As a result, while Google has boasted that they know "roughly who you are, roughly what you care about, roughly who your friends are," the same is true for the lead brands of many supply chains, though they generally prefer not to say so in public.[56] That's because their efforts to govern consumer behavior are more effective when consumers don't know that they're being targeted—at least for now. As it stands, most consumers are turned off when they realize how intensely they are being watched; Target reports that they intentionally intersperse irrelevant coupons with their personalized offers so that customers don't realize how closely their habits are being tracked.[57] But when supply chain professionals, data brokers, and others talk among themselves in the trade press, they are clear that their aim is, in the words of one digital marketer, "retraining customers"—retraining them not just to patronize their particular brand but also to habituate them to be the kinds of subjects who part willingly with their data.[58] The enthusiastic sharing of personal information over social media platforms has been significant here. Twitter provides its users with a free snapshot of the data it collects in order to induce them to pay for promotions to particular audiences; for example, of the roughly 1,100 people who follow me on the service, Twitter reports that 16 percent of them earn between $100,000 and $124,999 while 20 percent have a "consumer buying style" described as "value conscious" and 36 percent use AT&T as their wireless carrier.[59] Unsurprisingly in this context, many people are already resigned to the ubiquity of digital surveillance and can be readily induced to give up personal data for small discounts. As the fashion magazine *Allure* excitedly reported to its readers in an article about how the cosmetics company Ulta's "loyalty program" offers free samples of lipstick, "Typically, news of companies monitoring shopping habits and hoarding data gives us some major Big Brother vibes. But you're going to like what Ulta is doing with all of your shopping data: using it to send you free beauty swag . . . As long as the retailer keeps fighting to share more newness with its customers, we're down to share our shopping data to score some new beauty swag."[60]

There's good reason to be skeptical about some of the more grandiose claims that brands make about their ability to track their customers. While such statements risk temporarily alienating customers if they go viral, their real audience is often investors who need reassurance that the firm has a strategy for managing consumer behavior. Even taking these claims with a grain of salt, it's appropriate to describe customers as subjected to the supply chain in light of the practices used to try to govern their behavior. For a consumer to imagine that he only makes up a link in the chain when actually purchasing a good is thus a very consequential misunderstanding because, on that view, the natural method of resisting is by making different choices at the point of consumption, through boycotts and ethical consumption from responsible supply chains (after all, who wants their personal brand to be tarnished by association with injustice?).[61] To recognize that one is subject to the supply chain beyond the moment of exchange would already suggest that one's own freedom may be implicated in ways that go beyond choice in the market and point toward an alternative orientation to supply chains outside of their political rationality."

Though a neoliberal orientation may reject the distinctiveness of labor, workers themselves are still clearly essential to supply chains. Brands claim the authority to determine which workers count as part of the chain, typically including only those who are officially employed by firms with a direct contracting relationship. However, firms often place orders with suppliers on terms that are foreseeably impossible for the contracted supplier to meet, necessitating further outsourcing to other firms or even informal work performed by individuals outside the factory, sometimes in their own homes.[62] These workers contribute labor to their supply chain but are not recognized by lead brands as members of it, enabling them to disclaim knowledge of and responsibility for their wages and working conditions. Even for those workers who are recognized as included, taking the political rationality of supply chains at face value directs attention to workers in two ways: first, it normally focuses on the choice to accept factory employment as an exercise of market freedom, a voluntary choice to accept low wages and dangerous working conditions that prima facie deserves to be protected from government interference. Such employment is in fact preferable to most really available alternatives to them, but this should not direct attention away from the political and economic conditions that made the choice necessary

in the first place. Exclusive focus on the normative significance of the choice
to accept employment without a broader reflection on political context
not only reinforces neoliberal and libertarian defenses of sweatshops, but
overlooks other ways that workers express resistance to factory conditions—
union organizing, strikes, slowdowns, sick-ins, and other actions that attempt to change they options they face rather than to accept one they are
presented with.[63] Second, when every subject is defined as an enterprise,
then consumers and workers appear to have different investments with conflicting interests. Getting the best return for me as a consumer obviously
entails getting the lowest price possible for a garment so I can minimize my
expenditures, while the best return for a garment worker entails getting the
highest wage possible. It is not obvious what reason workers and consumers
would have to build coalitions to demand justice together.

This is the political effectiveness of the supply chain form: even as the political rationality of the supply chain includes and connects workers and consumers, consumers are habituated to think of their connection to the chain
as limited to the moment of purchase; meanwhile, workers are treated as dis-
posable, screened from the view of others, and often kept in the dark about
the identity of the lead brand for which they produce. Both workers and consumers are denied ready access to the information supply chain managers
have about their connection which would facilitate acting together. In light
of their respective experiences in isolation from each other, a neoliberal orientation can seem to them like a sensible way to make sense of supply chains.
But whether it's proffered by critics or defenders, accepting the picture of
supply chains as infinitely mobile dreams of neoliberal flexibility reinscribes
the ways that workers and consumers are weakest. When an individual
worker declines to take a sweatshop job or a single consumer refuses to buy
sweatshop clothing, there are enormous numbers of consumers and workers
who are willing to step in and do so instead. Unsurprisingly, then, strategies
to prevent injustices in supply chains based on this view have largely failed.
Public handwringing about the production of iPhones and worker suicides at
Foxconn have generated lots of headlines, but little change in consumer behavior or working conditions; the amount of illegal forced overtime in Foxconn
factories actually went up from 2013 to 2014.[64] What it has done is give rise to
a significant public relations effort on the part of lead brands to show concern,
often by establishing ethical sourcing departments and announcing "social
audits" of their suppliers. An ample literature attests to the failures of these
forms of self-regulation to change conditions for workers.[65] What they do in

practice is bolster the legitimacy of supply chain managers; as a matter of political rationality, these forms of self-regulation treat supply chain managers
and their firms as well-intentioned agents seeking to advance the common
good, only to be thwarted by the market itself, whose verdict of course must
be accepted. However, the market will not produce better wages and working
conditions simply through people preferring that it do so. A neoliberal orientation to supply chains thus offers no effective strategies for reforming them.

Neoliberal in Theory, Cooperative in Practice?

What then is an alternative strategy for resisting injustice in supply chains?
According to many critics of neoliberalism, we need to develop an entirely
different theoretical vocabulary to resist it. In 2003, Wendy Brown argued
that neoliberalism had so thoroughly hollowed out liberal democracy that
it no longer offers any critical potential; efforts to critique the economy for
subverting liberal democracy won't work when liberal democracy is itself
populated by citizen-entrepreneurs and justified on the economic terms of
neoliberalism.[66] David Harvey likewise has suggested that those who want
to resist neoliberalism need to abandon the language of freedom as incompatible with social justice because freedom has been so thoroughly appropriated and individualized by neoliberalism.[67] Such pessimism about freedom
and democratic politics might seem warranted for all I've said so far. On the
neoliberal understanding of supply chains, the existence of efficient supply
chains provides evidence that consumers and workers already understand
themselves as entrepreneurs, and this self-understanding in turn makes resistance ineffective. Likewise, when appeals to freedom and democracy can
be reduced to assertions of the importance of individual choice, then we end
up stuck with the neoliberal understanding of supply chains which treats
every link in the chain as fungible calculating units.

While neoliberal theory and practice can go hand in hand and economic
precarity can deepen the appeal of a neoliberal orientation, the gap between
political rationality and practices of governmentality provides an opportunity to reorient our experience of neoliberalism, as I argued in chapter 1.
Attending to the practices of neoliberal governmentality I've described
undermines neoliberalism's self-description as defending the economy
against politics; we can instead come to see what is already political about
features of social life that neoliberalism would have us see as economic.

Repoliticizing the economic realm by showing how it already centers around characteristic features of political life, like claims to legitimate authority, facilitates collective action that can be effectively guided by appeals to freedom and democracy. To that end, in this section, I develop the view of supply chains as political institutions by showing how, in actual practice, they more closely resemble the economic planning Hayek decried than the necessarily unknowable production process he praised. Even on the neoliberal view, the operations of supply chains—which are characterized by cooperation among a ruling elite who claim legitimate authority to govern the actions of others—can aptly be described as political; as a result, workers and consumers who are subject to supply chain governance can come to see each other as sharing a political status and work together to contest the authority that seeks to govern them.

Far from being separate enterprises engaging in individual contracts loosely organized around corporate nexuses, global supply chains centrally rely on *standardization* and *cooperation*, two features which resist incorporation into an orientation to society where the primary unit is the independent enterprise. To the extent that global supply chains are ruthlessly efficient, it is not merely because outsourcing functions enables specialization and lower costs, but because each link in the chain needs to abide by strict rules in order for the chain as a whole to be successful. Standardization of both material and information is required. Physically, for example, the entire logistics of transportation in global supply chains is only possible because of the standardization of shipping containers.[68] With respect to information, one can look at the International Organization for Standardization (ISO), an international NGO which sets standards for products and services—almost 20,000 standards that cover everything from the compatibility of computers to a uniform benchmark for the speed of photographic film. Notably, the ISO itself stands outside the logic of entrepreneurship. The importance of this was made clear in 2003, when they floated a plan to charge money for the use of the codes it employs to describe the standards; in other words, if two companies wanted to affirm that their products were compatible, they would both have to pay a fee to the ISO in order to "speak" in standards to each other. Imposing costs on the transmission of such information would have shaken the foundations of supply chains and the ISO backed away from the plan.[69] This resistance to turning standards into simply another form of capital that can bring a return is a telling break.

With respect to cooperation, though they have some conflicting interests when they negotiate over margins, orders, and profits, Apple and Foxconn are not competitors but neither is Foxconn merely a supplier of commodity goods; the relationship is rather one of interdependence and continuous coordination.[70] To be clear, not all iPhones are assembled by Foxconn and Foxconn does not assemble exclusively for Apple.[71] But neither could exist in anything like its current form without the other. The parts that go into an iPhone are not commodities just anyone can purchase; the batteries, screens, and other components used are custom engineered precisely to Apple's specifications. Indeed, Apple directly coordinates engineering details even with the firms that supply parts to the firms that supply parts to Foxconn— for example, the firms that make the parts that go into the batteries that go into iPhones—so they are directing supply chain activity even at firms with which they have no contractual commercial relationship. These firms, in turn, purchase inputs like tantalum and cobalt from commodity markets, which is where so-called conflict minerals enter the supply chain. Supply chains are thus not merely a matter of what corporations other corporations buy components from, even while it remains possible to maintain that fiction; as the CSCMP's definition indicated, multinational corporations are in practice defined as much by who they cooperate and collaborate with as by who they compete with.

So-called lean production and just-in-time manufacturing requires both clear communication about standards and extensive cooperation along the supply chain. On the one hand, "lean manufacturing" remorselessly strives for efficiency by constantly introducing innovations found anywhere else on the chain into the production process.[72] This evolving production process constantly asks more and more of workers to the point that it causes significant physical and psychological harm. Such production techniques often work in conjunction with "just-in-time" manufacturing in which inventory is kept to a minimum and production responds as quickly as possible to demands; as information about consumer demand and consequent production volume is disseminated, every link needs to be ready to deliver highly varying quantities of goods at precisely the time the next link requires.[73] Together, lean production techniques and just-in-time manufacturing can maximize responsiveness to consumer demand and generate tremendous efficiency for corporations, but require putting workers on extremely erratic schedules; in these supply chains, hours can vary by as much as 80 percent from week to week and illegal forced overtime is the norm.[74] But all this efficiency is only possible if buyers and sellers agree not to re-enter the marketplace for each transaction; they need to plan and act together in order to capture these gains. Yet only certain parties participate in this collaborative planning.

By contrast, neoliberal markets putatively produce a common good through independent actions; through price mechanisms, information about supply and demand becomes public and allows people to coordinate economic activity efficiently. Hayek writes, "Fundamentally, in a system where the knowledge of the relevant facts is dispersed among many people, prices can act to coordinate the separate actions of different people in the same way as subjective values help the individual to coordinate the parts of his plan . . . The whole acts as one market, not because any of its members survey the whole field, but because their limited individual fields of vision sufficiently overlap so that through many intermediaries the relevant information is communicated to all."[75] Yet supply chain managers do, in a sense, aspire to survey the whole field; their cooperation and mutual reliance is quite different from the impersonal coordination among anonymous actors that is Hayek's paradigm of an economic relation.

Indeed, while his view has affinities with Jensen and Meckling's "nexus of contracts" view, Hayek himself never developed a theory of the corporation, much less one that would be adequate to explain the relationship between Apple and Foxconn, which troubles his neat distinction between spontaneous order and planning.[76] Notably, in Hayek's account of how markets generate knowledge, he talks about how a factory manager needs to have "tiles for its roof, stationary for its forms" and other kinds of equipment available for purchase from the market; when he considers production inputs, his example is the price of tin.[77] In other words, he only imagines utterly fungible commodities available to all as the paradigm of the market rather than a world where Walmart can dictate to its suppliers the exact specifications and price of the goods it is purchasing.[78] Fungible commodities do enter into supply chains, as we've seen, but Hayek's account isn't adequate for understanding Apple's leverage over production not only at the plants that assemble iPhones but at the factories that make iPhone components and even at the factories that make components of its components. In short, supply chains much more resemble the kind of planning and regulation that Hayek rejected than a spontaneously arising order.[79] The central form of international trade in the global economy is thus more characterized by on-going interdependence rather than independence and by negotiations over terms of on-going cooperation than ephemeral exchanges. Combined with the practices of governmentality that supply chains use to steer the behavior of consumers and workers subject to them, this represents a fundamental challenge to the neoliberal orientation because it suggests politics and economics cannot be clearly separated, even conceptually—opening the door to politicizing the market and raising questions of justice and equality within it.

Importantly, Hayek's is not the only neoliberal way of seeing the market; the University of Chicago economist Ronald Coase offers another, more sophisticated neoliberal account of the corporation. However, as I'll now argue, Coase's account only deepens the problems for neoliberal political rationality and bolsters the case for considering supply chains as political institutions. Unlike the "nexus of contracts" account, which regards the corporation as a legal fiction draped over the reality of individual agreements, Coase's view recognizes that the internal workings of corporations are not examples of spontaneous order but of hierarchy; employees do what their bosses direct them to do.[80] In keeping with neoliberal theories of political legitimacy, Coase provides an economic reason why hierarchy, rather than market coordination, is employed: transaction costs.[81] It's not actually efficient to negotiate new contracts for every single task or product; sometimes it's more efficient to be directed by a "controlling authority."[82] Consequently, Coase defines a firm as "the system of relationships which comes into existence when the direction of resources is dependent on an entrepreneur."[83] Within a competitive market, the size of a corporation will be determined by how many functions it is efficient to direct hierarchically and how many are more efficiently determined by the price mechanism.

Coase's story complicates and improves upon the explanatory power of Hayek's account but remains essentially faithful to the neoliberal orientation in important ways. First, Coase retains the divide between the spontaneous order of the market and the coercive planning that is otherwise required to get people to do things. Coase makes his understanding of the nature of the employment relation especially clear in his analysis of what he calls "the legal relationship normally called that of 'master and servant' or 'employer and employee.'" He writes, "it is the fact of direction which is the essence" of the employment relation, both legally and economically.[84] Employees have agreed to unique contracts that are limited but open-ended about what kinds of performance are required; they have consented to submit not to the market but to their manager. This means, second, we can still reduce complex organizations to individuals because they are run by the entrepreneur who directs them; in that sense, we can effectively treat corporate actors as a unit in the same way that we treat individual actors who have preferences and seek to maximize returns. Above all, Coase's view suggests that so long as a firm survives in the market, corporate managers' authority is justified and that employment never entitles one to a voice at work; any attempt to incorporate worker voice into the operations of a firm is at the discretion of management. To the extent it makes sense to talk about "corporate responsibility" on this view, the employer's responsibility is to command their employees in a manner consonant with economic efficiency, since that is how the market serves the common good.[85] If an employer abuses his authority, the only mechanism for accountability is the market itself.

Coase's theory improves upon Hayek's by offering a tool to explain why huge swathes of the economy do not look like spontaneous order. However, his picture of authority in the workplace is both descriptively and normatively inadequate. I've already argued that relations between firms in supply chains overturn the strict distinction that Coase maintains between the spontaneous order of a market coordinated by the price mechanism and the internal life of a firm controlled by hierarchical authority. We have seen supply chain managers themselves describe how their work "integrates supply and demand management *within and across* companies"; the logic of the chain itself supersedes the boundaries of the firm and, as we've seen, involves negotiated planning in a way not aptly described as either market coordination or employer direction. Even within a single corporation, different departments compete for authority over decisions in a way that belies the assumption of a simple, univocal hierarchy; departments in charge of compliance with environmental and labor standards routinely compete with the departments in charge of operations and logistics for authority over decision-making, for example.[86]

Most importantly, in order to explain corporations within a neoliberal framework, Coase's theory of the firm has to acknowledge that hierarchical authority is intrinsic to contemporary economic activity. That acknowledgment is hugely significant because it captures the inadequacy of neoliberalism's central organizing distinction between politics as a space of coercive force and the economy as the site of market freedom. For Coase, economic efficiency remains the ultimate justification for that authority, just as Hayek and Friedman ground the legitimacy of political authority; however, by acknowledging that coercive authority is structurally part of the economy itself rather than just part of government that clears the way for economic activity, Coase's theory exposes a breakdown in neoliberalism's ability to orient us to the global economy as apolitical. This also suggests the grounds for an alternative orientation—one that takes note of the same hierarchical authority but calls its basis and legitimacy into question. In the next section, I examine what this contestation looks like.

Supply Chains as They Are, Laws as They Might Be?

In this section, I show how an orientation to supply chains as political entities can help contest their authority. By calling supply chains political entities, I mean that they are institutions that aim to govern individuals and make contestable appeals to authority that require justification; that these institutions are only possible given certain avowedly political decisions; and that they essentially implicate political values like freedom and justice. Seeing supply chains as simply the product of spontaneous economic development leaves the authority of supply chain managers untroubled; oriented to supply chains in this way, we are likely to approach their reform by providing ethical guidance to the supply chain managers, helping them to make tough decisions about how to use their power responsibly. By contrast, orienting ourselves to supply chains as political institutions facilitates the democratic contestation of economic hierarchy and repoliticizing the neoliberal economy in order to raise claims of justice within it.

The central exercise of authority that I want to consider here is the supply chain manager's claim to determine the boundaries of the chain itself. The political rationality of supply chains, as we've seen, can make these boundaries vague since the primary unit is held to be the interchange; supply chains are conceived as ways of relating different units, so it is always possible in principle for each unit to extend the chain, making it hard to know where the boundary lies. The supply chain of a t-shirt could be traced back not only to the cotton grower but from there to the company that provided fertilizer to grow the cotton and from there to the company that provides the fertilizer company with the natural gas that it will convert into ammonia, and so on.[87] Where does it end?

This question highlights the fact that the boundaries of a supply chain are not a pregiven fact. Rather, the decision where to draw the line between what's in the supply chain and what's out should be understood as essentially political; it's just that brands have claimed the exclusive authority to determine this. This appeal to authority is entirely consonant with Coase's view that what defines a firm is that it has a controlling authority who directs employees. Coase grounds the legitimacy of this authority on economic efficiency, but as the previous section showed, the actual exercise of corporate authority often does not resemble Coase's model. Corporations often exercise their authority in ways that cannot plausibly be justified by appeal to economic efficiency. For example, as Elizabeth Anderson has noted, employers routinely claim the authority to regulate their employees' behavior outside the workplace. In the United States, roughly half of all workers do not enjoy robust protection of their freedom of speech since their employer can fire them for off-duty speech.[88] Employers regularly compel their employees to engage in overtly political acts like attending rallies or lobbying for legislation that the firm's owners and managers favor.[89] And in many supply chain facilities like Foxconn's, there is never any completely "off duty" time at all since workers live in dorms attached to the factory and eat their meals in the factory cafeteria.

My argument here is not that economic efficiency can never support a claim to authority, but that the grounds and scope of corporate authority—as well as the responsibilities that accompany the exercise of that authority—are rightly subject to contestation by those subject to it. Importantly, that means supply chain managers do not always have final authority to determine who counts as subject to their power. We need not cede to Nike the legitimate authority to decisively determine who counts as a member of its supply chain. Recent years have seen many challenges to corporations' authority to determine who counts as an employee. Multiple lawsuits in several countries have argued that ridesharing apps like Uber have illegally classified their drivers as independent contractors when they treat them like employees.[90] Under the Obama administration, the US National Labor Relations Board determined that fast food companies were "joint employers" with their franchisees of the employees who worked in franchise restaurants that the corporation did not own.[91] Fast food corporations lobbied furiously against this determination and it was quickly rescinded by the Trump administration, but this only further illustrates how questions about the scope of corporate authority—about who counts as a corporate subject, if you will—are political questions that cannot simply be resolved by appeal to economic efficiency or existing law.

The same is true of supply chains. Coase's view suggests that if the supply chain that produces Nike sneakers always contained the same corporations, then the efficiency gains over a vertically integrated company would be slim to nonexistent. Supply chain managers often cycle among suppliers in the interests of efficiency and argue that these firms are not part of the supply chain except during those times when they are specifically contracted to produce goods. But this begs the question in an important way. As I detailed earlier, just-in-time production can be highly irregular with production for a lead brand occurring just a few months a year. Yet such just-in-time production is only possible with a reserve army of idle factories, as it were, ready to spring back to full production when called upon. What's more, these factories often produce for the same lead brand several times over many years on multiple short-term contracts. While it is convenient for supply chain managers to consider those factories part of the chain only at the moments of production, there is not a good reason to take their claim as authoritative. The same goes for production that authorized suppliers further outsource to other factories or even to individual workers performing informal labor, as detailed earlier. Many Western retailers had clothes produced in the factories that collapsed at Rana Plaza but have denied that the factories were part of their supply chain; they argued that they sourced from other factories in Bangladesh that in turned sourced from Rana Plaza factories without the brands' knowledge. In the aftermath of the collapse, workers who survived actively claimed belonging to the supply chain of, for example, Benetton and The Children's Place.[92] We are faced with two conflicting definitions: the workers argue that what defines belonging to the supply chain is the fact that the work done contributes to the final product (and, in this case, the companies do not dispute that their work did so); the corporations argue that what defines belonging to the supply chain is their explicit authorization. No facts in the matter are in dispute; rather, there is a political argument about who has the authority to define the supply chain.[93] Whether one counts as a subject, what conduct is proper to a subject, and the responsibilities a supply chain has to its subjects are matters to be contested.

Importantly, one way that supply chain managers govern people is precisely by *excluding* them from the chain. This is visible not only in the discursive exclusion of Rana Plaza workers with the aim of avoiding responsibility for providing them compensation, but also in the material deprivation suffered by workers through the decision to source work elsewhere. For example, Lordstown, Ohio, was devastated when General Motors closed its factory there at the same time that it allocated new production to factories in Mexico; the factory had been the main source of employment for the city's residents for decades.[94] It would be strange to say that the thousands of Lordstown workers who found themselves unemployed in a city with few other employment prospects had ceased to be subject to G.M.'s supply chain at a moment that so profoundly demonstrated the power of the supply chain to determine the course of their lives. The structure of their cities and their families were profoundly shaped by the supply chain and did not cease to be so when G.M. stopped production there. This suggests how an orientation to supply chains as political institutions facilitates a broader repoliticization and contestation of neoliberalism, which I explain further in the chapter's next and final section.

Next Steps?

Against outlooks that see neoliberal theory and practice as seamlessly reinforcing each other, I've tried to trace some gaps between them by looking at transnational supply chains and how their rationality and operations diverge from how most of us typically experience them. These gaps offer spaces for those subject to supply chains to reorient their view of them and try to govern themselves in other ways. Specifically, the gap between neoliberal views of markets and supply chain practices turned us to the need for a neoliberal theory of the corporation. But as Coase showed, that required acknowledging coercive authority as an intrinsic part of the modern economy, one that consequently requires a theory of legitimacy. Yet efforts to explain and justify hierarchical authority within what neoliberalism had designated as the space of freedom unsurprisingly produce new gaps, as these theories of legitimacy fail descriptively and normatively. On the one hand, the functioning of supply chains cannot be reduced to hierarchical commands backed up by coercion; many relations along the chain are better described as matters of cooperative interdependence (as firms relate to each other) or governmentality (as firms relate to consumers) than as obedience to commands. On the other hand, the coercion that workers do experience is not well justified by the theory; bosses' claims to authority routinely exceed the scope that can be justified by appeals to economic efficiency. Rather than see each other as rival independent enterprises, workers and consumers can instead see each other as sharing the political status of *supply chain subjects*. An orientation to supply chains as political institutions better captures their actual operations and makes it possible to see the inadequacy of prevailing efforts to legitimate those operations, facilitating efforts to contest that authority.

This account of supply chains as political entities is importantly different from the picture of supply chains as a corrosive force that transforms everything into a homogenous global market; on the contrary, supply chains rely upon workers, consumers, and managers all being differently positioned in order to operate. Rather than a cause of homogeneity, supply chain managers conceive of their work as a way of organizing difference. This provides a different explanation for our disorientation at supply chains' sprawling geographic scope than neoliberalism's appeal to our necessary ignorance. As Anna Tsing points out, we find supply chains dizzying because they characteristically model bigness *without* homogeneity.[95] In contrast to the sovereign state imagined as a big and unitary entity, supply chains connect diverse locations and functions into huge networks that still result in a single product. Crucially, economic efficiency does not always dictate erasing difference, but can reinforce it through optimizing around it. For example, supply chains depend on and exploit the existence of national differences; the mobility of apparel production makes it possible to pit different countries against each other in a "race to the bottom" that would be impossible if the world was a single unit with uniform labor and environmental regulations. Supply chains also take advantage of, and play a role in constituting, gender differences. Garment factories disproportionately employ women because managers see them as easier to control, leading workers to enact gendered submission in order to get hired and keep their jobs.[96] It reveals the extent to which supply chain operations are bound up with reproducing social differences that some men in Lordstown experienced the G.M. factory closure as making it impossible for them to continue performing traditional masculinity; changing their role in the chain led them to ask, "What am I as a man?"[97]

We misunderstand supply chains—and how to resist them—if we think that they are machines for turning diverse social relations into homogenous enterprise units; that view suggests we can resist them by staying out of them. But as we've seen, one way to be subjected to supply chains is precisely by being excluded from them. Seeing the question of whether one is in or out of the chain as a political question about who has the authority to determine the answer makes it easier to understand the relationship between the supply chain and the neoliberal policies and institutions that sustain it.[98] As I've already argued, global supply chains are part of and reliant on political arrangements that a neoliberal orientation will tend to depoliticize; because those arrangements have played an important role in determining supply chain boundaries, effectively contesting authority within the supply chain can require a broader resistance to the political institutions that make them possible.

In the absence of a more political understanding of supply chains, many brands have developed "codes of conduct" to govern the behavior of their suppliers and hired auditing teams to report on whether or not the nodes in their supply chain are behaving as requested. Corporate codes of conduct make explicit what was always implicit in the practice of supply chain management; it would be impossible for supply chains to function without clear rules and standards that every link in the chain knew about and the codes represent an acknowledgment that it is practically impossible to deny entirely the normative responsibilities that cooperation entails. Codes of conduct, which are typically issued by lead firms rather than developed in cooperation with the chain as a whole, represent an attempt for brands and retailers to retain their authority in the face of public contestation that asserts its illegitimacy. Nevertheless, they can serve as starting points for democratizing supply chains to the extent that they provide a common point of reference to workers and consumers, giving them a set of standards the supply chain has acknowledged but failed to meet. As we have seen, what links in the supply chains generally lack is common knowledge of their cooperation.[99] If we want to politicize supply chains in the service of achieving global justice, we could see codes of conduct representing a kind of incipient common knowledge; even when they are adopted and implemented insincerely, as efforts to distract attention from unjust wages and working conditions, they could mark the existence of a kind of public.

When workers and consumers jointly conceive of supply chains as a political form to which they are subjected, new self-understandings are possible that can facilitate cooperative relations among these disparate links of the chain and together they can perhaps transform these material relations. Workers and consumers have developed a small but growing number of solidarity campaigns where they have linked not only supply chain consumers to supply chain workers but also workers to each other from distant links; for example, workers at different factories producing for Adidas have created networks that include sites in Turkey, Indonesia, Nicaragua, El Salvador, and elsewhere.[100] Even when manufacturing has moved, these campaigns to improve wages and working conditions through the supply chain have continued, showing how workers are likely to continue contesting supply chains once they recognize their political form.[101] As I describe further in chapter 5, consumer participation in such campaigns puts the activity of "ethical consumption" in its place by showing that a supply chain can be contested in multiple, political ways which may include consumption-oriented activities like boycotts or purchasing "fair trade" goods but which are not reducible to neoliberal choosing.[102]

Practically, the political conception of supply chains should lead us to demand freedom of association for workers and consumers as a tool to achieve global justice. Through free association, workers can develop alternative accounts of legitimate authority and coordinate to press for the improvements that matter most to them. Free association also allows workers to organize connections with others along the chain, both workers and consumers. What's more, enjoying the freedom of association is a good in itself and the habitual exercise of this freedom provides an experiential ground for forms of identity that diverge from the neoliberal self-understanding of individuals as human capital fostered by constant competition for income—a point I return to in the book's conclusion. Some might note the enormous amount of turnover in most supply chain production facilities as a reason to be skeptical that workers will take meaningful advantage of the freedom of association. Why invest in developing cooperative relations at a particular factory if you won't be there long? Yet this skepticism is belied by the staggering number of job actions that workers undertake even in countries where the freedom of association is prohibited.[103] The flipside of the high amount of churn in factories is that workers are also emboldened to work together to strike, knowing that other factories will also have soon burned through their workers and be hiring again. The importance of freedom of association for challenging the legitimacy of authority in supply chains is also clearly recognized by firms themselves, who regard China as a desirable location for production at least in part because freedom of association is officially prohibited there.[104] Elsewhere, they push hard to prohibit freedom of association in export processing zones and blacklist workers who are known to have exercised their freedom of association by supporting unions.[105]

It's no coincidence that promoting and protecting freedom of association plays a key role in the most effective efforts to reform supply chains.[106]

Following the collapse of Rana Plaza, unions and worker organizations played a key role in founding the Accord on Fire and Building Safety in Bangladesh ("the Accord"), which grew to include 160 corporations from North America, Europe, Australia, and Asia; 10 unions, including 8 unions that represent workers in Bangaldeshi factories; and 4 NGOs.[107] As Alan Roberts, the international executive director of the Accord, explained, "the Accord contains provisions that ensure not just that workers can participate in the programme, but that workers can influence the programme, both in terms of what happens on the factory floor and at the highest levels of Accord decision-making through labour representatives in the Accord's governing body." [108] While it is not clear that the Accord fully embodied these lofty claims, they mark a significant recognition of the political logic of supply chains and the agency of workers. While companies like Walmart refused to take responsibility for the wages and working conditions in their suppliers, companies that signed the Accord were required to spend millions to improve the safety of 1,700 factories; as a result, workplace deaths in the Bangladesh garment industry declined, with twenty workers dying on the job in 2017. While these gains are limited, the importance of even the Accord's limited recognition of freedom of association is underscored by the fact that Bangladesh's garment manufacturers have pursued a lawsuit all the way to the Bangladeshi Supreme Court to prohibit the Accord from extending its operations beyond its original five-year contract.[109] It is likewise important to note the ways that the Accord has been taken up as a model elsewhere; for example, garment workers in Lesotho along with labor rights and women's rights advocates successfully pressured brands to sign a legally binding agreement like the Accord protecting their rights against sexual harassment and abuse there.[110]

Demanding and exercising the freedom of association is crucial to politicizing and contesting both corporate authority and neoliberalism broadly. It asserts the importance of collective organization against the neoliberal picture of a market of independent individuals and facilitates alternative self-understandings. Such collective organization also can exercise power in a way solitary individuals cannot while potentially offering an alternative source of authority within supply chains. In the end, any changes in supply chains will only be successful if supply chains are politicized so that workers and consumers can exercise their freedom not only through neoliberal exit and exchange, but also through democratic voice. Against the pessimism of those who see neoliberal theory and practice invariably reinforcing each other, this represents a great opportunity to repoliticize neoliberalism in the name of democracy and freedom. However, doing so requires a more fully developed account of freedom that can serve as a guiding ideal and alternative to neoliberalism's account of freedom as choice in the market. I turn to this task in the next chapter.

3

The Outer Limit of Freedom

I began this book by considering cases of egregious injustice: the Tazreen factory fire and the Rana Plaza building collapse. Some people do deny these are injustices, like the self-described neoliberal pundit who responded to Rana Plaza by arguing that "in a free society it's good that different people are able to make different choices on the risk–reward spectrum."[1] While my account does have something to say to those who hold such views, the primary problem I seek to address is somewhat different: it's about how those who are troubled by these events should be oriented to them. Calling them injustices is certainly important; it helps us to identify what's at issue as a political problem and not just a humanitarian one. But this isn't enough to orient us to these circumstances and facilitate effective political action to change them. As I've argued, an effective orientation to politics has three components: a description of how existing social and political arrangements operate; an explanation of the prevailing means of making those arrangements intelligible and legitimate; and an account of normative values that ought to be promoted. I've now explained how the key neoliberal institution of the supply chain is legitimated and offered another way of understanding its operation. But this is not enough to guide action. An effective orientation requires more than ad hoc normative judgments; it needs an account of values that can help organize our perceptions and lead us to act.

Neoliberalism represents a formidable challenge to egalitarians of all stripes because it offers an orientation that makes sense of contemporary circumstances and can guide action within it. Neoliberal sociodicy explains not only how things work but also why these arrangements are for the best: though they make the fate of any individual uncertain, markets are uniquely able to produce efficient outcomes that benefit everyone overall. At the same time, neoliberal thinkers like Friedrich Hayek and Milton Friedman offer an account of freedom that is attainable within these institutions and legitimates their adoption of neoliberal policies. On this view, the aim of politics is to protect the forward-looking freedom to choose from coercion; other elements of freedom, like the range and distribution of choices

Disorienting Neoliberalism. Benjamin L. McKean, Oxford University Press (2020). © Oxford University Press.
DOI: 10.1093/oso/9780190087807.001.0001.

available to individuals, are not normatively relevant. Freedom also means that individuals, rather than institutions, should be held responsible for the bad outcomes that come from their choosing among a bad set of options—like accepting a job in a sweatshop.

Resisting neoliberalism requires a different orientation and with it, a different conception of freedom. Flawed conceptions of freedom can seem to provide a path for resisting neoliberalism but instead reinforce it, as Nancy Fraser has argued. Fraser argues that the new social movements of the 1970s endorsed conceptions of freedom too disconnected from solidarity and, as a result, became inadvertent vehicles for neoliberalism by endowing it with their emancipatory sheen.[2] While Fraser's account of history is contested, the general concern she raises remains worth addressing.[3] It's easy to endorse a conception of freedom that has an elective affinity with neoliberalism in part because neoliberal freedom is so ambivalent: it isolates by seeing others primarily as obstacles to the expression of our freedom of choice, but also frees us from customary ties we want to break; its forward-looking orientation readily endows our present choices with the hope that these investments will produce great returns, but also holds us alone responsible for the circumstances we presently find ourselves in. Resistance to neoliberalism needs another conception of freedom—one with a broader view of what threatens freedom today; an explanation of how individual freedom is connected to equality with others; and an account of the temporality of freedom that does not allow the promise of the future to excuse the injustices of the present. The question is where to find this.

As I argued in the introduction, existing arrangements are susceptible to multiple orientations because they realize different, conflicting values; this is also part of what makes it possible to change them.[4] Iris Marion Young writes, "The method of critical theory, as I understand it, reflects on existing social relations and processes to identify what we experience as valuable in them, but as present only intermittently, partially, or potentially . . . looking for possibilities glimmering in it but which we nevertheless feel lacking."[5] An effective orientation directs us to those values and leads us to act in ways that realize their potential. In chapters 1 and 2, I emphasized the extent to which the actual practices of the global economy reveal a neoliberal orientation to be more disjointed and fragmentary than both supporters and critics recognize. In this chapter, I present an alternative account of freedom. In reorienting our view of supply chains, I made a practical case for the importance of associational freedom to resist neoliberalism; that kind of freedom suggests we can find freedom in our relations with others rather than seeing them as obstacles to the exercise of freedom. However, because we live in an unjust world where our relations with others are marked by oppression, we are denied the full experience of this freedom; consequently, this fuller freedom will sometimes mark our experience through feeling ourselves as blocked from realizing it, as unfree. It's not merely that we have a sense we're being subjected to forces we can't quite grasp. Pathologizing that experience entirely can lend itself to a fruitless search for control. As individuals, we're always subject to forces beyond our control; to desire a form of freedom that escapes that condition is to put freedom permanently beyond our reach.[6] What's needed is a conception of freedom that doesn't pretend we can be fully masters of our lives while still facilitating resistance to the neoliberal freedom that leaves us entirely at the mercy of market forces.

In this chapter and the next, I argue that we can draw this desirable and useful conception of freedom from Hegel, John Rawls, W. E. B. Du Bois, Gloria Anzaldúa, and Theodor Adorno, among others. This conception of freedom connects individual freedom to the freedom of others; gives us a different relationship to the past and future; and can ground alternative self-conceptions outside of neoliberal concepts like human capital. As I noted in the introduction, an account of freedom drawn from these sources should be appealing to and endorsable by adherents of a range of theoretical traditions. In this chapter, I show how Rawls's synthetic, widely appealing vision of social justice seeks to capture the relationship between freedom and equality in a way that can be used in opposition to neoliberal orientations. Much of the reception of Rawls's theory has focused on elaborating the implications of his principles of justice for ideal institutions, but comparatively little attention has focused on articulating the vision of freedom found in his work. Drawing out Rawls's Hegelian dimensions breaks from prevailing interpretations that badly orient us to our nonideal world, highlighting how the conception of freedom he shares provides an appealing alternative to market freedom. Emphasizing his connection to Hegel also helps us to see, as I believe Iris Marion Young did, important continuities between Rawls's work and critical theory that suggest further political and philosophical uses for his work.[7]

Yet Rawls's vision on its own is insufficient as a source of orientation; as has been widely noted, his theory of justice ascended in the academy precisely as neoliberal inequality ascended in the global economy. Rawls's method is useful for identifying the normative values embedded in existing circumstances that should be promoted, but taken on its own, his theory lacks an account of power that would enable us to see how institutions actually operate and the other values they promote.[8] That leaves him in the position of only being able to offer a partial orientation—orienting readers to the equality embedded in American institutions while overlooking their reproduction of white supremacy, for example. Consequently, while Rawls and Hegel develop a useful conception of freedom to aspire to, we need to look elsewhere for an account of how that freedom is realized in unjust circumstances. In the next chapter, I turn to Du Bois and others for help with that task.

Rawls and Hegel as Unlikely Theorists of Freedom

Drawing on Rawls and Hegel to resist neoliberalism might strike you as unlikely for a host of reasons, not least because with the ascendance of Rawls's work in political philosophy, it appeared to many that liberalism's face had thereby assumed a Kantian cast.[9] This belief seems well founded on the numerous explicit references to Kant found throughout Rawls's work. As early as 1958's article "Justice as Fairness," Rawls footnotes Kant when introducing the ancestors of his famous two principles of justice.[10] So it is no surprise to find that in his lectures on the history of moral philosophy, Rawls assigns his theory of justice as fairness to a tradition he calls "the liberalism of freedom" and places Kant's theory alongside it.[11] What may be cause for greater surprise is that Rawls also assigns Hegel's theory pride of place there. This may surprise for two reasons: first, because Hegel is not always understood to value liberalism and freedom very highly; second, because it is unexpected to find *Rawls* identifying himself with Hegel.[12] Insofar as Rawls is famous as an exponent of egalitarian liberalism, it may seem strange to attribute great influence to Hegel, who was no obvious friend of equality, given his repellent, hierarchical views about gender and race, among other things.[13] Rawls himself notably describes the Hegelian political state not as liberal but as a "decent consultation hierarchy"—the term he uses to describe the kinds of peoples that liberals must tolerate in international relations.[14] However, over the last decades, there has emerged a consistent and persuasive interpretation of Hegel as a theorist of freedom and restrained advocate for reform.[15] Rawls explicitly avows an interest in this Hegel; he says that he "[interprets] Hegel as a moderately progressive reform-minded liberal" and even says that John Stuart Mill is "less obviously" part of his freedom-loving pantheon.[16]

A contributing factor to the relative paucity of writing on Rawls's debt to Hegel is a hangover from the long debate between liberals and communitarians, with Rawls and Hegel typically assigned to opposing sides.[17] Roughly contemporaneous with the publication of *Political Liberalism*, that debate evolved into the somewhat less polarized dynamic between multiculturalists, who sought for forms of personal identity to be publicly recognized, and political liberals, who championed a concept of public reason that was said to prohibit such expressions and acknowledgments; given Charles Taylor's deployment of Hegel's *Phenomenology of Spirit* on behalf of multiculturalism, Hegel and Rawls were again rarely seen as compatriots.[18] In some quarters, that was resolved into a truce of so-called liberal nationalism—a development welcomed by Rawls in *The Law of Peoples*—which the contemporary global justice literature now pits against forms of cosmopolitanism.[19] By placing Rawls and Hegel in opposition to cosmopolitanism, this framing has made it easier to draw connections between them, but at the expense of making them unlikely resources for thinking about freedom and justice in transnational supply chains. My argument resists all these inherited ways of dividing up conceptual space by asking how their account of freedom can provide an alternative to market freedom.

Rawls's debt to Hegel is considerable and a failure to understand it has distorted many interpretations of Rawls's views. Rawls's Dewey Lectures are characteristic; though they are titled "Kantian Constructivism in Moral Theory," the actual view Rawls elaborates is avowedly Hegelian. In praising Dewey, he writes, "In elaborating his moral theory along somewhat Hegelian lines, Dewey opposes Kant, sometimes quite explicitly, and often at the same places at which justice as fairness also departs from Kant. Thus there are a number of affinities between justice as fairness and Dewey's moral theory which are explained by the common aim of overcoming the dualisms in Kant's doctrine."[20] Rawls reiterates this point in §40 of the revised *Theory of Justice*, which Rawls titles "The Kantian Interpretation of Justice as Fairness."[21] Again, while he pays tribute to Kant, his method of doing so is notably Hegelian. Rawls writes, "Kant's view is marked by a number of deep dualisms . . . His moral conception has a characteristic structure that is more clearly discernible when these dualisms are not taken in the sense he gave them but recast and their moral force reformulated within the scope of an empirical theory. What I have called the Kantian interpretation indicates how this can be done."[22] It is debatable whether or not a Kant freed of dualisms really represents the core of Kant's own thought as Kant understood it. But it is certainly the case that the project of recasting Kant's thought so that its dualisms are reformulated and reconciled by being realized in an empirical framework bears striking resemblance to key elements of Hegel's project.[23] Elsewhere, Rawls explicitly notes his acceptance of Hegel's views, including his criticisms of earlier social contract theories; for example, the final section of *Political Liberalism*'s lecture "The Basic Structure as Subject" is somewhat misleadingly titled "Reply to Hegel's Criticism" because there he repeats *and accepts* four such criticisms.[24]

Reading his corpus with this identification in mind shows that Rawls shares Hegel's conception of freedom as having subjective and objective components that are interdependent and expressed concretely in the dispositions of individuals. In striking contrast to the neoliberal freedom to choose, Rawls shows how a *disposition to reciprocity* both expresses freedom and contributes to the maintenance and reproduction of just social institutions. Of course, there are many obvious areas of disagreement between Rawls and Hegel when it comes to philosophy as a whole and political philosophy more specifically.[25] But Rawls's debt to Hegel is no novelty; those arguments where Rawls departs from Kant by drawing from Hegel are precisely those parts of his theory that make it possible for him to specify what it means to live freely in a stable society characterized by reciprocity and substantive equality.

Explicating the relation between Hegel and Rawls thus serves two purposes: first, it recontextualizes egalitarian liberalism in a way that clarifies its shared ancestors with critical theory and, second, it shows us how to develop a new account of freedom which can both orient us to the injustices of the global economy and be endorsed by adherents of multiple theoretical traditions. To achieve these aims, the following section lays out the traditional interpretation of Rawls's conception of freedom, which focuses on the priority of liberty in his principles of justice. However, this interpretation fails to capture an important element of his thought—what Rawls calls "the outer limit of our freedom."[26] To understand what this limit entails, I then explain the basics of Hegel's conception of freedom, highlighting those elements that Rawls draws upon. In explicating the relationship between political institutions and individuals, Hegel emphasizes habits, dispositions, and attitudes; ethical life (*Sittlichkeit*) constitutes the highest political ideal, subsuming the laws of Kantian politics and morality. This account of norms for individuals in political society has three features especially important to an account of freedom that can offer an appealing alternative to neoliberal market freedom: a sensitivity to the nature of the development and exercise of our choice-making capacity as shown in his account of habit; an explanation of the interdependence of individuals and institutions; and the view that freedom is fully instantiated when our subjective attitudes and habits are facilitated by and help to support political institutions. Freedom is thus both expressed and preserved by the durable dispositions of individuals and so I call this a habitual or *dispositional conception of freedom*.[27]

Having set out Hegel's account of freedom, I next explain how Rawls revises it for egalitarians.[28] Rather than the forward-looking freedom of choice defended by Hayek and Friedman, Rawls strikingly argues that the extent of a person's freedom can only be known retrospectively, as she looks back on how she has been shaped by and continues to live among forces that are largely beyond her control. Rawls believes that this Hegelian account of freedom as acceptance of forces beyond one's control is not an overly conservative view since he does not counsel accepting just any society as compatible with the outer limit of freedom; accepting unjust institutions neither expresses nor affirms freedom. This is crucial to employing a habitual conception of freedom in orienting us to our world, though Rawls himself never develops such an account. For this, I turn in the next chapter to Du Bois, whose conception of double consciousness provides a model account of habitual unfreedom.

Rawls's Liberalism of Free Persons

As the exemplary liberal of twentieth-century Anglo-American political philosophy, it may be assumed that Rawls holds an obvious or familiar view that would be compatible with or even reducible to neoliberal market freedom. When Rawls's conception of freedom is discussed, debate has most often concerned his justification for the priority of liberty, which sparked a famous objection from the British legal philosopher H. L. A. Hart. Rawls himself occasionally writes as though he has no distinct conception of freedom or believes that having one is undesirable. In *A Theory of Justice*, Rawls expresses a desire to "bypass the dispute about the meaning of liberty that has so often troubled this topic."[29] And in his *Lectures on the History of Political Philosophy*, Rawls describes what he calls the "Main Ideas of Liberalism" and says, "the essential thing is to stress the great significance that liberalism attaches to a certain list of liberties, rather than to liberties as such."[30] These quotes sound like attempts to deflate the concept of freedom so that it contains nothing more than an enumerated list of protected rights.

If Rawls thought freedom were nothing other than such a list of enumerated liberties, his account would not obviously offer an alternative to neoliberal market freedom (and Hegel would be a considerably less likely source of influence). However, the list of liberties is only part of Rawls's larger conception of freedom, which can be illuminated by the role that this list is meant to play in the principles of justice. Rawls's two principles of justice are meant to regulate the institutions that comprise what he calls the "basic structure" of society and so the liberties considered by the principles must be those that institutions can protect. As formulated in A Theory of Justice, the first principle of justice says, "Each person is to have an equal right to the most extensive total system of equal basic liberties compatible with a similar system of liberty for all."[31] This specific role for enumerated liberties in Rawls's larger theory does sometimes lead Rawls to sound dismissive of a more general concept of liberty. For example, in Political Liberalism, Rawls writes, "No priority is assigned to liberty as such, as if the exercise of something called 'liberty' has a preeminent value and is the main if not sole end of political and social justice."[32] However, contrary to appearances, Rawls is not arguing here against having a conception of liberty; instead, he is making the more limited claim that justice requires giving priority only to a particular list of liberties. A more general conception of freedom need not be given priority over the fair distribution of resources; in fact, Rawls has his own conception of freedom that is not abridged but instead realized in such distributional concerns.[33]

The shape of Rawls's conception becomes clear if we look at his response to Hart's critique. Hart argued that Rawls was incapable of defending the claim that a liberty could only be justly compromised for the sake of another liberty since he had failed to weigh properly how the use of a liberty by one person could affect the interests of another.[34] Rawls's responded that Hart was wrong about the ground of his view. The priority of liberty rests "on a conception of the person that would be recognized as liberal and not, as Hart thought, on considerations of rational interests alone."[35] Importantly, persons conceptualized as free and equal have the capacity to engage in social cooperation, which Rawls glosses as instantiating "reciprocity and mutuality."[36] Now the limits of an enumerated list become clearer. It won't do to say that a free person is one who enjoys the most extensive set of liberties compatible with others, since the conception of the free person is supposed to guide us in finding and justifying that same set. To meet Hart's criticism, a conception of the person needs to provide a basis for determining the extent of some liberties in order to protect others. Here, Rawls identifies what is most worth protecting as those liberties that make it possible for us to develop and exercise the capacities that enable cooperation.[37] Rawls calls these capacities the two moral powers, which he describes as (i) the capacity to develop and revise our own conception of the good, which gives us an interest in mutually beneficial cooperation, and (ii) a sense of justice, which is the capacity to understand, apply, and act because of fair terms of cooperation.[38] In other words, in Rawls's conception, a free person is someone whose capacity to reflect and act is developed and exercised within society. The priority of enumerated liberties is founded on the capacity to see cooperation as worthwhile and to be motivated to pursue it fairly.

This already suggests the extent to which Rawls's account of freedom provides resources for orientations and self-conceptions in opposition to neoliberal freedom, which sees cooperation as having at best a contingent relationship to freedom. Indeed, Rawls's conception of freedom shapes not only his first liberty-focused principle of justice, but also the redistributive second principle, which governs the distribution of offices and goods. Rawls writes, "Taking the two principles together, the basic structure is to be arranged to maximize the worth to the least advantaged of the complete scheme of equal liberty shared by all. This defines the end of social justice."[39] The larger aim of justice is to maximize not the formal extent of liberty but the worth of liberty, and this is accomplished by promoting the development and exercise of our capacity to cooperate fairly. Rawls describes the priority of liberty and the distribution of the primary goods that guarantees their worth as "a first step in combining liberty and equality into one coherent notion [of justice]."[40]

What marks the break from neoliberal logic is that Rawls's conception of freedom attends not only to the human faculty for choice, but also the egalitarian conditions required for its free development. According to Rawls, people are such that society shapes the development of the capacities that make meaningful choice and consent possible *within* a society. Yet Rawls does not suggest consent as a model for understanding how individuals can relate freely to the society that shaped them. Instead, Rawls writes:

> The government's authority cannot, then, be freely accepted in the sense that the bonds of society and culture, of history and social place of origin,

begin so early to shape our life and are normally so strong that the right of emigration (suitably qualified) does not suffice to make accepting its authority free, politically speaking, in the way that liberty of conscience suffices to make accepting ecclesiastical authority free, politically speaking. Nevertheless, we may over the course of life come freely to accept, as the outcome of reflective thought and reasoned judgment, the ideals, principles, and standards that specify our basic rights and liberties, and effectively guide and moderate the political power to which we are subject. This is *the outer limit of our freedom.*[41]

Freedom on this account is necessarily retrospective and reflective: we must exercise the choice-making capacities of our will in order to determine if we're free, but we can only do so after this choice-making capacity has itself been developed by an environment beyond our control. As Rawls makes clear here, freedom does not aspire to absolute self-determination but accepts the always situated and social character of human agency. To count as being free, it is not enough that a person simply be unconstrained to do whatever she happens to want to do. Nor is it enough that society actively protects a reasonably robust set of possible activities. An essential element of freedom—the outer limit of freedom, as Rawls has it—is an *affirmation* of our situatedness, even though we are shaped by that very situation in a fashion that is fundamentally unchosen and out of our control.

A view that combines an emphasis on the sociality of persons with a belief that freedom can be found by affirming what is unchosen might be expected from Hegel, but it cuts against well-known interpretations of Rawls. In the communitarian critique of Rawls's liberalism, for example, the unchosen encumbrances of human life are often set against a form of reflection that floats free of them; liberalism is said to conceive of a free person as a radical chooser whose relationship to the world is entirely self-determined. The very idea of being able to reflect and revise ends is even said to diminish the ends I do hold, reducing them from "a constituent of my identity" into a mere attribute that can be discarded like yesterday's fashion.[42] But to emphasize only the ability to choose and revise a lifeplan is to ignore Rawls's account of the circumstances required for such an ability to be possible. On Rawls's theory of freedom, reflection and encumbrance are necessarily intertwined. Individuals cannot develop their capacity for reflection on their own. The kind of freedom available to people necessarily includes the retrospective assessment of unchosen elements of their lives so that they may be accepted and affirmed as part of them. Such a conception of freedom is not best exemplified by changing who one is or by being alienated from one's ends. Rather, such freedom has the same structure as philosophical wisdom in Hegel's aphorism that "the owl of Minerva begins its flight only with the onset of dusk."[43] Far from being marginal to his account, what Rawls calls the outer limit of our freedom is where we must look to understand the concept fully—and this is not found in decision-making about the future but contemplation of the past, not in distancing oneself from society but in accepting it so that one can feel at home there.

Rawls's "Hegelian Expressivism"

I've argued that these features of Rawls's view can be used in a conception of freedom that helps orient resistance to neoliberalism. But these Hegelian dimensions of Rawls's view can be easy to overlook since, as I've noted, Rawls himself more often highlights what is Kantian about it. In a footnote commenting on the passage where he introduces the idea of the outer limit of freedom, Rawls writes,

> Here I accept the Kantian (not Kant's) view that what we affirm on the basis of free and informed reason and reflection is affirmed freely; and that insofar as conduct expresses what we affirm freely, our conduct is free to the extent it can be . . . Limits on freedom are at bottom limits on our reason: on its development and education, its knowledge and information, and on the scope of the actions in which it can be expressed, and therefore our freedom depends on the nature of the surrounding institutional and social context.[44]

Rawls notes that his own view is not Kant's, though he insists it is Kantian and it is surely reasonable (in the non-technical sense) to say that a view which links freedom to the exercise of reason has an importantly Kantian strand. So what *isn't* Kantian about this view? The Kantian and Hegelian strands can be disentangled by describing how actions can express freedom. A Kantian method can be drawn from Rawls's remark that "Kant held, I believe, that a person is acting autonomously when the principles of his action are chosen by him as the most adequate possible expression of his nature as a free and equal being."[45] This leads Charles Larmore to describe Rawls's view as "Kantian expressivism" because individuals express their nature as free and equal beings by giving priority to right and justice over the good.[46] Larmore's interpretation resembles the communitarian picture of Rawls in that freedom is expressed by distancing oneself from one's own conception of the good. Larmore believes that Rawls turned away from this view and describes the Dewey Lectures that mark Rawls's turn to political liberalism as anti-expressivist.[47] However, the inclusion of this footnote in *Political Liberalism* itself suggests that Rawls continued to find the expression of freedom to be important and did not believe that a political conception of justice as fairness needed to turn away from this concern. Consequently, a different understanding of how action can express freedom is needed.

Here, I want to point to what might be called Rawls's "Hegelian expressivism," since I will argue that it is foremost in the *disposition to reciprocity* that an individual expresses and affirms his or her nature as free and equal, according to Rawls. Rawls attributes to Kant "the idea that moral principles are the object of rational choice" where the principles are public and agreed to "under conditions that characterize men as free and equal rational beings."[48] But as I have shown, Rawls recognizes that in practice free people do not actually choose principles this way, as fully developed but blank individuals employing pure practical reason. People grow up in certain ways that develop their capabilities for reflection and desire. It is only after they are raised within a society and shaped by its particular ideals and principles that that they can choose freely, which means that they choose after already having particular desires and interests. So how *do* encumbered citizens express freedom at its outer limit? Since freedom requires certain social institutions to be in place so that capacities can develop appropriately, the expression will reflect not just the nature of the person but also of the institutions. Consequently, because justice requires institutions designed to promote freedom and equality, the way an individual growing up under such institutions will affirm his or her freedom will accordingly involve an egalitarian component. Thus, for Rawls, situated freedom is expressed and affirmed by a disposition to reciprocity.

Of course, for us to attribute a particular disposition to someone, she needs to perform actions that follow from that disposition with some regularity. In subsequent sections, I consider the acts that follow from the disposition to reciprocity, but first I want to consider the idea of freedom being expressed in *any* disposition. From the perspective of neoliberal freedom of choice, the actions that come from a disposition are not an obvious place to look for an expression of freedom since it suggests something done naturally or habitually rather than according to a consciously selected plan or prefer-ence. However, this captures perfectly how freedom can incorporate and af-firm the unchosen. This incorporation of the unchosen follows from the way in which Rawls and Hegel both hold conceptions of freedom that include subjective and objective elements that are interdependent. Subjective aspects of freedom are those that relate to the psychology or will of the person while objective aspects of freedom are those that relate to circumstances outside the individual. Conceptions of freedom that consider only one aspect can easily be imagined. A purely objective description of freedom would be one that bracketed psychological obstacles to the exercise of the will and maxi-mized the number of choices or actions hypothetically available to us; this is something like Hobbes's conception of freedom as the absence of "ex-ternal impediments to motion."[49] A purely subjective conception of freedom would be one in which freedom of the will is always possible and external circumstances regarded as irrelevant. Hegel interprets Fichte as having something like this view; where limits are encountered, they are understood as self-imposed.[50]

Kant himself provides a conception of freedom with both a subjective component—the inner freedom of setting one's own end—and an objective one—the external freedom that the state protects through coercion.[51] Kant's view tries to keep these two parts of freedom separate so that duties of right only concern external freedom. This leaves his conception of justice deeply inegalitarian; redistributing property appears to be a violation of external freedom and so, rather than have justice require material equality, Kant describes those who are economically reliant on others as "passive citizens" who are not entitled to exercise political will.[52] In contrast, Rawls stands with Hegel by adding a third component connecting these two parts of freedom. Freedom comes not only with the appropriate subjective mindset and the correct institutions, but from the way these two components can support each other and be expressed in the particular disposition of individuals—that is, their habitual attitudes. Habituating ourselves to certain kinds of physical activity frees us to virtuosic improvisation in its performance; habit-uating ourselves to thinking frees us from distractions; habituating ourselves to seeing society in certain ways disposes us to take the kind of political ac-tion that support just institutions. Habit is thus an outstanding figure for the general conception of freedom at work in both Hegel and Rawls, because freedom is understood to incorporate affirming parts of human life that are not experienced as the result of conscious choice.

Hegel on the Subjective and Objective Conditions of Freedom

In this section and the next, I begin to draw out the political implications of dispositional freedom by offering a reading of certain elements of Hegel's political philosophy as found in *Elements of the Philosophy of Right*. I highlight Hegel's linked arguments about three topics of particular importance to developing an alternative to neoliberal market freedom: the interdependence of the objective and subjective aspects of freedom; the nature and scope of the institutions of ethical life relevant to right; and, in the next section, the ideal stability of the ethical society as expressed in the dispositions of its citizens.

Though the relationship between objective and subjective aspects of freedom may seem like an abstract philosophical issue, it has significant practical consequences. For neoliberal market freedom, freedom of choice is protected so long as one is not subject to coercion by another; in that sense, the relevant subjective condition of freedom is an individual's bare capacity to formulate plans and preferences while the relevant objective condition of freedom is the presence or absence of other individuals who intentionally seeking to direct your actions to accord with their own plan. But these are fundamentally disconnected; their problem with coercion is not that it impedes your ability to formulate plans, but that it frustrates your ability to try to realize them. The alternative view I develop here not only defines different objective and subjective conditions of freedom, but also posits that these conditions must be related in the right way for individuals to be free. In Hegel's account, both subjective and objective conditions are required to experience concrete freedom—analogous to what Rawls calls the outer limit of freedom. Roughly, the subjective conditions of freedom exist when individuals face no psychological obstacles to the exercise of their will while objective freedom consists in the external institutional framework that makes it possible to act freely in the world. Concrete freedom is the resolution of these two into a single concept, in which individuals subjectively grasp the role that the external framework plays in enabling their freedom and so freely endorse it in the course of their everyday actions; this is why Hegel argues that the political state really exists in the dispositions—that is, the habitual attitudes—of its citizens.[53]

How does habit come to play such a fundamental role in expressing our freedom as an individual in society? The argument begins with Hegel's understanding of the subjective conditions of freedom. In §151 of the

Philosophy of Right, Hegel writes, "In habit, the opposition between the natural and the subjective will disappears, and the resistance of the subject is broken; to this extent, habit is part of ethics, just as it is part of philosophical thought, since the latter requires that the mind should be trained to resist arbitrary fancies and that these should be destroyed and overcome to clear the way for rational thought." For Hegel, it is habit that marks the transition from natural impulses to rational self-determination. Habits start with apparently insignificant matters, such as inuring ourselves to external stimuli, for example, accustoming us to hot and cold so that they don't distract us. But habit remains significant at a much higher level, as Hegel holds that it is even impossible to think seriously without habituating oneself to it. In the *Encyclopedia*, Hegel writes, "The essential determination is liberation, which the human being wins from sensations . . . through habit" and "when one is not in the habit, sustained thinking causes headaches."[54] As the considerable range between habituation to temperature and to thought implies, habits can be acquired intentionally or unintentionally and when they are acquired intentionally, they may be the product of education and training.

Habit thus plays an important role in Hegel's normative ideal, not only as a transitional stage which the individual must pass through as part of learning self-mastery but also one of continuing relevance to ethical and political action.[55] At §151, Hegel writes, "If it is simply *identical* with the actuality of individuals, the ethical [*das Sittliche*], as their general mode of behavior, appears as *custom* [*Sitte*]; and the *habit* of the ethical appears as a *second nature* which takes the place of the original and purely natural will and is the all-pervading soul, significance, and actuality of individual existence [*Dasein*]" (emphases in original). Hegel makes a cluster of claims here. Describing habit as a second nature indicates both that habit essentially replaces the first nature of our impulses but also that it becomes so natural that we do not necessarily notice its operation. Thomas A. Lewis puts it nicely when he writes, "Hegel's point is that our habits, our ways of doing things, and our background beliefs make up much of our identity and determine the vast majority of our activity in the world. These are acquired habits, but they have become part of us; they are no longer external or opposed to the self."[56] The way in which habit gets incorporated into the self, so that habitual action can become an expression of the individual, anticipates on a personal level how Hegel will apply these ideas politically. Hegel's ethical ideal is achieved when we are habituated to doing the right thing because it has become internalized from the customs of our society; in his terminology, it is only then that society becomes "actual" and realizes its rationality. This has significant implications for the experience of political freedom and justice, as it may be the case that actions of which we need not be aware play a crucial role in supporting even conscious acts of freedom. The contrast with market freedom understood simply as the deliberate exercise of the capacity for choice is clear.

If the maintenance of freedom requires that individuals be habituated in particular ways, the number and nature of the institutions relevant to justice expand beyond the state to encompass other parts of the social world that habituate us. This turns us to the objective conditions for Hegel's conception of freedom. Unlike the a priori identification of justice with the state found in Kant and some contemporary Kantians (discussed further in chapter 6), Hegel includes all the ethically relevant institutions of the social world—as Rawls puts it in his lectures on Hegel, "the whole ensemble of rational political and social institutions that make freedom possible: the family, civil society, and the state."[57] These three primary institutions together form the part of right that Hegel calls ethical life. Hegel regards family, civil society, and the state as all fitting together into a framework that is, taken as a whole, the complete instantiation of right. In this, it plays a role very much like society's basic structure does for Rawls, providing a unit of ideal evaluation comprised of multiple discrete institutions that constitute the background for individual action.[58] Though Hegel speaks of the state as the foremost institution of right, the other institutions are also essential to the achievement of concrete freedom; all these institutions are interdependent and need the others to serve their purposes in conditions of modernity. This is in part because of the nature of individuals, who require institutions in multiple areas of life to develop their rational capacities. It is also because these constituent elements can be in tension internally as well as with each other, so that each must play an essential role in correcting and thereby supporting the others. The assumption of institutions instantiating multiple conflicting values lays important groundwork for employing this view to resist neoliberal hegemony and perceive other possibilities in our unjust present, but Hegel himself described these conflicts as beneficially contributing to human development.[59]

To clarify how this occurs, consider Hegel's account of how the institutions of civil society habituate individuals and thereby shape their subjectivity. Though sometimes interpreted as being predominantly the economic institutions of the market, civil society is a notoriously complicated concept in Hegel with many disputed interpretations.[60] However, while the details of its institutional instantiation can be confusing, the overall principles and effects of civil society are comparatively clear. The market and other institutions of civil society have two primary effects: first, they treat people as private individuals with their own needs and desires, thereby reinforcing their individuality; second, they show how interdependent individuals in fact are when it comes to being able to satisfy those needs and desires (see §§181–183). Since these effects can be in tension, the institutions that habituate people to regard themselves as both atomistic individuals and interdependent cooperators are a diverse group, including not only private economic institutions like corporations, but also the administration of justice and what Hegel calls the police, which includes public works, economic regulation, and the public welfare system. Though we more commonly associate these government functions with the state, for Hegel, these belong to civil society because they treat people as private individuals with common needs.

This illustrates how institutions habituate individuals: when we continually experience public life in particular ways, we come to understand ourselves along those lines. Consequently, how individuals are treated in one area of their lives may affect their self-understanding in other contexts. This basic thought should be familiar from chapter 1's discussion of how habituation to experiences of the neoliberal market facilitated looking at the rest of society through an economic lens. As I argued, the pervasiveness of that orientation was the result of a political project that recognized neoliberal institutions would only operate successfully if those subject to them adopted particular ways of seeing themselves. Hegel too recognizes the political importance of promoting particular self-understandings and connects this directly to the institution of the corporation—a connection that is especially striking in light of the argument in chapter 2 that we should identify the supply chain as a political institution. He writes, "In providing for himself, the individual in civil society is also acting for others. But this unconscious necessity is not enough; only in the corporation does it become a knowing and thinking [part of] ethical life" (§255). Of course, corporations for Hegel are not the multinational firms that are central to neoliberal practice if awkward to account for in neoliberal theory; while some commentators compare them to medieval guilds, Hegel's corporations are better understood as something between trade associations and unions.[61] Corporations for Hegel serve as mediating institutions that make it possible for individuals to bridge the self-interest of the economy and the common good pursued by the state. As habit represents a kind of second nature, so the corporation "has the right to assume the role of a *second* family for its members" (§252) by training their habits, dispositions, and attitudes to incorporate a sense of their inter-dependence and thereby broaden individuals' interests beyond themselves. Corporations thus play a potentially pivotal role in habituating individuals so that they are prepared to be good citizens who can perceive and act for a common good.[62] But Hegel's particular conception of the corporation is flawed because it too readily assumes an identity of interests among the members of the corporation; this naturalizes the authority of those who are currently in charge, much the way that neoliberal theories like Ronald Coase's do. However, when the economy is organized hierarchically, we should ex-pect there to be conflicting interests, which means that those who are not in charge will often appropriately contest the legitimacy of those with authority over them. Nevertheless, Hegel's account of the corporation usefully marks the fact that dispositions can be trained intentionally by institutions set up in part to serve that purpose and further underscores the appropriateness of seeing economic arrangements like supply chains and multinational firms as political institutions. It also raises the question: Where can we look to find alternative sources of habituation? As I'll argue in the book's conclusion, we can see contemporary social movements play an important role in helping individuals to dispose themselves appropriately.

Dispositions and the Stability of Justice

In this section I introduce the key idea of a political disposition, which use-fully encapsulates the way that this account of freedom can be realized and thus how it can contribute to an effective orientation that can guide action. Recall that an orientation does not direct a particular action; rather, someone who is effectively oriented will habitually attend to the most salient parts of her circumstances. A political disposition is the habitual attitude that an in-dividual should take up that is appropriate to her social and political world; ideally, being appropriately disposed to one's circumstances facilitates judg-ment about what to do and makes meaningful action come naturally.

Framing this in terms of what individuals ought to do—how they should habituate themselves and so on—raises the question of what would moti-vate someone to comply with these normative demands. On the habitual conception of freedom, because the subjective and objective conditions of freedom are interdependent, duty and desire are intrinsically related. When a properly habituated individual inhabits social institutions that facilitate and protect the development and continued exercise of her capacities, then affirming her own freedom also affirms the institutions that have made possible her freedom and the freedom of others subject to them. Consequently, complying with the demands of right—doing her duty as specified by the laws, respecting the rights of others, and so on—does not feel like a constraint on her freedom but an expression of it, since she has already accepted these institutions and their requirements. In the world as Hegel conceived it, the complete expression of concrete freedom appears in the attitude he calls patriotism. However, in the unjust world I've described, the best expression of concrete freedom appears in a disposition to solidarity, as I'll argue in chapter 5.

First, though, I want to explain why it makes sense to think of freedom being paradigmatically expressed in a habitual political attitude rather than the exercise of our capacity for choice in the market. Consider Hegel's epigrammatic statement that "it is the self-awareness of individuals which constitutes the actuality of the state" (§265A). This sounds puzzling, to say the least: Why would the actuality of a state consist in the psychology of its citizens? Hegel's claim can seem like a category mistake. But for Hegel, this is what marks the fullest instantiation of the idea of a state—not only the right institutions, but also the right attitudes toward them. As argued earlier, these attitudes develop out of the experience of the family and civil society, so the self-aware freedom of individuals represents the ideal of all social institutions taken together: "In an ethical community, it is easy to say *what* someone must do and *what* the duties are which he has to fulfill in order to be virtuous. He must simply do what is prescribed, expressly stated, and known to him within his station" (§150, emphases in original). Concrete freedom consists in the individual and applicable social institutions having a transparent relationship so that the actions prescribed by those institutions have four characteristics: first, the activities are known to the individual; second, they promote the reproduction of the social institutions; three, they are feasible for an individual to perform; fourth they are in the individual's interest to the extent that the prescribed actions promote freedom by protecting the institutions or insofar as the activity itself more directly promotes freedom by training the individual (or both).[63] In short, when both the subjective and objective conditions of freedom exist, they reinforce each other. Actions that express concrete freedom thus also tend to its preservation.

Individuals habituated by the right kind of social institutions will find that action respecting the claims of those institutions can itself be an expression of their freedom. Hegel holds the view that the institutions which represent the fullest instantiation of right will lead individuals to support them freely—that is, the institutions will foster durable dispositions that conduce to social stability. Hegel expresses this by saying that, in the ethical society, duty and right coincide (§263). That is, what ought to be done and what people do freely as a matter of second nature coincide—an ideal Rawls too endorses in his conception of a well-ordered society, as I'll discuss in the remainder of this chapter.[64] It is this attitude—the attitude of doing one's part rather than any jingoism—that Hegel calls patriotism. He writes, "The political *disposition*, i.e. *patriotism* in general, is certainty based on *truth* . . . and a volition which has become *habitual*. As such, it is merely a consequence of the institutions within the state, a consequence in which rationality is *actually* present" (§268, emphases in original). Hegel contends that individual citizens do have actions that are required of them, but in a just society, to do so would be a habit, a largely unnoticed and unobtrusive second nature.[65] Indeed, in a fully ethical society we would not need to seek out this training, as the development of this attitude happens fluidly; individuals there are trained in the moral sentiments first by the family and then by civil society until one acquires the universal perspective appropriate to a citizen.[66]

The political disposition that Hegel calls patriotism is thus an expression of the existence of ethical institutions as well as an essential component of their perpetuation. Hegel writes, "Patriotism is frequently understood to mean only a willingness to perform *extraordinary* sacrifices and actions. But in essence, it is that disposition which, in the normal conditions and circumstances of life, habitually knows that the community is the substantial basis and end" (§268). Patriotism is simply the willingness to do one's part in an ethical community. In a similar formulation, Rawls writes, "We need not suppose, of course, that in everyday life persons never make substantial sacrifices for one another, since moved by affection and ties of sentiment they often do. But such actions are not demanded as a matter of justice by the basic structure of society."[67] Just as Hegel had contended that an ethical community would not require extraordinary demands, Rawls's ideal society is one that makes acting justly a matter of course. Once one accepts that the fullest freedom entails not only the right subjective and objective conditions but also individuals expressing their freedom by affirming their circumstances, then it follows that individuals with developed capacities enabling them to reflect and cooperate must all be able to endorse the institutions as compatible with their freedom rather than as alien impositions on it. In short, the outer limit of freedom can only be found once justice is achieved for each citizen in the state and, having been achieved, affirming that freedom helps make justice stable and enduring.

While Hegel and Rawls are sometimes criticized as thinkers with static and homogenous conceptions of society, this conception of freedom can effectively accommodate the experience of pluralism, tension, and complexity that characterizes modern societies even as it identifies feeling at home as a potentially emancipatory experience.[68] While being among people who are like us may be one feature that makes us feel at home (though it can equally be stultifying and make us long to escape), Hegel's account importantly shows that difference can also make us feel at home through its emphasis on interdependence and the way in which conflicting institutional influences contribute to individual freedom; individuals having different roles within these institutions is not only compatible with the political disposition of patriotism, but necessary for it. As a result, the disposition to patriotism can lead individuals to respect others precisely because of how they are different and how their differences contribute to the functioning of social and political institutions.

This discussion of patriotism in an ethical society illustrates how the commitment, shared by Hegel and Rawls, to ground Kant's political philosophy empirically reformulates the relation between individual and institution: the attitude of the former toward the latter invariably becomes a subject of justice because the subjective and objective components of political life are seen to be interdependent.[69] For Hegel, the state is made actual in individual self-consciousness because our habits, dispositions, and attitudes are essential to making a free society function stably. To orient one's conception of politics around coercion, as neoliberals like Hayek urge, is profoundly misguided. Hegel writes, "It does not occur to someone who walks the streets in safety at night that this might be otherwise, for this habit of [living in] safety has become second nature, and we scarcely stop to think that it is solely the effect of particular institutions. Representational thought often imagines that the state is held together by force; but what holds it together is simply the basic sense of order which everyone possesses" (§268A). As we saw in chapter 1, neoliberals define the political realm as coextensive with coercion; by contrast, Hegel argues that it is the *insufficiency* of coercion for maintaining a state which shows that compliance must be an expression of freedom.[70] This concrete freedom expresses a person's freedom in a way that befits people who can only develop their choice-making capacities in collaboration with others, through experiences of multiple institutions. Consequently, affirming the outer limit of freedom also affirms one's society. In the next section, I interpret Rawls as adopting and refining Hegel's approach to link this conception of freedom to material and social equality in a coherent conception of justice.

Rawls on How Freedom is Expressed

In order for this account of freedom to provide an alternative to market freedom and facilitate resistance to neoliberalism, we need to see why inequality should be seen as inimical to freedom. Rawls's conception of freedom explains this. As shown earlier, Rawls endorses a conception of freedom with both objective and subjective conditions; like Hegel, he holds a conception of freedom in which those conditions are interdependent and find their expression in dispositions. But where Hegel sees freedom expressed in the habitual attitude of patriotism, Rawls finds it in the *disposition to reciprocity*, forging an essential connection between freedom and equality. To show this, I first explain how Rawls sees the subjective and objective conditions of freedom as interdependent and then explain why he finds freedom expressed in reciprocity particularly.

As with Hegel, Rawls argues that the achievement and protection of freedom places particular requirements on social institutions, including the state and family, but also requires that individuals respond to those institutions—and to others subject to those institutions—with particular attitudes in order for their actions to preserve and express their freedom. The first direction of interdependence—that of subjective freedom upon objective social institutions—is made clear in Rawls's conception of the basic structure of society. Because multiple social institutions contribute to the development of our choice-making capacity and so condition our freedom, the basic structure of society—the primary unit of evaluation for social justice—takes in more than the state. It is a single structure only as a matter of convenient idealization and evaluation.[71] This view that multiple institutions are necessary to the exercise of freedom and the achievement of right stands in opposition to Kant's view, in which the singularity of the state was its defining feature; its sovereign capacity for uniting the will of all citizens is precisely what enabled it to establish external freedom and its own objective necessity.[72] By contrast, it is clear that Rawls always means to include a variety of discrete nonstate institutions among those which make freedom possible and to which the two principles of justice apply, much as Hegel also highlighted the contributions of the family and civil society to right. Nor does this social influence ever cease. He writes, "The social system shapes the wants and aspirations that its citizens come to have. It determines in part the sort of persons they want to be as well as the sort of persons they are. Thus an economic system is not only an institutional device for satisfying existing wants and needs but a way of creating and fashioning wants in the future."[73] This is very much like Hegel's view of how, for example, civil society itself generates new needs in order to induce further consumption (§191). But while Hegel describes how civil society is in tension with the family and must be moderated by corporations and the state even in an ethical society, for example, Rawls has comparatively little to say about possible tensions among social institutions in a well-ordered society—an issue that I return to in this chapter's conclusion.

Having established Rawls's view that objective institutions shape the subjective attitudes of individuals, I turn briefly to the second direction of interdependence and show that the functioning of institutions in turn depends upon individual attitudes. While Rawls's account of stability undergoes significant changes from A Theory of Justice to Political Liberalism as individuals shift from affirming a comprehensive liberalism to an overlapping consensus, what remains consistent—and what I emphasize here—is the form of the argument: individuals must adopt particular subjective attitudes toward each other in order for political and social institutions to function successfully.[74] On the instrumental utility of the affective dimensions of subjectivity for justice, Rawls writes straightforwardly, "Moral sentiments are necessary to insure that the basic structure is stable with respect to justice."[75] Institutions will only reproduce successfully if enough people want them to; as Hegel also recognized, there are practical limits to what coercion can accomplish. Rawls understands that a free, stable society needs citizens who not only endorse an overlapping consensus of principles, but who are also emotionally attached.

Recall that, for Rawls, the outer limit of our freedom is the affirmation of the society that has shaped us since long before we could choose it. Now we can bring this together with the role of habitual attitudes and sentiments to see why it is appropriate to describe Rawls as offering a dispositional account of freedom. The general adoption of an appropriate attitude toward the basic structure transforms the nature of a society, giving it three distinguishing features: (i) everyone endorses and knows that everyone endorses an overlapping consensus regarding the principles of justice; (ii) the institutions of the basic structure are publicly known to satisfy those principles; and (iii) citizens have "a normally effective sense of justice" and so generally comply with those institutions.[76] This resembles Hegel's conception of an ethical society, which emphasized the transparency of the requirements on citizens, the ease of compliance, the self-sustaining nature of the whole, and the provision of a motive to express freedom through compliance. By meeting Rawls's criteria, a well-ordered society is one that has no internal sources of instability; individuals have no reason to be alienated from their social institutions and so can feel at home while just social institutions are not threatened by a lack of individual investment in their continuation.

Each of these three features helps show how an individual's actions and attitudes can express an understanding and affirmation of a society that she did not choose. In remainder of this section, I reinterpret Rawls's account of an overlapping consensus along these lines, turning to publicity and the sense of justice in the next section. Some worry that an overlapping consensus about principles of justice would stifle debate by excluding certain points of view from the public sphere; others regret the move away from a more comprehensive agreement about value to a "merely" political arrangement. What I want to draw attention to is not the substance of agreement itself, but the general feature around which this contention is centered: the way in which individuals are directed to attend to each other. This returns us to Rawls's account of the role that citizenship plays in orientation, first discussed in the introduction. A well-ordered society is one in which seeking agreement is valuable because those subject to the same social institutions share an equal status; it matters what others think because each is oriented to the others as partners in a cooperative enterprise.

This return to Rawls's conception of orientation cements the description of Rawls as offering a dispositional account of freedom: in order for social institutions to be stable, those subject to them must grow to understand those institutions in a particular way and habitually hold certain attitudes about others subject to them. Where Hegel found freedom made actual in the political disposition of patriotism, Rawls argues that free citizen-cooperators exhibit the political disposition of reciprocity. Rawls tells us that citizens exhibit reciprocity "when, *viewing one another* as free and equal in a system of social cooperation over generations, they are *prepared to offer* one another fair terms of social cooperation (defined by principles and ideals) and they agree to act on those terms, even at the cost of their own interests in particular situations, provided that others also accept those terms."[77] As one of the underlying values of public reason, the familiar role of reciprocity is to describe limits on permissible public justification of political power.[78] It is less noted that reciprocity also encompasses the habits, attitudes, and dispositions that make up a form of life that fulfills the obligations associated with the status of citizen in a well-ordered society. Such a disposition shapes not only their actions toward each other, but also their perceptions of each other. It matters whether or not individuals perceive the institutions of their society as instantiating values consistent with their status as cooperators. Nancy Fraser nicely captures this relationship between institutional egalitarianism and the perceptions of the individuals subject to them. She writes, "Proposals to redistribute income through social welfare, for example, have an irreducible expressive dimension; they convey interpretations of the meaning and value of different activities, for example, 'childrearing' versus 'wage-earning,' while also constituting and ranking different subject positions, for example 'welfare mothers' versus 'taxpayers.'"[79] Rawls's egalitarian liberalism shows how questions of redistribution relate to the political status and identity of individuals, giving them resources other than their material self-interest to weigh in determining their actions; some candidate actions might be not only considered and rejected but never even contemplated because they are inappropriate to the self-understanding associated with the roles of cooperator to which citizens have been habituated.[80]

Such a disposition cannot be simply willed or coerced, but must be fostered. When it comes to the laws of the state for individuals, we expect compliance to be within our reach at any time; we are asked to do (or refrain from doing) things we already have the ability to do. Yet a disposition to reciprocity is not like this; it requires development and training. As Rawls puts it, the role of the criterion of reciprocity is "to specify the nature of political relation in a constitutional regime as one of civic friendship."[81] Looked at in this way, it is clear that many of the thought experiments in which Rawls engages throughout his corpus are not meant only to give reasons; they are also rituals and practices that, if properly undertaken, can help change dispositions and reorient our ways of seeing—or at least illuminate what it might be like to be so disposed. As Raymond Geuss notes, Rawls offers "imaginative constructs that have not primarily an analytic or cognitive function, but persuasive and transformational power."[82] Rawls calls such a constructed viewpoint a "device of representation" and is frank about how they are meant to shape ways of seeing.[83] They are tools to help us see political and social institutions from a new perspective—tools that can be particularly useful when neoliberal institutions train us to see each other in ways that normalize inegalitarian relations.

The original position is the best known such construct, so it may be useful to talk about its relationship to dispositions briefly. In the closing paragraph of *A Theory of Justice*, Rawls contends that the original position is "not a perspective from a certain place beyond the world, nor the point of view of a transcendent being; rather it is a certain form of *thought and feeling* that rational persons can adopt *within the world*."[84] When Rawls says of the original position that "it seems that we have simply materialized, as it were, from nowhere to this position in this social world with all its advantages and disadvantages, according to our good or bad fortune," he is not advocating that we think like this all the time.[85] Rather, he is suggesting that doing so provides another perspective on one's position in society, one achieved by resisting our habituation to injustice. When Rawls rather grandly concludes *A Theory of Justice* by extolling how occupying the original position can help us to "to see clearly and to act with grace and self-command," he is prescribing a way of training ourselves to be disposed to reciprocity.[86] For individuals living under unjust institutions that afford unjustified privileges to certain groups, this perspective may unsettle comfortable assumptions about how individuals have come to enjoy their present status.[87] I explore this function at greater length in chapter 4. For now, I want to note that, in a well-ordered society, the original position can be an affirmation of freedom—not because it alienates individuals from their society but because it helps to affirm and make them feel at home there.

Why Freedom Is Expressed

For all I've said so far, it is not yet clear that the habitual affirmation of society Rawls envisions is itself an affirmation of one's own freedom rather than the conditions that make it possible. That's critical for an account of freedom that offers a full alternative to market freedom. Ultimately, Rawls argues that a disposition to reciprocity expresses an affirmation of the self that makes this an attractive conception of freedom—one that has diagnostic value for those of us trying to orient ourselves in an unjust world. To see this, I turn from the overlapping consensus to reinterpreting the second and third features of a well-ordered society: publicity and the sense of justice.

Publicity in Rawls's sense requires the relationship between individuals and institutions to be in principle understandable if it is to be freely affirmed; the sense of justice concerns the affective resources that can move us to be disposed to reciprocity. What these features show is that when individual identity is understood as relational—that is, when one's identity is understood to be constituted by the institutions and relations under which one's desires, preferences, capacity to plan, and so on were developed—then affirming and expressing one's own freedom is necessarily an affirmation of the relations that have developed and continue to sustain that identity.[88] Market freedom, by contrast, assumes individuals are endowed with desires, preferences, and a capacity for free choice. Freedom is when relations with others allow for that capacity to be exercised unimpeded, but as we've seen, freedom is not relevant when it comes to what constitutes an individual's desires or other elements of their identity; nor does freedom require the possibility of understanding an individual's relationship to those who made the clothes on her back, since such relations of production necessarily escape human understanding, as we saw in chapter 2.

The importance of publicity to dispositional freedom is clear. Rawls describes publicity as obtaining when the political order does not "depend on historically accidental or established delusions, or other mistaken beliefs resting on the deceptive appears of institutions that mislead us as to how they work."[89] As he puts it, in such a society citizens are thereby "presented with a way of regarding themselves that otherwise they would most likely never be able to entertain. To realize the full publicity condition is to realize a social world within which the ideal of citizenship can be learned and may elicit an effective desire to be that kind of person."[90] Individuals must have attitudes toward social institutions that are well-grounded in the nature of those institutions themselves. That does not mean the relations and institutions that have constituted an individual's identity are fully transparent to that individual, but it does mean that in principle, when an individual interrogates the social sources of their identity, what they find is consistent with their self-conception. The affirmation of one's society is freely given in that it does not depend on deception, which would obviate the need for most ideology critique in a free society. This again suggests the fruitful connections between Rawls and critical theorists, for whom ideology represents a key means for stabilizing an unjust society; indeed, Rawls specifically says a well-ordered society will be one in which there is no need for "ideological, or false, consciousness."[91] Theodor Adorno expresses just such a thought when he says, "an action is free if it is related transparently to the freedom of society as a whole."[92] In such a society, individuals can freely affirm the circumstances that shape them, confident that they are not doing so simply as a result of those circumstances inducing them to do so.

However, for an affirmation to be freely given does not yet establish it as itself an expression of freedom. To see why a disposition to reciprocity expresses one's own freedom, recall that Rawls seeks to offer a theory of justice that makes freedom and equality coherent together. So meeting the demands of justice by complying with and affirming just institutions should not be experienced as an abridgement of freedom but rather as an expression of it. What makes people *want* to affirm those institutions? As in Hegel, the capacity for one's attitude to express the nature of the social institutions to which one is subject makes it possible for individuals to understand themselves in a new way. Indeed, Rawls argues that the possibility of seeing ourselves in this way can motivate individuals to act in ways that sustain just institutions. This is the third feature of a well-ordered society—that its citizens have a normally effective sense of justice. According to Rawls, individuals crucially develop their sense of justice from the way in which the institutions of the basic structure not only comply with the two principles of justice, but also express them in some broader sense, promoting a public culture in which those principles play a foundational role. Just institutions have to freely elicit particular dispositions from individuals or their justice will be for naught.

To a skeptic, Rawls's insistence on a sense of justice that motivates compliance might seem like a deus ex machina, and a Kantian one at that—one that succeeds by stipulating that people naturally prioritize the right over their own good. But even from the perspective of our unequal and unjust world, we can find reasons to think that "an effective desire to be that kind of person" can indeed be elicited. Desiring self-respect can lead people to desire fair cooperation and reject benefits from cooperating on unfair terms.[93] Experience in many parts of life attests to our interdependence so Rawls does not imagine that individuals aspire to an impossible form of self-control or self-creation. But he says that we can be disposed to want our accomplishments to be our own in the sense that we would feel our actions and self-conceptions to be less deserving of respect if they relied on deceiving, manipulating, or exploiting others. Cooperating on fair terms makes our interdependence as free as it can be; affirming our society as just thus also affirms our individual freedom, by showing that the institutions and relations that have constituted our identity are compatible with our self-understanding.

Note that Rawls is *not* arguing that our sense of justice as it has developed in an unjust and unequal world is so strong as to make a desire to cooperate on fair terms strong and widespread. If that were the case, then we would already be living in a just world and fair cooperation would prevail. He is more modestly arguing that people *in a just society* would desire to perpetuate it. But if this argument is to help orient us within a neoliberal global economy, then we should still be able to draw from some part of our experience to find this plausible. And we do find this; after all, it was the very discomfort with the injustices of our world that began this inquiry into how individuals should orient themselves today. Think again about the transnational supply chains in which thousands of workers die unjust deaths. People in the developed world are wearing clothes assembled by workers struggling to survive and consumers are often made profoundly uncomfortable when attention is drawn to this.[94] This reflects the kind of sense of justice that Rawls appeals to—a visceral discomfort at the way we literally wear violations of our principles against our skin.

It's hard to feel at home when you're uncomfortable in your own clothes. But under just institutions, the disposition to reciprocity enables one to feel at home in just the way that Hegel identified with patriotism. Actions that follow from the disposition to reciprocity express a person's freedom because they affirm that the social forces of a well-ordered society—forces out of an individual's control but which have nevertheless shaped her and developed her capacities—are not alien but freely accepted. The unchosen is not an obstacle to but a reflection of her convictions. Again, Rawls's argument connects the subjective and objective: this disposition is grounded in the objective features of that individual's social world and the political institutions that make it up; it makes sense to be disposed to reciprocity when you've benefited from just institutions that guarantee relative equality and when you have good reason to expect that your reciprocity will be reciprocated. Such arrangements give individuals good reasons to see the institutions of which they are subjects as expressions of egalitarian liberal values and also to take up a particular way of seeing others subject to them. Individuals can be motivated to adopt these attitudes and perspectives because doing so enables them to affirm that their self-understanding belongs with their political institutions and vice versa—and this is the very thing that Rawls identified as the outer limit of human freedom.

Unequal Status as a Violation of Freedom

Adopting the disposition of reciprocity thus contributes to stability not only for the instrumental way it enables the reproduction of social institutions; it also affirms the individual's status as a free and equal person. Rawls notably maintains precisely the same formulation of this view across his work, writing, "The most stable conception of justice, therefore, is presumably one that is perspicuous to our reason, congruent with our good, and rooted not in abnegation but in affirmation of the self."[95] In other words, justice affirms the political *status* of the individual—that is, the self regarded and treated by others as having the two capacities that make it possible to engage in politics as a free equal with similar others.[96] One will find understanding herself and doing her part as a social cooperator to be second nature—and an expression of herself and her freedom. Expressing human freedom thus becomes not a threat to the stability of a society, but rather, as in Hegel, the surest guarantee of it. Actions that express freedom also uphold justice; equality is not in conflict with freedom, but supports it.

Meeting the demands of justice in a well-ordered society is relatively easy. In keeping with the idea of freedom as entailing affirmation rather than abnegation, Rawls's argument here is attentive to the cost to individuals of compliance; for reasons discussed at greater length in chapter 5, Rawls even argues that the natural duty of justice requires only actions "without too much cost to ourselves."[97] Dispositions are thus an appropriate object of attention since the costs of habituation are repetitive but low. However, the focus on cost and on the right instead of the good should not blind us entirely to the benefits that may accompany meeting the requirements of justice. Rawls's conception of justice requiring only a thin theory of the good has too often led discussion away from the ways acting in accord with right stands to benefit the individual for fear of speaking too fully about the particular good that may result. But to shy away entirely from the topic of how acting in accord with the demands of justice changes individuals, including the potential subjective benefits that may follow, risks creating problems in the other direction by making it seem as though individuals experience only costs when acting justly. This needlessly exaggerates the strains of commitment and disables important resources for helping us understand why individuals might dispose themselves justly. This is especially important when we consider the challenges of using a dispositional conception of freedom as a source of orientation in an unjust world.

In the rest of this book, I turn to providing such an account. In concluding this chapter, I want to return to its opening question about why people might want to resist neoliberalism by suggesting some ways that they are denied freedom today, including its outer limit. Workers in factories like the Savar building that collapsed at Rana Plaza face many kinds of unfreedom. They are desperately poor. Most have migrated from other parts of Bangladesh with even fewer options, as anthropogenic climate change has made agriculture more difficult and precarious a source of income.[98] Most are women, which means they have even fewer opportunities to earn money. Once hired, they face not only punishing hours for little pay, but other clear violations of their freedom: harassment, abuse, denial of bathroom access. These are the urgent injustices that prompted my opening query about how consumers should be oriented to this situation. Now we can add that they are denied the outer limit of freedom. Workers cannot affirm the forces that have made them who they are and brought them into unsafe factories, though they often appeal to future hopes to reconcile themselves to their circumstances. From an individual perspective, they hope working these jobs will mean that their children don't have to; from a social perspective, the justification for permitting such jobs is that they contribute to economic development that makes them unnecessary in the future. Unfortunately, the empirical evidence for either hope is weak. Outside of China, garment worker wages have declined over the past decade.[99] Other evidence suggests that factory work does not even pay more than labor in the informal economy, despite coming with significant larger health risks.[100] Nor is there much evidence that export-oriented development generally has proven to be a reliable path to national wealth.[101]

However, even if these hopes were well-founded, these workers would still be denied the outer limit of freedom because this forward-looking justification depends on the future, not on freely accepting the past. Indeed, what makes these circumstances tolerable to the workers is precisely an acceptance of their purported necessity, of the thought that it could not be otherwise since, for example, economic development must pass through certain stages. But that is not a claim to freedom; it is a way of justifying unfreedom. Of course, libertarians will be quick to note that workers did agree to accept these jobs—and they're right that that fact is normatively significant and should condition how others respond to the injustices they face; as I'll argue in chapter 5, it's one of the reasons why consumers concerned about these injustices should generally defer to the workers' judgment about the best actions to take in response. But such constrained consent in unjust circumstances doesn't mean they are free.

The self-respect of consumers is threatened when they too face a constrained set of options that lead them to live their lives in contradiction with their principled beliefs in fairness. They cannot look back on a life that has been shaped by a habitual reliance on unjustly produced commodities and freely affirm the forces and relations that have shaped their self-conceptions. These supply chains also violate publicity in a way that denies consumers the outer limit of freedom; the systematic opacity of their sourcing—the impossibility of consumers even knowing the origins of many of their goods—makes it all but impossible to know the principles guiding a central institution of our lives. What's more, as I argued in chapter 2, supply chains also try to govern consumers, as lead brands gather and systematize unprecedented quantities of data in order to direct their conduct in visible and invisible ways. Consumers clicking "agree" on long, byzantine data security policies they haven't read is not a meaningful form of consent; not only are most consumers not sufficiently well informed to make sense of them, but they also have little opportunity to say "no" if they wish to engage in normal activities like reading the news or communicating with their friends.[102] And, of course, companies routinely violate these policies in any case.[103] In addition, most consumers are also workers themselves, facing an economy transformed by neoliberalism in a way that more directly constrains their own freedom as work becomes increasingly precarious and responsibility to invest in one's own human capital shifts from social institutions to individuals, resulting in unprecedented student debt, among other consequences.

How does the outer limit of freedom guide action as part of an effective orientation? We now have the first half of the story. Note that it won't do to simply tell those subject to the global economy to aspire to enjoy the outer limit of freedom since they will never be able to affirm the forces that have shaped them. While it is essential that we've clarified the normative value an effective orientation should promote, specifying that value entailed accepting a view in which individuals are deeply shaped by the institutions and relations to which they are subject and under which they develop. That means individuals in our world are habituated to injustice and will often normalize unjust relations and incorporate this into their self-conceptions. In other words, the account of motivation that underlies dispositional freedom means that an orientation to our neoliberal world has to be one that individuals who are accustomed to injustice can adopt but which facilitates action to promote justice. It needs to depict a world that they recognize but direct their attention in ways that may not come naturally. I begin this task in the next chapter.

4

Ugly Progress and Unhopeful Hope

In early 2003, workers at the Matamoros Garment factory in Puebla, Mexico, sought to improve the poor wages and working conditions at the factory by trying to organize an independent union. They were producing garments for sale in the US market for the German apparel and footwear firm Puma. These workers were denied union certification on the basis of a highly suspect technicality and suffered mass firings, harassment, and intimidation by factory management. Workers' attempts to resolve the violations via the appropriate legal domestic channels were unsuccessful, and so they pressed their claims in international forums. They argued that the Mexican government was failing to enforce its own laws, which would violate the North American Free Trade Agreement (NAFTA) and the related North American Agreement on Labor Cooperation (NAALC). With the assistance of NGOs in the United States and Canada, they filed a complaint under NAALC, which led to hearings in 2004 before panels in the United States and Mexico. Following the hearings, both panels found in favor of the workers and recommended what's called "Ministerial Consultation"—that is, the US and Canadian government officials who heard the complaints asked that their respective cabinet members for Labor meet with their Mexican counterpart to press them to resolve the situation.[1] Such recommendations were the strongest possible remedies available under NAALC. Four year later, the resultant consultations produced a joint declaration from the labor ministers announcing that Mexico's Secretariat of Labor and Social Welfare would convene a meeting of federal and state officials "for an exchange of information on best practices" regarding the administration of labor law; in addition, all three countries pledged to work together to produce better "informational materials" informing workers of their rights.[2] No remedies for the particular injustices suffered by the Matamoros workers were adopted. The Matamoros workers were denied a union and, in the years that followed the ministerial joint declaration, the United States officially announced a "general failure" to protect the freedom of association and right to organize in Mexico, contrary to its treaty commitment.[3]

Disorienting Neoliberalism. Benjamin L. McKean, Oxford University Press (2020). © Oxford University Press.
DOI: 10.1093/oso/9780190087807.001.0001.

How can the conception of freedom in the previous chapter inform an effective orientation to these events and to the broader neoliberal global economy of which they are a part? The answer cannot be straightforward. Anyone who wants to resist the injustices of neoliberalism today will never be able to enjoy the outer limit of freedom. They have already grown up under those institutions and their identity is already partly constituted by unjust relations with others; they will never be in a position to look back at the forces that have made them who they are and freely affirm them. Indeed, in light of the way existing political institutions typically realize multiple and contradictory values, some may suggest that the hope of anyone ever enjoying such freedom is a pious wish. What then is the orienting value of a conception of freedom that, while appealing, may not ever be fully realized?

Hegel and Rawls are of limited help here. For his part, Hegel argued that really existing political and social institutions already embody reason and express freedom—a view that Rawls understandably found impossible to accept after witnessing the horrors of the twentieth century.[4] Rawls thought that the best response to those horrors was to develop an ideal theory of justice as a form of consolation and a source of hope. But the resultant vision of society, which he called a "realistic utopia," doesn't readily orient us to our own nonideal world; while a realistic utopia may ameliorate despair in the face of injustice, it doesn't draw attention to our world's contradictions and flaws but rather encourages us to look beyond them. Yet Rawls clearly saw those flaws; he critiqued welfare state capitalism for creating a small ruling elite with a larger permanent underclass denied the equal political liberty required to realize justice.[5] The result is that while Rawls believed existing political and social institutions to be unjust, he provides inadequate tools to orient us to them.[6] Egalitarian liberals who want to resist neoliberal inequality will accordingly need to go beyond Rawls's conceptual tools if they are to realize the values they hold dear.

In Rawls's well-ordered society, the content of the ideal of the outer limit of freedom is supplied by what exists; one affirms the forces that have shaped their life. But that's not possible in an unjust society, so what gives the outer limit of freedom content and makes it potentially action guiding? What is it that can be freely affirmed and how does it help us orient ourselves to the injustices we face? For answers to these questions, I turn to W. E. B. Du Bois and the orientation to freedom that he provides in *The Souls of Black Folk*. Drawing from the same Hegelian framework that Rawls used to fashion his account of a well-ordered society, Du Bois illuminates the relevance of dispositional freedom to unjust circumstances by introducing the concepts of double consciousness, second sight, and the veil. Taken together, these concepts show how adopting the outer limit of freedom as an egalitarian ideal can inform our orientation to the real world injustices of contemporary neoliberalism—first, by providing a characterization of the distinctive deformations of individual identity that injustice causes; second, by illuminating the capacity of ordinary people to nevertheless find the normative grounds to reject those deformations by experiencing the resistance to injustice as an expression of freedom. In the way that it specifies the ideal to be promoted through the negation of really existing injustices, we can see Du Bois employing dispositional freedom along the lines of what Theodor Adorno called a negative dialectic. We cannot say precisely what fully free institutions would look like; on the contrary, we have good reason to believe that our view of them is distorted, since our vision is affected by the injustice that has shaped us. But we can see from our own experiences that we are not free and the negation of that unfreedom can inform an ideal that facilitates further resistance. The act of rejecting what exists can give content to the outer limit of freedom in a way that facilitates pursuing it further.

The Souls of Black Folk is a complicated, sometimes contradictory text with many different political strands running through it—alternatively elitist and egalitarian, promoting assimilation and self-assertion, endorsing political protest but concerned about respectability—and it draws on many different traditions of thought and expression. In this chapter, I trace just one key thread of the book: its analysis of how injustice impairs freedom, which employs and transforms the conception of freedom at its outer limit developed in the previous chapter. For Du Bois, the outer limit of freedom is unattainable for many Americans because they are subject to segregated institutions and habituated to racial injustice, either as victims or complicit beneficiaries.[7] In stark opposition to Milton Friedman's neoliberal vision of segregation as the unfortunate result of individuals freely choosing according to their preferences, Du Bois employs a dispositional framework to show how segregated institutions shape the self-conceptions of those subject to them; as a result, their desires and choices may express not their freedom but rather their adaptation to oppressive circumstances. Du Bois shows how taking the outer limit of freedom as an orienting ideal can help the privileged and the oppressed become aware of each others' circumstances and, through common knowledge of the veil between them and the freedom this denies them, be oriented to each other as partners.

Through its critical employment of the ideal of dispositional freedom, Du Bois's concepts can help provide a useful orientation to the circumstances like those faced by the Matamoros workers—one that suggests how workers and consumers might, in light of this ideal, perceive the political institutions that they are subject to as a shared obstacle to their enjoyment of the outer limit of freedom. However, many contemporary egalitarian liberals extend Rawls's account without accounting for how systematically it must be transformed in light of our unjust circumstances. To highlight the utility of my view, I conclude the chapter by showing how these unreconstructed views cannot effectively promote their values because they lack the tools to understand what individuals should do when institutions fail to operate as they ideally should. We can do a better job understanding what individuals should do in the face of global injustices when we see what leads Du Bois to argue that when we are oriented to injustice by the outer limit of freedom, we will recognize the need for a partnership between those who are directly oppressed and those who want to reject the advantages they enjoy as a result of others' oppression.

Injustice in Sight

The dispositional account of political duties in a well-ordered society relies on individuals readily acquiring appropriate habits and attitudes from their ordinary interactions with existing social and political institutions; in a just society, performing such duties expresses freedom by affirming one's own political status, though it was never the object of choice. But what happens when the institutions that exist are unjust? What attitudes should individuals take up toward their social world and others who are subject to its institutions? And how could habituating oneself in that way express freedom? To understand the challenges posed by the relationship between unjust institutions and individual dispositions, I turn to Du Bois's *The Souls of Black Folk*. Thanks to the work of Shamoon Zamir, Robert Gooding-Williams, Stephanie J. Shaw, and others, it is now widely accepted that Du Bois's arguments in *Souls*—particularly its first chapter, "Of Our Spiritual Strivings"—draw centrally on Hegelian themes with which Du Bois became familiar while studying at Harvard from 1888 to 1892 and at the University of Berlin from 1892 to 1894.[8] Du Bois's conception of double consciousness advances the dispositional account in three ways: it shows how to extend the framework to understand nonideal institutions; it introduces an important connection between perception and disposition through the concepts of "second sight" and the veil; and it shows why political action can be worth engaging in even though it will always reproduce injustice to some extent.

The idea of using Du Bois to think about circumstances like those of the Matamoros workers may seem surprising at first glance, since he is too rarely included in discussions of egalitarian justice.[9] In fact, Du Bois's conception of freedom in *Souls* draws on the same Hegelian resources already considered in order to understand the attitudes facilitated by unjust institutions that oppress some individuals and offer unjustified privileges to others.[10] Joel Williamson first noted that "It would be fruitless to search for a one-to-one appropriation of Hegelianism in Du Bois's essay. But yet it is fundamentally Hegelian, and it is useful to consider it in that light."[11] By contrast, Shamoon Zamir has gone so far as to write, " 'Of Our Spiritual Strivings' constitutes itself as a narrative structure by reference to key sections of the narrative that dominates the central part of Hegel's *Phenomenology*, from the differentiation of self-consciousness from consciousness to the vision of the ethical state, or *Sittlichkeit*."[12] In this section, however, I place Du Bois's essay in the context of the dispositional account of freedom I drew from Hegel's *Philosophy of Right* in the previous chapter. While Du Bois was undoubtedly influenced by the *Phenomenology*'s famous discussion of the struggle for recognition between master and slave, an emphasis on this dyadic encounter between two consciousness can obscure the institutional context and group dynamics that are crucial for understanding the relevant obstacles to and opportunities for freedom.[13] Reading *Souls* in the context of the *Philosophy of Right* rather than the *Phenomenology* also better fits the kind of expressivist view of freedom that we find there. In this, my argument both represents a novel contribution to our understanding of Du Bois's views and helps to illuminate further how a dispositional account can address unjust circumstances.

Du Bois is an outstanding guide for this task because the political circumstances he addressed prefigured our own in important respects. Du Bois published *Souls* in 1903, a time he identifies as "an age of unusual economic development" as well as "an age when the more advanced races are coming in closer contact with the less developed races, and the race-feeling is therefore intensified."[14] Though it predated neoliberal globalization, the context for Du Bois's writing was a time when economic thinking was of heightened salience and a globalizing economy meant that in his view, advocates of racial justice could never achieve success in one country without transnational transformation. In rejecting the idea that Black people could become

free by leaving the United States, Du Bois wrote, "nothing has more effec-
tually made this programme seem hopeless than the recent course of the
United States toward weaker and darker peoples in the West Indies, Hawaii,
and the Philippines—for where in the world may we go and be safe from
lying and brute force?"[15] In other words, Du Bois is writing in a world in
which political economy makes it a pressing question how to be oriented
across borders.[16]

Du Bois also notes how pervasive economic thinking can be an obstacle
to freedom. He laments that among Black people, "the habit is forming of
interpreting the world in dollars"—a habit acquired from whites, among
whom it is already widespread.[17] A key element of his famous critique of
Booker T. Washington is precisely that Washington promotes the adoption
of this habit and mistakenly sees it as facilitating Black people's freedom.
Much of Du Bois's critique of Washington concerns the practical impossibility of pursuing economic development without political power, but he also
sees Washington's endorsement of market freedom as constraining freedom
more directly. Du Bois writes of Washington, "so thoroughly did he learn the
speech and thought of triumphant commercialism, and the ideals of material
prosperity, that the picture of a lone black boy poring over a French grammar
amid the weeds and dirt of a neglected home soon seemed to him the acme
of absurdities. One wonders what Socrates and St. Francis of Assisi would
say to this."[18] Washington's political program, Du Bois concludes, appears
"almost completely to overshadow the higher aims of life."[19] Clearly Du Bois
isn't recommending learning French grammar as an investment in human
capital. But what kind of freedom does Du Bois envisage that leads him to
invoke Socrates here? How is such education and self-development related
to freedom?

Living in an avowedly racist society and mindful of the ways that existing
circumstances shape the desires and self-conceptions of individuals, Du Bois
offers a conception of freedom in which the ideal is revealed in part by the
shape of the obstacles we face to experiencing it. Here, Du Bois's account
of the double consciousness experienced by the oppressed and the veil that
divides them from the unjustly privileged provide invaluable models. Du
Bois famously writes:

> After the Egyptian and Indian, the Greek and Roman, the Teuton and
> Mongolian, the Negro is a sort of seventh son, born with a veil, and gifted
> with second-sight in this American world,—a world which yields him no

true self-consciousness, but only lets him see himself through the revelation of the other world. It is a peculiar sensation, this double-consciousness,
this sense of always looking at one's self through the eyes of others, of meas-
uring one's soul by the tape of a world that looks on in amused contempt
and pity. One ever feels his two-ness,—an American, a Negro; two souls,
two thoughts, two unreconciled strivings; two warring ideals in one dark
body, whose dogged strength alone keeps it from being torn asunder.[20]

This suggestive paragraph has been analyzed and recontextualized endlessly
since its publication.[21] In the context of developing an orientation to injustice, I wish to draw attention to three important elements: first, the way in
which it can be seen as a straightforward application of the dispositional account in providing a descriptive account of how individuals will be disposed
under systems of unjust privileges for some made possible by the oppression
of others; second, the way in which it introduces the potent visual metaphors
of second sight and the veil into the dispositional account, enabling a richer
description of the perceptions of both the oppressed and the privileged;
and third, the way in which these elaborations complicate the normative
demands on individuals and their dispositions by presenting the problem of
how to live among oppressive institutions.

   First, consider double consciousness as an application of the dispositional
approach to describing the effect of institutions that unjustly discriminate
so that some are oppressed and others concomitantly and unjustly privileged. Robert Gooding-Williams helpfully glosses double consciousness as
"the false self-consciousness that obtains among African Americans when
they observe and judge themselves from the perspective of a white, Jim
Crow American world that betrays the ideal of reciprocal recognition due
to a contemptuous, falsifying prejudice that inaccurately represents Negro
life."[22] We can see that Du Bois's account contains the same three moments
of freedom as does Hegel's and in the same relation, but now deployed to
explain an experience of unfreedom. Objectively, the institutions of enforced segregation and discrimination materially restricted the freedom of
Black people.[23] Subjectively, the pervasiveness of this experience in every
area of life invariably habituated individuals to its expectations. Concretely,
these objective and subjective elements find their expression in the double
consciousness of the individual—that is, the disposition of Black people
to judge themselves from the perspective of the Jim Crow institutions that
impair their freedom. As Zamir notes, "The process by which an external

struggle is internalized in Du Bois is also identical to that in Hegel."[24] But for Du Bois, the relevant political disposition both expresses the unfreedom of the segregated world and further impairs freedom by hampering action and autonomy. It is, after all, a *false* self-consciousness; discriminatory white institutions endorse false prejudicial views, which distort self-understanding when internalized. Rather than the easy comfort in and familiarity with the world expressed by Hegelian patriotism or Rawlsian reciprocity, double consciousness represents the dispositions developed from the experience of constant alienation and discomfort—precisely the feeling of an inability to be at home, even in one's own skin.

However, while alienation is a form of unfreedom, the distance from existing institutions that it creates also makes it possible to be oriented to them in a way that can facilitate resisting them. Double consciousness is thus importantly connected to but distinct from the useful concepts of second sight and the veil, which Du Bois uses to describe how perception operates under unjust institutions. Second sight is the capacity to perceive from the perspective of social institutions that are not one's own. On Du Bois's account, this can have a crippling effect on Black people under Jim Crow, as they persistently perceive themselves from the perspective of discriminatory white institutions. But Du Bois also notably refers to second sight as being "gifted" to Black people and second sight clearly possesses a certain efficacy of its own. As Thomas Holt argues, "Pressing the logic of Du Bois's formulation suggests a radical proposition: that African-Americans should celebrate their alienation, for *it* is the source of 'second-sight in this American world' . . . Because they live in two worlds at once, African-Americans possess the power to see where others are blind."[25] In other words, second sight helps its bearers to see injustice more clearly; painful as it is, the contrast and tension between the multiple perspectives they occupy is productive of knowledge.

The meaning of actions and events can look quite different depending upon one's status in a segregated society, as Du Bois emphasizes throughout *Souls*. In the chapter that serves as a biographical sketch of the minister and activist Alexander Crummell, Du Bois describes Crummell's efforts to go to school in New Hampshire, where "the godly farmers hitched ninety yoke of oxen to the abolition schoolhouse and dragged it into the middle of the swamp."[26] The ironic use of "godly farmers" deftly reveals both how they conceived of themselves as well as how they are perceived from the other side of the color line. This capacity to simultaneously perceive individuals, actions, and events against quite different contexts throws the entwining of objective circumstances and subjective attitudes into relief, giving perception a different quality than it has for people for whom the world seems already a home. In describing her own experience as a queer *chicana*, Gloria Anzaldúa calls this effect of second sight *la facultad*—"the capacity to see in surface phenomena the meaning of deeper realities, to see the deep structure below the surface . . . a kind of survival tactic that people caught between worlds unknowingly cultivate."[27] Second sight is thus a kind of embodied practical knowledge, a sense of how to navigate a world in which the meaning of things is not fixed by or for the powerless—though the powerful can often determine their fate. Where feeling at home in a just world allows one to be easily oriented and capable of navigating it effortlessly, alienation from unjust institutions accompanies the habitual need to navigate them strategically, wary of the consequences of any misstep. Those accustomed to being privileged in relation to racial injustice have not had to acquire such practical knowledge about how to navigate the world and, as a result, alienation from the status quo may require their conscious, deliberate effort as they try to retrain the way they see things—for example, by coming to see their "good," "safe" local public schools as the product of on-going, unjust racial exclusions and the lack of efforts to address the widening racial wealth gap. Note that seeing these schools as the product of injustice does not show that they aren't "good" and "safe," but recontextualizes those attributes, showing how they are tied to the position of others in society with a different and inferior status.

This has important implications for thinking about how injustice can impair the freedom even of those who materially benefit from it. When one benefits from racial hierarchy, there is rarely a felt need to look carefully to see how things are; precisely because they can make a home in the world as it is, social institutions can appear to whites as just and appropriate when they are anything but. Alternative perspectives are available, but there may be little obvious motivation to acknowledge or take them up explicitly. If anything, there is an aversion to them and an anxiety about being confronted with one's own bad faith.[28] As David S. Owen puts it, "It is the *content* of whiteness (the norms themselves) that is visible and the *function and operations* of whiteness within the social order that remain invisible (especially to whites)."[29] In other words, white people are perfectly well aware that Black people are treated differently; what they are disposed to avoid seeing is what the world looks like without having privilege normalize the injustice underlying their perspective. This disposition, which Charles Mills calls "white ignorance," is reinforced by legitimating concepts that purport to explain the lower status of Black people (biological inferiority, a culture of poverty, and so on) as well as the enshrinement of particular historical narratives in educational institutions, public monuments, and popular culture.[30]

While nowhere near as damaging to freedom as being oppressed, this incoherent form of perception born out of the receipt of unjustified benefits has its own disadvantages. Describing Southern whites as "deeply religious and intensely democratic," Du Bois charitably notes that "such an essentially honest-hearted and generous people cannot cite the caste-levelling precepts of Christianity, or believe in equality of opportunity for all men, without coming to feel more and more with each generation that the present drawing of the color-line is a flat contradiction to their beliefs and professions."[31] Living in contradiction with one's own deeply held convictions is compatible with enjoying material wealth, but generates its own quandaries. As Charles Mills describes the situation, whites and blacks in a segregated society "are not cognizers linked by a reciprocal ignorance but rather groups whose respective privilege and subordination tend to produce self-deception, bad faith, evasion, and misrepresentation, on the one hand, and more veridical perceptions, on the other hand."[32] Strategies of disavowal that seek to deny the existence of such contradiction can cause significant distortions in whites' self-conception and practical commitments; they can readily become averse to making an effort to live in accord with their egalitarian convictions when confronting the practical difficulties of implementing them in some areas can dislodge the mental coping mechanisms developed to deny the contradiction that remains protected in other realms.

These distortions suggest some of the cost of racial injustice to whites. To see how such injustice can prevent them from enjoying the outer limit of freedom, I turn to Du Bois's account of how a segregated society denies its inhabitants self-knowledge. Central to Du Bois's account of ethical perception is his figure of the veil. He writes, "It dawned upon me with a certain suddenness that I was different from the others; or like, mayhap, in heart and life and longing, but shut out from their world by a vast veil," and "In those sombre forests of his striving his own soul rose before him, and he saw himself,—darkly as through a veil; and yet he saw in himself some faint revelation of his power, of his mission."[33] Note that in the first passage, the veil stands between Du Bois and the world while in the second, the veil is internal to his self-perception. Du Bois thus gives us another way to understand the relationship between the objective and subjective as institutionalized prejudice gets internalized as the split figured by the veil. In other words, second sight is the ability to perceive the veil in the world which most whites try to avoid noticing—and which is in part constituted by this very obliviousness—while double consciousness is the disposition forced on Black people by the veil in the world that results in habitually taking up the white perspective. Black people in a segregated society are thus denied the outer limit of freedom not only in the sense that they cannot retrospectively affirm the forces that have shaped them, but further in the sense that the internalized veil denies access to a clear picture of one's undistorted self. As a result, it's difficult to see what it would be like to enjoy the outer limit of freedom when the individual who could freely accept the unchosen forces that shaped their identity could be so different from the individual they are.

By contrast, white people face different epistemic obstacles to enjoying the outer limit of freedom. Importantly, white people in a segregated society enjoy more freedom than Black people; denying that would itself be a form of white ignorance. But because white people fail to perceive the veil already in their world, they can affirm the false unity of their perspective—and thereby remain ignorant of the way in which they would reject the forces that have made them who they are if they better understood those forces. Such a society fails to be transparent in the way Hegel and Rawls saw as necessary for freedom. Feeling at home among institutions from which one's convictions ought to produce alienation generates barriers to self-knowledge that are not easily overcome. As the dispositional framework makes clear, the habits one acquires from developing in particular circumstances do not vanish in a single flash of insight. While one might come to recognize the existence of a social veil, that doesn't itself produce any knowledge of what's on the other side, for example. Nor does it stop the continuing existence of the veil in daily life from structuring one's opportunities for action in a way that perpetuates certain kinds of habituation. As a result, white people who are privileged with respect to racial injustice have good reason to distrust their intuitions about what parts of their lives they can freely affirm as consistent with their considered convictions—and they should expect that uncertainty to persist. So whites too face obstacles to self-knowledge that prevent them from enjoying the outer limit of freedom.

Recall that an effective orientation to politics has three components: a description of how existing social and political arrangements operate; an explanation of the prevailing means of making those arrangements intelligible and legitimate; and an account of normative values that ought to be promoted. In this section, I've focused on how Du Bois offers the resources to transform the account of freedom found in Rawls and Hegel so that it can be adequate to the first two components. Du Bois's account shows how injustice not only impairs the freedom of the oppressed directly, but also generates new obstacles to freedom, as individuals develop habits from being subjected to unjust circumstances. Those subject to injustice may perceive their unfreedom clearly while finding it hard to imagine a free self; those who unjustly benefit from that oppression may find self-knowledge so difficult and painful to acquire that they avoid it. How can the outer limit of freedom orient people to these circumstances in a way that facilitates effective political action?

Dwelling in Freedom Amid Injustice

To see the usefulness of Du Bois's transformation of the outer limit of freedom thus far, let's apply it to circumstances like those of the Matamoros workers. Using Du Bois's analysis of how unjust institutions habituate their subjects, we can readily imagine both some of the psychic barriers that supply chain workers face to contesting authority as well as why US consumers would be disposed to avoid acknowledging the unjust conditions of supply chain workers and even to actively reproduce the conditions that tend to leave them ignorant. But the relevance of Du Bois is not merely analogical; the veil of the color line is also present in relations along the supply chain, as workers of color in developing and often formerly colonized nations produce for predominantly white consumers in wealthier developed countries—that is, in states which those workers are generally prohibited from entering.[34] Consequently, it is entirely apt for Charles Mills to describe global inequality as perpetuated in part by "global white ignorance" and to describe many consumers as reproducing this phenomenon.[35] Remember that such ignorance need not entail total unawareness of suffering in the Global South; many consumers in the Global North regard the circumstances of sweatshop workers as unfortunate, for example. But they remain ignorant of the processes by which such oppression and violence is normalized as a necessary part of the global economy as well as their relationship to this normalizing process; they fail to perceive themselves as sharing with workers the status of being subjected to supply chains, as described in chapter 2, for example. Race often plays an important role in such normalization. Many people readily accept that deplorable wages and working conditions are the natural state of things in Mexico and Bangladesh; they may even find such conditions unjust, but think that no particular explanation is required for why such conditions are found there. Such consumers are like the sympathetic but ignorant whites who, lacking any idea what it would mean to treat Du Bois as a genuine equal, don't know how to talk with him and "instead of saying directly, How does it feel to be a problem? they say, I know an excellent colored man in my town."[36]

Having used double consciousness and the veil to describe the nature of the obstacles to freedom we experience amid injustice, in this section, I look at how freedom can nevertheless be experienced in some ways. That attention to how an orienting ideal can be partly realized amid injustice stands in contrast to Hegel's confidence in the rationality of existing political and social institutions as well as Rawls's vision of a realistic utopia, which directs our attention away from existing injustice in order to provide the hope that justice might one day be achieved.[37]

We can say that double consciousness is the appropriate disposition for Black people in Jim Crow America in the descriptive sense that it is the expression of a segregated social world. But double consciousness does not present itself phenomenologically as a settled or normatively desirable end state; it is rather a feeling of constantly being torn asunder. The practical question for Du Bois is, how can this experience of unfreedom be resolved or alleviated? What actions should follow from being oriented to its causes and the means of their legitimation? If the veil blocks the outer limit of freedom, what relationship can someone who desires freedom have to this ideal?

Recall Du Bois's objection to Booker T. Washington's endorsement of market freedom; Du Bois rejected Washington's scorn for the value of learning French grammar and wondered what Socrates and St. Francis would say. In his own vision of freedom, Du Bois returns to such figures, writing, "I sit with Shakespeare and he winces not. Across the color line I move arm in arm with Balzac and Dumas, where smiling men and welcoming women glide in gilded halls. From out the caves of evening that swing between the strong-limbed earth and the tracery of the stars, I summon Aristotle and Aurelius and what soul I will, and they come all graciously with no scorn nor condescension. So, wed with Truth, I dwell above the Veil."[38] Here Du Bois offers a vision of how to experience freedom amid injustice, if only temporarily: to dwell not behind but above the veil through the experience of unconstrained thought. The experience of philosophy and art makes it possible for him to imagine free, egalitarian relations emancipated from racial injustice, thereby providing an image that facilitates envisioning freedom at its outer limit. What's more, this imaginative vision is itself an expression of freedom despite the constraints imposed by existing injustice; above the veil, Du Bois can affirm that there is a true sense in which he enjoys his status as free and equal despite the white world's refusal to acknowledge it. This is a limited experience of freedom, but it is enough to make a temporary resolution of double consciousness's tension possible.

This experience of freedom does not look away from contemporary injustice, but is in an important sense made possible by it. Immediately preceding the paragraph on dwelling above the veil, Du Bois writes, "Herein the longing of black men must have respect: the rich and bitter depth of their experience, the unknown treasures of their inner life, the strange rendings of nature they have seen, may give the world new points of view and make their loving, living, and doing precious to all human hearts."[39] It is precisely the "rich and bitter depth of their experience" that makes genuinely new thinking and art possible. The truth that Du Bois connects with freedom— what he has to say in conversation with Shakespeare and Aristotle—is thus not an invocation of any "true" or authentic self that has been left untouched by injustice; rather than divest himself of the distorted parts of his identity, the free individual he imagines is still one shaped by his own history of encounters with injustice but now able to stand in a different relationship to those parts of his identity.[40] As Du Bois notes, he is himself permanently marked by the veil and cannot experience the outer limit of freedom that comes from freely affirming the unchosen forces that have shaped him. He writes, "Surely there shall yet dawn some mighty morning to lift the Veil and set the prisoned free. Not for me,—I shall die in my bonds,—but for fresh young souls who have not known the night and waken to the morning."[41] So Du Bois does not expect that his struggle with the veil, both internal and external, will end. But being able to dwell above the veil, even if only temporarily, gives him an experience of freedom that changes his perspective on and recontextualizes life within the veil. For one thing, it provides hope—not through a description of the institutions of another, more fully just world, but by providing some confidence that this world, which is decidedly not a home for him, is nevertheless not entirely inhospitable. Such hope is necessary because, as he notes, "the facing of so vast a prejudice could not but bring the inevitable self-questioning, self-disparagement, and lowering of ideals which ever accompany repression and breed in an atmosphere of contempt and hate."[42] But dwelling above the veil—the experience of a freedom that feels out of this world—makes it possible to develop other dispositions and habits of mind, to work toward a different self-conception than the one fostered by his circumstances. Freedom and self-development are thus importantly connected for Du Bois.

Isolated contemplation of great works is not the only way to dwell above the veil or to retrain one's habits of mind; Du Bois makes it clear that there can be other spaces for actions that express freedom amid injustice, though they are often narrow. Du Bois notably discusses dwelling above the veil in connection with his very first experience of double consciousness, which takes place not in the Jim Crow South but in his New England elementary school. Students there exchanged cards with each other but one girl refused his card because he was Black. As a result, he writes in a passage I quoted from briefly earlier, "it dawned upon me with a certain suddenness that I was different from the others; or like, mayhap, in heart and life and longing, but shut out from their world by a vast veil. I had thereafter no desire to tear down that veil, to creep through; I held all beyond it in common contempt, and lived above it in a region of blue sky and great wandering shadows." Du Bois here employs the trope of living above the veil as a place where he feels free because he thinks he has made himself indifferent to the effort to rectify racial injustice, having no desire to forge relations with whites. But this professed indifference is belied by Du Bois's experience that he feels most free when he could demonstrate his superiority in comparison to his white classmates. He continues, "That sky was bluest when I could beat my mates at examination-time, or beat them at a foot-race, or even beat their stringy heads. Alas, with the years all this fine contempt began to fade; for the worlds I longed for, and all their dazzling opportunities, were theirs, not mine."[43] In other words, Du Bois's actions expressed freedom when they were actions that affirmed himself and left double consciousness behind. But opportunities for such actions are constrained by circumstances and the freedom Du Bois experienced through his abilities as a child was increasingly denied as racial injustice widened the gap between where he and his white classmates were permitted; his focus had to shift from objective freedom to subjective freedom. Efforts at self-development that reshape one's self-conception consequently become increasingly important as opportunities to experience and express freedom.

Dwelling above the veil is consequently not an unmixed source of hope since the experience of freedom it provides also heightens the intolerability of really existing injustice. And it is impossible to remain above the veil for long. As Du Bois writes in the moving chapter about the death of his first child, in an unjust world, it is only at birth and in death that one can be entirely free of the veil. Admiring his infant son Burghardt, Du Bois feels "a vague unrest" as he contemplates the child's appearance; recognizing that the fairness of Burghardt's features is the product of a long history of racial mixing that has been disavowed by whites, Du Bois writes, "thus in the Land of the Color-line I saw, as it fell across my baby, the shadow of the Veil" (160).[44] One can be free of injustice's influence at birth, but not for much longer. Tragically, Burghardt contracted diphtheria and, refused care by Atlanta's white doctors, Du Bois watched "the shadow of the Veil" become "the Shadow of Death." Amidst his grief, Du Bois's reaction to his son's death includes a feeling of great relief that Burghardt has been spared further injustice and its attendant deformations of the self. He writes, "All that day and all that night there sat an awful gladness in my heart,—nay, blame me not if I see the world thus darkly through the Veil,—and my soul whispers ever to me saying, 'Not dead, not dead, but escaped; not bond, but free.' . . . Fool that I was to think or wish that this little soul should grow choked and deformed within the Veil!"[45] Du Bois's awful gladness that his son has escaped is a stunning illustration of the severity of the harms of injustice. As Annie Menzel puts it, Du Bois evinces "an agonizing paradox: the clearest expression of love for a child may be the wish for its corporeal death . . . Life's duration under these conditions means at least some degree of spiritual death; conversely, life in its expansive fullness may perhaps only be preserved by an early corporeal death."[46] Du Bois directly links this back to his vision of freedom, ending the chapter on Burghardt's death by writing, "Sleep, then, child,—sleep till I sleep and waken to a baby voice and the ceaseless patter of little feet—above the Veil."[47] Du Bois describes the freedom from injustice that Burdhardt finds in death with the same language that he uses to describe the freedom he experiences in the thinking that lets him dwell above the veil.[48]

Why associate freedom and death? Many have pointed to the echoes of German romanticism in this gesture, which arguably points to a sublime exit from the world, but I want to focus on its contribution to a practical ori-entation to resisting injustice.[49] The experience of dwelling above the veil is not an ideal that floats free from the world as it is, but is instead intimately linked to the pain of injustice. Such pain punctures the legitimations of our world and impels us to conceive ways of experiencing freedom; the experi-ence of freedom in turn both heightens the pain of injustice by revealing its contingent character and offers hope that can sustain resistance to injustice. Burghardt, whom Du Bois called "this revelation of the divine," functions as a totem of both ways in which one might dwell above the veil, symbolizing their intimate relation.

Anzaldúa argues for the general applicability of the perceptual intertwining of pain and freedom, writing that "anything that breaks into one's everyday mode of perception, that causes a break in one's defenses and resistance, anything that takes one from one's habitual grounding, causes the depths to open up, causes a shift in perception. This shift in perception deepens the way we see concrete objects and people."[50] By breaking through habitual ways of thinking about the world and about ourselves, pain from injustice opens up the possibility of something like second sight even to people who in other respects benefit from injustice. As Anzaldúa notes, such interruptions are inherently forms of loss: "We lose something in this mode of initiation, something is taken from us: our innocence, our unknowing ways, our safe and easy ignorance . . . Confronting anything that tears the fabric of our everyday mode of consciousness and that thrusts us into a less literal and more psychic sense of reality increases awareness and *la facultad*."[51] Though harm would be appear to be unambiguously negative in a world where the outer limit of freedom could actually be enjoyed, such loss can facilitate freedom in our unjust world by jarring us from the self-understandings we've developed under existing circumstances and making new critical perspectives possible, even necessary.[52] This has important implications not only for the oppressed who already regularly confront harm, but for those privileged in relation to existing injustice, highlighting a reason to welcome the loss of their privilege that justice entails.

Freedom's Negative Dialectic

One way to sum up what I've said so far is that employing the outer limit of freedom in an orientation to injustice interprets this ideal along the lines of what Adorno called a "negative dialectic."[53] Hegel affirms the fundamental rationality of what exists and argues that the failures and injustices of the past were necessary to the achievement of our society, vindicating the harms of the past and present as consistent with reason. By contrast, Adorno argues that "the smallest trace of senseless suffering in the empirical world belies all the identitarian philosophy that would talk us out of that suffering."[54] For Adorno, the pain of injustice serves as a standing refutation of any attempt to argue that the present can be affirmed. And like Du Bois and Anzaldúa,

Adorno argues that this pain is intimately linked to the kind of freedom we can experience; where Du Bois describes how the "bitter depth" of life also makes it temporarily possible to dwell above the veil, Adorno suggests we can experience freedom in "the power of the mind to retain its self-control in the face of the sorrow" caused by injustice.[55] Like Du Bois before him and Anzaldúa after, Adorno sees the capacity to engage in thinking as an experience of freedom that can change our orientation to the world as it is. Where Hegel sees the outer limit of freedom affirmed in a world where objectively and subjectively free individuals are disposed to readily express that freedom through patriotism, these thinkers see freedom expressed in a negation of the world as it is, which affords most people neither objective nor subjective freedom.[56]

This negation of the world is not a counsel of hopelessness. Instead, it promotes an attitude that better facilitates action against injustice than Rawls's image of a realistic utopia free of the injustices of our world. Oriented by the outer limit of freedom, people on both sides of the veil might come to see the act of working against injustice as itself an expression of their freedom and therefore worth undertaking together as partners, despite the uncertainty of success. Kwame Anthony Appiah describes the practical import of such negation, writing, "The history of our collective moral learning . . . starts with the rejection of some current actual practice or structure, which we come to see as wrong. You learn to be in favor of equality by noticing what is wrong with the unequal treatment of blacks, or women, or working-class or lower-caste people."[57] Notably, Du Bois characterizes his infant son's attitude toward the veil as "a hope not hopeless but unhopeful" and I will argue that this serves as an apt characterization of the attitude that Du Bois believes accompanies an orientation to the outer limit of freedom as an ideal.[58] Such unhopeful hope changes our view of political action, encouraging us to recognize that resisting injustice can be meaningful even though such actions are themselves not wholly free. Because injustice habituates us to its perpetuation, even our actions to resist it will often reproduce injustices since our self-conceptions remains shaped by them. As we've already seen, Du Bois makes it clear that life in the shadow of the veil has shaped him irreversibly so that he will never be entirely free. Du Bois's text itself reflects this habituation to injustice; even as it highlights the emancipatory possibilities found amid grave racial injustice, *Souls* reproduces oppressive tropes that normalize gender and class hierarchies.[59] Because it is generally true that individuals are habituated by such unjustified hierarchies, political action is pervasively imperfect and likely to reproduce elements of injustice. Consequently, we should not expect any political action to be an unambiguous expression or achievement of freedom—but neither should we become unduly discouraged when we find this to be the case.

One key way that unjust circumstances habituate individuals to reproducing injustice is through forcing them to make tragic choices in which any action possible for them produces some wrong. Du Bois writes, "To-day the young Negro of the South who would succeed cannot be frank and outspoken . . . he must flatter and be pleasant, endure petty insults with a smile, shut his eyes to wrong; in too many cases he sees positive personal advantage in deception and lying."[60] Racial domination pushes Black people to respond either by adapting themselves to its demands or by suffering potentially grave penalties for acting as they would prefer. Du Bois writes sympathetically of those who act as injustice demands, "With this sacrifice there is an economic opening, and perhaps peace and some prosperity. Without this there is riot, migration, or crime."[61] While it would be most hopeful to suggest that doing the right thing and standing up for oneself against injustice will invariably have good effects in the world, Du Bois denies this; perhaps refusing to comply with unjust demands is the right thing to do, but Du Bois acknowledges that it may nevertheless cause harm. Adorno put the point in general form when he wrote, "Wrong life cannot be lived rightly."[62] And strikingly, in *Souls*, Du Bois generalizes this tragic dilemma too, writing "Nor is this situation peculiar to the Southern United States, is it not rather the only method by which undeveloped races have gained the right to share modern culture? The price of culture is a Lie."[63] Du Bois's expansion of the critique here—from Black people in the South to all of what would come to be called the Third World—prefigures Adorno in its pithy formulation of the practical paradoxes faced by those who resist injustice, but attends to the racial dimensions of global injustice that Adorno largely ignored.[64] That recognition is crucial because "wrong life" means different things for the young Black man forced to lie and the alienated white man who cannot live in accord with his egalitarian convictions; those divergent circumstances matter when we think about who bears the costs of actions that unavoidably reproduce some injustice. For both authors, the paradigmatic form of guidance that philosophers and theorists can provide is not to identify a morally unimpeachable path forward that puts us above reproach, but to provide conceptual tools for orienting their readers to the practical dilemmas that they face.

Just because wrong life cannot be lived rightly does not mean that there are not better and worse ways to live.

Attending to the losses that accompany political action may seem to discourage people from resisting injustice—an interpretation bolstered by Adorno's reputation as an academic mandarin who disdained activism.[65] But I believe it is more in keeping with Du Bois's unhopeful hope to see how this critical employment of the outer limit of freedom helps us perceive new possibilities for action. I want to highlight two ways that attention to the loss that attends political action serves this function. First, we have already seen the way that loss itself can jar individuals into new perspectives and impel further efforts to express freedom. Efforts to identify unimpeachable acts that avoid loss will be self-defeating and falsely equate freedom with control over our actions, their meanings, and their effects. Such a conception of freedom emphasizes consent as the central experience of freedom, but as the outer limit of freedom shows, crucial experiences of freedom cannot be understood on that model; we can never consent to the unchosen forces that shape our lives before we're capable of choice, but we can aspire to be in a position to affirm them. In that spirit, Adorno argues that we will be freer if we accept that we do not always know where our freedom is to be found. He writes, "Good is what wrenches itself free, finds a language, opens its eyes. In its condition of wrestling free, it is interwoven in history that, without being organized unequivocally toward reconciliation, in the course of its movement allows the possibility of redemption to flash up."[66] In Du Bois's language, we might more readily find ourselves dwelling above the veil if we do not imagine that there is foolproof way to get there or that we already know what things will look like when we do. Conceding that our subjection to injustice limits us in ways that we cannot always anticipate or avoid thus better facilitates actions that do express freedom than the assumption that we might be able to identify and perform an unimpeachably free act. The acts we can perform are interwoven with injustice, but can still be expressions of freedom—even though they, in turn, have features that must themselves be negated. This negative dialectic is thus guided by the ideal of freedom at its outer limit without claiming to know under what circumstances such an ideal could be fully realized.

Second, this acknowledgment that actions under unjust circumstances can express freedom and resist injustice while nevertheless having a remainder of loss can contribute to resisting the sociodicy of neoliberalism. Neoliberalism sociodicy, which explains why market forces necessarily produce the best possible results despite the fact that no particular outcome can ever be predicted, is the latest iteration of the thought that progress is of unambiguous benefit to all. Du Bois recognized a version of this thought in Booker T. Washington's commitment to economic advancement as a cure-all and showed how his own experience belied such unjustified faith in progress. The chapter of *Souls* devoted to his two summers volunteering as a school teacher in rural Tennessee is entitled "Of the Meaning of Progress" and Du Bois closes the chapter by describing his experience returning a decade later and seeing what had changed. Of seeing what replaced the building where he taught, Du Bois writes, "My log schoolhouse was gone. In its place stood Progress; and Progress, I understand, is necessarily ugly . . . As I sat by the spring and looked on the Old and the New I felt glad, very glad, and yet—"[67] Where Du Bois surprises the reader with the awful gladness he felt at the sad event of his son's needless death, here he records the unexpected ambivalence he feels seeing material resources for the very poor happily improved. Du Bois's recognition of loss entails understanding that progress does not benefit all and is instead "necessarily ugly." This necessary ugliness leads Du Bois to hesitate—to feel "glad, and yet"—because he knows that this progress came at a cost and required leaving others behind. Du Bois has just learned the fates of his former students and found that Josie, his most enthusiastic student, essentially worked herself to death in her efforts to materially support her parents and sibling. This leads Du Bois to ask at the end of the chapter, "How shall man measure Progress there where the dark-faced Josie lies? How many heartfuls of sorrow shall balance a bushel of wheat?"[68] Du Bois suggests here that prevailing conceptions of progress, whether Hegel's philosophy of history or Washington's belief in economic development, fail to adequately register its necessary ugliness and, as a result, they overlook the oppression that accompanies the growth of what they identify as freedom. Drawing attention to the loss that accompanies action thus promotes freedom by helping to ensure we attend to real unfreedom; untroubled sociodicies that assure us rising material wealth benefits everyone mask the constraints on freedom that they impose. This is what Adorno calls "the absurdity that it is progress itself that inhibits progress."[69] Neoliberal sociodicy presents itself as a story of progress—the unshackling of the market that will, by definition, produce greater material for all over the long run—but the acceptance of this story as legitimating the inequalities and injustices produced by market freedom blocks the way to addressing those obstacles to freedom. The remedy is to focus on losses, which can jar us from our habitual perceptions in accord with the prevailing forms of legitimating existing arrangements: "Having arisen socially, the concept of progress requires critical confrontation with real society."[70] Attention to those who are left behind or are harmed by progress prevents the concept from becoming a tool for normalizing injustice and reproducing ignorance.

Partnerships Across the Veil

So let us return to "real society" and ask again, what does all this mean for an orientation to the circumstances of the Matamoros workers? Du Bois's analysis shows how injustice predictably divides society. Those who are most directly oppressed face distinctive subjective and objective obstacles to freedom, but their habituation to injustice also leads them to acquire a keener sense of society's actual operation; meanwhile, those who benefit from injustice—even if only from the comparative advantages they enjoy as a result of not being oppressed—tend to be averse to acknowledging the nature of their position and, as a result, face obstacles to enjoying both self-knowledge and self-respect. Individuals on either side of the veil have been shaped by forces that they would reject if they have egalitarian convictions and, as a result, cannot experience the outer limit of freedom. But there are other, more limited experiences of freedom available to them, including through the work of retraining their attitudes and habits. They are more likely to act to resist injustice when they recognize that, under unjust conditions, there is no perfect way to do so; any action will likely have some meaning or effect that reproduces injustice and will need to be negated in turn, leaving the struggle against injustice without a clear endpoint. Consequently, while the outer limit of freedom provides a guiding ideal, actions that seek to express freedom by resisting injustice do not require images of distant utopias, however "realistic," but can be oriented by more proximate concerns.

For Du Bois, this combination of features has an important practical upshot: people on both sides of the veil should work together to resist injustice. Du Bois's ideal of freedom thus facilitates the identification of injustice as a shared obstacle to freedom that at least some people on both sides of the veil have reason to work together to remove.[71] We can see this in two ways: first, the audience that *Souls* addresses; second, the actual argument of *Souls*. Du Bois models and anticipates the cross-racial coalition necessary to resist racial injustice with the audience to which he addresses *Souls*. *Souls* offers white and Black readers different paths to this conclusion. Second sight entails that Du Bois's Black readers already possess some understanding of the perspective of white institutions; to them, he addresses arguments that explain the mechanisms of double consciousness in order to explain what gives rise to such a widespread disposition and thereby facilitate actions that express freedom. For the same reason, he engages debates about Black political strategy, including his critique of Booker T. Washington. For his white readers, Du Bois positions himself as a guide who can show them a world otherwise hidden from them. As he explains in the "Forethought," "I have stepped within the Veil, raising it that you may view faintly its deeper recesses." Identifying himself as "bone of the bone and flesh of the flesh of them that live within the Veil," Du Bois seeks to model a cross-racial partnership through his engagement with a white reader.[72] As Melvin Rogers has argued, "In suggesting that they (speaker and listener) will arrive at shared judgments regarding the plight of blacks and the deficiencies of the polity, [Du Bois] also suggests that they will have tied themselves together in a community based on shared emotional dispositions regarding the subject matter."[73] In particular, Rogers argues that "the power of *Souls* is bound up with its aspiration to persuade through an appeal to affirmative and negative emotional states, namely, sympathy and shame."[74] In portraying terrible injustices like the unnecessary death of his son—and the way whites responded to his burial procession not merely with cold indifference but vituperative racial slurs—Du Bois aims to elicit from his white readers an empathetic identification with black suffering.[75]

On Rogers's interpretation, the unjust and unnecessary character of such suffering works to shame the concerned whites who would actually read *Souls*, making vivid the distance between their egalitarian convictions and the inegalitarian reality from which they benefit. Rogers writes, "Shame honors the judgment of the reader by encouraging a self-critical stance toward one's treatment of African-Americans that reflexively reveals the moral deficit within oneself and one's political community, which should in turn generate outrage regarding racial injustice."[76] As we've seen, this inward-looking work to retrain one's self-understanding is an important part of Du Bois's account of how freedom can be experienced. But it is not all of it; among other things, self-criticism by whites is likely to partially reproduce a lifetime of habituation to injustice. Centering this approach also risks instrumentalizing Black suffering to the furtherance of white self-improvement through sympathy. As Rogers puts it, "Du Bois thus attends to the 'souls' of black folk—both the work they may yet contribute and the deprivation they experience—in order to reveal and redirect the 'souls' of white folk."[77] If that formulation were the whole story, then relations between deprived Blacks and sympathetic whites would remain fundamentally inegalitarian, with whites addressed primarily as political agents and Blacks addressed primarily as suffering victims.

The avoidance of shame can undoubtedly be a powerful motivator to address racial injustice. As Christopher J. Lebron argues, "Shame, then, challenges us to display principled consistency between beliefs and attitudes and actions. I imagine this being a deeply valuable tool for a society largely populated by morally and ethically disadvantaged agents, for it is a mechanism whereby persons can come to affirm the principles of justice in accordance with their own account of basic principles of rightness and goodness."[78] Like Rogers's, Lebron's optimistic reading of the deployment of shame in politics suggests that it can drive whites to resolve the contradiction between their convictions and their habitual actions in favor of living a more consistently egalitarian life. However, other coping strategies exist and may be more readily adopted; an aversion to shame may instead drive whites to deepen segregation so that they live only among the likeminded and consequently need not fear the shameful exposure of their hypocrisy. Such an outcome may be even more likely in cases of pervasive injustice when wholly divesting oneself of unjustified privileges is all but impossible. After all, no individual white citizen can singlehandedly abolish white privilege and thereby live in accord with their considered convictions. That is not to say that they don't have an obligation to promote movements that seek racial justice—quite the contrary—but it is important to note that in such cases, even individuals acting in good faith to promote justice may find something shameful about their circumstances.

Shame thus has important limits as a political tool. Rather than centering shame, I interpret Du Bois as arguing that the best way to lift the veil is for concerned whites and Blacks to work together as partners who understand their interdependence. Addressing the question of how whites and Blacks should be oriented to each other, he writes, "the future of the South depends on the ability of the representatives of these opposing views to see and appreciate and sympathize with each other's position . . . They both act as reciprocal cause and effect, and a change in neither alone will bring the desired effect. Both must change, or neither can improve to any great extent."[79] The stakes of the struggle are, of course, very different for the two sides. Du Bois has already lost a son to the veil while sympathetic whites face threats to their self-respect and self-knowledge; such harms are not as grave as the oppression faced by Black people, though individuals who feel threats to the integrity of their self-conception may be more readily moved to action than those who rightly fear retaliatory violence. And it is obvious that white people in a Jim Crow society have vastly more power than Black people. With respect to social power, the testimony of a white person could send a Black person to jail or get them lynched; with respect to political power, most have some access to the ballot, which was largely denied to Blacks. That's one reason why it is useful for Black people to ally with concerned whites, who may protest where they cannot. But it is important to recognize the limits of a white individual's power; while unjust circumstances endow them with great power to harm Black people, that doesn't entail that they have great power to change the unjust circumstances which grant them this unjustified hierarchical status. What's more, they lack the knowledge necessary to remove the veil themselves because of the habitual ignorance of the veil and the lives behind it that even concerned whites are disposed to; lacking a certain self-knowledge, they often don't even know what they don't know. They too have reason to ally with Black people in order to realize their egalitarian convictions so they can achieve greater knowledge of the forces that have shaped them and acquire the self-respect that comes from the confidence that one's achievements are justly one's own.

In short, by employing the outer limit of freedom as an ideal and thereby identifying grounds for both Black and white people to understand racial injustice as impairing their freedom, Du Bois gives them reason to see the veil as a *shared* obstacle to freedom, one that they should address as partners in resistance. That orientation to the veil importantly differs from one centered on sympathy with others' suffering, which exhibits a more altruistic attitude. In that way, having whites avow their own interest in achieving racial justice better facilitates egalitarian relations than efforts to move them to act exclusively because of harms done to others. This returns us to the question of the appropriate orientation to the circumstances of the Matamoros workers, who endured terrible wages and working conditions in a factory in Mexico producing garments for a German brand that were sold to US and Canadian consumers. Following Du Bois's framework, workers and consumers should see the transnational supply chain as a shared obstacle to freedom. The Matamoros workers themselves had such an awareness as they reached out to US and Canadian groups for support; that's unsurprising as Du Bois's framework suggests that they're likely to be in a better epistemic position to navigate injustices than those who benefit from their oppression. But consumers generally should consider how injustices along the supply chains which they rely on threaten their own integrity and self-respect; they should reflect on the extent which their self-conceptions normalize injustices—for example, because of the race of the oppressed or the purported necessity of their oppression for the greater good—and engage in the work of retraining their habitual perceptions of the world. As I argued in chapter 2, consumers already tend to regard the products of transnational supply chains as uncanny when they reflect on them and it is difficult to overcome this uncanniness without changing the actual social relations that give rise to supply chains; as Anzaldúa argued that *la facultad* is "the capacity to see in surface phenomena the meaning of deeper realities," we can see in the experience of the supply chain's uncanniness an intuition of the great power that they have over our lives. For this reason, consumers seeking to resist their habituation to injustice have all the more reason to regard supply chain workers as partners and to take action with them to resist supply chain injustices—for example, by protesting the failure of Puma and the Mexican government to protect the freedom of association of the Matamoros workers. In doing so, they may find the experience of taking action against injustice to express their own freedom; by contesting supply chain authority, they are politicizing neoliberal policies that treat them unjustly as well, showing that durable freedom requires more than the freedom to choose in the market. As I argue in the next chapter, such solidarity between workers and consumers is the key to resisting not only supply chain injustices but neoliberalism more broadly.

Prevailing Perceptions of Global Injustice

In this chapter, I've shown how the ideal of the outer limit of freedom must be modified in order to guide action in a world of injustice and unfreedom. Du Bois suggests three important ways it can do so: first, by showing how the difficult work of retraining one's habitual attitudes can be an expression of freedom; second, by showing how working for justice can be meaningful even though the injustice of our world means that such work will not itself be fully free; third, by facilitating the identification of injustice as a shared obstacle to freedom that at least some people on both sides of the veil have reason to work together to remove. This orientation to solidaristic partnership in political action is quite different from the predominant way that Rawls's view has been applied in the egalitarian liberal literature on global justice, so I want to conclude this chapter by highlighting some of the problems with that way of proceeding before further developing my own view in the next chapter. Because Rawls's dispositional account of freedom has been overlooked, the focus of egalitarian liberals for the past several decades has been largely on principles of justice for institutions as well as the related questions of their legitimacy and appropriate scope. As a result, when they do consider the question of how individuals should respond to injustices in the global economy like those faced by the Matamoros workers, this literature tends to assume that individuals should draw their orientation from existing institutions. But as we've already seen, the orientations that individuals develop under unjust circumstances tend to facilitate actions that reproduce those circumstances. As a result, most egalitarian liberal arguments about why individuals have duties of justice that cross borders lack any account of how to specify them.

I've argued that egalitarian liberals can be an important part of a coalition to resist neoliberal injustice. That can be facilitated by breaking with these prevailing approaches, which assume that because principles of justice apply to institutions first of all, the focus of theorizing about global justice should be on determining the most just rules for international institutions. Liam Murphy captures the foundation of this conventional wisdom with his assertion that Rawls believed "the two practical problems of institutional design and personal conduct require, at the fundamental level, two different kinds of practical principle." Murphy objected to this position, which he called "dualism," and argued for "monism," which rejects the idea that "that there could be a plausible fundamental normative principle for the evaluation of legal and other institutions that does not apply in the realm of personal conduct."[80] These are complicated and abstract debates about the nature of normativity, but they have important stakes for how we should be oriented to existing institutions. Most importantly, Murphy's framing assumes that individuals and institutions are two distinct and separable kinds of things, where, as I argued in chapter 3, we should see them as co-constituting. That insight lends itself to the view that our principles for evaluating individuals and institutions stand in a relation of dialectical interdependence; principles for evaluating individual behavior should be attentive to their institutional context, principles for evaluating institutions should be attentive to the kind of individuals that growing up under such institutions tends to produce, and so on. As we've seen, Du Bois shows how this view should lead us to consider how our own development in unjust circumstances should condition our employment of an ideal that guides our actions; that we should expect our actions to reproduce injustice suggests that progress toward justice will necessarily be ugly rather than the clean, unmediated application of normative principles through individual action.

Rather than acknowledging how their own practice of theorizing is shaped by our unjust circumstances, many defenders of Rawlsian egalitarian liberalism against Murphy instead accept the latter's basic terms and argue in favor of dualism. Thomas Nagel identifies dualism—which he dubs "pluralism," to recognize multiple levels of principle—at the core of his rejection of global justice while Thomas Pogge's defense of global economic justice takes pains to show that it is compatible with dualism.[81] This conventional wisdom about Rawls's dualism fits neatly with a picture of individual political duty as primarily institutional compliance. Because dualism proclaims that principles for individuals and institutions are different in kind, this often entails a practical "division of labor" with institutions responsible for the basic rules of society and individuals responsible for following those rules.[82] But a dualist view has a hard time accounting for individual responsibility in the absence of just rules, other than an admonition to help change the rules in an unspecified manner; even then, institutional justice retains a kind of priority since it is assumed that one cannot effectively act against unjust institutions without a conception of the just rules that one should advocate for.[83] Monism and dualism share the hope that if you follow the right rules, you can otherwise stop worrying about justice; on this view, an important way to experience freedom is to be free of justice's demands.[84] But as I have argued, the negative or critical use of freedom better orients us and facilitates effective political action to promote justice. Given the way we are shaped by forces before we could ever choose them, there is no way to assure in advance that our actions will be entirely free of injustice and therefore free of evaluation from the perspective of justice.

Because it frames so much of the contemporary global justice literature, call *the standard view* the claim that the content of individuals' duties of justice derive from the rules of existing political institutions. On this view, individuals retain humanitarian and other moral duties, but their political obligations are exhausted by compliance with the rules of well-functioning institutions. Several elements of Rawls's thought support this reading. The first is the well-known formulation that "justice is the first virtue of social institutions, as truth is of systems of thought."[85] The priority that Rawls here accords to principles of social justice for institutions is often understood precisely as a way of minimizing the importance of individual duties. Along these lines, Rawls writes, "If this division of labor can be established, individuals and associations are then left free to advance their ends more effectively within the framework of the basic structure, secure in the knowledge that elsewhere in the social system the necessary corrections to preserve background justice are being made."[86] In other words, so long as you follow the rules, justice sounds like someone else's problem. Even more strikingly, he writes, "There is, I believe, no political obligation, strictly speaking, for citizens generally."[87] In a society that is just or nearly so, normal politics thereby becomes something most citizens need not worry about, from the perspective of justice, and so they have no additional political obligations.[88]

Taken together, these slogans leave the impression that egalitarian liberalism has little to say about what political actions individuals ought to take—a problem greatly exacerbated by the circumstances of international politics, where a multiplicity of institutions must be accounted for. Adherents to the standard view have pursued three different strategies for addressing these circumstances. As I discuss at greater length in chapter 6, Thomas Nagel holds that the standard view entails that duties of justice are limited to the nation-state; since the global economy is not properly political and consequently outside the scope of justice, individuals can buy coffee and clothes from abroad without considerations of justice ever entering.[89] By contrast, Thomas Pogge argues that the institutions of the global economy are political and characterized by unjust rules of sovereign recognition that, for example, allow dictators to reap the economic benefits of natural resources that really belong to the people they rule; individuals who benefit from these rules, he argues, have duties to "judge ourselves more harshly" and "not to support . . . an unfair institutional order."[90] For his part, David Miller tries to steer a middle path and writes, "our thinking about global justice should primarily be focused on institutions: we should be looking at the institutions at global level that primarily determine people's life chances, and asking which principles of justice apply to them" while also arguing that individuals have distinct but attenuated duties of justice internationally that derive from the fact that existing international institutions are weaker than domestic ones.[91] On this account, the strength of such duties proportionately tracks the strength of existing institutions. For all three varieties of the standard view—call them the *statist*, *globalist*, and *proportional* views, respectively—the paradigmatic political duty of individuals is not their being properly disposed but objective compliance with institutional rules.

Consider what each of the three variations of the standard view see as salient for orienting an American consumer to the unjust circumstances of the Matamoros workers. Recall that the Matamoros workers filed a complaint about the Mexican government's failure to protect their rights with the United States and Canada under the authority of the labor side agreement to NAFTA, known as NAALC. Each considers the primary determinant of the political action that American consumers ought to take—what their political obligations are—to be the institutional nature of NAALC, which lacks independent coercive enforcement capabilities. The statist view notes that these institutions fall short of statehood and concludes that they consequently give rise to no political obligations except insofar as they are laws of their respective states; NAFTA thus gives individual US citizens no reason to perceive citizens of Mexico or Matamoros workers in any particular way. By contrast, the globalist view concludes that the existence of such transnational institutions effectively brings about full political obligations between citizens of the member states. Because it holds that the global economic and political order as a whole is both sufficiently tightly integrated and sufficiently harmful that we should understand our political obligations as being effectively identical to individuals everywhere, there is nothing distinctive to say about how individuals should respond to this particular case; beyond the imperative to reform an unjust global order and perhaps reform NAALC particularly, there are no political duties that obviously apply to American consumers specifically in relation to the Matamoros workers. Pogge makes this failure especially clear with his self-regarding reference to "the global poor, whose best hope may be our moral reflection."[92] As we've seen, self-criticism undertaken by those privileged with respect to an injustice in isolation from the oppressed is likely to be flawed; here Pogge's globalist institutionalist approach to justice leads him to position consumers as the saviors of the poor rather than as their partners. The proportional view does distinguish among existing institutions and concludes that very weak institutions are accordingly subject to correspondingly weak egalitarian political norms; these norms apply in the first instance to the rules of the institution itself and duties for individuals derive from how egalitarian norms are instantiated in the institutions. For example, when Joshua Cohen and Charles Sabel consider individual duties in international politics, they ask, "Why not say that citizens in member states are expected to take account of WTO decisions . . . ?"[93] In the case of NAALC, one might charge that the decision-makers who fashioned the institution were insufficiently accountable to the workers but because standard views focus on rule compliance, it is unclear if the institution as it stands requires anything of individuals. Perhaps in this case, they could be said to have a weak duty to encourage the officials of their government to take seriously the recommendations for reform issued by the NAALC office, but again there is nothing particular to say about how individuals in the United States should perceive the status of oppressed Mexican workers. In each case, the standard view orients us to institutions to determine what we owe to others (and what they owe us); what the others themselves have to say—what they ask of us—is only relevant insofar as institutional rules direct it.[94]

The resultant orientation doesn't merely fail to guide political action effectively, but naturalizes the injustice of existing neoliberal institutions even as it purports to critically evaluate them. David Miller's description of his orientation to global injustice illustrates this process. He writes, "I switch on the television to watch the evening news. The main stories today are all from what we used to call the Third World, and they all speak of human suffering." Miller goes on to describe the images he sees: the corpses left by Baghdad car bombs, the flies on the faces of the starving children of Niger, would-be immigrants injured while trying to cross into the EU. Miller also describes his distinct emotional reactions to each of these situations of poor, wounded, dying people—sympathy and anger, but also confusion and incomprehension at what has caused these situations and even a touch of exasperation at those trying to enter the EU illegally.[95] Miller invites his reader to identify with him; given the daily routine implied by the fact that international injustice only comes into his awareness during the evening news, it appears quite natural that questions of international injustice seem to be about things happening to others elsewhere. Their suffering triggers the viewer's reflection, but it appears natural that these questions can be impartially answered by the viewer, on his own.

Miller's scenario is thus worth reflecting on because of the way it illustrates why the orientation that comes naturally from interacting with unjust institutions helps reproduce them—as well as our own ignorance. Because our focus is habitually directed to the events on screen, we are oriented away from the ways in which we viewers are ourselves in the midst of international politics all the time—for example, the economic and political relations that resulted in the TV being manufactured and imported; those that led to the production of the news program itself; and, indeed, the entire set of relations that make it the case that Anglo-American political philosophers could experience international politics through a screen. Miller's TV screen thus exemplifies the veil that operates in the global economy; while he can see through it, he doesn't note how it distorts his vision, rendering invisible the very structures he purports to scrutinize. Here again we see the importance of Du Bois's conceptual tools for developing an orientation to freedom that can promote effective political action, as this veil divides predominantly white viewers on one side from the minoritized people who suffer on the other side. As Charles Mills notes, the "virtual absence of any discussion of race and racism" is pervasive in the egalitarian liberal literature on global justice, but acknowledgment of the racial divide at work in global injustice may also spur recognition of the multiple ways that this veil disposes consumers to reproduce their ignorance and orients them away from taking effective action.[96] Or, as Mills puts the point, "Global justice demands . . . ending global white ignorance."[97]

By contrast with the standard view and its variants, the dispositional account makes it a question of justice not just what institutional rules are, but how institutions are inhabited and how others subject to them are perceived, which is more useful for understanding what individuals can do in an unjust society. While it is often uninformative to demand that individuals comply with rules of institutions like NAALC, it is clear that individuals can take up particular perspectives on those institutions and on others who are subject to them—and seeing things from a certain point of view can dispose us to act in particular ways. Orientation captures this connection: when we are oriented to a location, we see it not as a collection of structures but as a town that we know our way around. The spatial nature of the metaphorical concept of orientation indicates how a disposition to activity is related to the normative requirements on our perceptions; what we see guides how we act. Seeing things rightly facilitates acting rightly, but the standard views cannot incorporate this beyond the model of rule-following.

As I argued in the introduction, a theory that makes inequality presumptively illegitimate still has critical uses today, but realizing the values of egalitarian liberalism should move its adherents toward a theoretical practice more aligned with critical theory in three senses: first, by recognizing the importance of the connection between an ideal and the context of its social world; second, by acknowledging that our knowledge of the ideal is likely to be impaired by our own social development in inegalitarian conditions;

and third, by thinking self-reflexively about our theories as a source of self-conceptions. To claim this as a way to realize egalitarian liberal values may prompt skepticism. Stephen K. White argues that talk about dispositions is incompatible with political liberalism, because "an ethos inquires not only about the justness of basic structures but also about how we go about 'living . . . the structures' (in Charles Taylor's words)," implicating founda-tional issues addressed by comprehensive doctrines.[98] However, far from undermining them, the shift to political liberalism if anything deepens the importance of these requirements. First, as Rawls makes clear when he introduces the "duty of civility" as a moral duty derived from the guidelines of public reason, political liberalism does not preclude requirements on the attitudes that individuals display toward their institutions or each other.[99] Second, the kinds of attitudes and dispositions that are required of individ-uals are derived from their political status and the work of habituation need not touch any element of comprehensive doctrine, as it will occur signifi-cantly apart from propositional content; as we've already seen, significant transformations in an individual's orientation and self-conception are pos-sible without altering their principled convictions and can often make it pos-sible to realize those convictions more effectively.

Any egalitarian who wants to achieve distributive justice when individ-uals are shaped by neoliberal governmentality must think seriously about what kind of work is required for individuals to be appropriately oriented and disposed. As I'll argue in the rest of the book, the best way to retrain our self-conceptions and express dispositional freedom amid neoliberal in-justice is by joining transnational social movements that promote solidarity among those subject to neoliberal institutions. Participation in such social movements both promotes freedom by working to change existing social arrangements and expresses freedom by facilitating new relations and conse-quently new identities that can be more readily affirmed.

5

The Significance of Solidarity

How can we resist a neoliberal global economy that routinely violates our freedom and promotes inequality? Episodic catastrophes like the 2008 financial crisis and the Rana Plaza collapse can jar us out of habitual ways of seeing and provide opportunities to reorient ourselves, but that does not mean it is obvious how to take advantage of those opportunities and adopt an orientation that can more effectively promote freedom and equality. In the absence of a meaningful alternative orientation that can organize resistance, neoliberal institutions and policies endure and the widening inequalities that have characterized both the United States and the world persist. Capital remains highly mobile while restrictions on the mobility of persons have increased. Between 2007 and 2016, the value of financial assets continued to grow faster than the value of nonfinancial assets, leading to widening wealth inequality in every region of the world between 2007 and 2016.[1] Nor have trends changed with respect to income in the United States. Between July 2017 and July 2018, in an economy with a low official unemployment rate nominally not in a recession, the real value of average wages nevertheless declined. Despite the financial crisis and widespread protests by the Occupy movement, another 4 percent of national income has shifted from workers wages and salaries to corporate profits since 2000, continuing a trend since the early 1970s.[2]

In these circumstances, it can seem like your best shot at economic success and security is to embrace the necessity of your status as an entrepreneur of the self and try to build your brand in every area of life in the hopes that it pays off in one of them. Who knows? If you get lucky and play your cards right, the cute videos of your two-year-old that you post on Instagram could net you two million followers—and with them, enough corporate sponsorships to support your family.[3] But that's a long shot, and if you want to have any hope of getting it right, you'll need to habituate yourself and your family to be constantly on the lookout for viral content. You may even need to send your kids for training at Social Media Star Camp, "The first sleepaway camp dedicated to creating social media stars." As the Social Media Star Camp "Team" point out, the fact that anyone can post on social media and make their own bid

Disorienting Neoliberalism. Benjamin L. McKean, Oxford University Press (2020). © Oxford University Press.
DOI: 10.1093/oso/9780190087807.001.0001.

for the kind of fame that would give them financial security means that "the competition is fierce—When anyone can, everyone is."[4]

While the chance to succeed by extending the economic grid throughout your life and monetizing your intimate relations is slim, the costs are clear and immediate. When the best way to significantly change your economic position requires becoming an entrepreneur of self, you're always at work. As an enterprise of one, you have to train yourself to be constantly ready to perceive and act on opportunities to build your personal brand; whatever else they are, experiences and opportunities to act are necessarily perceived through the lens of potential future income. And, to the extent that brand-building requires the use of social media—or even just the extent to which economic opportunities of any kind require owning a smartphone—you are subjecting yourself to constant surveillance by the corporations that maintain the platforms on which you seek to appear. As we saw in chapter 2, it's no hyperbole to say that companies like Facebook and Google track all of our movements in the world and online; they track everything down to the movements of your mouse on the screen in order to monitor how you pay attention to your computer.[5] These corporations then aggregate this data in order to find patterns and learn ways to direct our attention even more effectively. They may not be particularly interested in you as an individual, but they ensure that through your actions, you are contributing to their efforts to guide your future behavior in ways that you may never notice—and if asked, they may share this information with government agencies interested in surveilling you specifically.[6] If your social media presence does go viral, you risk drawing the ire of your current employer, who may fire you if they don't like the attention it draws to them.

Opting out of all this feels impossible. We're told that jobs from professor to housecleaner increasingly require maintaining a personal brand; not only does this exacerbate the need to adopt neoliberal self-conceptions, but it also further entrenches inequality, as marketing skills and reliable internet access become necessary for even entry-level jobs.[7] What's more, the most recent generations to enter the workforce have done so with unprecedented debts, as neoliberal policies have largely shifted the costs of job training away from corporations onto individual workers, who are now held responsible for the development of their own human capital. Over the past thirty years, the real cost of tuition and fees at four-year nonprofit private colleges in the United States grew by 129 percent—and grew 212 percent at public colleges; not coincidentally, public spending per student for higher education is 13 percent lower per student than it was thirty years ago.[8] As a result, student debt is now the second-largest source of household debt after housing, with over $1.4 trillion in student loans outstanding.[9] For many people, even when their principles lead them to reject the justice and legitimacy of neoliberal institutions, it can feel like they have little choice but to adopt a neoliberal orientation in order to navigate daily life. In light of such material circumstances, it is unsurprising that the global financial crisis could throw neoliberal sociodicy into doubt without generating significant changes in how we act.

In this chapter, I propose an alternative orientation to the global economy that facilitates actions to promote egalitarian justice. As I've argued, an effective orientation combines an explanation of how things work, an account of how they are legitimated, and a conception of the values that should be promoted. To that end, I've argued that appreciating the actual operation of transnational supply chains should lead us to see how economic practices diverge from their neoliberal justifications; rather than the apolitical outcome of distributed and independent choices, transnational supply chains should instead be understood as political institutions to which both consumers and workers are subjected. I've also developed an alternative to the market freedom that has helped legitimate existing institutions, arguing that the outer limit of our freedom, when we can freely accept the unchosen forces that have shaped us, can provide an orienting ideal. I've argued that those of us living under unjust institutions cannot experience the outer limit of freedom, but we can express our freedom in actions and habits that resist injustice. I now bring together my account of an effective alternative orientation to the global economy by arguing that those who are subject to its unjust institutions should be *disposed to solidarity* with others who are also subjected. The disposition to solidarity promotes and expresses freedom and equality in a way appropriate to our unjust circumstances, reflecting our common entanglement in injustice and the need to cooperate if we are to meaningfully resist it.

As we've seen, leading contemporary approaches to global justice have generally overlooked the existing operations of the global economy to focus on debating the ideal scope of international institutions.[10] Yet manifest injustices abound every day in transnational supply chains—rape and sexual harassment in factories, mass layoffs of union activists, factories that shut down in the middle of the night to avoid paying wages for hours already worked. However, while injustices like these are obvious, what we should do in relation to them is not. By this I mean that we lack not only a good idea of what action to take, but also of why we should take it. Adopting a disposition to solidarity answers this need. By disposing ourselves to attend to others' calls for solidarity, we can determine the particular actions to take in a way that treats these others not exclusively as objects of concern but as political partners, which better models the freedom and equality we want to realize.

By acting this way, my partners and I meet what can broadly be called the demands of justice. The language of justice is indispensable for properly orienting ourselves to neoliberal policy outcomes like growing inequality as well as catastrophes like the Rana Plaza collapse, which are properly seen not as isolated tragedies but as evidence of an unjust system. By calling the global economy unjust, I'm identifying it as a political problem, contrary to the neoliberal depoliticization of market outcomes, and asserting that we need to do our part to reorganize our common life. Because justice concerns the nature of our relationships, it cannot be brought about unilaterally; it requires the coordination of many people to change our collective circumstances. In other words, acting to promote justice forces us to engage in politics. But in a world of unjust institutions, meeting the demands of justice can strike individuals as impossibly broad and the prospect of meeting its requirements paralyzing, especially since we know not everyone will even try to do so. That is why I say that the demands of justice can be met by individuals when they are disposed to solidarity with others who share an interest in resisting and replacing the unjust institutions to which they are subjected. On my view, cultivating and maintaining a disposition to solidarity is a sufficient (but not strictly necessary) condition for meeting our duty; while individuals may be able to find other ways that the duty can be met under our circumstances, my view best accounts for how reforming or replacing institutions requires collective political action by differently situated people. Individuals cannot generally decide on their own how best to advance this project, but must do so through coordination with others. To be effective, a judgment about how to make lasting institutionalized change needs to be taken up by others. As a result, meeting our duty is not as simple as following ethical rules that I can theoretically identify in isolation.

Given the complexity of our entanglement with existing injustice, the particular groups with whom we should act in solidarity often cannot be determined apart from actual calls for solidarity. Unjust institutions are detrimental to some of the interests of those subject to them, but in diverse ways. Consequently, we should extend the presumption to others that they too have an interest in living under institutions they regard as just and are willing to act to advance that interest, but we generally *act* in solidarity against injustice only when others are willing to do the same. We must therefore be alert to their *calls* for solidarity and when we are asked to support efforts to resist or replace unjust institutions to which we are subject, we must be willing to do so. In short, this disposition entails perceiving relevant others as potential partners in reform, being ready to take seriously their appeals to act alongside them, and understanding the achievement of one's own interest as dependent upon them attaining theirs. In the rest of this chapter, I elaborate this argument for orienting our actions to meeting the demands of justice, highlight the advantages of my account of solidarity in comparison to rival conceptions, and show how it applies to the garment factory cases I began with.

The Role of Interest in Justifying the Natural Duty of Justice

The egalitarian coalition of theoretical traditions that can endorse my account agree we ought to act against injustice, even if they may disagree about the reasons grounding that "ought." Accordingly, I do not engage with meta-ethical questions about the status of the demands of justice in this chapter because the answers to such questions do not help orient us to our practical circumstances. Instead, I focus on practical reasons for understanding our actions as oriented to meeting the demands of justice. In offering a political account of why we should orient ourselves this way, this chapter again extends and transforms John Rawls's egalitarian liberalism to make it useful for a range of people navigating an unjust world. Rawls similarly brackets the ultimate normative grounding of justice, but somewhat confusingly speaks of individuals having a "natural duty of justice," which may sound to some as though the duty stands outside politics. However, this duty is "natural" not in the sense that endorsing the duty relies on any particular deep claim about our innate, prepolitical nature or ontology, but in the sense that one does not need to do anything to acquire the duty; it's just part of what we mean when we say that something is unjust that people should do something to stop it. Nevertheless, making the natural duty of justice part of an effective orientation requires a transformation akin to the one that made the dispositional conception of freedom appropriate to unjust circumstances. In particular, Rawls's argument assumes a uniform practical interest in living in a just society, but an unjust society includes both those who are oppressed and those who are privileged in relation to any injustice. An argument that each group should meet the demands of justice needs to acknowledge the different senses in which they have an interest in achieving justice. In addition, the natural duty of justice applies differently to those who claim authority in unjust institutions and so act or direct others to act to cause injustice, such as apparel company executives. As I elaborate later in the chapter, such individuals are not partners in resisting injustice, but perpetrators of it; their duty is, first of all, to cease being so.

Solidarity is a fitting specification of the natural duty of justice in our unjust world because it best reflects the role that interest appropriately plays in orienting the actions and defining the political duties of individuals. Rawls argues that people have a natural duty of justice that not only "requires us to support and comply with just institutions that exist and apply to us," but that also "constrains us to further just arrangements not yet established, at least when this can be done without too much cost to ourselves." [11] Yet while Rawls's claim that this natural duty binds us to just institutions has been defended and contested at length, his accompanying claim that we must further just arrangements has received comparatively little attention. [12] Egalitarian liberal discussions of political obligation amid injustice have more often focused on civil disobedience and conscientious objection—that is, on exceptions to the duty to comply with partly just states—than on furthering just arrangements not yet established. [13]

Rawls himself did little to explore what the natural duty of justice requires in our unjust world. However, because his theory of justice is importantly relational—that is, he holds that the principles of justice apply to people subjected to the same basic structure rather than to humanity as a whole—many have assumed that when it comes to individuals' duties of justice, priority would evidently be determined by existing institutional relations and consequently go to co-nationals. But this moves too quickly. In fact, Rawls asserts that natural duties "hold between persons irrespective of their institutional relationships; they obtain between all as equal moral persons. In this sense the natural duties are owed not only to definite individuals, say to those cooperating together in a particular social arrangement, but to persons generally." [14] Here Rawls's own account again helps to identify injustice even as he failed to develop an effective orientation to it. Rawls recognized that in "our world as it is with its extreme injustices, crippling poverty, and inequalities," achieving justice requires that we look beyond existing national borders, but the "realistic utopia" he describes in his *Law of Peoples* envisions a world of distinct peoples who are not interdependent and who already enjoy political autonomy; it's unclear how such an ideal can effectively guide action in our world.[15]

A central feature of Rawls's view that can be usefully taken up by an effective orientation to these injustices is his argument that a natural duty of justice is in our interest. Rawls emphasizes this feature by addressing his argument to people who have taken up the perspective of the original position and, as he reminds us, "although the parties in the original position take no interest in each other's interest, they know that in society they need to be assured by the esteem of their associates."[16] Of course, one need not enter the original position to justify the natural duty of justice; the device of the original position is meant to restrict what we consider, but opening up our reasoning to consider how individuals actually care for each others' interests does nothing to undercut the case for a duty of justice. What's important is that the argument does not simply insist on the primacy of justice; rather, it appeals to an interest in living in a just society. This does not derive from a prudential worry that once the veil of ignorance is dropped, one may find oneself at the bottom rung of society; instead it comes from the fact that certain desirable goods necessary to live well are public goods and can only be enjoyed if everyone has access to them. Rawls illustrates this with his similar argument in favor of the duty of mutual aid. Given the vulnerability of human life, you may be put in a position to benefit narrowly from this duty—if you find yourself drowning in a pond, for example—but more important, Rawls says, is "its pervasive effect on the quality of everyday life." He writes, "The balance of gain, narrowly interpreted, may not matter. The primary value of the principle is not measured by the help we actually receive but rather by the sense of confidence and trust in other men's good intentions and the knowledge that they are there if we need them."[17] This is an important good—one essential to most life projects—that can be enjoyed every day; we can readily identify a self-interest in living in a society that publicly affirms its respect for duties of mutual aid.

People likewise have an interest in living in a just society where they can enjoy the outer limit of freedom. Not only do they benefit from knowing that they need not worry about structural injustice turning on them, but they also benefit from knowing that their relations with others under the same basic structure are characterized by freedom and equality. Because of these fair background conditions, one can expect that relations with others will generally be free of negative reactive attitudes like resentment, guilt, and distrust that are endemic to the public spheres of unjust societies. There is no need to worry that the projects one undertakes are only possible because of structural injustice; each can enjoy the self-respect that comes from knowing one's achievements are one's own and not achieved because of unfair advantage. This shared interest in justice also helps us to make sense of why Rawls limits the duty to promote just arrangements not yet established to those cases "when this can be done without too much cost to ourselves."[18] This is not an ad hoc addition since the duty is partly justified by appeal to self-interest. Of course, there is significant ambiguity about what counts as "too much cost" and as I will discuss, some people clearly benefit enough from their position in the structures perpetuating injustice that appealing to them on grounds of solidarity is inappropriate; though we may still want to say that they have an interest in living in a just society, their duties in relation to injustice will have a different character.

Understanding these public goods as common interests that we share a duty to promote helps address the collective actions problems that beset political life. Consider Rawls's argument for why the natural duty of justice best accounts for the duty to obey just institutions. Accounts that require individuals to undertake some intentional act in order to acquire the political obligation to obey—whether that be actual consent to the institution, the willing acceptance of its benefits, or something else entirely—all face two features of collective action that constitute what Rawls calls "the assurance problem."[19] First, rational individuals all prefer to free ride; second, they worry that others will free ride. This leads to instability, "since even with a sense of justice men's compliance with a cooperative venture is predicated on the belief that others will do their part, citizens may be tempted to avoid making a contribution when they believe, or with reason suspect, that others are not making theirs." As a result of this suspicion that others are not bound to do their part, Rawls notes that "a greater reliance on the coercive powers of the sovereign might be necessary to achieve stability."[20] But Rawls rejects the centrality of coercion to politics urged by neoliberals; like Hegel, he regards such extensive reliance on coercion as undesirable and ineffective at promoting stability over time. Instead, he argues, all of this can be avoided if we concede that no voluntary action is necessary in order to acquire political duties. He writes, "The parties in the original position do best when they acknowledge the natural duty of justice. Given the value of a public and effective sense of justice, it is important that the principle defining the duties of individuals be simple and clear, and that it insure the stability of just arrangements."[21] The common knowledge that just institutions are due obedience simply in virtue of their justice results in a more stable society than an account that focuses on voluntarily acquired obligations and thus better explains the grounds of the fundamental requirements on individual political action.

Assigning duties to individuals without them taking any voluntary action may seem to constrain their freedom, but it is deeply in accord with the logic of egalitarian liberalism and with dispositional freedom more generally. As Rawls notes, "The basic structure is the primary subject of justice because its effects are so profound and present from the start."[22] One reason why institutions should meet the standards of social justice is precisely that they affect us deeply before we could ever choose them. Consequently, it makes sense that the natural duty of justice requires no action in order to apply to individuals; the same interest in freedom and equality that justifies the application of the principles of justice to the basic structure of society likewise requires that individuals uphold those values.

However, when we consider the duty to obey just institutions, this line of thought gives rise to a well-known "particularity" problem: if this duty is grounded in an appeal to the value of freedom and equality generally, it is not clear why we should be bound to the particular institutions that claim to govern us rather than any institution that meets this standard.[23] Notably, even if one accepts this criticism that a nonrelational natural duty of justice fails to explain our duty to comply with our particular institutions, one can still accept the part of the duty I consider here—the duty to further just arrangements—since that part is not vulnerable to the particularity objection. Indeed, John Simmons, the foremost proponent of the particularity objection, writes, "I think that, as Rawls suggests, we do have a natural duty to support and assist in the formation of just institutions, at least so long as no great inconvenience to ourselves is involved."[24] But while there is no particularity objection to this part of the duty itself, we are faced instead with a problem of focus: in a world of many injustices, how can we judge what to respond to?

Rawls suggests that this is not an easy task; he says of the natural duties for individuals, "The real difficulty lies in their more detailed specification" and notes, "It would seem that the theory for the basic structure is actually simpler."[25] Nevertheless, as I argue in the next section, the concept of solidarity provides a clear framework for specifying how individuals who live among unjust institutions can meet the demands of justice. Because Rawls's duty is justified by the widespread compliance that is necessary to bring about a public good, nonideal circumstances where we must reckon with partial compliance change what the duty requires. Rawls writes, "The social system shapes the wants and aspirations that its citizens come to have. It determines in part the sort of persons they want to be as well as the sort of persons they are. Thus an economic system is not only an institutional device for satisfying existing wants and needs but a way of creating and fashioning wants in the future."[26] As I argued in chapters 3 and 4, this has significant implications for individuals who grow up in an unjust society that Rawls failed to grapple with. Not everyone will develop a fully functioning sense of justice in such circumstances and so partial compliance is to be expected; even those who do desire to meet their duty may have a distorted sense of themselves and their interests as a result of the profound influence of unjust institutions on their development. Moreover, since we lack a shared public basis for justification, both domestically and internationally, we cannot always appeal to the same kinds of shared values in determining what it is reasonable to expect of other people. So what does the natural duty of justice require of individuals when they cannot expect everyone to comply and when others may even disagree about the requirements of justice?

The Disposition to Solidarity as Nonideal Specification of the Natural Duty of Justice

I am hardly the first to suggest the relevance of solidarity to questions of global justice. Perhaps the most common usage is descriptive and associated with cultural or familial ties. Kwame Anthony Appiah describes that kind of solidarity as the thought that " 'Because I am an L,' an L will say, 'I should do this thing for that other L.' "[27] Starting from this definition, some then argue that global justice and international solidarity are impossible because national identity will always trump identification with humanity as a whole.[28] Others endorse international solidarity but seek to make it a value distinct from or even trumping justice.[29] However, there is another tradition that uses solidarity summarized by the slogan "An Injury to One is An Injury to All," which was popularized in the United States by the Industrial Workers of the World (IWW) union in the early twentieth century. This is the sense of solidarity "when people form a group to stand up for common interests," as Kurt Bayertz describes it.[30] Philosophically, this conception of solidarity has been developed most extensively within feminist philosophy.[31] Solidarity of this kind, which Sally Scholz calls *political solidarity*, directs our attention to how injustice experienced directly by relevant others can impair our own interests—paradigmatically, our exercise of freedom.

Political solidarity differs from two other normative senses of solidarity important in the philosophical literature: *cosmopolitan solidarity* simply in virtue of common humanity as well as the *civic solidarity* of the welfare state.[32] These forms aren't appropriate to the circumstances I consider; the existence of unjust institutions makes civic solidarity inappropriate and cosmopolitan solidarity fails to account for the existence of people who unambiguously benefit from injustice as well as the absence of general compliance. Political solidarity is an appropriate means of meeting the duty of justice in unjust circumstances because those who avow a shared interest can be expected to take action more readily, helping to address the assurance problems faced by those who can expect only partial compliance.[33] But if the relevant group is neither a nation-state nor all of humanity, which individuals share an interest in resisting unjust circumstances and consequently should act in solidarity with each other?

Most obviously, individuals who are directly oppressed or disadvantaged by such circumstances have an interest in making institutions more just in order to lessen their oppression. But the world is rarely divided simply into those who oppress and those who are oppressed, those who exclusively have an interest in preserving the status quo and those who entirely lack it; in most cases, circumstances are more complicated and the set of those with an interest in furthering just arrangements cannot be so easily delimited. As Chandra Talpade Mohanty notes, "The interwoven processes of sexism, racism, misogyny, and heterosexism are an integral part of our social fabric, wherever in the world we happen to be. We need to be aware that these ideologies, in conjunction with the regressive politics of ethnic nationalism and capitalist consumerism, are differentially constitutive of all our lives in the early twenty-first century."[34] Individuals stand in different relations to each of these axes of oppression, potentially benefitting from some while being constrained by others. What's more, even oppressed individuals often also receive some benefits from the unjust institutions that mistreat them—for example, when one is exploited but still receives some much-needed income—and retaining those benefits may appear impossible or uncertain if the institution is replaced. Likewise, individuals who are privileged in relation to an axis of oppression may still have an interest in resisting an injustice which grants them some advantages; a consumer who benefits from the exploitation of garment workers may still find that the governmentality of supply chains shapes them in ways they want to reject and that the neoliberal policies which makes transnational supply chains pervasive constrain their freedom in other ways.

Consequently, determining what is in one's interest overall requires judgment and can change even without significant shifts in one's material circumstances. As Roberto Mangabeira Unger puts it, our interests are often "substantively ambiguous in the sense that they are never unified or detailed enough to provide the occupants of any given social station with a single uncontroversial view of their interests."[35] Those who willingly profit from injustices that they have the power to stop may be net losers in the transition to a just society, but many others will find the balance of gain favors justice or is unclear. This is why meeting the demands of justice requires a *disposition* to solidarity; habitually perceiving others as potential partners in resisting injustice can and should play a role in how we judge our overall interests. Unjust institutions realize multiple, conflicting values so our habituation to injustice is never so complete that alternative self-conceptions are impossible. Seeing others as our partners can change how we see ourselves. In a similar vein, Allison Weir argues, "shared interests are not simply given or discovered, but are constructed through our attention to what is significant and meaningful to us. Thus, feminist solidarity plays an important role in constituting women's identity."[36] Which of our interests we prioritize depends on our self-conceptions and as we've seen in chapter 4, our desire to express our freedom can give us reason to work on shifting our conception of our self; though consumers of supply chain goods may most readily conceive of ourselves as entrepreneurs of self, we have also seen ample reason for discontent and frustration with this self-conception. Orienting ourselves to others as partners in resistance provides an alternative. While the expectation of partial compliance and uncertain prospects of institutional change can make it seem more rational to accept the status quo rather than shoulder the costs of resisting injustice if others fail to take part, a disposition to solidarity can shape judgment of our overall interests in a manner consistent with meeting the duty to further just arrangements not yet established.

That many people have interests in both the maintenance of an unjust status quo and in its replacement thus means that the boundary of the solidarity group cannot always be clearly defined in advance of calls for solidarity. Trying to antecedently impose boundaries on the group called to solidarity leads to a spurious clarity while allowing for vague boundaries better captures how most of us are complexly enmeshed in injustice. To see this, consider Tommie Shelby's account of Black political solidarity, which he also links to an interest in correcting injustice. He defines Black interests "in terms of the unfair social disadvantages that some individuals or groups face because they are (or their ancestors were) socially defined as members of the 'black race.'"[37] On the resultant conception of Black political solidarity, he writes, each Black person should promote "identifying, correcting, and ultimately eliminating race-based injustices. In this way, black political solidarity should be understood as black collective action in the interest of racial justice, not on behalf of an ideal of blackness."[38] Shelby assumes that being disadvantaged by racial injustice is on its own sufficient to create an overriding interest in promoting racial justice, thereby making it possible to clearly distinguish the group that should be in solidarity. However, as Robert Gooding-Williams points out, this assumption that every member of the group stands in the same relation to injustice creates important problems. Black feminist political theory has shown "there is no generic, antiblack racism that targets all blacks regardless of their gender, class, age, and sexuality—and that all blacks, qua blacks, have an interest in eliminating—but instead a multiplicity of intersecting antiblack racisms (again, clusters of antiblack stereotypes and beliefs), each of which targets some but not all blacks."[39] The result of this internal diversity of interests, obstacles, and views of justice is that the solidarity group should not be imagined as somehow objectively latent, waiting only to be roused.[40] Rather, it must be constructed by building coalitions—and the process of doing so does not only reflect pre-existing interests but shapes how people judge their interest.

The natural duty of justice is not merely a directive to pursue what is already one's unambiguous self-interest but rather gives a reason to weigh certain factors—for example, an interest in reducing exploitation, the work of others already acting to reduce exploitation, their requests for support—in the process of judging one's overall interest or deciding with which interest one wants to identify most closely. Solidarity thus takes the form of listening for a call to act in support of a shared interest and to be disposed to act in response. This is more appropriate than seeing the natural duty of justice as directing us to particular actions—both because judgment about one's interests can change when presented with a call to solidarity but also because, under conditions of partial compliance, it is more rational to act when there is some assurance that others will act with you.

For example, in June 2016, the Wal-Mart Chinese Workers Association (WCWA) reached out to a US-based group of Walmart workers called Organization United for Respect at Walmart (OUR Walmart) to ask for solidarity before the former began an illegal strike to protest work scheduling policies at Walmart stores in China.[41] It would be easy for American workers to orient themselves on the assumption that their interests are contrary to those of Chinese workers in a competitive world economy. However, these workers considered the call for solidarity and agreed to provide support because the Chinese workers articulated a shared interest; rather than seeing each other as competitors for scarce resources, they identified their subjection to the same corporation as a shared obstacle to justice and saw each other as partners in the effort to overcome it. Victories in China create useful precedents for workers in the United States to hold the company accountable, reduces the company's arbitrary power, and so on. By the same token, for people who see each other as partners, a setback for one is understood as a setback for the others; injustice done to a partner in solidarity both augments the obstacle to achieving justice and, by harming a partner, reduces the collective capacity to act effectively. In that sense, an injury to one *becomes* an injury to all.[42] Specifying the natural duty of justice as a disposition to solidarity thus provides the kind of assurance that is possible under conditions of partial compliance; by identifying a shared interest, it singles out the people who can most be relied on to act to be ready to do so when called upon. Where Rawls argues that a disposition to reciprocity in a well-ordered society requires citizens to view one another as "free and equal in a system of social cooperation over generations," we can see analogously that a disposition to solidarity requires seeing others as potential partners in a joint effort with a goal—to reform or replace unjust institutions for mutual advantage.[43]

It might be thought inappropriate to link solidarity to interest and justice in this way. From one perspective, solidarity is too independently valuable to be subordinated to justice; from another perspective, however, the requirements of justice are too weighty to be met by a mere disposition to solidarity. With respect to the first objection, Avery Kolers shares my view that solidarity is an appropriate response to structural injustice but nevertheless argues for distinguishing duties of solidarity from duties of justice because valuing solidarity as a means of achieving justice obscures solidarity's own distinctive value and overriding importance. Kolers argues that what he calls "teleological views" that emphasize solidarity's instrumental value to justice cannot explain why we should enter into solidarity when the prospects of achieving justice look grim. He writes, "Solidary actions often fail to achieve the justice that they seek, and the strong likelihood of failure is knowable in advance. Nonetheless some fights are worth joining even if defeat is virtually inevitable . . . This fact sits badly with teleological justification."[44] Kolers goes so far as to argue that the value of solidarity should trump justice, writing, "In solidarity one may, as it were, have an obligation to give oneself an injustice by refusing a deserved benefit simply because others cannot get their deserved benefits."[45] Kolers's project differs from my own in that I am not seeking to provide a context-independent conception of solidarity, but rather an account of the value of solidarity as part of an orientation to an unjust global economy legitimized by neoliberalism. In this context, a disposition to solidarity is both practically useful as a way to meet the demands of justice and, by facilitating acts of resistance to injustice, expresses freedom in a way appropriate to our circumstances; where neoliberal freedom sees others primarily as competitors, a person disposed to solidarity sees acting in partnership with others on basis of a shared interest in justice as the best expression of freedom's outer limit possible in our circumstances. Contra Kolers's critique, a solidaristic partnership aiming at justice can thus be desirable even when the chances of success are hard to discern.

In seeking to explain how solidarity could be of such overriding importance that we should understand it as paradigmatically independent from justice or any other value that we might have an interest in realizing, Kolers makes it more difficult for solidarity to guide action. Unlike my account, Kolers's justification of a duty to solidarity makes no reference to the interests of the individual who have a duty to be in solidarity. He writes, "Solidarity offers a general reason r for the choice of a particular object group G, saying that everyone should in principle be in solidarity with G. Solidarity is thus agent-neutral."[46] But this agent-neutrality makes orientation more difficult. It suggests that everyone stands in the same relationship to solidarity, which provides no help in thinking about, for example, the differing relations that workers, consumers, and supply chain managers have to neoliberal injustice. Kolers's commitment to providing a context-independent, agent-neutral account of solidarity as conceptually unconnected to justice or interest also ends up producing a counterintuitive view that departs significantly from the common understanding that solidarity entails valuing the relationship one has to the others in solidarity. Kolers writes, "Since solidarity is reason-driven rather than relationship-driven, it does not entail any longer-term arrangement or dedication to a particular movement or cause."[47] Kolers's view makes thus solidarity unduly ascetic and unappealing; rather than entering solidarity to express one's own freedom and find partnership with others in a world that often isolates individuals by training us as competitors, he sees solidarity as expressing "a Kantian 'purity of heart.'"[48]

Sally Scholz similarly makes the appeal of solidarity unnecessarily puzzling by preserving an attenuated link to justice but severing the link to interest. A group in political solidarity, she writes, "is unified not by shared attributes, location, or even shared interests. The unity is based on shared commitment to a cause."[49] However, while the cause itself furthers justice, Scholz rejects any natural duty of justice and asserts that "there is no inherent duty to join in political solidarity itself" because "there is no justification for mandating that someone form a relationship that carries potentially heavy obligations and even sacrifices with a non-familial person."[50] Instead, she argues, the commitment to solidarity stems from a kind of groundless existential decision: "In contrast to the liberal autonomous choice based on rational decision-making, an existential commitment encompasses all aspects of an individual's existence and merges the individual's project with the projects of others."[51] But as I've argued, when political solidarity is based in a shared interest in furthering just arrangements, it can be rational to be disposed to it. Conceptualizing solidarity as so burdensome a relation that not even justice can compel us to enter into it seems self-defeating; if we lack any interest or duty, entering into solidarity again appears unappealing and unreasonable. By contrast, when political solidarity advances a shared interest in justice, we can see not only what benefits would lead people to engage in it, but also why its justification places a limit on the costs it can require.

One might instead object that my view thus treats solidarity too lightly. A duty to be properly disposed may seem insufficiently weighty in light of the importance of justice and the significant injustice of existing institutions. But while they may seem inconsequential individually, promoting dispositions can be an appropriate response to structural injustice; when sufficiently widespread and public, individual dispositions can play an important role in rectifying and compensating for institutional failure. In his account of civil disobedience, Rawls notes, "By resisting injustice within the limits of fidelity to law, it serves to inhibit departures from justice and to correct them when they occur. A general disposition to engage in justified civil disobedience introduces stability into a well-ordered society, or one that is nearly just."[52] While the natural duty of justice has a broader scope than domestic civil

disobedience, this still provides a useful model. When a disposition to justified civil disobedience is required of individuals, they have an obligation to
regard themselves as potential political agents disposed to identify and act to
correct injustice; the same is true for the natural duty of justice more generally. The work of disposing oneself to be prepared to act should the opportunity arise has a comparatively low cost, but it comes with important political
consequences for one's own self-understanding. Seeing myself as being disposed to engage in political action to further just arrangements requires a
host of preparatory acts and attitudes if my self-conception is to be coherent.
I also have to be willing to take smaller actions, to defend my self-conception
to others, and to encourage others to dispose themselves similarly.

I further discuss ways in which participation in social movements can be
emancipatory in the book's conclusion. For now, I want to note that people
have undertaken precisely these tasks of shaping their self-understanding in
the face of international injustice since at least the anti-slavery sugar boycotts
of the late eighteenth century. What is consequential is not the efficacy of the
boycott alone, but the way that it helped spread a disposition to take action
to abolish the slave trade—a disposition that facilitated many more directly
political actions, such as petitions, mass meetings, and so on.[53] Once abolition became part of people's self-conceptions, they were often willing to bear
much greater costs. The American Civil War badly disrupted the economy of
Lancashire, England, where cotton mills had relied heavily on slave-picked
cotton from the US South; denied access to Southern cotton largely due to a
Union blockade, hundreds of thousands of people were thrown out of work.
The Manchester Chamber of Commerce pressured the English government
to recognize the South, but Manchester cotton workers assembled and passed
a resolution declaring their support for the Emancipation Proclamation and
for the very blockade that kept them starving and out of work.[54]

Solidarity and Deference

Meeting the demands of justice by cultivating a disposition to solidarity
and making specific actions dependent on a call to solidarity better reflects
the relationship between justice and interest in a nonideal world than other
leading accounts of solidarity. While my account presumes that individuals
are often willing to act when they share an interest in furthering justice, it
leaves open much else. Rather than bringing a comprehensive view of the

world to bear on others and insisting they must act for reasons that they may not recognize, a call to solidarity is public in seeking to offer a reason to act that, based in shared interest, one's partner can recognize. However, this does not mean that each individual has ultimate authority over his or her own interest. Instead, as other theorists of political solidarity have argued, individuals who benefit from existing institutions owe deference to those who do not. This goes back to the profound influence that institutions have on us before we can choose them; since nonideal institutions will tend to habituate people to existing injustice, as we saw in chapter 4, individuals may need to "look harder" to see if the intuitive interpretation of political life that we read off of official institutional status is the best available. In particular, those who are privileged in relationship to injustice will need to work hard to make sure that they do not take the perspective of their advantaged position to be natural.[55]

Consequently, justice requires us to cultivate a certain alienation from our habitual perceptions under unjust institutions and a greater openness to the claims of others that we share an interest with them in reforming existing institutions. In our world, while domestic norms like equality before the law and "one man, one vote" generate some imperfect force toward developing the disposition to acknowledge the equal political status of co-citizens, other domestic institutions—including elements of the criminal justice system like the "war on drugs" and felony disenfranchisement as well as entrenched systems of discrimination in civil society, including the media—encourage the development of dispositions that fail to acknowledge equal political status. Because of the deep influence of social institutions on our self-conceptions and on our ways of seeing, we should dispose ourselves to accept the ever-present possibility that we have failed to perceive accurately the political status of others, particularly the oppressed. Disruptive social movements like Black Lives Matter can be essential to prompting people to undertake these revisions.[56] In the international case, that means we should not be so quick to write off distant others as obviously standing in no relation to us, especially if they make claims to the contrary.

However, other theorists of solidarity go too far in suggesting that comparatively privileged individuals should invariably defer to others. Kolers's view of solidarity is again overly strong. He writes, "Solidarity involves the agent's choosing sides without confidence that the chosen side is in the right."[57] He gives the example of joining Amnesty International to support human rights and says that even if you disagree sharply with Amnesty's stance in favor of abolishing the death penalty, one must support their work to do so and "even show up to oppose the death penalty if asked."[58] He argues that deference to the group must be so strong because "if social movements worth the name are to be possible people must be disposed to both join and stay with the group despite lacking a rationally compelling justification of the group's aims and tactics."[59] But this is false, for both practical and conceptual reasons. Practically, Kolers's view implies a view of social change in which political organizations are so vulnerable that disagreements must be stifled for them to survive. Yet many successful social movements are internally democratic and do not require uniformity in order to succeed.

Conceptually, Kolers worries that people who link justice and solidarity will never truly be in solidarity so long as they retain their own judgment. He writes, "Since the justice of the goal and the necessity of extraordinary means are inevitably questions for the agent herself to determine, teleological solidarity cannot handle the deferential aspect of solidarity; the agent her- or himself is the ultimate judge of the moral and strategic challenges that confront the political struggle."[60] But this dichotomous view in which any exercise of judgment necessarily collapses into the sovereignty of individual conscience excludes a dispositional approach in which deference is habitual but not a matter of strict necessity. If someone privileged in relation to an injustice frequently refused to defer to the oppressed in cases of disagreement, then we can certainly say that he is not disposed to solidarity, but one does not need to entirely exclude the possibility of exercising one's own judgment to arrive at that conclusion. A dispositional approach that builds upon Du Bois's concepts of the veil and second sight provides ample reasons internal to the account for the privileged to generally defer. It also values partnership as a means of realizing and expressing freedom across the veil; it's hard to describe a relationship in which one party is required to refrain from exercising their judgment as a partnership. While the comparatively privileged have good reason to defer to the oppressed, exceptional circumstances may still require them to exercise their own judgment—not only because the reasoning of the oppressed is fallible and can be warped by the same unjust institutions that shape the privileged, but also because the privileged may have a better understanding of some political matters than the oppressed (e.g., American consumers may be better informed about how to pressure the US government than workers in Bangladesh).

On my conception of political solidarity, the privileged retain legitimate interests in their own freedom and do not become obliged to sacrifice them on the say-so of others. In the following sections, I elaborate on this interest and the practical uses of recognizing it. For now, I want to note that the legitimate interests of the privileged need not conflict with the interests of the oppressed—in contrast to perpetrators of injustice, for example—since which of our interests we identify with often changes once we've sought to meet the demands of justice and responded to calls for solidarity. For example, Mark R. Warren documents how involvement with movements for racial justice can transform whites' understanding of their interest. One white woman who reports being "raised in the lap of luxury" would seem likely to have little to gain from racial justice and thus participate for altruistic reasons, if at all. Instead she describes her actions to promote racial justice as "not really about contributing to someone else's cause. I feel that I'm contributing to the world that I would rather want to live in . . . So I see it as serving myself. I see it as working for what I want."[61] Of course, there will still be conflicts of interest, but because acting to promote justice can change how we understand our interests, we need not assume that what initially appears to be a conflict will still be one once a call to solidarity has been heeded.

How Institutions Shape Calls for Solidarity

How does the natural duty of justice help orient us to the unjust institutions of a neoliberal global economy? Contrary to other approaches to individual duties within global justice, I argue not that the existence of institutions *grounds* our duties but rather that existing institutions help *specify* how we should meet duties that are otherwise indeterminate.[62] As I've argued throughout this book, an effective orientation incorporates an understanding of relevant political status and we can say that those subjected to an institution have some political status with respect to it. Supply chain workers and supply chain consumers have many different interests, but their joint subjection to the governmentality of supply chains makes it appropriate to describe them as sharing a political status—one that can be incorporated in their orienting self-conceptions and which can lead them to identify more closely with their shared interest in resisting the institutions that seek to direct their actions.

This importantly differs from Iris Marion Young's influential account of this connection.[63] As I've noted throughout, my approach in this work draws from Young's spirit and method in many respects, but here I emphasize some problems with her specific account of how supply chains relate workers and consumers and how justice should lead them to act. Describing her view, Young writes, "The social connection model of responsibility says that individuals bear responsibility for structural injustice because they contribute by their actions to the processes that produce unjust outcomes." Because of their causal contribution through participation in social processes, Young argues, "All who dwell within the structures must take responsibility for remedying injustices they cause, though none is specifically liable for the harm in a legal sense."[64] By arguing that individuals acquire the responsibility to promote justice through their actions, Young's view diverges from the argument I've considered for viewing our relationship to justice as an unacquired, "natural" duty. At the same time, drawing from Anthony Giddens, William Sewell, and Pierre Bourdieu, Young offers a social theoretical account of the systematic causes of injustices like oppressive wages and working conditions in garment factories, which she describes as "a specific kind of moral wrong, structural injustice, which is distinct from wrongs traceable to specific individual actions or policies."[65] In other words, individual participation is not best understood as causing injustice, which diverges from Young's argument about how and why we acquire a responsibility for justice. Since individual consumer choices don't play a meaningful causal role in bringing about sweatshops, alternative consumption choices that they make are likely to have little effect on the circumstances of workers, as she acknowledges. She identifies "middle-class clothing consumers in the developed world" as "relatively privileged persons who have relatively little power as individuals or in their institutional positions, at least with respect to that issue of justice." Since this stands in tension with her claim that responsibility for justice rests on our participation causing injustice, she writes of such consumers that "As beneficiaries of the process, they have responsibilities." But that is a very different normative ground for assuming responsibility, since one can receive benefits from injustices caused entirely by others.[66]

In short, Young grounds a responsibility to further justice on one's participation in existing institutions, though she also argues that because of the nature of structural injustice, the particular participation of most individuals makes no causal difference. As many critics have noted, this is symptomatic of Young's failure to consistently reconcile her commitment to provide an account of responsibility focused on guiding future action to promote justice with her backward-looking invocation of participation as a cause of present injustice.[67] This has two important effects. First, because this view tends to make all forms of structural injustice functionally analogous, it provides an inadequate basis for orienting us to specific economic forms like supply chains. The emphasis on structural processes for which no one is responsible tends to direct attention away from the particular claims of authority made by brands that lead supply chains, for example. As Michael Goodhart observes, "Because she abjures considerations of culpability and causation and treats all connections as generating moral responsibility, the distinctiveness of power relations gets lost."[68]

Second, Young's account provides an unstable ground for the responsibility to further justice since institutional participation is invoked at the same time that its import is undercut.[69] This turns her to other descriptions of what constitutes the connection between garment worker and consumer, including the latter's receipt of benefits, as I noted earlier. Young's most sustained argument for a grounding connection is ultimately the idea that the consumer's action puts her into a relation with the garment workers where her action relying on or taking advantage of the worker's exploitation requires justification to the worker herself. She writes, "By the simple act of buying a shirt I presuppose the actions of all those people who are involved in growing the cotton, making the cloth, gathering the cutters and sewers to turn it into garments, the cutters and sewers themselves, and all the agents involved in shipping the garments and making them easily available to me."[70] This implicit reliance on an unjust process then generates a responsibility for justice even though my act itself may not cause any harm. Young argues, "To the extent that these practices result in harming workers, my intention to buy cheap shirts is implicated in that harm, even though I do not intend the workers harm, and even when I plausibly judge that my own constrained circumstances make it necessary for me to buy either inexpensive clothes or none at all."[71] The intuition here is that by taking advantage of a bad situation, I owe something to those disadvantaged by those circumstances. Note, though, my action needn't actually benefit me in order for me to acquire that responsibility; if I end up the subject of scorn and ridicule for the ugly shirt that I bought and rue the day I purchased it, this does nothing to diminish my act's reliance on other agents or my subsequent responsibility.

Though this approach avoids some of the issues associated with grounding a responsibility for justice in the receipt of benefits, it creates several other problems for Young's account. Onora O'Neill, on whose account Young draws here, says only that we are obliged to attend to the *well-being* of those we rely on, which is different and potentially more paternalistic than a shared interest in justice.[72] Given the causal story Young identifies, it's not obvious that I can't justify on those grounds the discrete act of buying the clothes to the workers I rely on. The worker would be no better off if the consumer instead did not purchase the garment; indeed, workers are often quite clear that they want consumers to employ boycotts sparingly.[73] What's unjustifiable is the larger supply chain structure, which requires a more detailed examination than Young provides. Yet focusing on the need for a justification of my individual act ends up fixing in place the very unjust institutions that should be the object of our resistance; my own "constrained circumstances" are taken for granted and the possibility that they are themselves related to the constraints faced by the workers is ignored.

This focus on justifying the discrete act of consumption places responsibility in the wrong place. To say that someone becomes responsible for sweatshop conditions in virtue of their consumption focuses our attention on the act where, as Young acknowledges, they actually exercise little power. It too readily accepts the supply chain manager's vision of the consumer as related to the worker only at the moment of consumption and doesn't incorporate the way that the consumer too is subjected to power. Disconnected from any urgent interest of the consumer and without real causal power, ethical consumption is easily reduced to an aesthetic preference—one readily perceived as sanctimonious and off-putting to others.[74] Holding individuals responsible for structural injustice that they didn't cause ironically echoes the neoliberal effort to hold individuals responsible for market outcomes that are simultaneously held to be out of their control.[75] Michael Goodhart aptly notes that Young never analyzes the importance of how "consumption is the primary modality of expressing freedom" today.[76] As a result, her account does not recognize resisting injustice as an opportunity to experience freedom by breaking from a neoliberal orientation, but instead sees a consumer's responsibility to promote justice as effectively reiterating the paradoxical neoliberal circumstances which likewise hold her responsible for causes beyond her control. Despite Young's official refusal to blame consumers, that is the all but inevitable result of her argument.

Finally, it's unclear how this argument about a connection grounded in reliance applies to the responsibility for justice of the worker herself. It's true that the workers' actions are reliant on consumers purchasing goods, but the temporal view here is different; it is a prospective reliance on a hypothetical consumer rather than a specific one. It need not be me that purchases the apparel so long as there is sufficient aggregate demand to keep her employed.

What's more, it's not clear on Young's account how this reliance is related to a responsibility for justice that would connect the worker to the consumer. It seems perverse to argue that a worker needs to justify her reliance on a consumer purchasing the goods she produces; that would seem to hold the worker responsible for her own disadvantaged position.

Overall, understanding our actions as guided by a natural duty of justice better reflects how subjection to unjust institutions shapes the interests of both garment workers and consumers. For Young, the connection between our interests and our acts to promote justice are contingent, which leads to her inconsistent reliance on causation to explain why responsible workers and consumers might promote justice together. As we've seen, Young makes no effort to explain what interest consumers might have in living in a more fully just society, despite recognizing the constraints that they face; instead, the focus is on the benefits that the consumer already enjoys. With respect to workers, Young writes, "Sometimes agents' interests coincide with the responsibility for justice. Victims of structural injustice in particular have an interest in undermining injustice, and they ought to take responsibility for doing so."[77] But here Young makes a symmetrical error. Where she ignores the interest that consumers have in a more just world, Young ignores the interests that workers have in the status quo. As a result, she makes it seem so obvious that workers' interests dictate resisting injustice that she overlooks the costs they would bear in doing so; by assuming workers' interests to be univocal, she risks holding them more responsible for their own oppression than the privileged. With respect to both workers and consumers, Young tells unappealing stories because she discounts the role that justice should play in our judgment of our interests and our actions.

An Interest in Freedom?

Consider again the situation of Bangladeshi workers like those who suffered the Tazreen factory fire. The incident is clearly an injustice and while the government of Bangladesh failed to protect its citizens, they are hardly the only ones culpable; Walmart and the other American corporations that produced there had some responsibility too. Indeed, they acknowledge this and a significant division of Walmart is now devoted to what they call "ethical sourcing." But they too failed. Despite claiming to have a comprehensive monitoring system to check for these problems, three different Walmart lines were produced at the factory even after potential fire safety issues were flagged. These corporate policies are fundamentally different than actions grounded in a shared status and shared interest in justice; they express not a form of political solidarity, but rather an effort to preserve the legitimacy of their authority by exercising their power more benevolently. Of course, it is usually better for power to be exercised with greater benevolence and less malevolence, but such interventions are ultimately better understood as aiming to preserve existing hierarchy rather than to improve workers' wages and working conditions. To the extent that they succeed at legitimating corporate authority, they entrench neoliberal orientations and privatize political power behind the technocratic logic of the efficient supply chain manager.[78]

Yet even by these technocratic standards, ethical sourcing audits have largely had no impact on workers. As discussed in chapter 2, their repeated failure to achieve even modest reductions in illegal mandatory overtime have been clearly demonstrated over the roughly two decades since ethical monitoring was first popularized.[79] That they persist anyway suggests that they have other functions that lead corporations to see them as worthwhile, such as directing attention away from the fundamental problems with the structure of supply chains that make injustice a predictable outcome.[80] These would be much more costly to change: the just-in-time production model that frees brands from needing to keep large inventories, the lack of collective bargaining, and the low prices brands offer to factories that make it impossible for them to offer the legal minimum.[81]

These institutional failures made the injustice of the fire possible and also make it reasonable for the workers there to appeal to Americans to act in solidarity and expect them to respond. This is not just because Walmart is an American corporation and Americans have Walmarts in their communities, but because of the whole system of bilateral and multilateral agreements and institutions that make it possible for Bangladesh to export $18 billion in apparel each year. These are agreements and institutions to which Americans are subjected too and which significantly affect their interests. Nevertheless, it would be inappropriate for Americans to try to meet the demands of justice by acting unilaterally. Such efforts can easily run afoul of the workers' interests; well-intentioned efforts to boycott Bangaldeshi goods might make the workers' situation more difficult, for example. This reflects solidarity's grounding in the need for coordinated collective action; the production of a shared good by diverse individuals typically requires consultation, as reflected in the requirement to attend to calls for solidarity.

So what acts of solidarity could these workers reasonably ask for? First, Americans could pressure the government of Bangladesh to improve its labor laws and enforcement. For example, the government promised the families of the workers who died at Rana Plaza roughly $20,000 each, but failed to deliver anything near that until international solidarity forced the government to make the payments and indict the factory owner for murder.[82] Second, the US government maintains significant relations with the government of Bangladesh and so American citizens have some standing to call for that relation to be reformed. This too has had some effect. In the wake of the Rana Plaza collapse, President Obama suspended some of Bangladesh's trading privileges and made progress toward protecting worker rights a condition of their restoration.[83] Finally, an appeal might ask those in solidarity to pressure Walmart or the other corporations producing at the factory to act directly to improve factory safety. Such action led directly to the formation of the legally binding Accord on Building and Fire in Bangaldesh signed by many major apparel brands, though Walmart itself notably refused to participate.[84]

Crucially, there are limits to solidarity because unjust institutions create a situation where some people have genuinely antagonistic interests. While consumers receive benefits like cheap clothes from unjust institutions, their role differs from those who have institutional decision-making power, like the CEOs of apparel companies. Such individuals are in a position to change the policies and structures that produce injustice and by failing to do so, they not only receive benefits but also actively perpetuate unjust institutions.[85] An appeal to interest is inappropriate for those individuals whose employment, wealth, or income is only possible because of injustice, such as supply chain managers themselves.[86] Any actions they take to promote justice should be understood under a different self-description. We might more readily identify it with a negative duty to avoid harm or with Rawls's account of the political obligation acquired by those who voluntarily advance their interests in a system; Rawls identifies that kind of obligation with *noblesse oblige*, which is quite different from solidarity.[87] Specifying principles of justice for supply chain managers to apply—or arguing that supply chain managers have a duty to quit their jobs to avoid complicity with injustice—is thus a different project from the one I pursue here. To the extent that supply chain managers habituate themselves to identify shared interests with workers and seek to perceive them as partners, I suspect that they will find their self-conception in tension with their role at work, where their position remains hierarchical; ethical supply chain managers and social responsibility auditors are likely to find that their jobs fit more readily with the humanitarian orientation I describe and critique in the conclusion.

The situation of a consumer who benefits from the low prices of goods produced through exploitation is different. Consider two kinds of consumers. One has been so disadvantaged by the neoliberal global economy that she has no choice but to seek out the cheapest possible goods in order to get by. She might understand herself to have an interest opposed to that of the Bangladeshi workers in that their sweatshop wages and working conditions make it possible for her buy fantastically cheap goods. But she can also understand herself to share an interest with the Bangladeshi workers in that they both would benefit from replacing existing international economic institutions and norms with more just alternatives. The natural duty of justice counsels individuals to habituate their attitudes so that they come to identify with the second interest without denying the full force of the first. Depending on how the consumer identifies their interests, they may articulate shared interests with garment workers in multiple ways. The overwhelming majority of garment workers are young women of color. American consumers of color may identify a shared interest in resisting the global color line that makes the exploitation of the developing world appear natural to so many. White American consumers may realize that their interest in resisting supply chains also leads them to share an interest in removing the racial veil that makes the exploitation of workers in the developing world seem natural. US women consumers may recognize that fighting sweatshops helps to resist the habitual assumption that women can be paid less because they are not supposed to be heads of household, so their wages should merely be sufficient to supplement a man's.[88]

These claims of a shared interest in solidarity might prompt greater skepticism when confronted with another, more privileged consumer—one who materially benefits from the global economy as currently constituted.[89] It might seem more rational to suffer the minor inconvenience of the injustice than the potential costs of action to further a more just arrangement. Earlier, I noted the public goods that are only available in a just society; here, drawing from my argument in chapters 3 and 4, I specify how supply chain injustice also affects the freedom of privileged individuals in a way that gives them a reason to be in solidarity. One needn't be a Hegel scholar to recognize that the institutions which help protect freedom need the compliance of many people to make them work; I can't durably enjoy freedom as a solitary individual.[90] But this compliance isn't the product of prepolitical individuals freely choosing to obey; we grow up under and are shaped by institutions from the very start, long before we're capable of anything like free choice. We need political institutions to enjoy freedom, but having such institutions also means that they shape us before we could possibly get to choose them. As I argued in chapter 3, our inability to choose the institutions under which we're born should shape the conception of individual freedom to which we can aspire. Because we are inevitably habituated by institutions we cannot choose, we can envision as an ideal being habituated by just institutions to understand the role that they play in enabling their freedom.[91] Consequently, complying with those institutions—by doing your duty as specified by the laws, by respecting the rights of others, and so on—wouldn't feel like a constraint on your freedom but an expression of it. Though individuals living under just institutions have not chosen their society, they can affirm it freely and so feel at home in it. This ready disposition to affirm the forces that are beyond our control but that make us who we are is the outer limit of freedom. For anyone who aspires to live under institutions we can freely affirm, injustice ensures that the social world cannot be a home in the fullest sense to either the privileged or the oppressed.

While the material benefits of unjustified privilege facilitate many possible actions, they prevent an individual from being able cooperate with others freely and fairly, since the other party is necessarily constrained. Given the structure of the global garment industry, it is impossible for me to purchase apparel manufactured in a manner consistent with justice; I am forced to wear a violation of my principles every day—and to become all but inured to this condition. In short, I am denied the outer limit of freedom. Obviously, many people choose to forgo exactly this kind of freedom every day, but at least we can say that it is possible, reasonable, and desirable to do otherwise—to identify the enjoyment of one's own freedom with that of others, not simply out of altruistic concern but as a way of affirming one's own interest in freedom. As I argued in chapters 3 and 4, living in a society that constrains the freedom to act in accord with one's conscientious beliefs about justice can do real damage. Knowing that one's accomplishments in life were only possible because of injustices done to others can rob them of meaning. Individuals constrained to act in a manner inconsistent with justice may have to deceive themselves or alter their character in order to cope, giving up their beliefs in order to maintain a consistent self-understanding.

Nor is it only at freedom's outer limit that most consumers face unjustified constraints. Consider some of the cases that I've already introduced.

Consumers of sweatshop goods are the same people who are facing a generation of stagnant real wages and widening inequality. They are the same people who feel pressured to build their brand on social media or on platform apps where they can solicit work. They live in a world in which freedom is identified with choice in the marketplace but in which they are constantly subject to corporate surveillance, which is justified as freedom-enhancing by helping them make better market choices. My own employer requires its employees to complete an extensive biometric and psychological profile every year in order to be eligible for a better health insurance rate; employees are also incentivized to install an app on their smartphone which, among other things, give you points that can reduce the cost of your health insurance if you let it monitor your fitness and count your steps.[92] In other words, the price of more affordable health insurance is giving your employer data about where you are at every moment. Under these circumstances, it is not surprising if individuals who enjoy real material benefits from neoliberalism nevertheless feel that circumstances constrain their freedom and they share an interest in resisting them with those who are more obviously oppressed.[93]

Practicing Solidarity

In arguing that a range of people subject to unjust institutions have an interest in meeting the demands of justice, I certainly do not mean to deny the powerful attractions of being privileged in relation to injustice, especially when so much else seems uncertain about one's fortunes under neoliberalism. Beyond the material comforts derived from such advantages, knowing that someone else is disadvantaged in comparison to you can be a great comfort. As Alexis de Tocqueville noted about the transition to a capitalist economy, "When the aristocracy of birth is supplanted by the aristocracy of money, things change . . . The immediate result of this is that all citizens are secretly at war with one another."[94] But this feeling of perpetual competition and perpetual uncertainty is hard to bear. On Tocqueville's analysis, white supremacy alleviates this feeling by installing "an aristocracy founded on visible and imperishable signs," which enables whites to feel like they needn't worry about competing with or falling below blacks.[95]

Similarly, Du Bois famously describes how white planters were able to defeat Reconstruction and install Jim Crow institutions because "the white group of laborers, while they received a low wage, were compensated in part by a sort of public and psychological wage." Whites received this psychological wage through their experience of a racialized public sphere: "They were given public deference and titles of courtesy because they were white. They were admitted freely with all classes of white people to public functions, public parks, and the best schools."[96] Even when schools for poor whites were bad, white parents could comfort themselves that they were better than the schools for Blacks. But the habitual receipt of this wage came with a high cost. As Du Bois put it in his 1920 essay pointedly titled "The Souls of White Folk," Du Bois notes that experience of this unjustified superiority and the ability to enter spaces from which others are restricted leads whites to think that "whiteness is the ownership of the earth forever and ever, Amen!"[97] With such wild self-aggrandizement, the existence of Black people in public comes to seem an affront, leading whites to take "fierce, vindictive joy" from seeing violence done to them.[98]

In the face of such grotesquely warped character, Du Bois still affirms the view of freedom that we saw him endorse in chapter 4: "A true and worthy ideal frees and uplifts a people; a false ideal imprisons and lowers." White folks are "a people imprisoned and enthralled, hampered and made miserable for such a cause, for such a phantasy" of white supremacy.[99] By choosing the material and psychological benefits of unjustified hierarchy over partnership in solidarity and the outer limit of freedom, they have been satisfied with fewer material benefits than they would otherwise accept and, in the process, denied themselves the benefits that come from living in a just society and warped themselves to justify what they've done. With respect to global injustice, American consumers who eagerly defend their status arguably do something analogous, choosing the psychological wage of nationalist identification with American hegemony over transnational partnerships to resist neoliberalism. But neoliberalism arguably makes this choice less and less attractive; as Nikhil Pal Singh and Thuy Linh Tu have argued, neoliberal austerity and inequality have led to "the stagnation of these wages of whiteness."[100]

Importantly, the number of individuals moved to act justly need not be large for solidarity to produce social change. Consider that in 1961, only 24 percent of white Americans supported the Freedom Riders' successful campaign to desegregate interstate buses.[101] On the eve of the March on Washington in 1963, only 23 percent had a favorable impression of the demonstration; even after he won the Nobel Peace Prize, more Americans had an unfavorable view of Martin Luther King Jr. than had a favorable view.[102]

Yet the fact that a majority of Americans never supported key leaders and actions by the civil rights movement did not prevent the movement from changing political institutions and policies. By the same token, the number of individuals who are disposed to solidarity and respond to calls for solidarity from transnational supply chain workers has been small but effective relative to their size. For example, in the period of 1999 to 2001, the group United Students Against Sweatshops (USAS) was active on roughly 180 campuses with groups ranging in size from 10 to 100 members. Despite being a network that almost certainly had fewer than 10,000 members in the United States, USAS was able to organize highly effective campaigns that resulted in the foundation of the Worker Rights Consortium (WRC), an independent monitoring organization that responds to worker complaints about injustices in the supply chains that produce university-licensed apparel.[103] More than 190 colleges and universities who collectively license the production of billions of dollars of apparel are now members of the WRC.[104] Ohio State University alone has a contract with Nike worth more than $250 million, giving them substantial leverage to press for improvements in the supply chain—when they care to use it.[105] USAS continues its solidarity work and has achieved other major changes to supply chains, including a successful campaign supporting workers in Honduras who organized unions in all of Fruit of the Loom's factories there.[106] These actions are obviously exceptional, but they suggest how effective a more widespread disposition to solidarity could be if more Americans came to identify their shared interests with supply chain workers.

Doing so need not involve a detailed explanation of how Hegel, Rawls, or Du Bois understand freedom. To see the way in which our unfreedom is clearly invoked in ordinary discourse, consider three kinds of rationalizations typically offered to justify the receipt of benefit from sweatshop exploitation. While each explanation purports to affirm existing institutions, each also makes it clear that they are not and cannot be affirmed freely, as is possible at freedom's outer limit. First and perhaps most common is simple avoidance; people are generally averse to thinking about the topic because it is discomfiting, as I noted in the book's introduction. Second, they might justify it by referring to exploitation's purported necessity for economic development. Again, the claim is essentially that we are not free to make things otherwise; insofar as existing arrangements are affirmed, it is not because we are capable of choosing them but precisely because they are put outside of our ability to choose. Third, privileged individuals may express a desire that it be otherwise but emphasize their own powerlessness to change things; this again suggests that even the privileged are not free to act or affirm as they wish. This list is not exhaustive of the ways that sweatshops might be defended as compatible with freedom, but it suggests the following general point: insofar as sweatshop defenders agree that these working conditions are regrettable, then they must explain why the institutions that produce them could be freely chosen by those who are exploited by them and so without recourse to claims about the necessity of these institutions. Libertarians and neoliberals of sincere conviction may be able to do so—though, as I argued in chapters 1 and 2, their orientation renders coercion and power in the work-place all but invisible—but others who find market freedom inadequate for articulating their own experience of unjustified constraints can find common cause with supply chain workers. However, some egalitarians argue that such transnational solidarity distracts us from a more effective tool to resist neo-liberalism: unconstrained state sovereignty. In the next chapter, I consider and critique that view.

6

Why Sovereignty Is Not the Solution

In this book, I have argued that resisting neoliberalism requires reorienting our view of the economy; rather than regarding it paradigmatically as an apolitical place where most people exercise market freedom, we should instead see it as saturated with coercive authority that aspires to legitimacy in order to function effectively and is thus appropriately subject to contestation, including democratic demands for representation by workers and consumers. This reorientation recognizes the supply chains traversing our globe as political entities, with their own governmentality and political rationality. By seeing supply chains as the essentially spontaneous product of independent private decisions by separate enterprises, a neoliberal orientation renders them apolitical. The actions to address supply chain injustices that naturally follow from that view—corporate codes of conduct enforced by lead brands, consumers expressing preferences for higher labor standards through purchases in the market, and so on—have proven to be largely ineffective over the past twenty years. Addressing the obvious injustices in supply chains like the Rana Plaza factory collapse is better facilitated by politicizing supply chains—and consequently neoliberalism more broadly—through promoting the freedom of association to build transnational coalitions of those the chains seek to govern and, ultimately, by seeing our own freedom expressed in a disposition to solidarity with each other.

That embrace of transnational politics runs counter to an alternative approach promoted by a broad and diverse group that seeks to resist global neoliberalism by revitalizing domestic politics against the international. This view appeals to an ideological common sense that attracts adherents from across the political spectrum. Notably, it seems to captures a key part of Donald Trump's electoral success. Trump often made rhetorical attacks on the global economy a centerpiece of his campaign, characteristically asserting that "this wave of globalization has wiped out totally, totally, our middle class. It does not have to be this way" and assailing "a leadership class that worships globalism over Americanism." Instead, Trump held out "Brexit," the United Kingdom's vote to leave the European Union, as a

Disorienting Neoliberalism. Benjamin L. McKean, Oxford University Press (2020). © Oxford University Press.
DOI: 10.1093/oso/9780190087807.001.0001.

model, approvingly noting that "Our friends in Britain recently voted to take back control of their economy, politics and borders."[1] We also see similar comments from Trump's political opponents; Senator Bernie Sanders has also described the global economy as one where other countries represent threats to the American working class. In one such tweet, he writes, "We must say to corporate America loud and clear: you can't continue sending our jobs to China while millions are looking for work."[2] Such rhetoric suggests that efforts to achieve domestic social democracy orient us in the first instance to workers abroad as threats or competitors rather than potential allies or coalition partners.

These arguments are not found only in partisan electoral politics; we also find related strains of thought among egalitarian liberals, critical theorists, and others who suggest that resisting neoliberalism needs to start at home—typically, by trying to restore the effective welfare state that purportedly preceded neoliberalism. Tony Judt argued along these lines that "if social democracy has a future, it will be as a social democracy of fear. Rather than seeking to restore a language of optimistic progress, we should begin by reacquainting ourselves with the recent past."[3] Likewise, Samuel Moyn argued that concern for human rights abroad has helped enable the erosion of the welfare state at home, writing, "in the long view, the search for rights beyond [the state] may have been at a considerable price: the loss of the inclusive space of membership that the concrete state, and even empire, had long provided in some form or other."[4] These views represent an important challenge to my project. The electoral success not only of Trump but also of Brexit demonstrates that the discursive framework of autarkic withdrawal from the global economy can move people to political action. To the extent my argument suggests that we need to repoliticize neoliberalism in order to resist it, the nation-state might then appear to be the most natural and efficacious site of such a project.

To take a concrete case, consider the political theorist Richard Tuck's arguments for "Lexit"—that is, left-wing reasons to support Brexit. Having the United Kingdom leave the European Union was originally the project of the virulently anti-immigrant UK Independence Party (UKIP) and was taken up by some leaders of the Conservative Party, but Tuck and others have argued that the left should welcome Brexit despite its origins as a right-wing project. For Tuck, Brexit offers the best opportunity to repoliticize and resist the injustice of the global economy through a renewed focus on the state's supremacy over the market. He writes, "The political debate the EU has closed down is the central question of our time, the debate over the role of the market, which dominated the 20th century and which has been revived across the world since the financial crash."[5] Settling whether or not the EU is most aptly described as "constitutionalised neoliberalism" (in the phrase of Lexit supporters Joe Guinan and Thomas Hanna) is beyond the scope of this chapter, but the logic of Tuck's turn to the state is characteristic of the larger view I'm tracing.[6] Tuck rebukes efforts to build transnational institutions and argues that in directing attention to forming transnational coalitions to democratize the EU, "the British left risks throwing away the one institution which it has, historically, been able to use effectively—the democratic state—in favor of a constitutional order tailor-made for the interests of global capitalism and managerial politics."[7] For Tuck, the only real tool that can address economic injustice is "an omnicompetent democratic legislature . . . not constrained by a constitution."[8] What matters to Tuck here is the state's ultimate authority, which grants it a free hand with respect to internal and external affairs; only a power that is unconstrained and capable of intervening wherever it sees fit can serve as a sufficient bulwark against the depoliticizing power of a neoliberalism that seeks to "encase the world economy."[9]

Life in the neoliberal market is necessarily unpredictable and success through one's own efforts can never be guaranteed; rather than seeking such power and self-determination, neoliberal subjects make life in the market tolerable by adhering to a "sociodicy" that justifies embracing market outcomes. Against this acceptance of powerlessness, Tuck desires a strong state; his rejection of constitutional constraints is not incidental.[10] A Lexit pamphlet that Tuck coauthored with political scientist Christopher Bickerton claims that British citizens became fearful when told that the United Kingdom is constrained from regulating immigration from EU member states. They write, "Though fear of this [constraint] was inevitably intertwined with hostility to immigration, the fact of powerlessness was *real*, and it presaged powerlessness in other areas in the future. This is the key thing Remainers, and especially Remainers on the Left, have to realize. Brexit is therefore above all about sovereignty."[11] It is only sovereignty—understood specifically as unconstrained state power with final, omnicompetent authority in a territory—that can take on global markets. Efforts to politicize neoliberalism transnationally will flounder because they fail to recognize that politics is essentially state-bound; in the absence of a sovereign in the form of a super-state or a world state, transnational relations will always be vulnerable to control by powerful nonstate actors like corporations.

This emphasis on unconstrained sovereignty as the key to resisting economic injustice is the through line of the views that I consider in this chapter. Some of the most prominent egalitarian liberals in the Rawlsian tradition argue that such sovereignty is a necessary precondition for even calling economic inequality an injustice at all—a claim they link to the argument that sovereignty is a practical precondition to making distributive justice effective. Critical theorists like Wendy Brown argue that "the neoliberal revolution takes place in the name of freedom—free markets, free countries, free men—but tears up freedom's grounding in sovereignty for states and subjects alike"[12] and "wholly abandons the project of individual or collective mastery of existence."[13] Resisting neoliberalism and reestablishing freedom, this line of thinking suggests, requires taking back up the mantle of unconstrained state sovereignty since it alone enables us to take control and achieve mastery. Similarly, Wolfgang Streeck argues that "the surrender of national sovereignty to supranational institutions, like international assistance and cross-border regulation, becomes a tool not only for the protection of financial investment and the collection of debt but also for the insulations of 'the markets' from political interference in the name of corrective social justice."[14] In response, he argues that the *Staatsvolk* must reclaim their national sovereignty from the *Marktvolk* who have taken it if social justice is ever to be achieved. Efforts to build transnational coalitions to democratize the global economy are counterproductive; Streeck writes, "Under today's conditions, a strategy that places its hopes in postnational democracy, following in the functionalist wake of capitalist progress, merely plays into the hands of the social engineers of self-regulating global market capitalism."[15] In line with Tuck's invoking border control as the key test of sovereignty, Streeck has prominently argued for immigration restrictions as part of resisting neoliberalism, writing, "By fighting for deregulation of national borders to allow for open and open-ended immigration, the Left abandons a central element of its historical pro-regulation agenda, which importantly involved restricting the supply of labor in order to limit competition in labor markets."[16]

Notably, Streeck develops his defense of national sovereignty in part through a critique of Jürgen Habermas's account of sovereignty, which does not see sovereignty as necessarily bound to the state or nation and which consequently opens conceptual space for transnational polities and transnational politics.[17] On the Habermasian view, sovereignty is not understood as the unconstrained power of unitary nation-states, but instead as the product of multiple institutions and consequently as sharable among them.

Adjudicating the overall merits of such a conception is beyond this chapter, but I do want to note two relevant features of it: first, precisely because the Habermasian account does not posit sovereignty as unconstrained but instead as dependent upon reciprocal relations among peoples and institutions, it cannot satisfy those who believe resisting neoliberal globalization requires a unilateral assertion of control; second, because the Habermasian account does not posit sovereignty as unconditional and unilateral but necessarily relational and conditional, it escapes the critique I develop in this chapter. My argument is aimed at those who see sovereignty's political value today stemming from the potential for unconstrained sovereignty to bolster the state over and against the market.[18] There are other potentially productive conceptions of sovereignty I do not consider; for example, indigenous assertions of sovereignty aimed at curtailing the power of settler-colonial states are also not the target of my critique here.[19]

The source of unconstrained sovereignty's broad appeal as a way of resisting globalization is obvious. Neoliberal thinkers like Hayek conspicuously critique sovereignty as an "unnecessary" and "misleading" concept, so resuscitating it naturally seems like a promising strategy for those who want to protect the achievements of social justice from being further undermined by neoliberalism.[20] But neoliberalism is not straightforwardly opposed to state sovereignty and efforts to bolster sovereignty can do more to reinforce neoliberalism than to undermine it. Neoliberals are not uniformly in favor of international institutions constraining state sovereignty; many of them opposed the creation of the EU and we find them on both sides of the Brexit debate.[21] Whether or not international institutions effectively encase markets or instead constitute an extension of state power that should be regarded as dangerous because it can be democratized and turned to other ends is a source of tactical disagreement among neoliberals themselves; taking sides in that debate is not enough to resist neoliberalism.

Hayek's view is representative of neoliberalism's ambivalence. On the one hand, sovereignty expansively justifies government power and indeed asserts the supremacy of political power, which contradicts the neoliberal view of legitimacy resting on economic efficacy. On the other hand, neoliberalism welcomes the way that sovereignty can not only justify government coercion, which it regards as necessary, but grant the government a monopoly on legitimate force within its territory.[22] As a result of this claim to monopoly, economic coercion becomes ultimately attributable to the government rather than intrinsic to the market; economic exchange—and

international economic activity in particular—becomes very difficult to recognize as political in the sense defended in chapter 2. In other words, appealing to sovereignty as an ultimate, omnicompetent authority will tend to
reinforce neoliberalism's depoliticization of the economy. What's more, such
aggrandizing of state power makes itself an all-too-convenient foil to neoliberalism; in seeking to critique state power, neoliberalism has developed a
more acute sense of the practical limits of what sovereign states can accomplish than those who counterfactually endow them with omnicompetent
mastery over all that transpires within them. In this chapter, I develop these
arguments to show that the elevation of unconstrained sovereignty is unlikely to be a successful path to resisting neoliberalism, whatever particular
justification is provided. After all, it's hard not to notice that while Trump and
Brexit supporters framed their campaigns as sovereign resistance to an unfair global economy, their victories have not resulted in the restoration of the
welfare state but rather continuing and deepening neoliberal austerity.

Sovereignty and the Space of Politics

Because the authors that propose a reassertion of national sovereignty
against global injustice represent a spectrum of political views and theoretical approaches, I should say a bit more to situate their views and explain
why it makes sense to consider them together. Taking politics to be a space
with distinct values whose scope is defined by sovereignty is often associated
with Carl Schmitt and, like the thinkers I'm discussing, Schmitt argues that
the state is "in the decisive case the ultimate authority" and criticizes efforts
to "subjugate [politics] to economics" by depoliticizing certain questions.[23]
For Schmitt, the sovereign's final, omnicompetent authority can never be
constrained by a constitution, but is in fact defined by the ability to depart
from it when necessary; in his famous formulation, the sovereign is "he who
decides on the exception."[24] But Schmitt's concept of the political purports
to be free of ethical content and ultimately grounds itself in the necessity of
"the real possibility of physical killing."[25] By contrast, the thinkers I'm considering here don't justify sovereignty as an existential necessity free of normative content; instead, they both see it as necessary *and* as an essential tool
to promote normative values like freedom and justice in a global economy
that undermines them. As a result, these views share an orientation in which

politics is the essential realm in which to realize those values, but in which international politics is only derivatively political.

Such an orientation is liable to practical incoherence in a world where, as I've argued, forms of economic organization that cross state borders are best understood as political entities. However, the role that necessity plays in justifying sovereignty on these views helps make them appear coherent. As I explained in the introduction, an effective orientation incorporates some explanation of how existing political and social arrangements work; a description of the prevailing justifications that make those existing arrangements seem justifiable or at least intelligible; and an account of the values political action should promote. Making sovereignty a necessary condition of politics, when politics is understood as the appropriate realm in which to realize certain values, runs these dimensions together in a way that produces a misleading understanding of really existing political institutions. Arguments about the necessary shape of political institutions risk confusing institutions as they are with institutions as they ought to be. Where neoliberal thinkers invariably explain market failures as the result of inappropriate constraints on the market rather than as resulting from any problem with markets themselves, those who elevate sovereignty can likewise suggest that the failure of the state to achieve its ends is the result of too many constraints on it. But invocations of practical necessity can stand in tension with the political values they seek to promote; these are two different kinds of normativity that may not always fit together. To put it more practically: insisting that we see the state as necessarily the site of an ultimate omnicompetent authority risks empowering real institutions that can use the purported necessity of being unconstrained to threaten the normative values we seek to promote. Note that I am *not* arguing really existing states are irrelevant as sites of resistance to neoliberalism; rather, my argument is that this view of sovereignty badly orients us to them for this purpose.

To draw this out, this chapter looks in detail at egalitarian liberal arguments for the state as the necessary site of justice. Though these views differ in important respects from others that yoke sovereignty to resistance to international economic injustices, I focus here for several reasons. These arguments have been foundational to the extensive literature on global justice that proliferated in the past fifteen years and many subsequent important contributions have been attempts to refute them. While these arguments do not always name neoliberalism explicitly, the distributive justice that they see sovereignty as a tool to realize is starkly opposed to it; they expressly oppose much economic inequality as unjustifiable and consequently seek for the state to curb market outcomes. In doing so, these arguments posit politics as the space in which social justice is pursued and achieved. Against the Schmittian view of politics as an agonistic space of contention, which valorizes the form of politics rather than its content, I share with these authors the view that politics is better understood in normative terms as where injustice is resisted and freedom is sought. However, by tightly linking justice and sovereignty, these liberal egalitarians offer an exceptionally clear example of how arguments for an omnicompetent ultimate authority come into conflict with the normative values such arguments are meant to support. As I will argue, these views readily facilitate seeing transnational supply chains as neoliberalism portrays them. Their focus on unconstrained sovereignty leads them to see political power as chiefly wielded through coercion, which brings their view of supply chain injustices startlingly close to libertarian defenders of sweatshops. More generally, holding up unconstrained sovereignty as the sine qua non of politics orients us to the global economy as a constitutively apolitical, even ahistorical space and makes it harder to conceptualize both domestic and transnational social movements as essential and fully political means for achieving justice.

This argument may seem quixotic. Few distinctions within political science seem better secured than that between domestic and international politics. The division between them organizes both the common sense and the disciplinary structure of the field, shaping conceptual imaginaries, journals, panels, and all manner of other aspects of our practice and theory. Even political theory and philosophy that takes transnational issues of global justice as its focus often assumes domestic politics as the norm and registers questions of global justice as both a historical and theoretical departure. For example, Laura Valentini describes her egalitarian liberal project as one of "offering a plausible answer to *the question of extension*: 'Can principles of justice be meaningfully extended from the domestic context to the world at large?'"[26] Consistent with this framing is an emphasis on global justice as a question only arising *now* as a new problem to confront, as though previously domestic politics occurred in isolation from events elsewhere. Again, Valentini offers a standard characterization: "Nowadays, if we want to get a sense of what is, or might be, happening at home, we also need to take a look at what is, or might be, happening abroad . . . Globalization opens up new possibilities and generates new challenges." While Valentini, like many others, accompanies this with a de rigueur citation to Kant's claim in *Perpetual Peace* that even in his time, "a violation of rights in one part of the world is felt everywhere," this literature offers comparatively little reflection on the actual historical transformations that took place between 1795 and today.[27]

What is the character of this globalization that opens up the question of global justice for egalitarian liberal theorists like Valentini? Absent any historical background—other than perhaps the fall of the Soviet Union, understood as the end of organized state opposition to capitalism—these global justice theorists tend to default to the belief that the global economy has somehow, due to forces internal to it, outstripped or exceeded the boundaries of our state-bound political arrangements, which now need to catch up.[28] Such a framing overlooks the political developments required to create contemporary globalization and, by making them virtually natural facts about the world, hampers consequent theorizing about how to respond. The period of decolonization from the end of World War II to the mid-1960s; the dramatic economic developments of the 1970s, from Nixon's ending the use of the gold standard to the oil crises of 1973 and 1979; and the rise of neoliberalism and its spread through the Washington Consensus implemented by the IMF and WTO through the 1980s are all rarely given even lip service.[29] Without some account of these historical transformations, it is unclear what makes the present moment unique since the economy of Kant's time saw similarly impressive and increasing global interdependence. Not only did the sale of chattel slaves create the Atlantic "triangle trade" that connected the Americas to Africa, but the same transportation network also facilitated the harvest of seal skins off South America and Australia for sale to China; fortunes in Massachusetts rose and fell with fashions in Guangzhou even then.[30]

With this long history of global interdependence in mind, how does the distinction between domestic and international politics retain its character as a self-evident fact? Among other factors, an unconstrained conception of sovereignty enables so much contemporary theorizing about *global* justice to accept this distinction as foundational and, as a result, perpetually restage globalization as though nations are today encountering each other for the first time. Taking the autarkic sovereign state as the normal point of departure almost invariably leads globalization to be understood as a practical but fundamentally *apolitical* organizational challenge to that form of government—something alien that comes from outside it. To pose "the question of extension" is then to ask if existing tools can master these apolitical outside forces and make them familiar and controllable. Such theories are ill-suited to orient us to the thoroughly political character of neoliberalism and consequently unlikely to facilitate effective political action in relation to these real obstacles to justice. Even if one is concerned only with domestic economic injustice, the neoliberal forces that produce inequality and constrain our freedom are themselves transnational.[31] Consequently, I argue that effective political movements seeking to achieving social and political equality must also be transnational if they are to be successful. Such transnational movement will often operate through and against particular states, as when the survivors of the Rana Plaza factory collapse in Bangladesh appealed to supporters in the United States to urge the US government to sanction the government of Bangladesh until it provided improved worker protections. My argument thus does not entail any belief that state power is waning or irrelevant; on the contrary, it suggests that state capacity is an empirical question rather than a matter of conceptual or a priori argument. The ideological common sense that makes "the question of extension" seem like a natural approach even to advocates of global justice thus needs to be undermined in order to clear space for effective orientations to constitutively transnational politics.

Coercion and the Burdens of Justice

The ideological common sense that sovereignty divides the world into normal, domestic politics and derivative, international politics has a particularly stark effect on egalitarian liberal thinkers in the Rawlsian tradition, which requires justifying a social order to its worst-off members. This represents a shift from some earlier liberal thinkers, for whom the protection of rights against unwarranted interference constituted the bulk of the work of justice. Ensuring the effective protection of such rights seems to place relatively few burdens on individuals; it does not seem too difficult to refrain from violating the rights of others. This appearance may turn out to be deceptive, but the intuitive impression of straightforward obligations that are easy to meet often remains.[32] In seeming contrast, egalitarian liberalism appears to require much more from individuals—not least their active participation in a redistributive scheme that could limit inequality by requiring them to give up access to or use of some resources.

These potentially demanding burdens lead to the question: How far must concern for relative standing take us? How widely are we obliged by justice to redistribute in a world of enormous inequalities? As I've noted, this debate about expanding concern across the globe in thought coincided with the implementation of policies to limit or rollback existing domestic redistribution; philosophers debated the possibility of extending the "difference principle" to the globe while the public political culture that supported its domestic application was undercut by neoliberalism. It is in that context that some liberal egalitarians have advanced arguments to limit the scope of concern about inequality to the fellow members of one's state. If the welfare state is already imperiled, one way to diffuse antagonism to it might be to assure its opponents that it does not push us down a slippery slope to global redistribution. Enter sovereignty, understood as the condition of possibility of legitimate political power. If states have a singular ability to coerce people legitimately, it seems quite natural to think that those people share a special relationship unlike what they have with others. I'll call *coercion theory* this family of views which hold that political borders represent the limits of obligations of egalitarian justice because of the nature of state coercion and the possibilities for its legitimation.[33]

Yet while its adherents seek to defend the normative uniqueness of the sovereign state in order to promote redistributive social welfare policies, coercion theory fatally undermines itself. Justifying state sovereignty because of its unique relationship to the legitimacy of coercion leads them to conceptualize purely economic relations as apolitical and free of coercion— with fatal effects for the view's ability to resist neoliberalism, which shares this same basic orientation to the market and the government. Moreover, by imagining that economic inequality can be rectified simply by strengthening the state, coercion theorists shore up the legitimacy of the state's penal power even while they conceptually concede that the state could recede from the market. In the end, I will argue that these efforts to defend what might be called "Rawlsianism in One Country" represent a dead end and suggest that this failure has important lessons for other egalitarian views that share its conception of unconstrained sovereignty. Centering this view of political power directs our attention away from other exercises of coercive authority that the state cannot control, notably social norms, and delegitimizes forms of political power actually in reach of ordinary citizens, such as participation in social movements.

If sovereignty is understood as the omnicompetent authority to determine what transpires within state borders, then coercion is the sovereign's indispensable tool for wielding that power. I understand coercion to be that species of force which has the effect of securing compliance with some aims through the threat of sanction.[34] Other forms of force, which might be called direct applications of force, are those which don't depend on my altering my behavior in order to succeed. So, mugging me to get my wallet involves coercion since I turn over the wallet in order to avoid being killed whereas simply assassinating me without warning is a lot of bad things but does not coerce me (it may, however, be coercive of others insofar as it is meant to intimidate, silence, etc.). Obviously, coercive force may depend on direct force for its efficacy; I comply with your coercive threat because I believe you have the means and the will to use your direct force against me. Coercion is generally more efficient than the simple use of direct force itself since it often requires less effort to threaten consequences and secure compliance, and it is partly this aspect that makes it so important to the political realm of coordinating behavior in groups.

Coercion is undeniably important to states, then. But according to what I'm calling coercion theory, what makes states unique is not their use of coercion; rather, coercion theory asserts that the uniqueness of states stems from their ability to *legitimate* this coercion by the state itself and other designated agents. As a result, the scope of our obligations of justice is coextensive with the scope of the state's legitimate ability to coerce. In other words, when citizens get the state to coerce other citizens, they are also obliged to be attentive to the relative equality of those individuals if that coercion is to be justifiable. Understanding justice in this way frames further questions in a particular direction: Namely, in what kinds of relations do obligations of justice obtain? And what kinds of relations must be formed to satisfy those obligations?

Coercion theory represents a particularly stark and distinctive example of a larger family of egalitarian liberal views which offer similar answers to these questions and which hold that there is necessarily a marked discontinuity between domestic and international justice. Proponents of discontinuity hold that there is something unalterably distinctive about the state that ties the idea of justice to domestic institutions; this may be coercion, but it may also be the public political culture or something else.[35] Regardless of the trait they hold to be distinctive, discontinuity theorists—coercion theorists included—agree that we may have various moral obligations to others outside our borders; these obligations may even be significant and onerous, but they will primarily be obligations of an apolitical and *humanitarian* kind.[36]

As I've said, these discontinuity views face a potential tension between their endorsement of sovereignty as a practical necessity and the normative values of freedom and justice that they want to promote. That tension reveals itself with exemplary clarity in the work of coercion theorists, who endorse two premises that are common within egalitarian liberal approaches to global justice. First is the view that achieving justice is primarily a matter of having the right kinds of institutions and so duties of justice for individuals primarily concern compliance with institutional rules. This view, which I looked at in chapter 4, echoes (often self-consciously) the argument for the necessity of the sovereign state found in Kant's political philosophy, so I will call it the *Kantian premise*. For Kant, justice is characterized as the state of everyone enjoying their rights through proper protection and enforcement of those rights by the coercive institution of the state. Kant links rights to institutions because he believes that an institution with universal jurisdiction in its territory is a priori the only possible method of rights enforcement. His basic point is that cases in which the rights of two individuals seem to conflict must rationally admit of a definitive resolution; such a resolution is only possible if everyone gives up their right to be judge of their own rights and delegates this capacity to a single final authority—the state. For Kant, this is not a probabilistic, empirical argument but a conceptual, a priori truth. The state is the condition of possibility of justice, and so there can only be relations of justice where institutions make authoritative decisions with no further possibility of appeal.[37] As Thomas Nagel writes in a seminal paper critical of global justice that structured much of the subsequent debate, "What creates the link between justice and sovereignty is something common to a wide range of conceptions of justice: they all depend on the coordinated conduct of large numbers of people, which cannot be achieved without law backed up by a monopoly of force."[38] Note that this argument for an ultimate, omnicompetent authority is not one that appeals only to liberal egalitarians, but echoes other views that see sovereignty as necessary to politics. Strikingly, it justifies a state monopoly of force with reference to its effects rather than to any popular authorization; in that, it structurally mirrors neoliberal justifications for state coercion, which likewise see state power as justified by its capacity to counter private coercion, regardless of whether the government is democratically authorized.

But this is only half the story. As we have already seen, coercion theorists also endorse a second premise: that justice requires relative social equality. Call this the *egalitarian premise*. Kant himself seems to have been content to accept great inequality; rather than prescribe economic redistribution to remedy the domination created by economic and social inequalities, he classed those who were economically dependent on others, including vir-tually all women in his time, as "passive citizens" properly regarded as in-capable of exercising their own political will.[39] This solution is found to be insufficient once egalitarian liberals accept that inequality cannot always be justified to the worst-off; for them, political institutions must operate so that they preserve and reproduce a justifiable level of social and economic equality. As Michael Blake writes, "The political and legal institutions we share at the national level create a need for distinct forms of justification. A concern with relative economic shares, I argue, is a plausible interpreta-tion of liberal principles only when those principles are applied to individ-uals who share liability to the coercive network of state governance."[40] This links justice and coercive institutions in a quite different way than Kant did since such equality is concerned with relative position (or at least the reason-able expectation of it). This is an extremely important shift, as it means that arguments about justice cannot be made completely a priori. Our duty of jus-tice may still require living under a state and complying with its rules, as Kant held, but the state now in turn must demonstrate its bona fides by showing that it is actually capable not merely of resolving disputes between conflicting rights but also of reproducing a permissible level of equality. This additional requirement of justice changes the conceptual nature of states considerably and stands in some tension with the first premise I've considered.

Because it concerns adopting rules that can reasonably be expected to have an appropriately egalitarian outcome, this liberal framework stands in tension with traditional understandings of state sovereignty. The approach is "anti-sovereigntist" in the sense of placing exterior moral limits on state action that are not simply self-limiting. By contrast, the Kantian premise assumes sovereignty as supreme authority. As Blake puts it, "[The state] is right, because it is final; it is not final because it is right"; any law with the appropriate legal form defines right within its territory.[41] The shift from formal to substantive equality thus complicates the normativity of sover-eignty significantly. Rawls makes this explicit in his *Lectures on the History of Moral Philosophy*, where he asserts, "a liberal conception will deny that states have the two traditional powers of sovereignty: the right to war to pursue their own rational interests and the right to internal autonomy."[42] Note how broad the claim is; Rawls says *any* liberal view must limit the internal and external sovereignty of states, constraining its purported omnicompetence and setting up other values in opposition to its ultimate authority.[43] Once a theory extends justice beyond the legal form of the state into a broader sense of relations, it will necessarily direct state action so as not to interfere with the establishment of justice in civil society, limiting the state's internal sovereignty and potentially the circumstances under which war with internally just states is permitted. When these kinds of limits are required, then sovereignty understood as an end in itself for states of all kinds must be renounced by the theory; sovereign authority must be justified by reference to other values and potentially balanced against other considerations, like human rights.

The tension in justifying an ultimate omnicompetent authority on grounds of both necessity and particular normative values confronts all the views that counsel unconstrained sovereignty as the decisive tool to resist a neoliberal global economy, with important implications for how individuals should orient themselves. Kantian justice is easy to determine since it is a matter of evaluating whether one's actions comply with sovereign legislation. In egalitarian liberal justice, on the other hand, the potential for a relation to be justice-relevant is much greater because one cannot prejudge whether a relation contributes to unacceptable relative inequality without examining it in the context of all the other potentially justice-relevant relations in the basic structure. Rawls suggests as much when he writes, "the spheres of the political and the public, of the nonpublic and the private, fall out from the content and application of the conception of justice and its principles. If the so-called private sphere is alleged to be a space exempt from justice, then there is no such thing."[44] From the perspective of this egalitarian premise, it is not immediately obvious how supply chain consumers in the developed world should be oriented to workers in the developing world that manufacture their clothes; it is a partly empirical question whether these relations are relevant to social justice, but it is conceptually possible that workers and consumers should regard each other as political partners acting against a common injustice, as I argue in chapter 5. This makes vivid the task of the coercion theorist: to find a justification for sovereignty that conforms with their egalitarian premise while still maintaining a strict domestic/international divide.

Coercion and Necessity

In the ideal world described by coercion theorists, states should coerce only their own citizens and those citizens thereby owe obligations of egalitarian justice only to each other, rendering domestic and international politics discontinuous realms.[45] Of course, as an empirical matter, states often coerce noncitizens; in addition to the domestic case of resident aliens, states often exert their power and influence internationally through war and other forms of intervention. These cases have given rise to an important debate about whether or not coercion can ever successfully ground discontinuity between domestic and international politics.[46] In this section, I want to bracket that question and argue that even domestically, the view that state sovereignty necessarily defines political power fails to orient us effectively to economic inequality and injustice. While coercion theory argues that state sovereignty and distributive justice are necessarily coextensive, it focuses on an unjustifiably narrow range of constraints on freedom, one surprisingly consistent with both neoliberalism and libertarian defenses of sweatshops. Even on those narrow grounds, because it aggrandizes the state, coercion theory overlooks the essential role that norms play in sustaining political and social life—a recognition crucial to reorienting our view of neoliberalism, as I argued in chapter 1.

With respect to their understanding of how coercion violates freedom, coercion theorists again see themselves as broadly in the Kantian tradition. According to Michael Blake, coercion is objectionable because it violates autonomy, which "reduces the will of one person to the will of another," while Thomas Nagel asserts that coercion is objectionable because it "claims our active cooperation" in some way without our so choosing.[47] Coercion theorists appeal here to a view of unfreedom not unlike the one articulated by Hayek and Milton Friedman; coercion is presumptively wrong because of how it forces us to choose something that we wouldn't otherwise. What distinguishes the state is its unique ability to justify and legitimate its coercion successfully by returning freedom to its subjects, thereby redeeming its coercive violations of freedom. Subjects of state coercion become the recipients of justice so that as much autonomy as possible can be restored to them—and to the extent that you can be held responsible for the state of which you are citizen, you thereby acquire obligations of justice to others who are similarly coerced. As Nagel puts it, "This complex fact—that we are both putative joint authors of the coercively imposed system, and subject to its norms, that is, expected to accept their authority even when the collective decision diverges from our personal preferences—that creates the special presumption against arbitrary inequalities in our treatment by the system."[48] Note again that this differs from Kant's own argument for the state, which is an a priori argument for the state based on the conditions of possibility of freedom. Here we find a posteriori justifications of the state which presume the existence of state coercion and see that as orienting subsequent political action and duties; as Blake puts it, "coercive enforcement might be legitimated with reference to reciprocity—but the coercion itself begins our story, and we do well to keep it in mind."[49] That priority of bare coercion is striking. What makes sovereignty so normatively special that we should invariably orient our political relations around it is not that it *is* legitimate, but that it is *potentially* legitimate. Where Kant defends an account of the state that relies on pure practical reason, coercion theorists must rely on some claim to practical efficacy in achieving equality. Yet on their account, a proper orientation to politics centers even on sovereigns that fail to achieve such equality, since they are the condition of possibility of a fully political relation in which inequality can be unjust.

The political primacy of bare coercion places these egalitarian liberals in some decidedly inegalitarian company. As I noted earlier, the forward-looking component of this argument rests the legitimacy of sovereignty on the consequences of its actions rather than, for example, on its democratic credentials; in that way, it orients us to the state in a manner similar to Milton Friedman's ledger, which looks to the consequences of government action to determine its legitimacy without regard for how the decision to act is arrived at. Nagel does refer to subjects of sovereign power as "putative joint authors," but as I will discuss, this putative authorship requires only that the sovereign act in the name of its subjects, not that the subjects themselves have any control over or democratic voice in the acts in question. Indeed, as we have seen, Hayek suggests such voice may not even be desirable since benevolent authoritarians can be more judicious in their use of force than a democratic people and Friedman praises undemocratic 1980s Hong Kong as his ideal state.

While coercion theories obviously depart from neoliberal thinking in demanding state action to achieve and preserve economic equality in order to be legitimate, their view of the unfreedom that triggers this requirement importantly echoes neoliberal market freedom. Blake's view is representative. Blake grounds his overall account in autonomy, which he says entails "more than the simple exercise of practical reasoning. It demands that the set of options provide adequate materials within which to construct a plan of life that can be understood as chosen rather than as forced upon us from without."[50] In other words, freedom understood as full autonomy has material preconditions that mere market freedom lacks; many things other than coercion can violate autonomy, including poverty. However, despite this more robust account of freedom, Blake argues that it is state coercion alone that orients us to others as fellow citizens and requires our relations to be characterized by social justice. He writes, "Whether an individual faces a denial of autonomy resulting from coercion cannot be read off simply from the number of options open to her. Coercion is not simply a matter of what options are available; it has to do with the reasons the set of options is as constrained as it is. Coercion is an intentional action, designed to replace the chosen option with the choice of another."[51] While coercion theorists believe that citizens deserve to enjoy a wide range of options, that governments ought to provide material benefits that help citizens learn how to choose well, and so on, they also believe that the failure to ensure these things does not trigger obligations of justice in the absence of state coercion.[52] The more expansive conception of autonomy is only relevant on the back end; what triggers the demands of social justice on the front end remains "the coercive nature of the laws, and not simply their effects upon welfare."[53] Violations of the freedom to choose still orient us to the state, in the first instance. While the failure to enjoy autonomy due to, for example, earning a subsistence wage may violate one's freedom, the only relationship that requires being oriented to that situation as a political problem is co-citizenship; the roles of consumer, employer, and so on have no particular status here.

As a result, coercion theory orients us to transnational supply chains in a way that startlingly resembles libertarian defenders of sweatshops. Consider the workers who took jobs in the Rana Plaza factories that collapsed in 2013. They accepted jobs with subsistence wages in dangerous conditions because they were poor and had few other options. To use Blake's terminology, we can certainly say that these workers do not enjoy full autonomy, but were they coerced into taking the job? As Benjamin Powell and Matt Zwolinski note, "No participant in the current debate [about sweatshops] holds that typical workers are coerced into *taking* sweatshop jobs."[54] Under the definition of coercion shared by Nagel, Blake, Hayek, and others, there is no coercion here because no one has manipulated the wills of the individual workers in order to force them to take the job; neither does any law force them to work there. Consequently, making coercion the beginning of the story means that for coercion theorists and libertarians alike, there's no reason for developed world consumers to be oriented to workers being forced to accept sweatshop jobs as a political problem.[55]

Now let's consider the situation of the workers who noticed the cracks in the factory building and entered anyway because a manager told them they would be fired if they didn't get to work. Were they coerced? Powell and Zwolinski conclude that, in such cases, what these workers are being asked to do might be wrong but it is not a coercive demand. Notice their reasoning: "If the demands above indeed qualify as coercive . . . then so too does almost any instance of an employer demanding her employee to X or else be fired—even the demand that the employee show up regularly to work at the scheduled time. If these are genuine examples of coercion, then coercion is everywhere in the workplace. And an account of coercion that has this implication seems too overinclusive to be much use in moral theorizing."[56] As I argued in chapter 2 by reading the work of economist Ronald Coase against the grain, it is absolutely correct to see that coercion is everywhere in the workplace; that is a key part of why we should be oriented to transnational supply chains as political entities. But coercion theorists, like libertarians, have to reject this conclusion because they argue that coercive authority is uniquely tied to the state.

Indeed, since poverty constrains autonomy without counting as coercion, focusing on coercion makes it appear that laws to regulate sweatshops are a bigger constraint on freedom than sweatshops themselves. Zwolinski writes, "Poverty reduces a worker's options, but so long as he is still free to choose from among the set of options available to him, we will do him no favors by reducing his options still further [through minimum wage legislation, building safety regulation, and so on]. Indeed, to do so would be a *further* form of coercion."[57] In other words, we have an apolitical, though perhaps unfortunate, situation where individuals are exercising market freedom until the state enters. On this view, workers who act collectively against their employers may be engaged in economic bargaining, but absent state coercion as a trigger, their contestation is not properly political; a developed world consumer might take a humanitarian interest in the workers' circumstances, but there is no reason to see it as a shared political struggle. In light of their argument, coercion theorists have no choice but to agree with the libertarians' description of the situation, though they will of course argue that coercively enforced state regulations are a justifiable form of interference.

State Sovereignty and Social Order

What makes state coercion so different from other violations of autonomy that it alone triggers duties of distributive justice and makes great inequality impermissible? As described earlier, the argument is that state coercion is a practically necessary condition of an ordered society, and that this necessity is what generates special obligations of justice as a kind of recompense for being subjected to that coercion. All other forms of coercion are in principle unnecessary and so can be rectified through their cessation, but because state coercion is necessary and cannot cease, its coercion can be rectified and legitimized through distributive justice. As Blake puts it, "Since the institution of the state is not likely to disappear at any point soon, and because some form of political coercion seems necessary for autonomous functioning, I think we must instead seek principles by which state coercion could be justified."[58] The way Blake separates these clauses is a telling equivocation that recalls neoliberal sociodicy. Do we need to justify the state because it is a coercive apparatus that we seem stuck with, and living with an unjustified imposition would be psychologically difficult? Or do we justify the state because it is actually necessary? Assuming that he means to put forward the latter, the argument is that we all share something like a rational interest in social order as a precondition to our other desires and consequently, state coercion is necessary in practice to achieve social order.[59] Since it is practically necessary, the bare existence of the sovereign does not need to be justified, but the particular laws it enforces do; only laws that produce appropriate levels of equality can be justified to all who are subject to them. Notice the Hobbesian dimension of the argument—not only does the practical importance of creating order ground the necessity of the sovereign, but the orientation that this argument produces is aptly pictured by the famous frontispiece of *Leviathan*: citizens turned in the first instance to the sovereign as the head of politics, their political equality a product not of their relation to each other but of their mutual subjection.

Let us accept this view that the state is a practical necessity for the sake of argument, though people have lived under various nonstate arrangements for much of history.[60] Note that accepting the practical necessity of state coercion does not show that state coercion is a *sufficient* condition to create an ordered society, so there may well be other necessary conditions to which we should be oriented. It is plain, in fact, that state coercion is not sufficient to create order. At least as necessary to the maintenance of order are the norms and practices of a society, as I showed Hegel and Rawls to argue in chapter 3. For the most part, society continues in virtue of the fact that its participants do not desire to stop its functioning. Yet in order to ground the importance of unconstrained sovereignty, coercion theory overlooks the crucial political importance of the practical acceptance of the legitimacy of state coercion found in the everyday practices of citizens. Neither stage of the coercion theorists' argument—not the bare necessity of the sovereign nor the justification of the particular sets of coercive laws enforced—makes any reference to citizens as political agents or their actual acceptance of the state and its laws; what matters is the nature of the state and not the actions of its subjects. This leaves it vulnerable to neoliberals who are better attuned to the practical limits of state power and the political importance of citizens' self-conceptions. As Hayek puts it, "The basic source of social order, however, is not a deliberate decision to adopt certain common rules, but the existence among the people of certain opinions of what is right and wrong."[61] While the state has the capacity to coerce and control any single individual, it cannot successfully coerce an entirely or even largely unwilling populace. To be practically effective, most people have to *want* to comply and these socially sustaining desires and behavioral regularities are reproduced through social practices and norms, not through state coercion.

To focus entirely on the state's relationship to violence and enforcement produces a poor understanding of how society functions and badly orients us to its institutions. This has not gone unnoticed by neoliberals themselves, whose recognition that neoliberal subjects need to be produced makes them more cognizant of the importance of social norms and practices. Though it sits awkwardly with their association of politics with state coercion, neoliberals do acknowledge that contracts and market exchanges need social norms to work; no market can function if market-bypassing behavior like fraud is pervasive.[62] Indeed, as I argued in chapter 1, this grudging recognition of the importance of social norms opens the way for a reorientation that can facilitate resistance to neoliberalism. But coercion theorists deny themselves this opportunity. If the reason for believing state coercion should orient our politics and demands for justice is that it is necessary to create order, then one could argue that the self-conceptions, norms, and practices of ordinary citizens are just as important to defining the scope of politics and justice because they are just as necessary. But if that's so, then coercion theorists have failed to identify anything unique about the state while conceding to neoliberals both that the state's primary function is to constrain freedom of choice through coercion and that the legitimacy of this coercion rests on its having efficacious consequences rather than any democratic authorization. Defining the state through its use of coercion doesn't even orient us properly to the welfare state that these theorists seek to defend; a focus on coercion obscures the other ways states wield political power as well as the tremendous variety of social service and regulatory activities that states undertake. Indeed, rendering such activities nonessential to the real business of government further reinforces the neoliberal view that promotes limiting government functions to the punitive sphere.

Monopoly and Legitimacy

Against my view that we should be oriented to the global economy as a political realm saturated with coercive authority that crosses borders and which should be contested through international movements that bring together the workers and consumers subjected to transnational supply chains, rival accounts argue that we should instead focus on domestic politics and resuscitate state sovereignty as the essential tool for resisting neoliberalism. So far, I've argued that views positing unconstrained sovereignty as a precondition to politicizing and resisting neoliberal globalization face a tension between the asserted necessity of unconstrained sovereignty and the normative values of justice and freedom that they seek to promote. I've shown that coercion theory tries to resolve this tension by making sovereignty necessary for social order, but that it fails to do so because the argument relies on a fatally incomplete social theory. This failure is consequential because, in orienting their conception of politics around state coercion, theorists like Nagel and Blake reinforce key elements of neoliberalism. Not every conception of sovereignty faces these problems, but in the remainder of this chapter, I want to show how these problems are endemic to arguments that assert both that politics and unconstrained sovereignty are coextensive and that politics is the proper domain in which to advance freedom and justice. Recall that sovereignty here is understood as the state's ultimate, omnicompetent authority; while these authors seek to empower the state in order to promote particular values, to do so, they first establish that state power is conceptually unconstrained by those values or any others. Recall how Bickerton and Tuck talk about the state's unconstrained power alleviating citizens' feeling of powerlessness and Wendy Brown's objection that neoliberalism "wholly abandons the project of individual or collective mastery of existence."[63] These claims suggest the powerful appeal of envisioning the state as an institution capable of controlling everything that happens in its territory, especially when neoliberals promote the very unpredictability of market outcomes as their signal virtue.[64]

In light of this desire for sovereignty as a means of control, it's notable that Nagel asserts the possibility of justice depends on "law backed up by a monopoly of force."[65] Nagel's phrase, of course, recalls Max Weber's definition of the state in "Politics as a Vocation" as "a human community that (successfully) claims the *monopoly of the legitimate use of physical force* within a given territory."[66] Weber elaborates: "The state is considered the sole source of the 'right' to use violence. Hence, 'politics' for us means striving to share power or striving to influence the distribution of power, either among states or among groups within a state."[67] This offers a different and perhaps more promising way of making politics and state sovereignty coextensive; rather than define the state by its necessity to creating order, Weber argues that "one can define the modern state sociologically only in terms of the specific *means* peculiar to it," not its end.[68] What makes sovereignty definitive of politics is its monopoly on the use of force itself, not any order-creating end for which it has purportedly acquired this monopoly. What's more, Weber's definition of the state incorporates successful claims to legitimacy, which appears to address the importance of individuals actually desiring and participating in the daily reproduction of their society, which coercion theorists overlooked.

Yet despite these advantages, Weber's view doesn't solve the problems faced by those who insist neoliberalism can only be resisted through the sovereign state. First, Weber's claim that the right to force always derives from the state depoliticizes the economy by positioning it as a place where force only exists as a result of the state's withdrawal; particularly when invoked as a failsafe tool against neoliberalism, it inflates the state's power by suggesting that it can unilaterally determine market outcomes while depoliticizing the market by not seeing the coercion that noncontingently has its home there. Second, it implies that government force is essentially homogenous—that all those subject to it stand in the same relation to it. But this assumption is dangerous and can facilitate policies that reinforce existing unjust inequalities, contrary to the aims of those invoking sovereignty. Ultimately, Weber's view preserves the tension between exercising sovereign power and its underlying legitimating values that characterizes all these views; the state's claim to monopolize force in its territory counterfactually endows the state with unconstrained power that resists any limits that would legitimate it. In particular, defining the state by its monopoly on legitimate violence supports sovereignty understood as an omnicompetent, ultimate authority but hollows out claims that this is legitimate because it constitutes a form of *popular* sovereignty. The conceptions of the people that result from trying to marry these ideas oscillate between making state power the people's in name only and assuming a homogenous, prepolitical people that matches the homogenous relationship citizens are imagined to have to state violence.

To show this, I want to reflect on what it means to monopolize force. Though it's now familiar, the idea of a monopoly on the legitimate use of physical force is a peculiar idea. To say that the state can determine what force is legitimate assumes that the state is capable of preventing or punishing unauthorized violence; repeated, visible failures to do so ensure the state's claim to monopoly will fail. In other words, other forces exist within its borders only through the state's tolerance of them; the state must be endowed with the unlimited powers that sovereignty protects, lest some other force have more resources at its disposal by virtue of being unconstrained. So states need to establish an overwhelming capacity for force in order for questions about legitimacy to be in order. But that means the violence establishing state capacity precedes questions of legitimacy and is in a sense prepolitical; it is bare violence. Unsurprisingly, this echoes the way coercion theory defends the state's existence as practically necessary in a way that initiates politics but isn't itself political. Nagel clearly recognizes the character of this movement of thought. In his view, this shows that "the path from anarchy to justice must go through injustice" since the task of establishing a monopoly requires wielding force that cannot yet be legitimated.[69] Kant is likewise clear in *Perpetual Peace* that the formation of government, however it occurs, is "a great step . . . taken *toward* morality (though it is not yet a moral step)."[70] This reliance on prepolitical force that stands outside of legitimation at the same time that it establishes the possibility of political legitimacy is inherent in the idea of a monopoly that can be the "sole source" of right and politics.

One effect of this equation of politics with a sovereign state that can comprehensively determine what force is allowed within its territory is an orientation that again neglects how coercive authority might structure other areas of life and thereby helps naturalize inequality in those areas. These theories are consequently ill-equipped to help us see coercion in the economy as anything other than incidental, which suggests that they are not well-placed to defend distributive justice against a neoliberalism that likewise enjoins us to see the market as a space of freedom and the government as reducible to violence. Coercion theorists again offer a particularly clear illustration of this, here in their accounts of property and trade. Domestically, Michael Blake writes, "Real property in the United States must be—in theory, if not in legal practice—traced back to an original grant from the sovereign for it to be legally cognizable as property."[71] While coercion theorists intend for this to give property a political basis, its effect is to orient us away from economic power in the marketplace, effectively making economic issues only derivatively political. Within the state, struggles about ownership, working conditions, wages, and the scope of an employers' authority are never really fights directly between employer and employees or between classes but rather are ultimately efforts by two sides to appeal to the sovereign to make a determination in their favor; we can always interpret the sovereign's failure to intervene as a kind of implicit legitimation of the balance of forces. What's more, by exaggerating the sovereign's power in order to establish the supremacy of politics over economics, coercion theory lends itself to overlooking the ways that economic power invariably shapes the exercise of political power. Even beyond the general influence of money in politics, sovereigns themselves directly acquire debt and sovereignty itself being bought and sold is not a historical anomaly.[72]

Internationally, coercion theory turns the global economy into a politics-free zone by asserting that (a) international trade exists as a result of agreements between sovereign states and (b) since no one is sovereign over those states, their agreements cannot be matters of justice. Nagel writes, "I doubt that the rules of international trade rise to the level of collective action needed to trigger demands for justice, even in diluted form. The relation remains essentially one of bargaining, until a leap has been made to the creation of collectively authorized sovereign authority . . . contracts between sovereign states have no such background [of collectively imposed property and tax law]: They are 'pure' contracts, and nothing guarantees the justice of their results."[73] Coercion theorists here essentially replicate the neoliberal view of complex social organizations as entirely reducible to a nexus of individual contracts. This does not mean that they are completely free from normative evaluation. Nagel notes that "even self-interested bargaining between states should be tempered by considerations of humanity" and Blake concedes that "international practices can indeed be coercive—we might understand certain sorts of exploitative trade relationships under this heading, and so a theory concerned with autonomy must condemn such relationships."[74] Nevertheless, the global economy is not properly understood as political because the coercive practices found in the global economy are contingent and we should consequently be oriented to them primarily as matters that concern us as humanitarians rather than as political agents. The aggrandizement of state power by coercion theorists thus offers little help in understanding neoliberal forms of governmentality like trans-national supply chains or export processing zones and works to depoliticize economic development.

These problems stem from being oriented to the global economy as a threat coming from outside politics rather than as a set of political arrangements with a political genesis. Consequently, they are not limited to coercion theorists, but shared by all the views that define sovereignty as unconstrained, omnicompetent power. Weber says politics occurs "either among states or among groups within a state," which leaves no conceptual space for transnational supply chains or the social movements that con-test them. Weber's definition of politics does allow for the international economy to be a matter of politics but reduces it to a contest for power be-tween states, without regard for its differential effects among citizens. This isn't incidental to the framework; orienting politics around unconstrained sovereignty means that the only real international politics is a nationalist competition between states. Much as Bernie Sanders sometimes implicitly pits US workers against Chinese workers, Richard Tuck's sovereignty-based argument for Lexit denies that the British working class has any reason to ally with, for example, the Polish working class; what matters in the first instance is the former reasserting their right not to share territory with the latter. By focusing on unconstrained sovereignty, we orient ourselves away from the different political statuses of classes and groups within the state; from the perspective of a Weberian orientation, what matters is that they are all ulti-mately vulnerable to violence and subject to the state's monopoly over it. This purportedly homogenous relation to the state has profound implications for invocations of popular sovereignty, as I explore in the next section.

The Effects of Depoliticization

I want to reiterate that my criticism here concerns views that see sover-eignty as an appealing lever against neoliberalism precisely because it is unconstrained, but as I noted earlier, these are not the only views of sover-eignty possible. For example, Jean Cohen argues that sovereignty remains an important defense against imperialism, but asserts that "the absolutist conception of sovereignty . . . has long since been abandoned" and that "limited sovereignty is not an oxymoron."[75] This acceptance of constraint is internal to Cohen's conception of sovereignty; she writes, "The discourse of popular sovereignty implies that government is representative government. Precisely because sovereignty is a relational concept, it cannot be located in any political body."[76] In Cohen's view, it is not the state itself that is sovereign and so the state's capacity is neither conceptually nor practically unconstrained. Cohen's view of sovereignty as constrained and relational consequently stands in very different relation to international politics; ultimately, while it maintains a domestic/international divide, it does not naturalize this divide and to some extent even prioritizes international politics over the domestic. She writes, "The mere fact that there are rules obligating states or rules that ascribe competence over what were once considered internal matters to supranational bodies does not mean that states are no longer sovereign, for it is the rules of international law that tell us in what sovereignty consists."[77] On this conception, transnational structures like the European Union may be flawed but they are not constitutively opposed to sovereignty and may be fashioned into useful tools for realizing democratic values.[78]

By contrast, for views that defend sovereignty as ultimate and omnicompetent state authority, international law can only ever be a constraint. As I've shown, the defense of unconstrained sovereignty against neoliberalism makes force the defining feature of the state and posits a homogenous relationship between citizens and state violence. But though the state is defined by force, that force can be legitimized by associating it with *popular* sovereignty. But who are the people, on this view? As Nagel puts it, they are "putative joint authors of the coercively imposed system."[79] But because of how defenses of sovereignty prioritize bare force, their putative authorship comes *after* they are coerced, not before. As a result, their authorship has more to do with how the sovereign regards them than how they regard themselves. One can see this in Nagel's odd claim that "if a colonial or occupying power claims political authority over a population, it purports not to rule by force alone. It is providing and enforcing a system of law that those subject to it are expected to uphold as participants, and which is intended to serve their interests even if they are not its legislators."[80] In other words, what makes this a political relationship has nothing to do with those who are ruled, but the self-description of the sovereign as ruling in their name. On this account, the orientation and duties of citizens to each other are no different under colonial rule than in a democratic state; both entail what Nagel calls the "special involvement of agency or the will that is inseparable from membership in a political society."[81]

This homogenous account of political relations under an unconstrained sovereign empties the content of the "popular" in "popular sovereignty." Ironically, this thin, homogenous characterization of the people who legitimize such sovereignty makes it all the more important to distinguish between insiders and outsiders. It's not a coincidence that immigration thus becomes a flashpoint. Tuck's case for Lexit makes this explicit. He writes, "The left should also appreciate that the traditional heart of modern left-wing politics, a planned welfare state, is rendered virtually impossible if Britain stays in the EU, since no one will have any idea of the population numbers in the United Kingdom even in the near future. This is an illustration of the way the free movement of people, as well as of goods and capital, in the EU almost necessarily entrenches markets rather than collective planning."[82] When they see unconstrained sovereignty as the best way to fight neoliberalism, purportedly left-wing arguments for Brexit end up in the same place as the right-wing arguments they are meant to be distinguished from: in favor of closing borders. This follows from the nationalism of the underlying conception of politics; rich and poor Britons are united by being subjected to the same monopoly on force while the working classes in the United Kingdom and Poland, lacking a common sovereign, have no fundamentally political relation. And who is it precisely that counts as a member of the British people that is a deserving recipient of state welfare? What is it rich and poor Britons share? Surely not equal opportunities to exercise sovereign power. Despite the official lack of cultural or racial content in the citizenship relation, such categories are often employed here to fill the gap.[83]

Consider the so-called Windrush generation who came to the United Kingdom from the Caribbean after World War II. Many were children who accompanied parents that moved for work and more than 50,000 of them have been long-term residents of the United Kingdom for decades; their residency was authorized by the 1971 Immigration Act and many did not even know that they were not technically British citizens. But under policies implemented by Theresa May, first as Home Secretary and then, after the Brexit vote, as prime minister, the UK government began to deny them government services, jail them in detention centers, and deport them to countries of which they had little or no memory.[84] Much like so-called DREAMers or DACA recipients in the United States, these people have ambiguous political status but in both cases, the same governments that promote sovereign autarky decided in favor of resolving that ambiguity through closure when it comes to groups that are racially coded.

States have an interest in making the claim to monopoly on legitimate force because it contributes to the practical consolidation of their power. But that is not a reason for people with an interest in resisting neoliberalism to accede to this claim. States do not have monopolies on force for the same reason that they are not sufficient to create order; there are some forces in politics that they cannot defeat or eliminate, actually or counterfactually. In particular, many social norms cannot be eliminated through applications of force; they have to be replaced by other norms, which the state itself cannot accomplish on its own. But as I've argued, such norms are at the heart of political life and are essential to achieving and maintaining equal status. Given the great force at the hands of most states, the state can surely control any given individual. Social norms, however, are distributed throughout society in such a fashion that coercing any single individual is all but irrelevant. Even more efficient than the threat of incarceration by the state, which can be costly, can be the threat of sanctions by peers, who each need only exert a small effort in order to have a cumulatively devastating effect.[85] The confusion is that states are good at killing people—the best around, even today—but that does not mean we should be oriented to them as the sole source of legitimate force.

The claim that other forms of force exist only at the sufferance of the state does not survive reflection when we consider the social practices that shape our lives. Racism and sexism—or, more generally, social practices of race, gender, and sexuality—are coercive. But could a state counterfactually eliminate such norms, and thereby retain its monopoly? Or must democracy and civil society—and with them, a less-sovereign-centered and more pluralist conception of politics—enter into the picture not just as the passive recipients of state force but also as an active contributor that is equally necessary? After all, the task of changing norms can be slow, complicated work—a long process of changing minds and habits of which altering state-sanction-based cost/benefit calculations is only one part. Effectively changing norms means, among other things, that sanctions also have to come from social peers; there is a need for collective political action.[86] For example, challenging white supremacy in this country made crucial advances with the passage of the Civil Rights Act of 1964 and the Voting Rights Act of 1965, but such institutional reforms did not end racist patterns of coercive behavior nor could they do so. That work requires a continuing social movement to accomplish, as the Black Lives Matter movement has sought to do. Such practices are of course mutable and the state can play a role in changing them. But in no kind of plausible counterfactual world can the state alone be imagined to end them by fiat; their constitutively political nature and potential legitimacy is not derivative of the state's. Neoliberals see this limit to the state's power as evidence that the market must be left to its own devices—and if that means people choose to live in whites-only neighborhoods, then that is unfortunate but there is no alternative. Those who want to resist neoliberalism through sovereignty, on the other hand, want to rule out such an inegalitarian outcome but lack the resources to do so because they cannot account for the political importance of citizens' dispositions and habitual attitudes toward each other.

By offering justifications for unconstrained sovereignty in the hope of defending domestic social democracy where it exists, these theorists counterproductively affirm the oppressive exercise of coercive state power and render themselves unable to analyze the neoliberal politics undermining the redistributive policies they want to preserve. Their focus on state sovereignty as a homogenous source of power ignores the differential impact of coercive relations that such practices entail. For example, women of color bear a disproportionate burden of violence in the United States. Many communities of color are reluctant to call the police to stop partner abuse and other coercive acts because they experience state force directly in police brutality and elsewhere; some women of color in such communities who are victims of domestic violence then become caught on the horns of a dilemma—to potentially experience great violence by the state or remain subject to local force and patriarchal violence.[87] Theories that respond to this injustice by granting the state further powers or duties cannot effectively orient us. Yet the concept of a monopoly of force hides these important differential experiences, giving institutional membership in the state a particularly untextured import by refusing the possibility of justice-relevant distinctions among relations; centering unconstrained state sovereignty in our resistance to neoliberalism thus orients us away from important forms of injustice. The problem is not just that shoring up the legitimacy of sovereign force in order to resist neoliberalism will make no sense to Black Lives Matter activists protesting police brutality. It is also that theorists of unconstrained sovereignty have no way of orienting themselves to such social movements since their political power is not well conceptualized as deriving from the sovereign. Considering such movements in our theorizing is important because without them, the values we promote will not be realized.[88] Consequently, I complete my account of an effective orientation to the global economy in the conclusion by showing how participation in social movements can help us meet the demands of justice and express freedom in an unjust world.

Conclusion

Freedom and Resentment Amid Neoliberalism

In developing my account of freedom, I've emphasized how our actions and attitudes are shaped by unjust circumstances, which they tend to reproduce. Mindful of that, I want to begin this concluding chapter by reflecting briefly on the circumstances that have shaped my own thinking and the field of argument that I am contributing to. Reflecting on the forces which have shaped you can be an experience of freedom, and in some respects, this book is itself the product of such a process. But I have no doubt that in the arguments made here, I have reproduced the imperfections of the movements that I have participated in as well as added some imperfections of my own. My hope is that others take up these arguments and negate them in turn in a spirit of solidarity so that we can better understand what justice requires of us today.

In the first instance, I became an activist against supply chain injustices as a college student. Jarred out of my habits by the beginning of freshman year, I looked for familiarity and found that the only other student on campus from my high school was involved in labor activism; within a month, largely due to the contingency of this social network connection, I was participating in protests to demand that the school publicly disclose the locations of the factories that made its licensed apparel. I quickly found that my participation in this movement was meaningful and helped me to put my other activities in perspective. After graduation, I worked full time as an organizer for United Students Against Sweatshops for a few years before deciding to attend graduate school. Studying political theory, I encountered the burgeoning literature in global justice and was surprised by what I found. The kinds of debates and demands for justice that I saw theorists considering didn't track my experience of the global justice movement, where people tended to be much more concerned about the distribution and abuses of power than, for example, the viability of global luck egalitarianism. This divergence was deepened when al Qaeda's attack on the World Trade Center led activist attention to focus on protesting the Bush administration's invasions of Afghanistan and

Disorienting Neoliberalism. Benjamin L. McKean, Oxford University Press (2020). © Oxford University Press.
DOI: 10.1093/oso/9780190087807.001.0001.

Iraq. The 1999 WTO protests in Seattle, as well as the subsequent protests of International Monetary Fund and World Bank meetings that followed, had very effectively raised questions of global justice and politicized neoliberalism, demonstrating publicly that the global economy is the product of contestable political decisions.[1] As the "War on Terror" proceeded, philosophers continued to debate global inequality, but many of the voices that might have drawn their attention to the specific injustices and violence generated by neoliberal political and economic institutions were otherwise occupied. This book is very much a product of my own dawning realization of how I understood these circumstances and my actions within them rather than an attempt to develop action-guiding principles through philosophical reflection independent of politics.

The egalitarian liberalism I encountered in graduate school is one of the most extensively developed political theories of the past century. By making unjustified inequality the paradigm of injustice, it should be well placed to critique a neoliberal world of widening inequality, but it has largely failed to develop an effective orientation to the global economy. Susan Buck-Morss offers an explanation in keeping with W. E. B. Du Bois's insights about the epistemic disadvantage of having oppressive power. She writes, "Rather than collective wisdom being the product of civilizational dominance, these two variables may well be inversely correlated: The greater the power a civilization wields in the world, the less capable its thinkers may be to recognize the naiveté of their own beliefs."[2] In other words, it is because of the veil that accompanied Western power and prosperity that Rawls's two principles of justice could have appeared to affirm the basic structure of really existing American society rather than requiring a transformation of it. As neoliberalism became hegemonic, the legacy of postwar wealth made it possible for those on one side of the veil to see widening inequality as an unfortunate deviation from the norm. But the 2008 financial crisis jarred many from this habitual understanding of our institutions, opening up possibilities for new actions as well as new modes of legitimation, both progressive and reactionary. I've offered an account of freedom that can help orient us to each other in a way that facilitates resistance to neoliberal inequality and promotes equality, but the disposition to solidarity that I propose is obviously not how most people have responded to this political moment; the Tea Party movement has arguably proven even more consequential than Occupy Wall Street, for example. In chapter 6, I argued that attempts to resist neoliberalism by appealing to unconstrained state sovereignty badly orient us to our circumstances and are likely to be counterproductive. Here, I conclude my account by, first, analyzing other widespread orientations that appear to break with neoliberalism but which are more likely to reinforce it, including reactionary resentment and humanitarian concern. Second, I explain how and why the disposition to solidarity can become widespread through participation in social movements. As my own story attests, people do not need to be moved to action in the first instance by deeply held convictions or well-formulated principles in order to find these experiences of solidarity meaningful and emancipatory.

Circuits of Pity and Resentment

Instead of solidarity, many have responded to widening neoliberal inequality with reactionary resentment or compassionate concern. These orientations have been effective in the sense that they have successfully galvanized popular social and political movements that have adopted them in the years since the financial crisis, but as I will argue, they are not effective orientations for resisting neoliberalism. First, the past decade has seen the resurgence of a reactionary orientation that departs from neoliberal forms of justification while nevertheless legitimizing its institutions. This way of seeing rejects the neoliberal sociodicy that reconciles its subjects to the experience of economic precarity by offering them assurance that markets make everyone winners in the long run; in its place, this reactionary orientation defiantly asserts the justice of a world in which there are definite winners and losers and provides some assurance that its adherents are, if not winners themselves, at least on the side of the winners. That assurance is typically provided by an overtly nationalist claim with clear racial implications. We can see the global popularity of such an appeal in the ascendance of a right-wing xenophobia that targets immigrants and minorities but which accepts or even embraces elements of the economic elite. Consider the way that the popular politics of Donald Trump rhetorically breaks from a neoliberal orientation while reinforcing most of its institutions. Trump's embrace of the "birther" conspiracy that claimed Barack Obama was not a natural-born citizen of the United States launched his political career by making it clear that from his perspective, not all citizens of the United States are "real Americans." Trump's promise has been to ensure that the economy's "winners" are real Americans, who belong at the top of a global hierarchy. Trump's view departs from neoliberalism in connecting market outcomes with merit—he wants to see the people who deserve to win be the winners—but sticks close to neoliberalism in suggesting that the best way to see who deserves to win is generally by seeing who has already won; under normal circumstances, wealth is presumptively justified as evidence of previous victories.[3]

How then can Trump's orientation explain why many real Americans who deserve to be winners seem to have been denied their birthright? On this view of the global economy, the United States has been a loser because its trading partners are cheating; that's why the actual winners aren't always the deserved winners. In a reactionary orientation, Americans ought to see workers in China and Bangladesh as our opponents in a zero-sum game; the explanation for the unfair, "rigged" outcomes in the US economy is that some foreigners are taking advantage of us, whether by breaking the rules of trade or by sneaking into the country.[4] These accusations of unfairness are often underwritten by a sense of racial hierarchy, as Trump made explicit in the bigoted comments about Mexico with which he launched his presidential campaign.[5] This orientation does not leave neoliberal policy totally untouched; the Trump administration's moves to raise tariffs on Chinese goods to advance the interests of particular industries do depart from neoliberal orthodoxies.[6] But this scapegoating also acts as a kind of release valve. By orienting us to entire nations as winner or losers, it directs attention away from the inequalities within countries, allowing Americans to identify as winners and overlooking how, for example, Chinese trade rules do not uniformly benefit everyone in China. A nationalist orientation not only badly orients us to multinational corporations and their global supply chains by identifying them exclusively with a particular country, but it also overlooks the way that neoliberal policies make it all but impossible for some people and communities ever to become "winners." Such an orientation thus perpetuates the inequality brought about by neoliberalism by naturalizing a hierarchy of winners and losers as the appropriate state of the world.[7] This organizes widely felt resentment at an unfair system by directing anger at "rightful" losers who refuse to accept their place, such as by publicly objecting to the race and gender hierarchies that have so long been used to identify winners. While such an orientation is plainly incompatible with egalitarian convictions, many Americans have found it to be a plausible way of making sense of a world in which the rise of supply chains has contributed to wage stagnation and the erosion of global labor standards. Yet to the extent it allows them to identify as winners while legitimating the institutions that continue to sustain enormous inequalities, this orientation does not facilitate actions that will bring about the conditions its adherents desire.

Another alternative orientation rejects the reactionary pleasure of looking on the world's "losers" as confirmation of one's own status as a "winner," but instead attends to them with concern for their suffering. A diverse coalition converges on the idea that we should conceive of our duties to distant others primarily as a humanitarian moral duty. Among them are liberal egalitarians who reject the idea of duties of international justice, a group I considered in chapter 6. For them, there is no such thing as "global justice" or an international politics of freedom; instead, they support engagement on the basis of a disinterested and humanitarian sympathy.[8] The group also includes thinkers like Richard Rorty, Stephen K. White, and Peter Singer, who emphasize understanding our shared vulnerability to suffering or death as the key to orienting us to injustice generally.[9] A leading promoter of this orientation in recent years has been the "effective altruism" movement, which tries to improve the efficiency of charitable giving and altruistic concern more generally.[10] Singer famously analogizes the situation of the global poor to a drowning child, arguing we have a duty to act because of their suffering. Shared interests with drowning strangers are irrelevant; rather than embracing the solidaristic slogan "An Injury to One is an Injury to All," he might say, "An Injury to Anyone is An Injury"—it should be attended to regardless of institutional context. For this reason, despite the deep and important differences among these accounts, I treat them together as promoting humanitarian concern as the appropriate response to events like the Tazreen fire and Rana Plaza collapse.

Political solidarity and humanitarian concern lead to very different orientations to international politics. Humanitarian concern directs us to attend to distant others as victims of a violation; we care for them not because of who or what caused the violation, but in virtue of their suffering. Political solidarity, by contrast, disposes us to see them as partners in efforts to replace or reform institutions to which we are both subjected in different ways. In addition, acting on the basis of humanitarian concern leads to particular self-conceptions on the part of the agent—when there are significant disparities in power at work, as there are in many forms of international injustice, humanitarianism can easily lead us to identify ourselves as benevolent paternalists acting in the best interests of our object of concern while political solidarity calls for deference and the identification of shared interests.

Rorty is quite clear about the imperial structure of this orientation. His conception of solidarity is explicitly meant to promote "the ethnocentrism of a 'we' ('we liberals') which is dedicated to enlarging itself, to creating an

ever larger and more variegated *ethnos*."[11] This reference to ethnocentric en-
largement is entirely consistent with an orientation that emphasizes one's
own agency while minimizing the agency of the oppressed. The privileged—
liberals, in Rorty's telling—are the ones who must act while the suffering and
humiliated others are acted upon; their only possible contribution to the en-
largement of the ethnos is to accept it. An orientation to pity thus directs
us away from the voice and agency of the oppressed, making an attitude of
partnership difficult to maintain. As Jennifer Rubenstein documents, this
orientation leads its adherents to see themselves as "heroic rescuers," special
protagonists in an unfeeling world who are helping the helpless.[12] The appeal of such a self-understanding in a neoliberal context is obvious; neoliberal institutions really do constrain people and habituate them to prioritize
self-interest, so to experience empathetic agency can feel like a break from
prevailing ways of being.

However, it is important to remember that there are good reasons for the
oppressed to be suspicious about acting in solidarity with those who have
benefited from their oppression. Many Bangladeshi workers are justifiably
suspicious of US consumers given the history of American imperialism and
the continuing power disparity between parties. My conception of solidarity
can alleviate some of these worries while an emphasis on humanitarian concern may deepen them.[13] Individuals disposed to solidarity in my sense understand their actions as political interventions that also promote their own
interest, not as altruistic charity; this can lead privileged parties to articulate
nonpaternalistic and self-interested reasons for their actions, which in turn
makes it easier for workers to challenge the privileged when they overstep
their appropriate role. By contrast, a humanitarian orientation more closely
resembles the ethical sourcing approach that lets supply chain managers treat
workers as the objects of concern rather than partners in reform; because humanitarian concern directs us away from the causes of injustice to the fact of
suffering itself, it can reinforce institutional hierarchies that thwart freedom.

If the reactionary orientation doesn't turn out to be an alternative to neoliberalism because it ultimately legitimizes existing hierarchies, the humanitarian orientation likewise doesn't provide an alternative to neoliberalism
because it too incorporates those hierarchies into the self-understanding it
promotes, with varying degrees of explicitness. Orienting an approach to
global injustice around the suffering of others and reserving political agency
for the privileged can lead humanitarians to tolerate or even valorize neoliberal inequality because of how some of the wealthy make use of their power.

For example, Singer writes, "It isn't clear that making the rich richer without making the poor poorer has bad consequences, overall. It increases the ability of the rich to help the poor, and some of the world's richest people, including Bill Gates and Warren Buffett, have done precisely that."[14] Similarly, William MacAskill, cofounder of the effective altruist movement, inverts Occupy's focus on American inequality between the "1%" and the "99%" and instead emphasizes that many working class and middle class Americans are themselves the "Global 1%." Where Occupy sought a more egalitarian society, MacAskill happily notes, "The fact that we've found ourselves at the top of the heap, globally speaking, provides us with a tremendous opportunity to make a difference."[15] Rather than seek to change the structures that generate this inequality, MacAskill encourages altruists to pursue lucrative careers in finance and consulting (with sales and marketing as less lucrative back-up options for those who lack math skills) so that they can donate more money to humanitarian charities.[16] As one effective altruist puts it, "Earning a lot of money is another way of doing good in the world."[17]

Humanitarian concern thus tends to emphasize and reinforce the differences between the privileged and the oppressed rather than any shared benefits or interests. Indeed, Singer goes so far as to claim that all Americans have reliable access to quality health care in order to highlight the importance of providing health care in Africa and Haiti.[18] This represents a great missed opportunity. Rather than emphasizing a common interest in the provision of health care that might motivate a coalition of those demanding better health care that stretches across national boundaries, Singer suggests that poorer Americans should minimize their own interests in favor of attending to those of distant others who are even worse off.[19] This is more likely to foster resentment than solidarity. If we perceive distant others as akin to drowning children, we will never expect to see any return or benefit from our assistance and consequently will be more likely to perceive only the costs of our action— and perhaps less likely to act.[20] As Singer himself writes, "Asking people to give more than almost anyone else risks turning them off, and at some level might cause them to question the point of striving to live an ethical life at all." We can see here how humanitarian and reactionary orientations form a circuit: humanitarian demands produce resentment that fuels adoption of the reactionary orientation, which encourages people to be angry at "losers" who are concerned about undeserved disadvantage; humanitarians, in turn, can feel their righteous acts are validated by the reactionaries' ostentatious indifference to others. Singer recognizes his view can provoke a backlash but his solution is simply to ask people to do less than he believes justice requires; since they can't handle the truth, he suggests, "we should advocate a level of giving that will lead to a positive response," even though this will lead people to wrongly affirm themselves as just.[21]

This ad hoc response does not address the underlying problem. Consider estimates that as many as 2.4 million US workers lost work as a result of import growth from China between 1999 and 2011.[22] The reactionary orientation sees this as a zero-sum competition that the United States has unfairly lost, but the humanitarian orientation does little better; it gives its adherents nothing to say to these workers that is likely to move them to action or draw them away from a reactionary orientation that can at least articulate their grievances. From the perspective of humanitarianism, the poverty alleviated by growing wealth in China is more significant than the suffering inflicted by lost jobs in the United States. This suffering can also make unemployed US workers an object of humanitarian concern, but it gives the workers themselves no way to conceive of their own agency nor any reason to think that they have any shared interests with Chinese workers that would lead them to perceive each other as partners rather than opponents. Here again we see the humanitarian and reactionary orientations forming a circuit.

This is not a small problem, but gets to the heart of what it means to be effectively oriented to the global economy today. According to Christoph Lanker and Branko Milanovic, the story of the global economy over the past generation is summarized by what's come to be called an "elephant graph" of global income distribution; looking at the relative gain in real household per capita income between 1988 and 2008, they argue that we can see the rise of a "global middle class" in places like China while the world's very richest have grown much, much wealthier and income has stagnated for lower- and middle-class Americans.[23] How should unemployed Americans think about this situation? Should they regard the improved economic circumstances of many people in China as evidence that they are rightfully seen as competitors? Or should they instead identify what Milanovic calls "the emergence of a global plutocracy" as an obstacle to justice that they share with the majority of the world's population, including most people in China?[24]

After all, rising wealth in China has also been distributed very unevenly; while China now has more billionaires than the United States, rising real estate prices are already squeezing the new urban middle class.[25] The same capital mobility that led transnational supply chains to manufacture in China is now at work within the country, moving production around various regions to avoid paying higher wages. Despite prohibitions on the freedom of association, the combination of great inequality with low wages and unstable employment has led to an enormous growth in worker protests as factories have closed.[26] Meanwhile, as workers in both the United States and China face some similar challenges, the wealth of global plutocrats has more than doubled as a share of global GDP.[27] According to Oxfam International, there are slightly more than 2,000 billionaires and their wealth increased by $762 billion over the course of 2017; the sixty-one richest billionaires own as much wealth as the poorest 50% of the planet.[28] In other words, it is not necessary for Americans who lost their jobs as a result of trade with China to see Chinese workers as competitors since it is not those workers who have received the majority of the gains over this period—or who determined how those gains were distributed. Rather than adopt a reactionary orientation that demonizes their Chinese or Mexican counterparts, they can instead see the world's plutocrats as a shared obstacle to more just circumstances. When disposed to respond to calls for solidarity by identifying and acting on shared interests, we can see that "An Injury to One is An Injury to All" can be not merely a slogan but a guide to our own freedom.

Theories Of and In Social Movements

In the remainder of this conclusion, I will argue that participation in social movements to resist injustices in supply chains is one of the best available ways to meet the demands of justice and express freedom amid injustice. I also explain why individuals find that participation is in their interest, in keeping with my account of meeting the demands of justice in chapter 5. In the following section, I look specifically at the experience of agency associated with movement participation and show how it offers an exemplary experience of freedom and equality that stands in contrast to market freedom, reactionary resentment, and humanitarian concern.

The centrality of solidarity reminds us that the actions that promote egalitarian justice cannot be unilaterally determined. As I've argued, a freedom that genuinely breaks with neoliberalism cannot take as its exemplar the consenting individual who aspires to a life in which nothing happens without his permission. By disavowing our complex interdependence, such an aspiration is likely to generate resentment when confronted with evidence of its failure and consequently often converges with the reactionary orientation just discussed; both tend to channel frustrations at economic outcomes through identification with the coercive power of the sovereign nation-state. What's more, effective resistance to unjust institutions requires collective action. Consequently, we can see how the action of participating in social movements to resist neoliberalism expresses freedom as it is possible for us. Doing so provides a model of how to negate forces that shape us but without reasserting a conception of freedom that ultimately reinscribes individual choice in the market as its implicit ideal. This is the first use of social movements that I want to emphasize: social movements are an apt form of political organization for those disposed by solidarity to see each other as partners.

This also helps explain the importance of listening for calls for solidarity. In light of our habituation to existing injustice, it can be hard to see beyond the veils that we've grown up with.[29] The idea of a "call" to solidarity is thus an especially useful figure because of how it reminds us that we can hear things we cannot see. We may not know what the sounds mean, at first, but if they are loud enough, they may be able to get our attention even while we cannot at first see where they come from. Cultivating this posture of listening and attentiveness to the voice of others is thus of particular importance to individuals who have been habituated by the global color line to regard themselves as the agents of history paternalistically charged with a responsibility to promote the development of others. As James Tully notes, genuine partnership across such lines requires people "to see their role, not as superior judges and guardians but as treaty partners in an intercultural dialogue."[30]

Such dialogue requires translators, which is the second function of social movements essential to the achievement of justice. I mean translation in two related senses: first, translating events into demands; second, literally translating between languages. First, while attentive individual consumers in the United States can read about disasters like the collapse of the factories at Rana Plaza in the English-language press, these articles may not convey the demands being made in response to such injustices, since they often reproduce the assumptions that poverty and suffering are the natural state of the developing world. Transnational activist networks can and do convey this information, connecting social movement participants more directly.[31] Second, this kind of work requires literal translators who can speak, for example, Bengali and English so that genuine dialogue can be conducted. These functions of social movements are crucial. We have many ways we can disavow our knowledge of injustice, so we shouldn't think that this information is sufficient, but it is nevertheless necessary. For this reason, some international institutions that lack coercive authority may still be important for their role in facilitating communication and circulating information. This potential is obscured if we regard political institutions as reducible to coercively enforceable rules, as some views I've critiqued do.

Third, social movements reduce the cost of political action for individuals, who do not need to heroically reinvent the wheel in order to meet their duty of justice. In addition to information, social movements provide important context and models for action, helping people see what to do in response to the information they've learned about injustice. As I discussed in chapter 5, individuals responding to injustice face a collective action problem since actions to promote justice can be costly and ineffective if taken in isolation from others. Social movements help to solve this by specifying an injustice to be targeted, reducing the cost of political action by providing accessible models to emulate, and creating reliable norms that can be incorporated into planning one's own projects. Individuals concerned about supply chain injustice can rely on social movements to inform them about the particular circumstances where actions can make a difference, such as a pressuring US brands to sign the Accord on Fire and Building Safety in Bangladesh. These movements make it possible to play a role in furthering just institutions without making it necessary for every participant to be a "role entrepreneur" who must invent or discern the particular requirements of her political status.

Fourth, social movements create networks of commitment and accountability. Such movements provide an entitlement to assume some others will be disposed to act along with you and can reasonably be held accountable for their failures to do so; if you claim to be disposed to solidarity but never respond to any calls to action, I can tell you that you are failing to live up to your own commitments. Both empirically and normatively, it is reasonable for me to plan my projects in a way that relies upon the assumption that social movement participants will take some actions aimed at meeting their stated objective.

Fifth, being involved in social movements can be transformative of our self-conceptions in emancipatory ways. For one thing, the experience of actually being accountable to others can further deepen our appreciation for the social nature of our freedom. Allison Weir calls this "transformative identification" and writes that it "involves a recognition of the other that transforms our relation to each other, that shifts our relation from indifference to a recognition of interdependence. Thus identification with the other becomes not an act of recognizing that we are the same, or feeling the same as the other, or sharing the same experiences. Identification becomes a process of remaking meaning."[32] In other words, if we see others in the movement as partners, we may no longer experience international politics as an overwhelming and distant phenomenon, but recognize ourselves as already engaged in a shared political enterprise with fellow human beings.

This experience of standing together can help counteract the uncanny alienation workers and consumers alike experience from supply chains. From the perspective of workers who object to being treated like fungible units, there is ample testimony of how standing together changes their relationship to the world. Writing about the role of such self-assertion in the US civil rights movement, Richard H. King writes, "To (re-)gain self-respect, in this view, one must assert his or her equality of moral worth or capacity; and one way of doing this may be to engage in public protest against the conditions producing this injured sense of self. To quote . . . A. C. Searles of Albany, Georgia: 'What did we win? We won self-respect. It changed all my attitudes.'"[33] In circumstances that deny people agency in part by individualizing them and setting them against each other, standing together can ironically restore their feeling of efficacy as individual agents.

Something similar can be true of consumers who stand with workers. As a consumer, one doesn't face the same oppression one does as a worker, of course. However, by being made reliant on unjustly produced goods to advance their own plans and projects, neoliberal consumers are denied the self-respect that comes from knowing their achievements are truly their own. Acting in solidarity with workers does not itself change the fact that, for example, we live in a neoliberal economy that only makes available for purchase apparel produced through exploitation contrary to my convictions, but while the outer limit of freedom is denied me, I may be able to do more to make a home in an unjust world knowing that I am trying to change it. As one labor organizer put it, "The only way I can live in this racist and oppressive society is to feel like I'm part of a struggle to build a more just world."[34] By bringing together individuals who seek to further just arrangements not yet established, social movements can create counterpublics that sustain alternative self-conceptions that break with those facilitated by hegemonic neoliberal circumstances.[35] Engaging in a community-building social movement in the context of an individualizing neoliberal world can be freeing. One global justice activist notes, "That sense of community helps me keep going in a world that is really, really disempowering and really, really degrading in a lot of ways."[36]

Finally, participation in social movements is also freedom-enhancing in that the skills one acquires through political action make it easier to navigate the world and reveal new ways of experiencing freedom in our relations of equality with others. Participating in social movements can involve learning skills like public speaking, negotiating, cooperating with diverse others, deliberation, and assessing the value and meaning of information.[37] As John Medearis puts it, "A march or sit-in may be geared toward some apparently external end, but planning it, organizing it, and carrying it out are often valued in themselves as both an exercise and a development of one's political powers—as a chance to enjoy the experience of one's agency, one's ability to overcome resistance, to intervene in the troubled political world, and to enjoy active cooperation and camaraderie."[38] It's no wonder that many social movement participants report that they find their engagement to be in their own self-interest, as the range of skills one can acquire appeals to many different people.[39]

Messy Agents in Messy Movements

Importantly, the experience of agency that one has through social movement participation is not the experience of a solitary individual imposing his will in an effort to control his environment. Social movements themselves are irreducibly messy; they are more complicated than the membership organizations and NGOs which partly constitute them. As Charles Tilly and Lesley J. Wood note, "Social movements organizations (SMOs) and social movements are by no means identical; movements are interactive campaigns, not organizations. SMOs sometimes outlast campaigns, and campaigns almost always involve multiple organizations, shifting coalitions, and unnamed informal networks."[40] That messiness and lack of clear boundaries has led much of analytic liberal political philosophy to avoid engaging with the centrality of social movements to achieving justice, since they largely fail to conform to the best models of collective action that they have developed.[41] These accounts of joint action, while useful and sophisticated for understanding some important cases, seek to draw sharp lines between participants and nonparticipants and thus rely on elements that are often lacking in social movement participation, such as individuals being linked by formal institutional procedures and common knowledge of the shared intentions of participants.[42] This reliance on participants linked by a common public structure makes these accounts inapt for understanding neoliberal forms of governance that privatize power, like transnational supply chains, as well as the messiness of the social movements that arise to resist the resultant injustices.[43]

In fact, there is no clear boundary between who counts as a social movement participant and who does not. As Ziad W. Munson argues, becoming a social movement participant is generally "a dynamic, multistage process, not a singular event or discrete decision."[44] As a result, it does not make sense to think of joining a social movement to resist neoliberalism on the model of a kind of existential leap into solidarity, as Sally Scholz describes in an account I critiqued in chapter 5. People decide to take action for all kinds of reasons and "action in the movement actually precedes commitment" to its ideas in most cases.[45] Jarred out of their habits, they may just be curious or bored. One of the most common reasons to become involved is simply because other members of one's social network are, as friends ask them to spend an afternoon together at a march and so on.[46] Finding oneself a committed social movement participant who can articulate and defend consistent principles is a *result* of action, not a cause; rather than an existential leap, the change is more akin to a dawning awareness where one retrospectively acknowledges undergoing a process that was less clear as it was being experienced.[47] The messiness of movements facilitates this. My own organizing experience reflects both the role of social networks in recruiting participants and the way commitment is often something recognized retrospectively. Did I become a participant the first time I attended a protest? When I tried to bring friends to a protest? Or when I first organized a protest myself?

The porousness of movement boundaries means that barriers to entry can be low since one doesn't need to have fully articulated principles in order to be moved to participate, but this does not render membership meaningless. On the contrary, the core activities of social movement participants can be meaningful experiences of freedom. Hahrie Han usefully distinguishes between the political activities of organizing and mobilizing. Social movements contain both activities and they can look similar; each involves political groups trying to get people to engage in public support of their positions. Mobilizing is about trying to "maximize participation by minimizing costs" while organizing concerns "developing people's capacity to act on behalf of their interests."[48] For example, e-activist "clicktivism" that generates lots of petition signatures but no other engagement is an example of mobilizing, as is getting lots of people to attend a rally without expecting them to participate in any future activities. By contrast, as Han uses the term, organizing refers to efforts to deepen an individual's relationships to movement participants and to engage them in activities that develop their skills so that they can become more effective movement participants themselves. To nonparticipants, much of the organizing work of movements is invisible and so they are likely to associate movements exclusively with mobilizing, which can make them appear less durable and expressive of freedom than they are.

Both mobilizing and organizing can be experiences of freedom for movement participants. One needn't be a movement leader in order to engage in either activity; someone who has decided to attend a rally and asks their friends to come along is mobilizing them while someone who works on recruiting a friend to come along to a planning meeting is organizing them. Mobilizing for public assembly can play a vital role in reconstituting an experience of the public; physically sharing the same space can exceed the individualizing and privatizing orientation fostered by neoliberal circumstances.[49] Nonphysical manifestations of group size can also be meaningful; generating petition signatures from multiple countries can be a powerful sign of transnational connection and evidence that one's local struggle is perceived as a matter of shared concern. But I want to focus on the experience of organizing, because it is often less public and consequently its connection to freedom is in some ways less obvious. In particular, I return to Michel Foucault, whose analysis of neoliberalism as a way of shaping self-conceptions remains an important starting point for analyzing both its appeal and its injustice. Foucault provides a language for understanding how we can experience and express freedom and equality through organizing.

Organizing is, in essence, a form of governmentality available to individuals in their relations with each other. Foucault writes, "Perhaps the equivocal nature of the term 'conduct' is one of the best aids for coming to terms with the specificity of power relations . . . The exercise of power is a 'conduct of conducts' and a management of possibilities. Basically, power is less a confrontation between two adversaries or their mutual engagement than a question of 'government.'"[50] This idea of a conduct of conducts is an apt description of the activity of organizing. Individual social movement participants aren't the state; they can't coerce people to take particular actions to promote justice. Nor can they employ the forms of governmentality deployed by firms to habituate consumers to purchase the products of their supply chains. Rather, if they want to promote justice, they must take other kinds of actions if they are to change how others understand their own interests and come to identify with social movements. These exercises of power are available to ordinary people and represent an essential means of resisting neoliberalism. By conducting the conduct of others, individuals not only experience an efficacy that neoliberalism may otherwise deny them, but they can express their freedom and equality with those they seek to conduct. This may seem like a strange claim to make, but as Foucault notes, "power relations are not something that is bad in itself, that we have to break free of." Rather, he says, our aim is "not to try to dissolve them in the utopia of completely transparent communication but to acquire the rules of law, the management techniques, and also the morality, the *ēthos*, the practice of the self, that will allow us to play these games of power with as little domination as possible."[51] Effective organizing models this practice, treating the individuals one organizes as free and, when oriented to them as a partner, as equals who can likewise hold the organizer accountable for continuing his or her own work to promote justice. In that way, social movement organizing can exhibit precisely the kind of "reversibility" in a relationship that Foucault argued was a sign of nondomination.[52] Where Hayekian neoliberalism emphasizes how the market is a form of order that emerges spontaneously from independent individuals making self-regarding choices, successful social movement organizing is a form of intentional but fluid ordering that shows how free and equal people can cooperate.

I emphasize these advantages of participating in social movements resisting neoliberalism in order to counteract the prevailing assumption that meeting a duty of justice does not benefit the agent herself. This is not to idealize such movements inappropriately; of course, many existing social movements work for unjust ends, are ineffective at attaining their stated aims, and lack internal accountability. After all, social movement participants have themselves developed in unjust circumstances that have habituated them to injustice. The unjust inequalities that make movements for justice necessary also make it difficult for them to succeed; asymmetries of knowledge, power, and cultural capital all lead social movements to reproduce the oppression that they purport to confront.[53]

Partly because of this but also because of the pervasiveness of good faith political disagreements, individuals disposed to solidarity will still need to exercise their own judgment. Calls to solidarity rarely come from a completely unified group. Solidarity requires individuals who are privileged with respect to injustice to defer to the oppressed, but when the oppressed disagree among themselves, there can be a question of whom to defer to. Kate MacDonald recounts the story of rival groups in Nicaragua who each presented themselves as the voice of workers asking for solidarity—a predominantly male union that sought a confrontational strategy and a more risk-averse NGO with women leaders. As MacDonald points out, this makes it possible for solidarity movements to exercise discretion and support "selective groups of workers whose interest and preferences most closely aligned to their own."[54] As I argued in chapter 4, injustice makes tragic choices common and leaves us with no way to remain above reproach; no matter which organization one decides to support, there may be grounds for the other to rebuke you. In such circumstances, those who are privileged in relation to an injustice should do what they can to be held accountable for their actions by those who ask for their solidarity.[55]

As challenging as such circumstances are, I hope to have shown that they are worth confronting. Throughout this book, I've developed an argument to show how neoliberalism can be understood to impair the freedom of many people, including some of those whom it materially benefits. Avoiding difficult judgments about which calls to solidarity to heed does nothing to change that. We face a global economy of great inequality where the rich get richer and the circumstances of most others only seem to get more precarious; where the ubiquitous commodities of everyday life in the developed world are unavoidably the product of unfair treatment in the developing world; where the prevailing conception of freedom trains individuals to think of themselves on the model of an entrepreneur of human capital, making them feel like they are always at work; and where the decisions that produced these outcomes are veiled by a technocratic form of justification that appears to put them beyond political contestation. There is widespread interest in changing these circumstances, but because neoliberalism combines a way of seeing and valuing with a set of policies implemented by a range of actors, its diffuse hegemony can be difficult to target, especially for people who have been habituated to the attitudes and forms of perception that make a neoliberal orientation seem like common sense. I've taken the workers and consumers linked by transnational supply chains as exemplary because their common political status as subject to governance by supply chains creates a shared interest in resisting them. That specifies a more proximate target than neoliberalism in its entirety, but by politicizing corporate authority, such demands create an opportunity to contest neoliberalism more broadly by making visible and challenging its common sense assumptions and the disparities in political power they obscure.

When the people whom supply chains seek to govern become partners in resisting those claims to authority, their actions express the freedom they have and may expand the opportunities for further exercising freedom. As a result of their habituation to injustice, they may not know and may not share an image of what freedom looks like, but they know it's not here. As I argued in chapter 4, giving content to an ideal of freedom in our world requires negating rather than affirming existing injustice; unlike the outer limit of freedom available in a just society, in an unjust world, actions express freedom not through acceptance of what has shaped individuals but through the refusal and negation of a specific obstacle to fuller freedom. The way that we express freedom is thus at least partly determined by the injustice we oppose rather than determined independently. Consequently, we can see freedom expressed in the demand that corporations act in ways that are responsive not to the market logic of efficiency but rather the democratic logic of accountability to those they seek to govern.

The experience of making and winning such demands also creates the possibility of larger breaks with neoliberal ways of seeing and acting. The importance of demanding better wages and working conditions in supply chains is consequently not reducible to the importance of the policy changes themselves. If we counterfactually imagine such changes being unilaterally implemented by beneficent supply chain managers, they would be changes for the better but their implementation would not undermine the putatively authoritative hierarchy of the supply chain—as they can when those changes are brought about because they are demanded by those who are normally excluded from decision-making. That is why consumers can have an interest in workers' demands even when they do not directly benefit from them. Demonstrating that supply chains can be responsive to such claims can pave the way for demands that are more obviously mutually beneficial, such as demanding respect for freedom of association, understood to include not only the right of workers to organize in response to workplace problems without fear of retaliation but also, for example, data privacy protections for consumers so that they can be assured that their actions won't make them and their friends subject to corporate surveillance.

By facilitating the transformation of self-conceptions from competing entrepreneurs of our own human capital to partners in political action, the disposition to solidarity thus helps individuals meet their duty of justice while also expressing their freedom. Retraining ourselves so that we no longer habitually adopt the self-conceptions fostered by unjust circumstances can be an important expression of freedom. In this case, the perception of workers and consumers as partners in political action expresses the equal status that egalitarian justice promotes because it sees freedom as only possible under conditions of fair interdependence. Neoliberalism denies the relevance of such standards of fairness in the service of legitimating unequal outcomes and endorses a narrow understanding of freedom sustained by a hierarchical politics. Justice cannot be immediately realized in a neoliberal world where the wealthy have disproportionate political power, but by working together, we can prefigure in our attitudes and actions the fuller freedom and equality that we seek.

Acknowledgments

I'm the kind of person who reads the acknowledgments section of an academic book first. It's fascinating to learn about its conditions of production. What networks were drafts circulated in? What support did the author receive? How did that shape the questions that the book chooses to address? Do personal touches reveal the socioeconomic status of the author's upbringing? (Are parents thanked for providing models of balancing academic work with family?) Acknowledgments are also often a place where authors let their hair down; free to depart from the stiff norms of academic prose, you can more easily catch a glimpse of an author's own personality in their wry acknowledgments of the tolerant friends and family who put up with the intensive time commitment required to finish a monograph. Oh, the author had a kid while working on the book—what a cute way to work that in! And then there's the inevitable, self-centered question: Am I myself acknowledged at all?

All of which is to say: I feel a little self-conscious about writing my own acknowledgments, especially since this book has taken so long to come together and I consequently have so many people to be grateful for. This project initially took shape in a much different form as a dissertation in the Princeton Department of Politics. Thanks are due to my dissertation advisors, Charles Beitz and Jan-Werner Müller, whose differing orientations helped spur my thinking. My experience of Princeton also benefitted immeasurably from the support and provocations offered by George Kateb, Jeffrey Stout, and Cornel West, among others. Undoubtedly the most important part of graduate school—intellectually but also just in terms of my personal well-being— was my classmates. I'm especially grateful to Evan Oxman, Alex Levitov, Sam Arnold, Loubna El Amine, Katie Gallagher, Rob Hunter, Daniel Lee, John Lombardini, Herschel Nachlis, Julie Rose, Genevieve Rousseliere, Ian Ward, and Jim Wilson for their friendship and insights.

After receiving my PhD, I was lucky enough to be a Harper-Schmidt fellow in the University of Chicago Society of Fellows. The junior fellows were an unbelievable group who did amazing work to sustain a vibrant and truly interdisciplinary intellectual community. I'm also grateful to

Chicago's political theory community, who were all exceptionally welcoming and supportive of me. Thank you Andrew Dilts, Sina Kramer, Julia Klein, Emma Mackinnon, Rafeeq Hasan, Fadi Bardawil, Nathan Bauer, Michael Gallope, Robert Gooding-Williams, Nick Gaskill, Daragh Grant, Sarah Johnson, Reha Kadakal, Steven Klein, Leigh Claire La Berge, Ainsley LeSure, Birte Löschenkohl, Toussaint Losier, Daniel Luban, Patchen Markell, John McCormick, Mara Marin, Timothy Michael, Laura Montanaro, Sankar Muthu, Daniel Nichanian, Jennifer Pitts, Ethan Porter, Lauren Silvers, Bettina Stoetzer, Karl Swinehart, Nathan Tarcov, Jonny Thakkar, Zhivka Valiavicharska, Neil Verma, Jim Wilson (again), Audrey Wasser, and Linda Zerilli. Thanks also to the Harper-Schmidts who fought for and won a union contract through SEIU Local 73 and to the Trauma Center Coalition and Southside Together Organizing for Power for holding the University of Chicago accountable for its abuses of power.

Ohio State University has been a wonderful place to write this book. Michael Neblo and Eric MacGilvray have been the kind of supportive and generous senior faculty mentors that every junior professor deserves to have. Alex Wendt's support of me and this project has also been unstinting. Starting on the tenure track at the same time as Inés Valdez has been a godsend. Her intellectual and professional insight has been invaluable, about this project and so much more. I'm also grateful to many others at OSU and in Columbus for intellectual community and camaraderie, including Amna Akbar, Roger Beebe, Micah Berman, Rachel Bloomekatz, Jonathan Combs-Schilling, Adam Fazio, Ari Glogower, Matt Ides, Erin Lin, Joachim Moortgat, Sa'dia Rehman, Katy Rivlin, Amanda Robinson, Emma Saunders-Hastings, Lauren Squires, Amanda Robinson, Karl Whittington. Thanks also to Black Queer Intersectional Columbus, Columbus Freedom Fund, People's Justice Project, and the other local groups and activists that have done so much to show central Ohio what solidarity looks like.

A generous grant from OSU's Mershon Center for International Security Studies paid for a course release that gave me more time to work on this book. A grant from OSU's Institute for Democratic Engagement and Accountability (then the Democracy Studies program) and support from the Department of Political Science paid for an invaluable workshop at which an earlier draft of this manuscript was presented. I cannot thank Sharon Krause, Stephen K. White, and Joshua Cohen enough for agreeing to participate in the workshop and for their feedback; it immeasurably enriched this work. Drafts of parts of this book were also presented to multiple audiences at the Western

Political Science Association, American Political Science Association, and Association for Political Theory as well as at the Quinlan School of Business at Loyola University of Chicago, the George Mason University Politics Philosophy & Economics Speaker Series, the UC San Diego Political Theory Workshop, the George Washington University Political Theory Workshop, and Dartmouth College's Moral, Social, and Political Philosophy Workshop.

I'm extremely grateful to Angela Chnapko at Oxford University Press for seeing promise in this project and being patient as it came to fruition. I'm likewise grateful to the organizers of the Association for Political Theory's book proposal workshop for putting my proposal in her hands. Many thanks also to the two anonymous readers of the manuscript for the press who provided extensive, thoughtful feedback; to Michael Kupperman for his fabulous cover illustration; to Suzanne Sherman Aboulfadl for constructing the index; to Alexcee Bechthold for working as OUP's assistant editor on the book; to Anne Sanow for her copyediting; and to Narayanan Srinivavan for his work as project manager supervising the book's production.

As I've indicated in the book's conclusion, this book's argument was deeply informed by my experiences organizing, principally with the Progressive Student Labor Movement's Harvard Living Wage Campaign and with United Students Against Sweatshops. The number of people who were involved in these groups are too numerous for me to name, but I'm grateful beyond words to all of them for showing me what solidarity looks like.

My parents, Grover McKean and Judi Laing, have always encouraged learning, even when they found the mechanics of an academic career bewildering. Their political commitments have shaped my own both through the model provided by their decades of political action and through the life-long conversations about politics we have shared. I'm grateful to them for all their support over the years, as well as the encouragement from my brother Jacob.

Finally, I could not have done any of this without Dana Howard, whom I am cosmically lucky to have as both my partner in life and a daily intellectual interlocutor. This would be unimaginable without you. Also, hey, we had a kid while I was writing this book! This is dedicated to Elka, who I hope gets to live in a world with more freedom, justice, and solidarity than we can see today.

Notes

Introduction

1. Matthew Most and Rhonda Schwartz, "Bangladesh Factory Inferno Witness: Managers Ignored Fire," *ABC News*, November 28, 2012, https://abcnews.go.com/Blotter/bangladesh-factory-inferno-witness-managers-fire/story?id=17826499.
2. Vikas Bajaj, "Fatal Fire in Bangladesh Highlights the Dangers Facing Garment Workers," *New York Times*, November 25, 2012, https://www.nytimes.com/2012/11/26/world/asia/bangladesh-fire-kills-more-than-100-and-injures-many.html.
3. Quoted in "Bangladesh: After Fire, Companies Evade Compensation," *Human Rights Watch*, November 23, 2014, https://www.hrw.org/news/2014/11/23/bangladesh-after-fire-companies-evade-compensation.
4. "Payment on Claims From Survivors and Families Affected By Tazreen Factory Fire Completed," *Clean Clothes Campaign*, July 8, 2016, https://cleanclothes.org/news/2016/07/08/payment-on-claims-from-survivors-and-families-affected-by-tazreen-factory-fire-completed. See Mahmudul H. Sumon, Nazneen Shifa, and Saydia Gulrukh, "Discourses of Compensation and the Normalization of Negligence: The Experience of the Tazreen Factory Fire," in *Unmaking the Global Sweatshop: Health and Safety of the World's Garment Workers*, ed. Rebecca Prentice and Geert De Neve (Philadelphia: University of Pennsylvania Press, 2017), 147–172.
5. "International Labour Standards on Occupational Safety and Health," International Labour Organization, accessed July 15, 2018, http://www.ilo.org/global/standards/subjects-covered-by-international-labour-standards/occupational-safety-and-health/lang--en/index.htm.
6. Jim Yardley, "Report on Deadly Factory Collapse in Bangladesh Finds Widespread Blame," *New York Times*, May 23, 2013, http://www.nytimes.com/2013/05/23/world/asia/report-on-bangladesh-building-collapse-finds-widespread-blame.html.
7. "Readymade Garment Industries Going Green," RMG Bangladesh, August 7, 2017, http://rmgbd.net/2017/08/readymade-garment-industries-going-green/.
8. Saurav Sarkar, "Why 50,000 Garment Workers in Bangladesh Went on Strike," *In These Times*, February 5, 2019, https://inthesetimes.com/working/entry/21715/garment_workers_bangladesh_rana_plaza_garment_industry_workers_conditions.
9. Michelle Chen, "6 Years After the Rana Plaza Collapse, Are Garment Workers Any Safer?" *The Nation*, July 15, 2019, https://www.thenation.com/article/rana-plaza-unions-world/.
10. Charles R. Beitz, "Justice and International Relations," *Philosophy & Public Affairs* 4, no. 4 (Summer 1975): 360–389.

11. Raymond Geuss, *Outside Ethics* (Princeton, NJ: Princeton University Press, 2005), 11–39. See also Katrina Forrester, *In the Shadow of Justice: Postwar Liberalism and the Remaking of Political Philosophy* (Princeton, NJ: Princeton University Press, 2019).

12. Inés Valdez, "Association, Reciprocity, and Emancipation: A Transnational Account of the Politics of Global Justice," in *Empire, Race, and Global Justice*, ed. Duncan Bell (New York: Cambridge University Press, 2019), 120–144.

13. Branko Milanovic, *Global Inequality: A New Approach for the Age of Globalization* (Cambridge, MA: Harvard University Press, 2016), chapter 2.

14. Justin R. Pierce and Peter K. Schott, "The Surprisingly Swift Decline of US Manufacturing Employment," *American Economic Review* 106, no. 7 (July 2016): 1632–1662.

15. Eduardo Porter, "Recession's True Cost Is Still Being Tallied," *New York Times*, January 22, 2014, https://www.nytimes.com/2014/01/22/business/economy/the-cost-of-the-financial-crisis-is-still-being-tallied.html; Chris Isidore, "America's Lost Trillions," *CNNMoney*, June 9, 2011, http://money.cnn.com/2011/06/09/news/economy/household_wealth/index.htm.

16. Thomas Biebricher, *The Political Theory of Neoliberalism* (Stanford, CA: Stanford University Press, 2018), 167–168.

17. Rana Foroohar, *Makers and Takers: How Wall Street Destroyed Main Street* (New York: Crown Business, 2017).

18. David Dayen, *Chain of Title* (New York: The New Press, 2016).

19. The literature on neoliberalism is voluminous and discussed at greater length in chapter 1, but for the influence of neoliberal thinkers on international financial institutions, see Sarah Babb and Alexander Kentikelenis, "International Financial Institutions as Agents of Neoliberalism," in *The SAGE Handbook of Neoliberalism*, ed. Damien Cahill, Melinda Cooper, Martijn Konings, and David Primrose (Thousand Oaks, CA: SAGE Publications, 2018), 16–27. For neoliberal influence specifically on the IMF, see Stephen Nelson, "Playing Favorites: How Shared Beliefs Shape the IMF's Lending Decisions," *International Organization* 68, no. 2 (2014): 297–328. For neo-liberal influence specifically on the WTO, see Quinn Slobodian, *Globalists: The End of Empire and the Birth of Neoliberalism* (Cambridge, MA: Harvard University Press, 2018). For the influence of Friedrich Hayek on Paul Volcker and the Federal Reserve, see William L. Silver, *Volcker: The Triumph of Persistence* (New York: Bloomsbury Press, 2013).

20. Katrin Flikschuh also notes the lack of an adequate orientation to global politics, but in responding to this lack, she deliberately "excludes consideration of ordinary liberal citizens' perspectives" and seeks to provide an orientation just for "academic philosophers" because, in her view, ordinary people do not "genuinely believe the problem of global justice to be of a kind that puts them in a heightened state of anxiety." Her account of orientation accordingly does not engage with political practices or their legitimation, as mine does, but remains at the level of conceptual analysis. See Flikschuh, *What Is Orientation in Global Thinking? A Kantian Inquiry* (New York: Cambridge University Press, 2017), 23.

21. Marx, "On the Jewish Question," in *The Marx-Engels Reader*, ed. Robert Tucker (New York: Norton, 1978), 26–46.

22. The extent to which Marx should be understood as opposed to liberal rights is a matter of dispute and was one of the central debates for analytic Marxists thinking about the relationship between Marx and Rawlsian egalitarian liberalism in the 1970s and 1980s. Unfortunately, perhaps because analytic Marxists generally scanted the common Hegelian heritage that Marxists and egalitarian liberals share, they interpreted the relation between these views primarily as a debate about competing schemes of ideal distribution. Such debates were largely detached from questions of political agency and action and did little to challenge neoliberal conceptions of freedom. See Forrester, *In the Shadow of Justice*, 214–227.

23. Lawrence Summers, "Global Trade Should Be Remade from the Bottom Up," *Financial Times*, April 10, 2016, https://www.ft.com/content/5e9f4a5e-ff09-11e5-99cb-83242733f755.

24. Jonathan D. Ostry, Prakash Loungani, and Davide Furceri "Neoliberalism: Oversold?," *Finance & Development* 53, no. 2 (June 2016): 38–41. Note, though, that this new public-facing focus on inequality has not translated into significant change in the policies that the IMF promotes for member states. See Alex Nunn and Paul White, "The IMF and a New Global Politics of Inequality," *Journal of Australian Political Economy* 78 (2017): 186–231.

25. Jim Tankersley, "Trump Just Ripped Up Nafta. Here's What's in the New Deal," *New York Times*, October 1, 2018, https://www.nytimes.com/2018/10/01/business/trump-nafta-usmca-differences.html.

26. Tom Wraight argues that "Trump's trade policy represents not a rejection of neoliberalism but an extreme articulation of it" because it uses the power of the US state to coerce other countries into adopting more market-oriented policies. See Wraight, "From Reagan to Trump: The Origins of US Neoliberal Protectionism," *Political Quarterly* 90, no. 4 (2019): 735–742.

27. Simon Parry, "The True Cost of Your Cheap Clothes: Slave Wages for Bangladesh Factory Workers," *South China Morning Post*, June 11, 2016, http://www.scmp.com/magazines/post-magazine/article/1970431/true-cost-your-cheap-clothes-slave-wages-bangladesh-factory.

28. Samuel Scheffler, *Boundaries and Allegiances: Problems of Justice and Responsibility in Liberal Thought* (New York: Oxford University Press, 2001), 43.

29. See Raymond Geuss, *History and Illusion in Politics* (New York: Cambridge University Press, 2001), vii.

30. Benjamin McKean, "What Makes a Utopia Inconvenient? On the Advantages and Disadvantages of a Realist Orientation to Politics," *American Political Science Review* 110, no. 4 (2016): 876–888.

31. Cruz, "What the GOP Should Stand For: Opportunity," *Washington Post*, January 3, 2013, https://www.washingtonpost.com/opinions/ted-cruz-gop-needs-message-of-opportunity-conservatism/2013/01/03/c9536c8e-550e-11e2-8b9e-dd8773594efc_print.html.

32. In this, I differ from critics of the egalitarian liberal global justice literature like Michael Goodhart, who argues that the central problem is the understanding of normativity found there. Criticism on this level itself tends to remain philosophical rather than political. That is, specific views about the nature of normativity are rarely a practical obstacle to political actions like forming coalitions, which tend to founder on disagreements with more practical stakes. See Michael Goodhart, *Injustice: Political Theory for the Real World* (New York: Oxford University Press, 2018).

33. John Rawls, *Justice as Fairness: A Restatement*, ed. Erin Kelly (Cambridge, MA: Harvard University Press, 2001), 2–3. Orientation is one of four practical aims that Rawls identifies. On the other practical aims, see Benjamin McKean, "Ideal Theory After Auschwitz? The Practical Uses and Ideological Abuses of Political Theory as Reconciliation," *Journal of Politics* 79, no. 4 (October 2017): 1177–1190.

34. An important political dispute concerns whether American political institutions imperfectly realize political equality or whether invocations of equality are merely an ideological veil over institutions exclusively intended to realize values of white supremacy, which would produce a different orientation. See McKean, "What Makes a Utopia Inconvenient?"

35. Arguably, one reason for this is that Rawlsians have seen their traditional antagonists as libertarians like Robert Nozick, who endorses prepolitical property rights. But while neoliberals and philosophical libertarians converge on supporting many policies, they offer quite different orientations and ways of legitimating political power. I explore this connection further in chapter 6.

36. See, for example, Joshua Cohen and Charles Sabel, "Extra Republicam Nulla Justitia?" *Philosophy & Public Affairs* 34, no. 2 (Spring 2006): 147–175; Arash Abizadeh, "Cooperation, Pervasive Impact, and Coercion: On the Scope (not Site) of Distributive Justice," *Philosophy & Public Affairs* 35, no. 4 (Fall 2007): 318–358.

37. Scheffler, *Boundaries and Allegiances*, 45.

38. Taylor St. John, *The Rise of Investor–State Arbitration: Politics, Law, and Unintended Consequences* (New York: Oxford University Press, 2018).

39. One could also do this for the linked experiences of financialization, as households have become increasingly reliant on credit. See Michel Feher, *Rated Agency: Investee Politics in a Speculative Age* (Brooklyn: Zone Books, 2018).

40. See Forrester, *In the Shadow of Justice*, 278.

41. See John Rawls, *The Law of Peoples; with "The Idea of Public Reason Revisited"* (Cambridge, MA: Harvard University Press, 1999). On the problems with using Rawls's vision of self-sufficient peoples to guide action in the world today, see Allen Buchanan, "Rawls's Law of Peoples: Rules for a Vanished Westphalian World," *Ethics* 110, no. 4 (July 2000): 697–721 and McKean, "Ideal Theory After Auschwitz?".

42. See, e.g., Chandra Talpade Mohanty, *Feminism Without Borders: Decolonizing Theory, Practicing Solidarity* (Durham, NC: Duke University Press, 2003); Serene Khader, "Neoliberalism, Global Justice, and Transnational Feminisms," in *The Routledge Companion to Feminist Philosophy*, ed. Ann Garry, Serene J. Khader, and Alison Stone (New York: Routledge, 2017), 607–620; Monique Deveaux, "Poor-Led Social Movements and Global Justice," *Political Theory* 46, no. 5 (2018): 698–725.

43. Iris Marion Young, "Responsibility and Global Labor Justice," *Journal of Political Philosophy* 12, no. 4 (2004): 365–388; and "Responsibility and Global Justice: A Social Connection Model," *Social Philosophy and Policy* 23, no. 1 (2006): 102–130; and *Responsibility for Justice* (New York: Oxford University Press, 2011), chapter 4.

44. Iris Marion Young, *Justice and the Politics of Difference* (Princeton, NJ: Princeton University Press, 1990), 3.

45. Young, *Justice and the Politics of Difference,* 15–38.

46. Young, *Justice and the Politics of Difference,* 7.

Chapter 1

1. Ellen Meiksins Wood, "The Separation of the Economic and the Political in Capitalism," *New Left Review* 127 (May/June 1981): 66–95, at 82; 161, John Rawls, *The Law of Peoples; with "The Idea of Public Reason Revisited"* (Cambridge, MA: Harvard University Press, 1999).

2. For criticism of promiscuous usage, Taylor C. Boas and Jordan Gans-Morse, "Neoliberalism: From New Liberal Philosophy to Anti-Liberal Slogan" *Studies in Comparative International Development* 44, no. 2 (June 2009): 137–161.

3. For neoliberalism's intellectual history, see Rob Van Horn and Philip Mirowski, "The Rise of the Chicago School of Economics and the Birth of Neoliberalism," in *The Road from Mont Pelerin: The Making of the Neoliberal Thought Collective*, ed. Philip Mirowski and Dieter Plehwe (Cambridge, MA: Harvard University Press, 2009), 139–178; Angus Burgin, *The Great Persuasion: Reinventing Free Markets since the Depression* (Cambridge, MA: Harvard University Press, 2012); Quinn Slobodian, *Globalists: The End of Empire and the Birth of Neoliberalism* (Cambridge, MA: Harvard University Press, 2018); and Thomas Biebricher, *The Political Theory of Neoliberalism* (Stanford, CA: Stanford University Press, 2019); among others.

4. Burgin, *The Great Persuasion,* 55–86.

5. Other sites of organized influence include the economics department at the University of Chicago with which Gary Becker, Ronald Coase, and Milton Friedman, among many others, were affiliated; Friedrich Hayek was also there, though his primary appointment was with the Committee on Social Thought. For a survey of recent history work on the department's influence, see Douglas A. Irwin, "The Midway and Beyond: Recent Work on Economics at Chicago," *History of Political Economy* 50, no. 4 (2018): 735–775.

6. Philip Mirowski, *Never Let a Serious Crisis Go to Waste: How Neoliberalism Survived the Financial Meltdown* (New York: Verso, 2013).

7. Wendy Brown, *Undoing the Demos: Neoliberalism's Stealth Revolution* (Brooklyn, NY: Zone Books, 2015), 17–46.

8. For a defense of this view, see Andrew Moravcsik, "Is There a 'Democratic Deficit' in World Politics? A Framework for Analysis," *Government and Opposition* 39, no. 2 (2004): 336–363. For a critique, see Wolfgang Streeck, *Buying Time: The Delayed Crisis of Democratic Capitalism* (New York: Verso Books, 2014).

9. Slobodian, *Globalists*, 10. Slobodian cites the influence of Carl Schmitt's use of the distinction between imperium (government of people) and dominium (ownership of property) on neoliberals. I return to Schmitt in chapter 6.

10. Friedrich Hayek, *The Road to Serfdom* (New York: Routledge, 2001), 226.

11. Nancy Fraser and Rahel Jaeggi, *Capitalism: A Conversation in Critical Theory* (Medford, MA: Polity Press, 2018).

12. Mark Blyth, *Austerity: The History of a Dangerous Idea* (New York: Oxford University Press, 2013).

13. Robert Hartley, Carlos Lamarche, and James P. Ziliak, *Welfare Reform and the Intergenerational Transmission of Dependence*, IZA Discussion Paper No. 10942, available at https://ssrn.com/abstract=3029813.

14. Peter S. Goodman, "In Britain, Austerity Is Changing Everything," *New York Times*, May 28, 2018, https://www.nytimes.com/2018/05/28/world/europe/uk-austerity-poverty.html.

15. Jacob Hacker and Paul Pierson, *Winner-Take-All Politics* (New York: Simon & Schuster, 2010).

16. M. Ayhan Kose, Eswar Prasad, Kenneth Rogoff, and Shang-Jin Wei, "Financial Globalization: A Reappraisal," *IMF Staff Papers* 56, no. 1 (2009): 8–62.

17. On the tendency of capital mobility to reduce the effectiveness of national standards, see Ronald B. Davies and Krishna Chaitanya Vadlamannatid, "A Race to the Bottom in Labor Standards? An Empirical Investigation," *Journal of Development Economics* 103 (July 2013): 1–14. The link between financial openness and financial crises is well summarized in Aaron James, *Fairness in Practice: A Social Contract for a Global Economy* (New York: Oxford University Press, 2012), chapter 9.

18. Slobodian, *Globalists*, 54.

19. Michael Blake and Patrick Taylor Smith, "International Distributive Justice," in *The Stanford Encyclopedia of Philosophy (Spring 2015 Edition)*, ed. Edward N. Zalta, https://plato.stanford.edu/archives/spr2015/entries/international-justice/.

20. Debapriya Bhattacharya, "Export Processing Zones in Bangladesh: Economic Impact and Social Issues," Multinational Enterprises Programme Working Paper No. 80 (Geneva: International Labor Office, 1998).

21. "Executive Chairman of BEPZA promoted to Lieutenant General," *The New Nation*, March 8, 2019, http://thedailynewnation.com/news/208556/executive-chairman-of-bepza-promoted-to-lieutenant-general.

22. On the political production of EPZs as extrapolitical spaces, see Aihwa Ong, *Neoliberalism as Exception: Mutations in Citizenship and Sovereignty* (Durham, NC: Duke University Press, 2006), 102–116.

23. 78th Annual Report of the Foreign-Trade Zones Board to the Congress of the United States (Springfield, VA: National Technical Information Service, 2017)

24. United Nations Conference on Trade and Development, World Investment Report 2013 (Geneva: United Nations Division on Investment and Enterprise, 2013), http://unctad.org/en/PublicationsLibrary/wir2013_en.pdf

25. Steven Greenhouse, "Our Economic Pickle," *New York Times*, January 12, 2013, http://www.nytimes.com/2013/01/13/sunday-review/americas-productivity-climbs-but-wages-stagnate.html.

26. Chuck Collins and Josh Hoxie, *Billionaires Bonanza: The Forbes 400 and the Rest of Us* (Washington, DC: Institute for Policy Studies, 2017).

27. Lawrence Mishel and Jessica Schieder, *CEO Compensation Surged in 2017* (Washington, DC: Economic Policy Institute, 2018).

28. Facundo Alvaredo, Lucas Chancel, Thomas Piketty, Emmanuel Saez, and Gabriel Zucman, *World Inequality Report*, https://wir2018.wid.world/files/download/wir2018-full-report-english.pdf.

29. Michael Pollan, "Voting With Your Fork," *New York Times "On the Table" Blog*, May 7, 2006, https://michaelpollan.com/articles-archive/voting-with-your-fork/.

30. Milton Friedman, "Neo-Liberalism and its Prospects," *Farmand*, February 17, 1951, 89–93; available online as part of *The Collected Works of Milton Friedman*, compiled and edited by Robert Leeson and Charles G. Palm, https://miltonfriedman.hoover.org/friedman_images/Collections/2016c21/Farmand_02_17_1951.pdf. For skepticism about this understanding of *laissez-faire*, see Rune Møller Stahl, "Economic Liberalism and the State: Dismantling the Myth of Naïve Laissez-Faire," *New Political Economy* 24, no. 4 (2019): 473–486.

31. Biebricher, *Political Theory of Neoliberalism*, 26.

32. For the view that neoliberalism lacks a theory of state legitimacy, see William Davies, *The Limits of Neoliberalism: Authority, Sovereignty and the Logic of Competition* (Thousand Oaks, CA: Sage Publications, 2014).

33. Harvey, *A Brief History of Neoliberalism*, 2.

34. For the history of this line of argument, see Eric MacGilvray, *The Invention of Market Freedom* (New York: Cambridge University Press, 2011).

35. Slobodian, *Globalists*, 269.

36. Friedman, "Neo-Liberalism and its Prospects."

37. Adom Getachew, *Worldmaking After Empire: The Rise and Fall of Self-Determination* (Princeton, NJ: Princeton University Press, 2019).

38. Fraser, *Fortunes of Feminism*, 224.

39. See, e.g., Jürgen Habermas, *Legitimation Crisis*, trans. Thomas McCarthy (Boston: Beacon Press, 1975).

40. Gary S. Becker, *Human Capital: A Theoretical and Empirical Analysis with Special Reference to Education, Third Edition* (Chicago: University of Chicago Press, 1993); Robert A. Pollak, "A Transaction Cost Approach to Families and Households," *Journal of Economic Literature* 23, no. 2 (1985): 581–608.

41. Wendy Brown, *Undoing the Demos: Neoliberalism's Stealth Revolution* (Brooklyn, NY: Zone Books, 2015), 116.

42. See Charles Peters, "A Neo-Liberal's Manifesto," *Washington Post*, September 5, 1982, https://www.washingtonpost.com/archive/opinions/1982/09/05/a-neo-liberals-manifesto/21cf41ca-e60e-404e-9a66-124592c9f70d/?utm_term=.54477af2307d.

43. On Bill Clinton's role in advancing neoliberal policies, see Gary Gerstle, "The Rise and Fall(?) of America's Neoliberal Order," *Transactions of the Royal Historical*

Society 28 (2018): 241–264. Specifically on Clinton's welfare reform and neoliberalism, see Melinda Cooper, *Family Values: Between Neoliberalism and the New Social Conservativism* (Brooklyn, NY: Zone Books, 2017), 67–117.

44. On the Chicago, Freiburg, and Geneva schools of neoliberalism, see Slobodian, *Globalists*, 8.

45. Burgin, *Great Persuasion*, 87–89.

46. Jennifer Schuessler, "Hayek: The Back Story," *New York Times*, July 9, 2010, https://www.nytimes.com/2010/07/11/books/review/Schuessler-t.html.

47. Lanny Ebenstein, *Milton Friedman* (New York: St. Martin's Press, 2007), 197–204.

48. Quoted in Slobodian, *Globalists*, 213.

49. Friedrich Hayek, *The Road to Serfdom* (New York: Routledge, 2001), 209, emphasis in original.

50. Hayek, *Road to Serfdom*, 210.

51. On sociodicy and neoliberalism, see Pierre Bourdieu, "The 'Globalization' Myth and the European Welfare State," in *Acts of Resistance*, trans. Richard Nice (New York: The New Press, 1998), 29–44. On the connection between neoliberal sociodicy and evangelical theodicy, see Bethany Moreton, *To Serve God and Wal-Mart: The Making of Christian Free Enterprise* (Cambridge, MA: Harvard University Press, 2009).

52. Friedrich Hayek, *The Constitution of Liberty* (Chicago: University of Chicago, 1978), 12.

53. MacGilvray, *Invention of Market Freedom*, 181–182.

54. Hayek, *Constitution of Liberty*, 13.

55. Milton Friedman, *Capitalism and Freedom* (Chicago: University of Chicago Press, 1982), 13. Officially, Friedman is describing households here, but when Friedman discusses families as a unit in later in that chapter, he notes that their inclusion "rests in considerable part on expediency rather than principle" (33). See also Wendy Brown's analysis of this passage in Brown, *Undoing the Demos: Neoliberalism's Stealth Revolution* (Brooklyn. NY: Zone Books, 2015), 99–107.

56. Hayek, *Road to Serfdom*, 63.

57. Hayek, *Constitution of Liberty*, 20–21.

58. Hayek, *Constitution of Liberty*, 137.

59. Friedrich Hayek, "The Use of Knowledge in Society," *American Economic Review* 35, no. 4 (Sep., 1945): 519–530.

60. See Adam Kotsko, "Neoliberalism's Demons," *Theory & Event* 20, no. 2 (2017): 493–509.

61. Friedrich Hayek, *Law, Legislation and Liberty*, Volume 2 (New York: Routledge, 1982), 115.

62. Hayek, *Law, Legislation and Liberty*, Volume 2, 33.

63. Hayek, *Law, Legislation and Liberty*, Volume 2, 110.

64. MacGilvray offers an insightful analysis of this oscillation between individual freedom and common good in defenses of market freedom in *Invention of Market Freedom*, 141–146.

65. Friedrich Hayek, *Law, Legislation and Liberty*, Volume 3 (New York: Routledge, 1982), 128. See also Friedman, *Free to Choose*, 28 for a virtually identical quote.

66. Hayek, *Law, Legislation and Liberty, Volume 2*, 113.

67. Friedman, *Capitalism and Freedom*, 34.

68. Hayek, *Law, Legislation and Liberty, Volume 1*, 48.

69. Friedman, *Free to Choose*, 299.

70. Friedrich Hayek, *Law, Legislation and Liberty, Volume 1* (New York: Routledge, 1982), 115–118. Hayek is offering an even stronger version of Ronald Coase's seminal law and economics argument for how judges should rule in Coase, "The Problem of Social Cost," *Journal of Law and Economics* 3 (October 1960): 1–44.

71. Friedman, *Capitalism and Freedom*, 16–17 and Hayek, *Road to Serfdom*, 73.

72. Hayek, *Constitution of Liberty*, 13–14; Friedman, *Capitalism and Freedom*, 21.

73. Biebricher, *Political Theory of Neoliberalism*, 86.

74. Friedman, *Free to Choose*, 34. Hong Kong was held to be such a political model that the Mont Pelerin Society paid tribute by holding its first-ever meeting outside the US and Europe there in 1978. See Slobodian, *Globalists*, 235–6.

75. Bernard Harcourt, *The Illusion of Free Markets: Punishment and the Myth of Natural Order* (Cambridge, MA: Harvard University Press, 2011).

76. Juan Gabriel Valdés, *Pincohet's Economists: The Chicago School in Chile* (New York: Cambridge University Press, 1995); Karin Fischer, "The Influence of Neoliberals in Chile before, during, and after Pincohet," in *The Road from Mont Pelerin: The Making of the Neoliberal Thought Collective*, ed. Philip Mirowski and Dieter Plehwe (Cambridge, MA: Harvard University Press, 2009), 305–346.

77. Friedman, "What is America?" in *The Economics of Freedom* (Cleveland: Standard Oil Company of Ohio, 1978), available online in *From The Collected Works of Milton Friedman*, compiled and edited by Robert Leeson and Charles G. Palm, https://miltonfriedman.hoover.org/friedman_images/Collections/2016c21/BP_1978_2.pdf.

78. Slobodian, *Globalists*, 178–181.

79. Friedman, *Free to Choose*, 65–66.

80. Hayek, *Road to Serfdom*, 73–74.

81. Martin Gilens and Benjamin I. Page, "Testing Theories of American Politics: Elites, Interest Groups, and Average Citizens," *Perspectives on Politics* 12, no. 3 (2014): 564–581; Joshua Kalla and Ethan Porter, "Correcting Bias in Perceptions of Public Opinion Among American Elected Officials: Results from Two Field Experiments," OSF Preprints, July 7, 2019, doi:10.31219/osf.io/c2sp6.

82. Friedman, *Capitalism and Freedom*, 29.

83. Hayek, *Law, Legislation and Liberty, Volume 3*, 76.

84. Hayek, *Constitution of Liberty*, 18.

85. Friedman, *Capitalism and Freedom*, 23.

86. Biebricher notes the difficulties neoliberals face in theorizing the transition to neoliberalism, "at least not without violating the very assumptions that underlie its own analyses and critiques of the shortcomings of democratic politics." See Biebricher, *Political Theory of Neoliberalism*, 31.

87. Cf. Tomas J. Philipson and Richard A. Posner, *Private Choices and Public Health: The AIDS Epidemic in an Economic Perspective* (Cambridge, MA: Harvard University Press, 1993) and the discussion of this work in Cooper, *Family Values*, 167–175.

88. Michel Foucault, "The Ethics of the Concern for Self as a Practice of Freedom," in *Ethics: Subjectivity and Truth*, ed. Paul Rabinow, trans. Robert Hurley (New York: The New Press, 1997), 281–301 at 300.

89. Cooper, *Family Values*, 167–175. In using governmentality to analyze this facet of neoliberalism, I differ with Cooper, who asserts that it eludes Foucault's analysis.

90. Michel Foucault, *The Birth of Biopolitics: Lectures at the Collège de France, 1978–1979*, trans. Graham Burchell, ed. Michel Senellart (New York: Picador, 2008), 270.

91. Foucault, *Birth of Biopolitics*, 246.

92. Foucault, *Birth of Biopolitics*, 243

93. Hayek, *Road to Serfdom*, 92.

94. Or if not powerless entirely, our efforts are doomed to have perverse unintended consequences. See Daniel Luban, "What is Spontaneous Order?," *American Political Science Review* 114, no. 1 (February 2020): 68–80.

95. Friedman, *Capitalism and Freedom*, 120. See the similar argument in Hayek, *Studies in Philosophy, Politics and Economics* (Chicago: University of Chicago Press, 1967), 300–312.

96. Gary Becker, *Human Capital: A Theoretical and Empirical Analysis, with Special Reference to Education, 3rd Edition* (Chicago: University of Chicago Press, 1994).

97. Foucault, *Birth of Biopolitics*, 225.

98. Indeed, the appeal is such that Foucault himself is sometimes understood to endorse neoliberalism. See Michael C. Behrent, "Liberalism Without Humanism: Michel Foucault and the Free-Market Creed, 1976–1979," *Modern Intellectual History* 6, no. 3 (2009): 539–568; and Daniel Zamora, "Can We Criticize Foucault?," *Jacobin* December 10, 2014, https://www.jacobinmag.com/2014/12/foucault-interview/. This overstates the case considerably; for a nuanced account of neoliberalism's influence on Foucault, see Andrew Dilts, "From 'Entrepreneur of the Self' to 'Care of the Self': Neo-liberal Governmentality and Foucault's Ethics," *Foucault Studies* 12 (October 2011): 130–146. More bluntly, François Ewald, Foucault's assistant at the time of his lectures on neoliberalism, said in 2015 it "makes absolutely no sense" to see Foucault as sympathizing with neoliberalism. See François Ewald, "Foucault & Neoliberalism," *Foucault 13/13* January 24, 2016, http://blogs.law.columbia.edu/foucault1313/2016/01/24/ewaldneoliberalism/.

99. Tom Peters, "Brand You: 2015," *Tom Peters Blog*, November 23, 2015, http://tompeters.com/2015/11/brand-you-2015/. This post defends his original enthused account of these developments in Peters, "The Brand Called You: You Can't Move Up if You Don't Stand Out" *Fast Company* August 31, 1997, https://www.fastcompany.com/28905/brand-called-you.

100. Elisabeth R. Anker, *Orgies of Feeling: Melodrama and the Politics of Freedom* (Durham, NC: Duke University Press, 2014).

101. Lawrence F. Katz and Alan B. Krueger, "The Rise and Nature of Alternative Work Arrangements in the United States, 1995–2015," *ILR Review* 72, no. 2

(2019): 382–416. Notably, this phenomenon is not limited to low-wage employers; half of Google's workforce are contractors. See Mark Bergen and Josh Eidelson, "Inside Google's Shadow Workforce," *Bloomberg*, July 25, 2018, https://www. bloomberg.com/news/articles/2018-07-25/inside-google-s-shadow-workforce.

102. James Cook, "Uber's Internal Charts Show How Its Driver-Rating System Actually Works," *Business Insider*, February 11, 2015, http://www.businessinsider.com/leaked-charts-show-how-ubers-driver-rating-system-works-2015-2.

103. Julia Ticona, Alexandra Mateescu, and Alex Rosenblat, *Beyond Disruption: How Tech Shapes Labor Across Domestic Work & Ridehailing* (New York: Data & Society Research Institute, 2018), 16–19.

104. Ronen Shamir, "The Age of Responsibilization: On Market-Embedded Morality," *Economy and Society* 31, no. 1 (2008): 1–19.

105. Malcolm Harris, *Kids These Days: Human Capital and the Making of Millennials* (Boston: Little, Brown, 2017), 13–41.

106. Leslie T. Chang, *Factory Girls: From Village to City in a Changing China* (New York: Spiegel & Grau. 2009), 183. On migrant media and multilevel marketing, see Chang, chapter 3; on classes for developing human capital, see Chang, 171–205.

107. Students & Scholars Against Corporate Misbehaviour, "Workers as Machines: Military Management in Foxconn," October 12, 2010, https://goodelectronics.org/workers-as-machines-military-management-in-foxconn/.

108. Tim Bartley, Sebastian Koos, Hiram Samel, Gustavo Setrini, and Nik Summers. *Looking Behind the Label: Global Industries and the Conscientious Consumer* (Bloomington, IN: Indiana University Press, 2015), 202.

109. Hayek, *Law, Legislation and Liberty, Volume 2*, 111.

110. Hayek, *Law, Legislation and Liberty, Volume 2*, 94.

111. Friedman, *Capitalism and Freedom*, 111.

Chapter 2

1. Tim Laseter and Keith Oliver, "When Will Supply Chain Management Grow Up?," *strategy+business* 32 (Fall 2003), https://www.strategy-business.com/article/03304?gko=95df5.

2. Gina Binole, "Maine Workers Would Make Nike Shoes Again," *Portland Business Journal*, November 16, 1997, http://www.bizjournals.com/portland/stories/1997/11/17/newscolumn3.html; and Locke, *Promise and Limits of Private Power*, 48.

3. Matthew Kish, "How Much Do Nike Contract Factory Workers Get Paid?," *Portland Business Journal*, May 20, 2014, https://www.bizjournals.com/portland/blog/threads_and_laces/2014/05/how-much-do-nike-contract-factory-workers-get-paid.html.

4. Nelson Lichtenstein, *Walter Reuther: The Most Dangerous Man in Detroit* (New York: Basic Books, 1995), 17.

5. See cached version of http://americanapparel.net/aboutus/verticalint/usa/ preserved at https://archive.li/OC2W0, accessed July 26, 2018.

6. Shan Li, "American Apparel Is Sold at Auction to Canada's Gildan Activewear," *Los Angeles Times*, January 10, 2017, http://www.latimes.com/business/la-fi-american-apparel-gildan-bankruptcy-20170110-story.html; and Noor Ibrahim, "The New American Apparel: Claims of 'Ethically Made' Abroad Clash with Reality," *The Guardian* November 12, 2017, https://www.theguardian.com/business/2017/nov/12/the-new-american-apparel-claims-of-ethically-made-abroad-clash-with-reality.

7. International Labour Organization, *World Employment and Social Outlook: The Changing Nature of Jobs* (Geneva: ILO Research Department, 2015), 132.

8. See Lauren Wolfe, "How Dodd-Frank Is Failing Congo," *Foreign Affairs*, February 2, 2015, https://foreignpolicy.com/2015/02/02/how-dodd-frank-is-failing-congo-mining-conflict-minerals/.

9. Michael Gold and Yimou Lee, "Apple Supplier Foxconn Seeks to Slim Workforce Over Time, Eyes Robotics," *Reuters*, January 28, 2015, http://www.reuters.com/article/2015/01/28/us-hon-hai-labor-idUSKBN0L00Z520150128.

10. Stanley Reed, "Saudi Aramco is World's Most Profitable Company, Beating Apple by Far," *New York Times*, April 1, 2019, https://www.nytimes.com/2019/04/01/business/saudi-aramco-profit.html.

11. Jonathan Standing, "Another Foxconn Worker Dies, Family Blames Overwork," *Reuters*, June 3, 2010, http://www.reuters.com/article/idUSTRE6520K420100603. See also David Barboza, "Supply Chain for iPhone Highlights Costs in China," *New York Times*, July 6, 2010, http://www.nytimes.com/2010/07/06/technology/06iphone.html.

12. Andreas Wieland and Robert Handfield, "The Socially Responsible Supply Chain: An Imperative for Global Corporations," *Supply Chain Management Review* 17, no. 5 (September/October 2013): 22–29. For a summary of the Rana Plaza tragedy, see Jim Yardley, "Report on Deadly Factory Collapse in Bangladesh Finds Widespread Blame," *New York Times*, May 23, 2013, http://www.nytimes.com/2013/05/23/world/asia/report-on-bangladesh-building-collapse-finds-widespread-blame.html.

13. Jason Dedrick, Kenneth L. Kraemer, and Greg Linden, "Who Profits from Innovation in Global Value Chains? A Study of the iPod and Notebook PCs," *Industrial and Corporate Change* 19, no. 1 (2010): 81–116.

14. Jennifer Bair, "Global Capitalism and Commodity Chains: Looking Back, Going Forward," *Competition & Change* 9, no. 2 (June 2005): 153–180 at 159.

15. As I note in the introduction, this blindspot is arguably related to a broader tendency in egalitarian liberalism to overlook the process of production in order to focus exclusively on the distribution of goods. See Iris Marion Young, *Justice and the Politics of Difference* (Princeton, NJ: Princeton University Press, 1990), 15–38.

16. Richard M. Locke, *The Promise and Limits of Private Power: Promoting Labor Standards in a Global Economy* (New York: Cambridge University Press, 2013), 4–6. Locke in turn draws his account from John Ryan and Alan Thein, *Stuff: The Secret Lives of Everyday Things* (Seattle: Northwest Environment Watch, 1998).

17. However, as electronics products have become smaller and their lifecycles shorter, they have increasingly been flown into the US. For example, iPhones can now be assembled in Zhengzhou, China, and then after a layover in Anchorage, be in San Francisco stores three days later. See David Barboza, "An iPhone's Journey, From the Factory Floor to the Retail Store," *New York Times*, December 29, 2016, https://www.nytimes.com/2016/12/29/technology/iphone-china-apple-stores.html.

18. Deborah Cowen, *The Deadly Life of Logistics: Mapping Violence in Global Trade* (Minneapolis: University of Minnesota Press, 2014), 96.

19. "ITF Organizes Dockers' Unions to Pressure DP World," *The Maritime Executive*, June 7, 2017, https://www.maritime-executive.com/article/itf-organizes-dockers-unions-to-pressure-dp-world.

20. Rose George, *Ninety Percent of Everything: Inside Shipping, the Invisible Industry That Puts Clothes on Your Back, Gas in Your Car, and Food on Your Plate* (New York: Metropolitan Books, 2013).

21. "What Should My Wages Be?," *International Transportation Workers' Federation*, accessed February 13, 2018, http://www.itfseafarers.org/what_wages.cfm.

22. Brett Murphy, "Retail Giants Enable Trucker Exploitation," *USA Today*, June 29, 2017, https://www.usatoday.com/pages/interactives/news/rigged-retail-giants-enable-trucker-exploitation/.

23. Walter Lippmann, *An Inquiry into the Principles of the Good Society* (Boston: Little, Brown, 1938), 30. See also the discussion of this passage and its influence in Quinn Slobodian, *Globalists: The End of Empire and the Birth of Neoliberalism* (Cambridge, MA: Harvard University Press, 2018), 79–84.

24. Leonard Read, *I Pencil: My Family Tree as told to Leonard E. Read* (Irvington-on-Hudson, New York: Foundation for Economic Education, Inc., 1999). https://oll.libertyfund.org/titles/112

25. Foucault, *Birth of Biopolitics*, 225.

26. On the importance of transaction speed to neoliberalism, see Saskia Sassen, *Losing Control? Sovereignty in An Age of Globalization* (New York: Columbia University Press, 1996).

27. Wieland and Handfield, "The Socially Responsible Supply Chain," 24.

28. Karl Marx, *Capital: A Critique of Political Economy, Volume One*, trans. Ben Fowkes (New York: Penguin Books, 1990), 279.

29. Michael C. Jensen and William H. Meckling, "Theory of the Firm: Managerial Behavior, Agency Costs and Ownership Structure," *Journal of Financial Economics* 3, no. 4 (1976): 305–360. See also Frank H. Easterbrook and Daniel R. Fischel, *The Economic Structure of Corporate Law* (Cambridge, MA: Harvard University Press, 1996).

30. Benjamin Barber, *Jihad vs McWorld: Terrorism's Challenge to Democracy* (New York: Random House, 1995), 4. For similar worries, see Zygmunt Bauman, *Globalization: The Human Consequences* (Columbia University Press, 1998); Naomi Klein, *No Logo* (New York: Picador, 1999).

31. Thomas Friedman, *The World is Flat: A Brief History of the Twenty-First Century* (New York: Picador, 2005), 79 and 128.

32. Friedman, *The World is Flat*, 48.

33. Marx, *Capital*, 163–164.

34. Marx, *Capital*, 176–177.

35. For examples of this trope, see National Resource Defense Council, "Your T-Shirt's Life Story (Before It Met You)," March 5, 2010, reprinted by Mother Nature Network, accessed January 17, 2018, http://www.mnn.com/lifestyle/natural-beauty-fashion/stories/your-t-shirts-life-story-before-it-met-you; similarly Pietra Rivoli, *The Travels of a T-Shirt in the Global Economy* (Hoboken, NJ: John Wiley & Sons, 2015) purports to tell "my T-shirt's life story" (xii).

36. Branden Eastwood, "The Threads That Tie Your Clothes to the World," *Seattle Times*, September 21, 2013, http://old.seattletimes.com/html/businesstechnology/2021859613_nikehuskiesxml.html.

37. Wendy Brown, *Undoing the Demos: Neoliberalism's Stealth Revolution* (Brooklyn, NY: Zone Books, 2015), 116.

38. Peter Gibbon and Stefano Ponte, "Global Value Chains: From Governance to Governmentality?," *Economy and Society* 37, no. 3 (2008): 365–392 at 366. Another excellent introduction to this expert discourse is Jamie Peck, *Offshore: Exploring the Worlds of Global Outsourcing* (New York: Oxford University Press, 2017), 91–126.

39. Kate Vitasek, "Supply Chain Management Terms and Glossary," Council of Supply Chain Management Professionals (August 2013), 187, emphasis mine, https://cscmp.org/CSCMP/Educate/SCM_Definitions_and_Glossary_of_Terms/CSCMP/Educate/SCM_Definitions_and_Glossary_of_Terms.aspx.

40. Peter Dicken, Philip F. Kelly, Kris Olds, and Henry Wai-Chung Yeung, "Chains and Networks, Territories and Scales: Towards a Relational Framework for Analysing the Global Economy," *Global Networks* 1, no. 2 (2001): 89–112.

41. On logistics as a "global spatial imaginary," see Charmaine Chua, Martin Danyluk, Deborah Cowen, and Laleh Khalili, "Turbulent Circulation: Building a Critical Engagement with Logistics," *Environment and Planning D: Society and Space* 36, no. 4 (August 2018): 617–629.

42. Carlotta Benvegnù, Niccolò Cuppini, Mattia Frapporti, Floriano Milesi, and Maurilio Pirone, "Logistical Gazes: Introduction to a Special Issue of Work Organisation, Labour and Globalisation," *Work Organisation, Labour & Globalisation* 13, no. 1 (2019): 9–14.

43. For an analysis of the software that manages this data as itself an expression of political rationality, see Miriam Posner, "See No Evil," *Logic Magazine*, April 1, 2018, https://logicmag.io/scale/see-no-evil/.

44. International Labour Organization, *World Employment and Social Outlook*, 143; Worker Rights Consortium, Global Wage Trends for Apparel Workers, 2001–2011 (Washington, DC: Center for American Progress, 2013); Nathan Wilmers, "Wage Stagnation and Buyer Power: How Buyer-Supplier Relations Affect U.S. Workers' Wages, 1978 to 2014," *American Sociological Review* 83, no. 2 (2018): 213–242; Cristopher Adolph, Vanessa Quince, and Aseem Prakash, "The Shanghai Effect: Do Exports to China Affect Labor Practices in Africa?," *World Development* 89, no. 1 (2017): 1–18.

45. Gary Gereffi, Miguel Korzeniewicz, and Roberto P. Korzeniewicz, "Introduction: Global Commodity Chains," in *Commodity Chains and Global Capitalism*, ed. Gary Gereffi and Miguel Korzeniewicz (Westport, CT: Praeger Publishers, 1994), 1–14, at 2.

46. Gary Gereffi, "Global Production Systems and Third World Development," in *Global Change, Regional Response: The New International Context of Development*, ed. Barbara Stallings (New York: Cambridge University Press, 1995), 100–142, at 113.

47. Gary Gereffi, John Humphrey, and Timothy Sturgeon, "The Governance of Global Value Chains," *Review of International Political Economy* 12, no. 1 (2005): 78–104.

48. Peter Gibbon, Jennifer Bair, and Stefano Ponte, "Governing Global Value Chains: An Introduction," *Economy and Society* 37, no. 3 (2008): 315–338.

49. Jason Dedrick, Greg Linden, and Kenneth L. Kraemer, "The Guts of an Apple iPhone Show Exactly What Trump Gets Wrong About Trade," *The Conversation*, June 25, 2019, https://theconversation.com/the-guts-of-an-apple-iphone-show-exactly-what-trump-gets-wrong-about-trade-119223. On the continuities between this distribution of profits and the resource extraction of colonialism, see Intan Suwandi, R. Jamil Jonna, and John Bellamy Foster, "Global Commodity Chains and the New Imperialism," *Monthly Review* 70, no. 10 (March 2019): 1–24.

50. On the academic study of supply chain literature taking up the perspective of managers rather than workers, see David L. Levy, "Hegemony in the Global Factory: Power, Ideology, and Value in Global Production Networks," *Academy of Management Proceedings* no. 1 (2005): 1–6; Benjamin Selwyn, "Beyond Firm-Centrism: Re-integrating Labour and Capitalism into Global Commodity Chain Analysis," *Journal of Economic Geography* 12 (2012): 205–226.

51. Nikolas Rose, *Powers of Freedom: Reframing Political Thought* (New York: Cambridge University Press, 2004), 246.

52. Bernard Harcourt, *Exposed: Desire and Disobedience in the Digital Age* (Cambridge, MA: Harvard University Press, 2015).

53. Lee Rainie and Andrew Perrin, "10 Facts About Smartphones as the iPhone Turns 10," *FacTank*, June 28, 2017, http://www.pewresearch.org/fact-tank/2017/06/28/10-facts-about-smartphones/.

54. Joseph Turow, *The Aisles Have Eyes: How Retailers Track Your Shopping, Strip Your Privacy, and Define Your Power* (New Haven, CT: Yale University Press, 2017), 116–123 and 134–136.

55. Turow, *Aisles Have Eyes*, 154–168.

56. Turow, *Aisles Have Eyes*, 151.

57. Charles Duhigg, *The Power of Habit: Why We Do What We Do in Life and Business* (New York: Random House, 2014), 209–210.

58. Turow, *Aisles Have Eyes*, 219.

59. Data from Twitter Analytics for @BLMcKean on August 7, 2019.

60. Macaela Mackenzie, "Here's What Ulta Is Really Doing With All Your Shopping Data," *Allure*, June 21, 2017, https://www.allure.com/story/ulta-loyalty-free-products.

61. For example, Dara O'Rourke, *Shopping for Good* (Cambridge, MA: MIT Press, 2012).

62. Kalyan Sanyal and Rajesh Bhattacharyya, "Beyond the Factory: Globalisation, Informalisation of Production and the New Locations of Labour," *Economic and Political Weekly* 44, no. 22 (May 30–June 5, 2009): 35–44; Marlese von Broembsen, Jenna Harvey, and Marty Chen, "Realizing Rights for Homeworkers: An Analysis of Governance Mechanisms," Carr Center Discussion Paper 2019-004, March 5, 2019.

63. For an example of a libertarian defense of sweatshops that emphasizes how such employment both maximizes well-being and expresses free choice, see Matt Zwolinski, "Sweatshops, Choice, and Exploitation," *Business Ethics Quarterly* 17, no. 4 (2007): 689–727. For a critique of the well-being justification, see Mathew Coakley and Michael Kates, "The Ethical and Economic Case for Sweatshop Regulation," *Journal of Business Ethics* 117, no. 3 (October 2013): 553–558; for a critique of such employment as a free choice, see G. A. Cohen, "The Structure of Proletarian Unfreedom," *Philosophy & Public Affairs* 10, no. 2 (Winter 1983): 3–33.

64. Hayley Tsukayama, "Conditions for People Who Make Your Gadgets Are Improving—Barely," *Washington Post*, February 19, 2015, http://www.washingtonpost.com/blogs/the-switch/wp/2015/02/19/conditions-for-people-who-make-your-gadgets-are-improving-barely/. For a general critique and empirical analysis of the ethical consumption model, see Timothy M. Devinney, Pat Auger, and Giana M. Eckhardt, *The Myth of the Ethical Consumer* (New York: Cambridge University Press, 2010), chapter 4.

65. See Dara O'Rourke, "Outsourcing Regulation: Analyzing Nongovernmental Systems of Labor Standards and Monitoring," *Policy Studies Journal* 31, no. 1 (2003), 1–29; Jill Esbenshade, *Monitoring Sweatshops: Workers, Consumers and the Global Apparel Industry* (Philadelphia: Temple University Press, 2004); Locke, *The Promise and Limits of Private Power*; Tim Bartley, Sebastian Koos, Hiram Samel, Gustavo Setrini, and Nik Summers, *Looking Behind the Label: Global Industries and the Conscientious Consumer* (Bloomington: Indiana University Press, 2015); Richard P. Applebaum and Nelson Lichtenstein, "Achieving Workers' Rights in the Global Economy," in *Achieving Workers' Rights in the Global Economy*, ed. Richard P. Applebaum and Nelson Lichtenstein (Ithaca, NY: Cornell University Press, 2016), 1–16.

66. Wendy Brown, "Neo-liberalism and the End of Liberal Democracy," *Theory and Event* 7, no. 1 (2003) doi:10.1353/tae.2003.0020. More recently, Brown has sought to revive an interest in the public as a necessary component of "the project of individual or collective mastery of existence" (see Brown, *Undoing the Demos*, 221). This approach has its own pitfalls, which I discuss in chapter 6.

67. See David Harvey, *A Brief History of Neoliberalism* (New York: Oxford University Press, 2005), 41–43.

68. Marc Levinson, *The Box: How the Shipping Container Made the World Smaller and the World Economy Bigger* (Princeton, NJ: Princeton University Press, 2006), 264–278.

69. Paul Festa, "ISO Rules Out Code Fee Plan," *C|Net News*, September 30, 2003, https://www.cnet.com/news/iso-rules-out-code-fee-plan/.

70. A similar relationship exists between Nike and Yue Yuen, which is the world's largest sports shoemaker. See Donny Kwok, "China Sports Shoe Maker Yue Yuen Hit

by Factory Strike," *Reuters*, March 18, 2015, http://www.reuters.com/article/2015/03/18/yue-yuen-strike-idUSL3N0WK1PY20150318.

71. Thanks to Joshua Cohen for helpful discussions about this and for pushing me to be clearer about the details of this process.

72. Matthias Holweg, "The Genealogy of Lean Production," *Journal of Operations Management* 25, no. 2 (March 2007): 420–437; and Chris Brooks, "Volkswagen in Tennessee: Productivity's Price," *Labor Notes* 432, March 12, 2015, http://labornotes.org/2015/03/volkswagen-tennessee-productivitys-price.

73. Kim Moody, *Workers in a Lean World: Unions in the International Economy* (New York: Verso, 1997), 85–113; and Locke, *Promise and Limits of Private Power*, 126–155.

74. See Locke, *Promise and Limits of Private Power*, 144–146.

75. Friedrich Hayek, "The Use of Knowledge in Society," *American Economic Review* 35, no. 4 (September 1945): 519–530, at 526.

76. Hayek even argues against theorizing relations within the corporation, writing, "it is necessary in the interest of the efficient use of resources that the corporation be regarded primarily as an aggregate of *material* assets" (emphasis mine). See Friedrich Hayek, "The Corporation in a Democratic Society: In Whose Interest Ought It To and Will It Be Run?," in Hayek, *Studies in Philosophy, Politics And Economics* (Chicago: University of Chicago Press, 1967), 300–312, at 303.

77. Hayek, "Use of Knowledge," 524, 526.

78. Nelson Lichtenstein, *The Retail Revolution: How Wal-Mart Created a Brave New World of Business* (New York: Picador, 2010).

79. Elizabeth Anderson polemically compares the internal operations of corporations to communist dictatorships in *Private Government: How Employers Rule Our Lives (and Why We Don't Talk about It)* (Princeton, NJ: Princeton University Press, 2017). While Anderson means this as a criticism, Leigh Phillips and Michal Rozworski argue that the resemblance between supply chain management and central planning demonstrate the viability of socialism. See *The People's Republic of Walmart: How the World's Biggest Corporations are Laying the Foundation for Socialism* (New York: Verso, 2019).

80. For an excellent account of Coase's theory of the corporation, see Abraham A. Singer, *The Form of the Firm: A Normative Political Theory of the Corporation* (New York: Oxford University Press, 2018), 52–72.

81. Ronald Coase, "The Nature of the Firm," *Economica* 4, no. 16 (November, 1937): 386–405. As Jennifer Bair observes, the transaction cost account of the corporation also grounds Gereffi's approach to supply chains, making it particularly appropriate to consider here. See Bair, "Global Capitalism and Commodity Chains: Looking Back, Going Forward," 163.

82. Coase, "The Nature of the Firm," 388.

83. Coase, "The Nature of the Firm," 393.

84. Coase, "The Nature of the Firm," 403–404.

85. Milton Friedman, "The Social Responsibility of Business Is to Increase Its Profits," *New York Times Magazine*, September 13, 1970, 122–126.

86. For a thick description of such competition, see Marina Welker, *Enacting the Corporation: An American Mining Firm in Post-Authoritarian Indonesia* (Berkeley: University of California Press, 2014).

87. For a positive argument in favor of including inputs like fertilizer in our understanding of supply chains, see Paul Ciccantell and David A. Smith, "Rethinking Global Commodity Chains: Integrating Extraction, Transport, and Manufacturing," *International Journal of Comparative Sociology* 50, no. 3–4 (2009): 361–384.

88. Anderson, *Private Government*, 40.

89. Alex Hertel-Fernandez, *Politics at Work: How Companies Turn Their Workers into Lobbyists* (New York: Oxford University Press, 2018).

90. For example, see Dana Rubinstein, "State Labor Judge Finds Uber an 'Employer,'" *Politico New York*, June 13, 2017, https://www.politico.com/states/new-york/albany/story/2017/06/13/state-labor-court-finds-uber-an-employer-112733.

91. Lydia Wheeler, "Labor Department Rescinds Obama-Era Guidance on Joint-Employers," *The Hill*, June 6, 2017, http://thehill.com/regulation/business/336733-labor-department-rescinds-obama-era-guidance-on-joint-employers.

92. Joan Verdon, "Protesters at Children's Place Headquarters in Secaucus Arrested," *North Jersey Record*, March 12, 2015, http://www.northjersey.com/news/business/protesters-at-children-s-place-headquarters-arrested-1.1287744.

93. Note that this distinguishes my view from the stakeholder theory of the corporation in business ethics, which urges managers to listen to the voices of other parties with an interest in the firm but generally assumes the legitimacy of their authority. See, for example, Thomas Donaldson and Lee E. Preston, "The Stakeholder Theory of the Corporation: Concepts, Evidence, and Implications," *Academy of Management Review* 20, no. 1 (January, 1995): 65–91. My approach here is closer to the skepticism about the legitimacy of workplace hierarchy found in Iris Marion Young, *Justice and the Politics of Difference*, 214–222.

94. Sabrina Tavernise, "With His Job Gone, an Autoworker Wonders, 'What Am I as a Man?,'" *New York Times*, May 27, 2019, https://www.nytimes.com/2019/05/27/us/auto-worker-jobs-lost.html.

95. Anna Tsing, "Supply Chains and the Human Condition," *Rethinking Marxism* 21, no. 2 (2009): 148–176, at 150.

96. Leslie Salzinger, *Genders in Production: Making Workers in Mexico's Global Factories* (Berkeley: University of California Press, 2003)

97. Tavernise, "With His Job Gone, an Autoworker Wonders, 'What Am I as a Man?'"

98. As scholars of the "disarticulation approach" to supply chain analysis have written, "Rather than an advancing frontier that proceeds by incorporating territorial and social relations *inside* a hierarchical core–periphery structure of global capitalism ... the commodity chain is a constantly shifting boundary that demarcates an *outside within* and *reproduces uneven relations at a variety of scales*." See Jennifer Bair, Christian Berndt, Marc Boeckler, and Marion Werner, "Dis/articulating Producers, Markets, and Regions: New Directions in Critical Studies of Commodity Chains," *Environment and Planning A* 45, no. 11 (2013): 2544–2552, at 2544.

99. For this reason, anti-sweatshop efforts that emphasize transparency in the hope that information will speak for itself are flawed; they essentially treat consumers as private individuals making independent decisions rather than as members of a democratic public. See Archon Fung, Dara O'Rourke, and Charles Sabel, *Can We Put an End to Sweatshops?* (Boston: Beacon Press, 2001).

100. "First Public Declaration of the International Union League for Brand Responsibility," February 10, 2013, http://www.union-league.org/first_declaration.

101. Ralph Armbruster-Sandoval, "Globalization and Cross-Border Labor Organizing: The Guatemalan Maquiladora Industry and the Phillips Van Heusen Workers' Movement," *Latin American Perspectives* 26, no. 2 (1999): 109–128.

102. On the variety of possible relations between ethical consumption and political action, see Margaret M. Willis and Juliet B. Schor, "Does Changing a Light Bulb Lead to Changing the World? Political Action and the Conscious Consumer," *Annals of the American Academy of Political and Social Science* 644, no. 1 (November 2012): 160–190.

103. *China on Strike: Narratives of Workers' Resistance*, ed. Hao Ren, Zhongjin Li, and Eli Friedman (Chicago: Haymarket Books, 2016).

104. Trini Leung, "ACFTU and Union Organizing," *China Labour Bulletin*, April 26, 2002, http://www.clb.org.hk/en/content/acftu-and-union-organizing.

105. On the importance to employers of preventing freedom of association in EPZs, see "Govt Rushes to Amend Labour Law," *Star Business Report*, May 11, 2018, https://www.thedailystar.net/business/govt-rushes-amend-labour-law-1574659; on blacklisting workers, see Tim Bartley and Doug Kincaid, "The Mobility of Industries and the Limits of Corporate Social Responsibility: Labor Codes of Conduct in Indonesian Factories," in *Corporate Social Responsibility in a Globalizing World*, ed. Kiyoteru Tsutsui and Alwyn Lim (New York: Cambridge University Press, 2015), 393–429.

106. Kate MacDonald says the "central lesson" of her research is that worker participation enhances the effectiveness of monitoring. See MaDonald, *The Politics of Global Supply Chains* (Malden, MA: Polity, 2014), 175.

107. Steven Greenhouse and Elizabeth A. Harris, "Battling for a Safer Bangladesh," *New York Times*, April 21, 2014, http://www.nytimes.com/2014/04/22/business/international/battling-for-a-safer-bangladesh.html; "Signatories," Accord on Fire and Building Safety in Bangladesh, accessed March 7, 2016, http://bangladeshaccord.org/signatories/.

108. Alan Roberts, "The Bangladesh Accord Factory Audits Finds More than 80,000 Safety Hazards," *Guardian Sustainable Business*, October 15, 2014, http://www.theguardian.com/sustainable-business/2014/oct/15/bangladesh-accord-factory-hazards-protect-worker-safety-fashion.

109. Michelle Chen, "6 Years After the Rana Plaza Collapse, Are Garment Workers Any Safer?," *The Nation*, July 15, 2019, https://www.thenation.com/article/rana-plaza-unions-world/; Saurav Sarker, "Bangladesh Accord Gets a Lifeline While Workers Organize Wildcat Strikes," *Labor Notes*, August 6, 2019, https://www.labornotes.org/2019/08/bangladesh-accord-gets-lifeline-while-workers-organize-wildcat-strikes.

110. Kate Hodal, "Bosses Force Female Workers Making Jeans for Levis and Wrangler into Sex," *The Guardian*, August 15, 2019, https://www.theguardian.com/global-development/2019/aug/15/bosses-force-female-workers-making-jeans-for-levis-and-wrangler-into-sex-report-claims.

Chapter 3

1. Matthew Yglesias, "Different Places Have Different Safety Rules and That's OK," *Slate*, April 24, 2013, http://www.slate.com/blogs/moneybox/2013/04/24/international_factory_safety.html.
2. See Nancy Fraser, "Feminism, Capitalism, and the Cunning of History," in *Fortunes of Feminism: From State-Managed Capitalism to Neoliberal Crisis* (Brooklyn, NY: Verso Books, 2013), 209–226.
3. Özlem Aslan and Zynep Gambetti, "Provincializing Fraser's History: Feminism and Neoliberalism Revisited," *History of the Present* 1, no. 1 (2011): 130–147; Johanna Brenner, "There Was No Such Thing as 'Progressive Neoliberalism,'" *Dissent*, January 14, 2017, https://www.dissentmagazine.org/online_articles/nancy-fraser-progressive-neoliberalism-social-movements-response.
4. William H. Sewell Jr., "A Theory of Structure: Duality, Agency, and Transformation," *American Journal of Sociology* 99, no. 1 (1992): 1–29.
5. Iris Marion Young, *Inclusion and Democracy* (New York: Oxford University Press, 2000), 10.
6. Patchen Markell, *Bound by Recognition* (Princeton, NJ: Princeton University Press, 2003), 10–17; Sharon Krause, *Freedom Beyond Sovereignty: Reconstructing Liberal Individualism* (Chicago: University of Chicago Press, 2015), 4–7.
7. Tony Smith has also argued for such continuity, noting "Marx's call for a society in which 'the full and free development of every individual forms the ruling principle' and 'the free development of each is the condition for the free development of all' makes explicit the principles underlying his normative assessments . . . Liberal egalitarians have repeated, clarified, elaborated, and complemented these same principles." See Smith, *Beyond Liberal Egalitarianism: Marx and Normative Social Theory in the Twenty-first Century* (Chicago: Haymarket Books, 2018), 341.
8. See Benjamin L. McKean, "What Makes a Utopia Inconvenient? On the Advantages and Disadvantages of a Realist Orientation to Politics" *American Political Science Review* 110, no. 4 (November 2016): 876–888.
9. For example, Arnold I. Davidson argues that "justice as fairness" is straightforwardly a development of Kant's moral philosophy in Davidson, "Is Rawls a Kantian?," *Pacific Philosophical Quarterly* 66, no. 1 (1985): 49–77.
10. John Rawls, "Justice as Fairness" in *Collected Papers*, ed. Samuel Freeman (Cambridge, MA: Harvard University Press, 1999), 48 footnote 2. However, Katrina Forrester persuasively argues that Rawls's key political ideas were formulated before he gave them a Kantian interpretation. See Forrester, *In the Shadow of Justice: Postwar Liberalism*

and the Remaking of Political Philosophy (Princeton, NJ: Princeton University Press, 2019), 1–40.

11. John Rawls, *Lectures on the History of Moral Philosophy*, ed. Barbara Herman (Cambridge, MA: Harvard University Press, 2000), 330.

12. In addition to the enduring legacy of Karl Popper's interpretation of Hegel as a totalitarian, see Jeremy Waldron, "Theoretical Foundations of Liberalism," *Philosophical Quarterly* 37, no. 147 (1987): 127–150, at 132.

13. See Rocío Zambrana, "Hegel, History, and Race," in *The Oxford Handbook of Philosophy and Race*, ed. Naomi Zack (New York: Oxford University Press, 2017), 251–260; Robert Bernasconi, "Hegel at the Court of the Ashanti," in *Hegel after Derrida*, ed. S. Barnett (New York: Routledge, 1998), 41–63. Kant's views about gender and race were, for the most part, equally hierarchical. See Robert Bernasconi, "Kant as an Unfamiliar Source of Racism," in *Philosophers on Race: Critical Essays*, ed. Julie K. Ward and Tommy L. Lott (New York: Blackwell Publishers, 2002), 145–166; Pauline Kleingeld, "Kant's Second Thoughts on Race," *Philosophical Quarterly* 57, no. 229 (2007): 573–592; Inder S. Marwah, "What Nature Makes of Her: Kant's Gendered Metaphysics," *Hypatia* 28, no. 3 (2013): 551–567.

14. Rawls, *Justice as Fairness*, 357 and Rawls, *The Law of Peoples; with "The Idea of Public Reason Revisited"* (Cambridge, MA: Harvard University Press, 19990, 73. For the argument that Rawls's view of "peoples" shares important features with Hegel's decent consultation hierarchy, see Maria G. Kowalski, "Toleration, Social Identity, and International Justice in Rawls and Hegel," in *Hegel and Global Justice*, ed. Andrew Buchwalter (New York: Springer, 2012): 85–110.

15. See, e.g., Thom Brooks, *Hegel's Political Philosophy: A Systematic Reading of The Philosophy of Right* (Edinburgh: Edinburgh University Press, 2007); Michael O. Hardimon, *Hegel's Social Philosophy: The Project of Reconciliation* (New York: Cambridge University Press, 1994); Frederick Neuhouser, *Hegel's Social Theory: Actualizing Freedom* (Cambridge, MA: Harvard University Press, 2000); Robert B. Pippin, *Hegel's Practical Philosophy: Rational Agency as Ethical Life* (New York: Cambridge University Press, 2008); Molly Farneth, *Hegel's Social Ethics: Religion, Conflict, and Rituals of Reconciliation* (Princeton, NJ: Princeton University Press, 2017).

16. Rawls, *History of Moral Philosophy*, 330.

17. See, for example, Allen Wood, *Hegel's Ethical Thought* (New York: Cambridge University Press, 1990), 258.

18. Charles Taylor, "The Politics of Recognition," in *Multiculturalism: Examining the Politics of Recognition*, ed. Amy Gutmann (Princeton, NJ: Princeton University Press, 1994), 25–74, at 36.

19. Thus we could have Stephen Houlgate saying that both Hegel and Rawls "have a claim to be regarded as liberal communitarians." See Houlgate, "Hegel, Rawls, and the Rational State," in *Beyond Liberalism and Communitarianism: Studies in Hegel's Philosophy of Right*, ed. Robert R. Williams (Albany: State University of New York Press, 2001), 249–273, at 249. For an example of Rawls's welcoming of liberal nationalism, see Rawls, *Law of Peoples*, 25 footnote 20, where he says his notion of the people

follows both John Stuart Mill and "Yael Tamir's highly instructive *Liberal Nationalism*." See Tamir, *Liberal Nationalism* (Princeton, NJ: Princeton University Press, 1993).

20. John Rawls, "Kantian Constructivism in Moral Theory," in *John Rawls: Collected Papers*, ed. Samuel Freeman (Cambridge, MA: Harvard University Press, 199), 303–358, at 304.

21. Rawls, *Theory of Justice*, 221–227.

22. Rawls, *Theory of Justice*, 226. Notably, this section was revised considerably from the first edition of *Theory*. There, Rawls makes no reference to recasting Kant's dualisms. Instead he writes that he believes that Kant meant his theory to accommodate humanity's "social situation," though he acknowledges his interpretation may be mistaken and says "if I am mistaken, the Kantian interpretation of justice as fairness is less faithful to Kant's intentions than I am presently inclined to suppose." See Rawls, *A Theory of Justice, Original Edition* (Cambridge, MA: Harvard University Press, 1971), 257.

23. Robert B. Pippin, *The Persistence of Subjectivity: On the Kantian Aftermath* (New York: Cambridge University Press, 2005), 27–55; Robert Brandom, *Tales of the Mighty Dead: Historical Essays in the Metaphysics of Intentionality* (Cambridge, MA: Harvard University Press, 2002), 45–57 and 210–234.

24. Rawls, *Political Liberalism*, 285–288. Rawls also lays out many of these critiques again in *Lectures on the History of Moral Philosophy* and again explicitly demonstrates how his view accommodates them. Rawls, *History of Moral Philosophy*, 365–371.

25. Rawls picks out Hegel's views about war and the highest form of good in politics as two of the most obvious areas of dispute. Rawls, *History of Moral Philosophy*, 358–362 and 369–371.

26. John Rawls, *Justice as Fairness: A Restatement*, ed. Erin Kelly (Cambridge, MA: Harvard University Press, 2001), 94.

27. By dispositions, I mean the habitual attitudes and propensities to action that individuals exhibit. I take this conception to be distinct from the philosophical literature on the dispositions of objects, which treats the modality and metaphysics of their properties—for example, the disposition of a lamp to shatter when dropped.

28. Many others have noted the Hegelian elements of Rawls's thought. See Jürgen Habermas, *Between Facts and Norms*, trans. William Rehg (Cambridge, MA: MIT Press, 1996), 56–66; Joshua Cohen, "Moral Pluralism and Political Consensus," in *Philosophy, Politics, Democracy: Selected Essays* (Cambridge, MA: Harvard University Press, 2009), 38–60; Jan-Werner Müller, "Rawls in Germany," *European Journal of Political Theory* 1, no. 2 (2002): 163–179; Jeffrey Stout, *Democracy and Tradition* (Princeton, NJ: Princeton University Press, 2004), 77–85; Ragip Ege and Herrade Igersheim, "Rawls with Hegel: The concept of 'Liberalism of Freedom,'" *European Journal of the History of Economic Thought* 15, no. 1 (2008): 25–47; and Margaret Meek Lange, "Exploring the Theme of Reflective Stability: John Rawls' Hegelian Reading of David Hume," *Public Reason* 1, no. 1 (2009): 75–90. Others argue that Rawls and Hegel share a dispositional approach to the norms of politics, but do not see this as an expression of freedom; see Jeffrey Bercuson, *Rawls and the History of Political Thought* (New York: Taylor & Francis, 2014) and Kiran Banerjee and Jeffrey Bercuson, "Rawls

on the Embedded Self: Liberalism as an Affective Regime," *European Journal of Political Theory* 14, no. 2 (2015): 209–228. On the other hand, for the claim that "the theoretical model of Hegel's *Philosophy of Right* plays no decisive part" in Rawls's political theory, see Axel Honneth, *The Pathologies of Individual Freedom: Hegel's Social Theory*, trans. Ladislaus Löb (Princeton, NJ: Princeton University Press, 2010), 1.

29. John Rawls, *A Theory of Justice, Revised Edition* (Cambridge, MA: Harvard University Press, 1999), 176.

30. John Rawls, *Lectures on the History of Political Philosophy*, ed. Samuel Freeman. (Cambridge, MA: Harvard University Press, 2007), 12.

31. Rawls, *Theory of Justice*, 266.

32. John Rawls, *Political Liberalism* (New York: Columbia University Press, 1996), 291–292.

33. The failure to recognize this distinction between the role freedom plays in the first principle and the way Rawls's theory overall expresses freedom is what generates the tension between freedom and equality that Samuel Arnold describes in "Putting Liberty in Its Place: Rawlsian Liberialism without the Liberalism," *European Journal of Philosophy* 26, no. 1 (March 2018): 213–237.

34. H. L. A. Hart, "Rawls on Liberty and Its Priority." *University of Chicago Law Review* 40, no. 3 (1973): 534–555.

35. Rawls, *Political Liberalism*, 290.

36. Rawls, *Political Liberalism*, 300.

37. Rawls, *Political Liberalism*, 335.

38. Rawls, *Political Liberalism*, 19; Rawls, *Theory of Justice*, 442; Rawls, *Justice as Fairness*, 18–20.

39. Rawls, *Theory of Justice*, 179.

40. Rawls, *Political Liberalism*, 326–327.

41. Rawls, *Political Liberalism*, 222; repeated verbatim in Rawls, *Justice as Fairness*, 94. Emphasis mine.

42. Michael J. Sandel, *Liberalism and the Limits of Justice*, 2nd ed. (New York: Cambridge University Press, 1998), 58.

43. Georg Wilhelm Friedrich Hegel, *Elements of the Philosophy of Right*, ed. Allen W. Wood, trans. H. B. Nisbet (New York: Cambridge University Press, 1991), 23.

44. Rawls, *Political Liberalism*, 222–223, footnote 9.

45. Rawls, *Theory of Justice*, 222.

46. Charles Larmore, *Patterns of Moral Complexity* (New York: Cambridge University Press, 1987), 120.

47. Larmore, *Patterns*, 126.

48. Rawls, *Theory of Justice*, 221.

49. Thomas Hobbes, *Leviathan: with Selected Variants from the Latin Edition of 1668*, ed. Edwin Curley (Indianapolis, IN: Hackett Publishing Company, 1994), 136.

50. Georg Wilhelm Friedrich Hegel, *Lectures on the History of Philosophy, 1825–26, Volume III: Medieval and Modern Philosophy, Revised Edition*, ed. and trans. Robert. F. Brown (New York: Oxford University Press, 2009), 178–184.

51. Immanuel Kant, "The Metaphysics of Morals," in *Practical Philosophy (The Cambridge Edition of the Works of Immanuel Kant)*, trans. and ed. Mary J. Gregor (New York: Cambridge University Press, 1996), 512–514.

52. I defend this interpretation of Kant in Benjamin McKean, "Kant, Coercion, and the Legitimation of Inequality," *Critical Review of International Social and Political Philosophy*, published online August 24, 2019: 1–23. https://doi.org/10.1080/13698230.2019.1658481

53. Citations are to Hegel, *Philosophy of Right* with section number indicated. See §142–145 and also the discussion in Alan Patten, *Hegel's Idea of Freedom* (New York: Oxford University Press, 1999), 43–47. Part of Hegel's critique of Kant is his charge that Kant has a purely subjective understanding of freedom owing to Kant's contention that everyone is free to act morally at any time. This is a misreading of Kant by Hegel, given the extensive institutional story Kant tells in the *Metaphysics of Morals* about the state's necessity to external freedom. Hegel's error seems to encourage Rawls to read Hegel as being entirely opposed to Kant's account of morality (see Rawls, *History of Moral Philosophy*, 333–335), when a more accurate reading of Hegel's view would see that he subsumes Kant's views; Hegel sees Kant's account as radically incomplete, but nevertheless sees the Kantian moral view as essential to understanding subjective freedom. For an account of Hegel's relation to Kant's moral philosophy along these lines, see Thom Brooks, *Hegel's Political Philosophy*, 52–61.

54. §410A, quoted in Thomas A. Lewis, *Freedom and Tradition in Hegel: Reconsidering Anthropology, Ethics, and Religion* (Notre Dame, IN: University of Notre Dame Press, 2005), 57.

55. See also Paul Franco, *Hegel's Philosophy of Freedom* (New Haven, CT: Yale University Press, 1999), 229–232. Franco argues that unreflective action is the highest form of ethics for Hegel, rather simply an element of a fully developed ethical life, as I maintain here.

56. Lewis, *Freedom and Tradition in Hegel*, 57.

57. Rawls, *History of Moral Philosophy*, 333.

58. Hardimon recognizes this connection between Hegel's social world and Rawls's basic structure in *Hegel's Social Philosophy*, 16. Notably, Rawls was a supervisor of the dissertation on which Hardimon's book is based. See also Houlgate, "Hegel, Rawls, and the Rational State," 251–252, and Sibyl Schwarzenbach, "Rawls, Hegel, and Communitarianism," *Political Theory* 19, no. 4 (1991): 555–560.

59. However, where Hegel acknowledges tension within and between the public and private, Rawls denies that they are in tension. See John Rawls, *Political Liberalism* (New York: Columbia University Press, 1996), 412. In these senses, Rawls might very well be understood to be a more unitary thinker than Hegel, as Andrew Buchwalter suggests. See Buchwalter, "Political Pluralism in Hegel and Rawls," in *Dialectics, Politics, and the Contemporary Value of Hegel's Practical Philosophy* (New York: Routledge, 2012): 97–110.

60. Jean Cohen and Andrew Arato, *Civil Society and Political Theory* (Cambridge, MA: MIT Press, 1992).

61. See Shlomo Avineri, *Hegel's Theory of the Modern State* (New York: Cambridge University Press, 1972), especially 164–167. For an instructive comparison between Hegel's corporations and modern firms, see Thomas Klikauer, *Hegel's Moral Corporation* (New York: Palgrave Macmillan, 2016), 25–36.

62. For the argument that Rawls endorses a similar vision, see Waheed Hussain, "Nurturing the Sense of Justice: The Rawlsian Argument for Democratic Corporatism," in *Property-Owning Democracy: Rawls and Beyond*, ed. Martin O'Neill and Thad Williamson (Malden, MA: Blackwell Publishing, 2012): 180–200.

63. See Patten, *Hegel's Idea of Freedom*, 36, where he puts the point nicely, noting that Hegel "thinks that a whole series of activities—from obeying the law, to the deliberations of public officials, to going to war—can potentially be viewed as part of the organic process in which a free society sustains and reproduces itself through, as he puts it in one passage, 'a constant negation of all that threatens to destroy freedom.'"

64. Rawls, *Political Liberalism*, xlii-xlvii and 41.

65. See Joshua D. Goldstein, "The 'Bees Problem' in Hegel's Political Philosophy: Habit, Phronêsis, and Experience of the Good," *History of Political Thought* 25, no. 3 (Autumn 2004): 481–507.

66. The theory of moral development that Rawls offers in *A Theory of Justice* strikingly parallels this, as individuals are said to proceed from a morality of authority (family) to a morality of association (civil society) before arriving at a morality of principle (state); notably, Rawls interprets the universality of the final stage in a more Kantian manner by emphasizing the self-consciousness with which one acts out of principle (405–420). See Rawls, *Political Liberalism*, 77–81 for how this model is transformed by the move to political liberalism.

67. Rawls, *Theory of Justice*, 155.

68. On Hegel as theorist of emotion, see Katrin Pahl, *Tropes of Transport: Hegel and Emotion* (Evanston, IL: Northwestern University Press, 2012).

69. A negative illustration of this phenomenon can be seen in Hegel's discussion of poverty in an otherwise rational state. This status has the effect of making people subjectively free but objectively constrained; moreover, he argues that "the disposition associated with poverty" is a kind of "inward rebellion against the rich" (§242). Hegel's discussion here prefigures Rawls on envy (*Theory of Justice*, 464–474); see also Jeffrey Edward Green, "Rawls and the Forgotten Figure of the Most Advantaged: In Defense of Reasonable Envy toward the Superrich," *American Political Science Review* 107, no. 1 (2013): 123–138.

70. This helps explain why both Hegel and Rawls believe that one of the most important functions of philosophy is to reconcile us to existing institutions; philosophy *can* make individuals reevaluate their relationships to existing institutions and thereby help shape their attitudes and dispositions. More generally, Hegel provides a framework for normatively evaluating the attitudes individuals have relative to the institutions they inhabit. See Hardimon, *Hegel's Social Philosophy*, 37–39, for an introduction to this topic of evaluating attitudes in Hegel. For a critique of Rawls's account of reconciliation, see Benjamin L. McKean, "Ideal Theory after Auschwitz?

The Practical Uses and Ideological Abuses of Political Theory as Reconciliation," *Journal of Politics* 79, no. 4 (October 2017): 1177–1190.

71. Rawls, *Theory of Justice*, 6; Rawls, *Political Liberalism*, xliii footnote 7.

72. Kant, "Metaphysics of Morals," 455–459.

73. Rawls, *Theory of Justice*, 229.

74. As Sharon Krause instructively argues, "sentiments run through Rawls's theory of justice from beginning to end, and they influence—in fact, they help determine— the practical deliberation that generates and justifies the principles of justice." See Krause, *Civil Passions: Moral Sentiment and Democratic Deliberation* (Princeton, NJ: Princeton University Press, 2008), 37. See also Banerjee and Bercuson, "Rawls on the Embedded Self" and Michael L. Frazer, "John Rawls: Between Two Enlightenments," *Political Theory*, 35 no. 6 (2007): 756–780. For the contrary argument that Rawls denies any role for the sentiments, see Robert C. Solomon, *A Passion for Justice: Emotions and the Origins of the Social Contract* (Lanham, MD: Rowman & Littlefield, 1995).

75. Rawls, *Theory of Justice*, 401; see also 420.

76. Rawls, *Political Liberalism*, 35; see also Rawls, *Theory of Justice*, 4.

77. Rawls, *Political Liberalism*, xliv, emphases mine. In *The Metaphysics of Morals*, Kant does assert that people ought to develop a "disposition to reciprocity" as expressed in "agreeableness, tolerance, mutual love and respect," but counts this as a duty of virtue when engaged in social intercourse; it is not a duty of right and lacks the connection to cooperative interdependence so important to Rawls's view (588).

78. Rawls, *Political Liberalism*, 217.

79. Nancy Fraser and Axel Honneth, *Redistribution or Recognition? A Political-Philosophical Exchange*, trans. Joel Golb, James Ingram, and Christiane Wilke (New York: Verso, 2003), 64.

80. This dispositional reading shows the extent to which G. A. Cohen's criticism of Rawls misses the mark. On Cohen's view, fundamental justice is fact-insensitive and its demands apply directly to individuals; as a result, egalitarian liberal views that take political and institutional status into account when determining an individual's duty of justice are flawed. Simply to comply with the rules laid down by just institutions is not enough to guarantee a distribution in which all inequalities are justified because an individual could withhold labor that would help the least-advantaged—unless he receives additional incentives which only need to be introduced because of his unwillingness to act otherwise. Cohen argues Rawlsians ought to condemn such an individual for acting unjustly but claims that they are unable to do so because they deny that the difference principle applies directly to individuals. But Rawls's own view does require individuals to realize justice in their lives, though not by applying institutional principles to them directly; as a matter of justice, which requires them to be disposed to reciprocity, individuals ought to perceive other members of society as their partners in collective social cooperation and equal in political status. To see others as less worthy of their share of the benefits produced by cooperation among equals violates this subjective dimension of the duty of justice and so egalitarian liberals can indeed condemn individuals in a well-ordered society who demand

purely self-interested incentives because they are failing in their political relationship with others. Indeed, this is a more plausible duty than Cohen's requirement that they ensure their individual actions contribute to bringing about the correct distribution. What's more, the account of interdependence between individuals and institutions provides a more plausible mechanism for relating individuals' attitudes to their duties than his invocation of the importance of social ethos, which appears as something of a *deus ex machina* lacking an underlying causal mechanism. See Cohen, *Rescuing Justice and Equality* (Cambridge, MA: Harvard University Press, 2008), 116–150.

81. Rawls, *Law of Peoples*, 137.

82. Raymond Geuss, *Philosophy and Real Politics* (Princeton, NJ: Princeton University Press, 2004), 86.

83. Rawls, *Political Liberalism*, 27.

84. Rawls, *Theory of Justice*, 514.

85. Rawls, *Political Liberalism*, 135.

86. Rawls, *Theory of Justice*, 514.

87. Compare this with Patchen Markell's preferred reading of contemporary constitutional patriotism, which he calls "a habit or practice that *refuses* or *resists* the very identifications on which citizens also depend." See Markell, "Making Affect Safe for Democracy? On 'Constitutional Patriotism,'" *Political Theory* 28, no. 1 (2000): 38–63, at 54, emphasis in original.

88. Allison Weir offers an extended defense of this conception of freedom, which she variously calls "freedom in connection," "freedom in belonging itself," and "social freedom." See Weir, *Identities and Freedom: Feminist Theory Between Power and Connection* (New York: Oxford University Press, 2013), 14.

89. Rawls, *Political Liberalism*, 68.

90. Rawls, *Political Liberalism*, 71.

91. Rawls, *Political Liberalism*, 68–69 footnote 21.

92. Theodor Adorno, *History and Freedom, Lectures 1964–1965* ed. Rolf Tiedemann, trans. Rodney Livingstone (Malden, MA: Polity Press, 2006), 266. See also Bernard Williams's "Critical Theory Principle," which calls for making sure that the structure of domination does not manipulate people into accepting the status quo (*In the Beginning*, 14).

93. Rawls, *Political Liberalism*, 81–82.

94. See the survey of relevant survey research on consumer attitudes in Fredrica Rudell, "Shopping With a Social Conscience: Consumer Attitudes Toward Sweatshop Labor," *Clothing and Textiles Research Journal* 24, no. 4 (2006): 282–296.

95. Rawls, *Theory of Justice, Original Edition*, 499; Rawls, *Theory of Justice*, 436; Rawls, *Political Liberalism*, 317.

96. Jeffrey Bercuson also notes the Hegelian resonances of Rawls's argument, but interprets them in a way that overlooks this crucial role for individual agency. Bercuson writes, "Rawls and Hegel share the foundational belief that institutions (and their guiding principles) *determine* the kind of people we become." See Bercuson, *John Rawls and the History of Political Thought: The Rousseauvian and Hegelian Heritage of Justice as Fairness* (New York: Routledge, 2014), 31. But this is too strong;

Rawls does not think the importance of institutions evacuates the space for individual agency and responsibility. It is more plausible to see institutions—even ideal ones—embodying conflicting values to which individuals can be oriented in several ways. Bercuson's confidence in institutions' capacity to determine the character of individuals subject to them leads him to adopt an overly optimistic view of the progressive realization of egalitarian justice. He writes, "institutional justice *produces* the social ethos that initially supplements it but that eventually gains a transformative power over it: the kind of society described forty years ago in *Theory* is *still coming into being*" (*Rawls and History*, 140). This seems belied by recent history.

97. Rawls, *Theory of Justice*, 99; also 293–294.
98. George Black, "Your Clothes Were Made by a Bangladeshi Climate Refugee," *Mother Jones*, July 30, 2013, https://www.motherjones.com/environment/2013/07/bangladesh-garment-workers-climate-change/.
99. Worker Rights Consortium, "Global Wage Trends for Apparel Workers, 2001–2011," July 11, 2013, https://www.americanprogress.org/issues/economy/reports/2013/07/11/69255/global-wage-trends-for-apparel-workers-2001-2011/; Jasmin Malik Chua, "Why Is It So Hard for Clothing Manufacturers to Pay a Living Wage?," *Racked*, February 27, 2018, https://www.racked.com/2018/2/27/17016704/living-wage-clothing-factories.
100. Christopher Blattman and Stefan Dercon, "The Impacts of Industrial and Entrepreneurial Work on Income and Health: Experimental Evidence from Ethiopia," *American Economic Journal: Applied Economics* 10, no. 3 (July 2018): 1–38.
101. Bruce E. Moon, "Exports, Outward-Oriented Development, and Economic Growth," *Political Research Quarterly* 51, no. 1 (1998): 7–36; Ha-Joon Chang, *Kicking Away the Ladder: Development Strategy in Historical Perspective* (New York: Anthem Press, 2002).
102. Social media makes the relationality of this freedom even clearer; as things are currently arranged, if all your friends opt into a system, you may have little choice but to follow suit. See Bernard Harcourt, *Exposed: Desire and Disobedience in the Digital Age* (Cambridge, MA: Harvard University Press, 2015), 31–53.
103. Gabriel J. X. Dance, Nicholas Confessore, and Michael LaForgia, "Facebook Gave Device Makers Deep Access to Data on Users and Friends," *New York Times*, June 3, 2018, https://www.nytimes.com/interactive/2018/06/03/technology/facebook-device-partners-users-friends-data.html.

Chapter 4

1. North American Agreement on Labor Cooperation, "Report of Review of NAO Submission No. 2003-01 (Puebla)," August 3, 2004, https://www.dol.gov/ilab/reports/pdf/Sub2003-01.pdf.
2. Department of Labor of the United States, Secretariat of Labor and Social Welfare of the United Mexican States, and the Labour Program of the Government of Canada,

"Ministerial Consultations Joint Declaration," April 24, 2008, https://www.dol.gov/ilab/submissions/pdf/us_2003-1_puebla_agreement.pdf.

3. US Department of State, *Mexico 2014 Human Rights Report*, accessed February 6, 2017, https://www.state.gov/documents/organization/236914.pdf, 32.

4. Benjamin L. McKean, "Ideal Theory after Auschwitz? The Practical Uses and Ideological Abuses of Political Theory as Reconciliation," *Journal of Politics* 79, no. 4 (October 2017): 1177–1190.

5. John Rawls, *Justice as Fairness: A Restatement* (Cambridge, MA: Harvard University Press, 2001), 135–140.

6. As Kiran Banerjee and Abraham Singer put it, Rawls lacks a theory of "meso-level" politics. See Banerjee and Singer, "Race and the Meso-Level Sources of Domination," *Political Research Quarterly* 71, no. 1 (2018): 215–227.

7. I say "many Americans" because committed white supremacists could certainly affirm the unchosen forces that shaped their lives. Du Bois addresses *Souls* to both African Americans and concerned whites, much as this book is primarily addressed to those who already recognize events like the collapse of the factories at Rana Plaza as injustices. I further discuss how to think about those reflectively committed to injustice in the next chapter.

8. Robert Gooding-Williams, "Philosophy of History and Social Critique in *The Souls of Black Folk*," *Social Science Information* 26, no. 1 (1987): 99–114; Shamoon Zamir, *Dark Voices: W. E. B. Du Bois and American Thought, 1888–1903* (Chicago: University of Chicago Press, 1995), chapter 4; Stephanie J. Shaw, *W. E. B. Du Bois and* The Souls of Black Folk (Chapel Hill: University of North Carolina, 2013).

9. For exceptions, see Terrence L. Johnson, "Rethinking Justice from the Margins: W. E. B. Du Bois and the Limits of Political Liberalism," *Journal of the Society of Christian Ethics* 29, no. 2 (Fall/Winter 2009): 61–79 and Elvira Basevich, "W. E. B. Du Bois's Critique of American Democracy during the Jim Crow Era: On the Limitations of Rawls and Honneth," *Journal of Political Philosophy* 27, no 3 (2019): 318–340.

10. Du Bois studied Hegel in a course with George Santayana while a student at Harvard, is likely to have had further exposure through his work with Royce and James, and wrote of reading further in Hegel while a student in Berlin. For a biographical overview of Du Bois's *Lehrjahre*, see David Levering Lewis, *W. E. B. Du Bois: Biography of a Race, 1868–1919* (New York: Holt, 1993), 117–149.

11. Joel Williamson, *The Crucible of Race: Black-White Relations in the American South Since Emancipation* (New York: Oxford University Press, 1984), 403.

12. Zamir, *Dark Voices*, 114. While accepting the influence of Hegel and of the *Phenomenology* more specifically, Robert Gooding-Williams critiques Zamir's claim about exact parallels in *In the Shadow of Du Bois: Afro-Modern Political Thought in America* (Cambridge, MA: Harvard University Press, 2009), 284–285, footnote 37.

13. For a reading of double consciousness that centers the master/slave dialectic, see David S. Owen, "Whiteness in Du Bois's *The Souls of Black Folk*," *Philosophia Africana* 10, no. 2 (August 2007): 107–126.

14. W. E. B. Du Bois, "The Souls of Black Folk," in *Writings* (New York: Library of America, 1986), 398.

15. Du Bois, "Souls," 400.

16. On Du Bois as a theorist of the transnational throughout his writings, see Inés Valdez, *Transnational Cosmopolitanism: Kant, Du Bois, and Justice as a Political Craft* (New York: Cambridge University Press, 2019).

17. Du Bois, "Souls," 418.

18. Du Bois, "Souls," 393. Du Bois is referring to a passage in Washington's memoir *Up from Slavery* where he describes "a young man, who had attended some high school, sitting down in a one-room cabin, with grease on his clothing, filth all around him, and weeds in the yard and garden, engaged in studying a French grammar" as "one of the saddest things I saw." See Booker T. Washington, *Up from Slavery* (New York: Oxford University Press, 2000), 71.

19. Du Bois, "Souls," 398.

20. Du Bois, "Souls," 364–365.

21. As Williamson notes, the peoples enumerated at the beginning of the passage are precisely those which Hegel identifies as world-historical peoples in his *Lectures on the Philosophy of History*. See Williamson, *Crucible of Race*, 404.

22. Gooding-Williams, *In the Shadow of Du Bois*, 80.

23. Importantly, Du Bois believed that separatism could sometimes be necessary in order for African Americans to freely define themselves. See the excellent discussion in Valdez, *Transnational Cosmopolitanism*, 141–147.

24. Zamir, *Dark Voices*, 146.

25. 306, Thomas C. Holt, "The Political Uses of Alienation: W. E. B. Du Bois on Politics, Race, and Culture, 1903–1940," *American Quarterly* 42, no. 2 (June 1990): 306; emphasis in original.

26. Du Bois, "Souls," 513.

27. See Gloria Anzaldúa, *Borderlands/La Frontera* (San Francisco, CA: Aunt Lute Book Company, 1987), 38–39.

28. See Linda Martín Alcoff, *The Future of Whiteness* (Malden, MA: Polity Press, 2015), 141–143. Alcoff develops this into a conception of "white double consciousness," though I think the symmetrical term risks mischaracterizing the asymmetry of these positions. See Alcoff, *Future*, 168–177.

29. Owen, "Whiteness in Du Bois's *The Souls of Black Folk*," 121, emphasis in original.

30. Charles Mills, "White Ignorance," in *Race and Epistemologies of Ignorance*, ed. Shannon Sullivan and Nancy Tuana (Albany: State University of New York Press, 2007), 11–38.

31. Du Bois, "Souls," 491.

32. Mills, "White Ignorance," 17.

33. Du Bois, "Souls," 364 and 368, respectively.

34. On the continuities between colonialism and transnational corporate resource extraction, see Sundhya Pahuja, "Corporations, Universalism, and the Domestication of Race in International Law," in *Empire, Race and Global Justice*, ed. Duncan Bell (New York: Cambridge University Press, 2019): 74–93.

35. Charles Mills, "Global White Ignorance," in *The Routledge International Handbook of Ignorance Studies* (New York: Routledge, 2015), 217–227.

36. Du Bois, "Souls," 363.

37. On Du Bois's transformation of Hegel to address oppression, see also Winfried Siemerling, "W. E. B. Du Bois, Hegel, and the Staging of Alterity." *Callaloo* 24, no. 1 (2001): 325–333.

38. Du Bois, "Souls," 438. While Du Bois here cites canonical figures of Western thought, he does not mean to suggest that they are the only source of truth or freedom. On Du Bois's "globalism" in *Souls*, see Vilashini Cooppan, "The Double Politics of Double Consciousness: Nationalism and Globalism in The Souls of Black Folk," *Public Culture* 17, no. 2 (2005): 299–318.

39. Du Bois, "Souls," 438.

40. In reading Du Bois this way, I depart from Robert Gooding-Williams's interpretation of Du Bois as inspired by Bismarck to seek a means of expressing an authentic *geist* animating African Americans as a people. See *In the Shadow of Du Bois*, 19–65.

41. Du Bois, "Souls," 510.

42. Du Bois, "Souls," 369.

43. Du Bois, "Souls," 364.

44. Du Bois, "Souls," 507. For a clarifying analysis that puts this passage in the context of prevailing prejudicial views about "the mulatto," see Annie Menzel, " 'Awful Gladness': The Dual Political Rhetorics of Du Bois's 'Of the Passing of the First—Born,' " *Political Theory* 47, no. 1 (2019): 32–56, at 40–43.

45. Du Bois, "Souls," 510.

46. Menzel, "Awful Gladness," 46.

47. Du Bois, "Souls," 511.

48. See also discussion of this passage in Shannon Mariotti, "On the Passing of the First-Born Son: Emerson's 'Focal Distancing,' Du Bois' "Second Sight," and Disruptive Particularity *Political Theory* 37, no. 3 (June 2009): 351–374.

49. For example, Kwame Anthony Appiah calls Du Bois "America's last romantic" in *Lines of Descent: W. E. B. Du Bois and the Emergence of Identity* (Cambridge, MA: Harvard University Press, 2014), 22. On the role of the sublime in *Souls*, see Gooding-Williams, *In the Shadow of Du Bois*, 66–95.

50. Anzaldúa, *Borderlands/La Frontera*, 39.

51. Anzaldúa, *Borderlands/La Frontera*, 39.

52. See the account of knowledge as loss in Robyn Marasco, *The Highway of Despair: Critical Theory After Hegel* (New York: Columbia University Press, 2015).

53. For a clear explanation of Adorno's conception of the negative dialectic, see Terry Pinkard, "What is Negative Dialectics? Adorno's Reevaluation of Hegel," in *A Companion to Adorno (Blackwell Companions to Philosophy)*, ed. Peter E. Gordon, Espen Hammer, and Max Pensky (Malden, MA: Wiley-Blackwell, 2020): 459–472.

54. Theodor Adorno, *Negative Dialectics*, trans. E. B. Ashton (New York: Continuum Publishing, 1973), 203.

55. Theodor Adorno, *History and Freedom: Lectures, 1964–1965*, ed. Rolf Tiedemann, trans. Rodney Livingstone (Malden, MA: Polity, 2006), 137.

56. Others who explicitly link *Souls* to Adorno include Mariotti, "On the Passing of the First Born Son" and Joseph Winters, *Hope Draped in Black: Race, Melancholy, and the Agony of Progress* (Durham, NC: Duke University Press, 2016), 33–42.

57. Kwame Anthony Appiah, *As If: Idealization and Ideals* (Cambridge, MA: Harvard University Press, 2017), 168. Note that this argument about improvement through negation differs from Amartya Sen's argument that we do not need ideal theory because we can engage in comparative justice to weigh imperfect alternatives. See Sen, *The Idea of Justice* (Cambridge, MA: Harvard University Press, 2009).

58. Du Bois, "Souls," 507. An unhopeful hope is also an apt characterization of the "sorrow songs" with which Du Bois begins each chapter. See Paul E. Kirkland, "Sorrow Songs and Self-Knowledge: The Politics of Recognition and Tragedy in W. E. B. Du Bois's Souls of Black Folk," *American Political Thought: A Journal of Ideas, Institutions, and Culture* 4 (Summer 2015): 412–437.

59. See Menzel, "'Awful Gladness.'" For the argument that a focus on double consciousness serves to perpetuate bourgeois politics that minimize class differences within the African American community, see Adolph L. Reed Jr. *W. E. B. Du Bois and American Political Thought: Fabianism and the Color Line* (New York: Oxford University Press, 1999).

60. Du Bois, "Souls," 503.

61. Du Bois, "Souls," 504.

62. Theodor Adorno, *Minima Moralia: Reflections on a Damaged Life*, trans. E. F. N. Jephcott (New York: Verso, 2005), 39.

63. Du Bois, "Souls," 504.

64. Bruce Baum, "Decolonizing Critical Theory," *Constellations* 22, no. 3 (September 2015): 420–434.

65. McKean, "Ideal Theory after Auschwitz?"

66. Theodor Adorno, "Progress," in *Critical Models: Interventions and Catchwords*, trans. Henry W. Pickford (New York: Columbia University Press, 1998), 148.

67. Du Bois, "Souls," 412.

68. Du Bois, "Souls," 414.

69. Adorno, "Progress," 147.

70. Adorno, "Progress," 148.

71. As I argue in "Ideal Theory After Auschwitz?" Adorno's own understanding of negative dialectic does not lead in this direction but rather tends to divide the world into cold philosophers and suffering others.

72. Du Bois, "Souls," 359–360.

73. Melvin Rogers, "The People, Rhetoric, and Affect: On the Political Force of Du Bois's The Souls of Black Folk," *American Political Science Review* 106, no. 1 (Februrary 2012): 188–203, at 198.

74. Rogers, "People, Rhetoric, and Affect," 194.

75. As Menzel highlights, this strategy leads Du Bois to engage in a politics of respectability that frames suffering in the way most recognizable to bourgeois whites, which risks marginalizing other forms of black experience. See Menzel, "'Awful Gladness.'"

76. Rogers, "People, Rhetoric, and Affect," 201.

77. Rogers, "People, Rhetoric, and Affect," 195.

78. Christopher J. Lebron, *The Color of Our Shame: Race and Justice in Our Time* (New York: Oxford University Press, 2013), 13.

79. Du Bois, "Souls," 492.

80. Liam Murphy, "Institutions and the Demands of Justice," *Philosophy & Public Affairs* 27, no. 4 (Fall 1998): 254–291. A. J. Julius similarly attributes what he calls the "separation view" to Rawls in "Basic Structure and the Value of Equality," *Philosophy & Public Affairs* 31, no. 4 (October 2003): 321–355.

81. Thomas Nagel, "The Problem of Global Justice," *Philosophy & Public Affairs*, 33, no. 2 (March 2005): 113–147; Thomas Pogge, "Moral Universalism and Global Economic Justice," *Politics Philosophy & Economics* 1, no 1 (2002): 29–58.

82. As Arash Abizadeh notes, one does not need to endorse dualism in order to endorse a "division of labor" argument, which could rest on other grounds, including monism. See Abizadeh, "Cooperation, Pervasive Impact, and Coercion: On the Scope (not Site) of Distributive Justice," *Philosophy & Public Affairs* 35, no 4 (2007): 318–358, at 329 footnote 20.

83. See, for example, A. John Simmons, "Ideal and Nonideal Theory," *Philosophy & Public Affairs* 38, no. 1 (2010): 5–36.

84. We might see Rawls endorsing a version of this thought and refusing Du Bois's acknowledgment of the tragic choices forced by injustice when he writes, "Acting with deliberative rationality can only insure that our conduct is above reproach" (TJ99, 371). Stanley Cavell notes that this claim is in keeping with Rawls's earlier approach in "Two Concepts of Rules" (1955). See Cavell, *Conditions Handsome and Unhandsome: The Constitution of Emersonian Perfectionism* (Chicago: University of Chicago Press, 1990), 101–126.

85. Rawls, *Theory of Justice*, 3.

86. Rawls, *Political Liberalism*, 269.

87. Rawls, *Theory of Justice*, 98.

88. Rawls acknowledges what he calls the "formidable complication" of actually distinguishing normal politics and interest group legislation from legislation that touches on constitutional essentials and basic justice. This relates to the difficulty of determining which individual actions affect background conditions. See Rawls, *Political Liberalism*, 397 footnote 34.

89. Nagel, "Problem of Global Justice," 141.

90. Thomas Pogge, "'Assisting' the Global Poor," in *The Ethics of Assistance: Morality and the Distant Needy*, ed. Deen K. Chatterjee (New York: Cambridge University Press, 2004), 260–288, at 279.

91. David Miller, *National Responsibility and Global Justice* (New York: Oxford University Press, 2007), 17. Similar proportional views are also endorsed in Joshua Cohen and Charles Sabel, "Extra Rempublicam Nulla Justitia?," *Philosophy & Public Affairs* 34, no. 2 (March 2006): 147–175, and in Anna Stilz, *Liberal Loyalty: Freedom, Obligation, and the State* (Princeton, NJ: Princeton University Press, 2009), 101–109.

92. Thomas Pogge, *World Poverty and Human Rights* (Malden, MA: Polity Press, 2002), 26.

93. Cohen and Sabel, "Extra Rempublicam Nulla Justitia?", 167.

94. Andrea Sangiovanni offers a liberal egalitarian account that does direct us to attend to our co-citizens, but does so at the cost of making it sound as though existing domestic politics already embodies reciprocity and cooperation for everyone. He writes, "We owe obligations of egalitarian reciprocity to fellow citizens and residents in the state, who provide us with the basic conditions and guarantees necessary to develop and act on a plan of life, but not to noncitizens, who do not." See Sangiovanni, "Global Justice, Reciprocity, and the State" *Philosophy & Public Affairs* 35, no 1 (2007): 3–39, at 20.

95. Miller, *National Responsibility and Global Justice*, 1–5. Miller is just one of many to emphasize television as the primary trigger for reflection on global injustice. For example, Peter Singer writes, "rich and poor are now linked in ways they never were before. Moving images, in real time, of people on the edge of survival are beamed into our living rooms." See Singer, *The Life You Can Save: Acting Now to End World Poverty* (New York: Random House, 2009), xii.

96. Charles Mills, "Race and Global Justice," in *Domination and Global Political Justice: Conceptual, Historical and Institutional Perspectives*, ed. Barbara Buckinx, Jonathan Trejo-Mathys, and Timothy Waligore (New York: Routledge, 2015), 181–205, at 183.

97. Mills, "Global White Ignorance," 225.

98. Stephen K. White, *The Ethos of a Late Modern Citizen* (Cambridge, MA: Harvard University Press, 2009), 16–17.

99. Rawls, *Political Liberalism*, 217.

Chapter 5

1. Credit Suisse Research Institute, *Global Wealth Report 2017* (Zurich: Credit Suisse AG Research Institute, 2017), http://publications.credit-suisse.com/index.cfm/publikationen-shop/research-institute/global-wealth-report-2017-en/.

2. Patricia Cohen, "Paychecks Lag as Profits Soar, and Prices Erode Wage Gains," *New York Times*, July 13, 2018, http://www.nytimes.com/2018/07/13/business/economy/wages-workers-profits.html.

3. Katherine Rosman, "Why Isn't Your Toddler Paying the Mortgage?," *New York Times*, September 27, 2017, http://www.nytimes.com/2017/09/27/style/viral-toddler-videos.html.

4. "A Letter to Parents," Social Star Creator Camp, accessed July 16, 2018, http://socialstarcreatorcamp.com/letter-to-parents/.

5. Letter from Facebook, Inc to Chairman John Thune and Ranking Member Bill Nelson, US Senate Committee on Commerce, Science, and Transportation, June 8, 2018, https://www.commerce.senate.gov/public/_cache/files/9d8e069d-2670-4530-bcdc-d3a63a8831c4/7C8DE61421D13E86FC6855CC2EA7AEA7.senate-commerce-committee-combined-qfrs-06.11.2018.pdf.

6. Claire Cain Miller, "Tech Companies Concede to Surveillance Program," *New York Times*, June 7, 2013, https://www.nytimes.com/2013/06/08/technology/tech-companies-bristling-concede-to-government-surveillance-efforts.html.

7. Kelli Marshall, "Branding Yourself As An Academic," *ChronicleVitae*, January 30, 2017, https://chroniclevitae.com/news/1681-branding-yourself-as-an-academic?cid=VTEVPMSED1; Alex Rosenblat, "There's an App for Wrecking Nannies' Lives," *New York Times*, July 12, 2018, https://www.nytimes.com/2018/07/12/opinion/gig-economy-domestic-workers-uber.html.

8. Jennifer Ma, Sandy Baum, Matea Pender, and Meredith Welch, *Trends in College Pricing 2017* (New York: The College Board, 2017), https://trends.collegeboard.org/sites/default/files/2017-trends-in-college-pricing_1.pdf.

9. Judith Scott-Clayton, "The Looming Student Loan Default Crisis Is Worse Than We Thought," *Economics Studies at Brookings Evidence Speaks Reports* 2, no. 34, January 10, 2018, https://www.brookings.edu/research/the-looming-student-loan-default-crisis-is-worse-than-we-thought/.

10. This approach is well represented by Michael Blake and Patrick Taylor Smith, "International Distributive Justice," *The Stanford Encyclopedia of Philosophy* (Spring 2015 Edition), ed. Edward N. Zalta, https://plato.stanford.edu/archives/spr2015/entries/international-justice/.

11. John Rawls, *A Theory of Justice, Revised Edition* (Cambridge, MA: Harvard University Press, 1999), 99.

12. In support of the natural duty of justice as grounding the political obligation to obey just institutions, see Jeremy Waldron, "Special Ties and Natural Duties," *Philosophy & Public Affairs* 22, no. 1 (Winter, 1993): 3–30 and Allen Buchanan, "Political Legitimacy and Democracy," *Ethics* 112 (July 2002): 689–719. For criticisms of that view, see George Klosko, "Political Obligation and the Natural Duties of Justice," *Philosophy & Public Affairs* 23, no. 3 (Summer 1994): 251–270 and A. John Simmons, "The Duty to Obey and Our Natural Moral Duties," in *Is There a Duty to Obey the Law?*, ed. Christopher Heath Wellman and A. John Simmons (New York: Cambridge University Press, 2005), 93–196.

13. Some recent work has moved beyond the paradigm of civil disobedience to consider justifications of outright resistance to domestic and international institutions. See Tommie Shelby, "Justice, Deviance, and the Dark Ghetto," *Philosophy & Public Affairs* 35, no. 2 (2007): 126–160; Javier Hidalgo, "Resistance to Unjust Immigration Restrictions," *Journal of Political Philosophy* 23, no. 4 (December 2015): 450–470; Candice Delmas, *A Duty to Resist: When Disobedience Should Be Uncivil* (New York: Oxford University Press, 2018).

14. Rawls, *Theory of Justice*, 99.

15. John Rawls, *The Law of Peoples; with "The Idea of Public Reason Revisited"* (Cambridge, MA: Harvard University Press, 1999), 117.

16. Rawls, *Theory of Justice*, 297.

17. Rawls, *Theory of Justice*, 298.

18. Rawls, *Theory of Justice*, 99.

19. Rawls, *Theory of Justice*, 99; see also 238.

20. Rawls, *Theory of Justice*, 296.
21. Rawls, *Theory of Justice*, 296.
22. Rawls, *Theory of Justice*, 7.
23. John Simmons, "The Particularity Problem," *APA Newsletter on Philosophy and Law* 7 (2007): 18–27.
24. John Simmons, *Moral Principles and Political Obligations* (Princeton, NJ: Princeton University Press, 1981), 154.
25. Rawls, *Theory of Justice*, 298–299.
26. Rawls, *Theory of Justice*, 229.
27. Kwame Anthony Appiah, *The Ethics of Identity* (Princeton, NJ: Princeton University Press, 2007), 184–185.
28. On the purported impossibility of international solidarity as an objection to global justice, see David Heyd, "Justice and Solidarity: The Contractarian Case against Global Justice," *Journal of Social Philosophy* 38, no. 1 (Spring 2007): 112–130. In her account of racial injustice, Juliet Hooker likewise argues that solidarity is a precondition to redistribution and rejects the idea that solidarity can be based in common interests. See Hooker, *Race and the Politics of Solidarity* (New York: Oxford University Press, 2009).
29. Avery Kolers, "The Priority of Solidarity Over Justice," *Journal of Applied Philosophy* 31, no. 4 (November 2014): 420–433.
30. Kurt Bayertz, "Four Uses of 'Solidarity,'" in *Solidarity*, ed. Kurt Bayertz (Dordrecht: Kluwer, 1999), 3–28 at 16.
31. See, for example, Jodi Dean, *Solidarity of Strangers: Feminism after Identity Politics* (Berkeley: University of California Press, 1996); Sally J. Scholz, *Political Solidarity* (Princeton, NJ: Princeton University Press, 2008); Carol C. Gould, "Transnational Solidarities," *Journal of Social Philosophy* 38, no. 1 (Spring 2007): 148–164; Chandra Talpade Mohanty, *Feminism Without Borders: Decolonizing Theory, Practicing Solidarity* (Durham, NC: Duke University Press, 2003); Edwina Barvosa, "Mestiza Consciousness in Relation to Sustained Political Solidarity: A Chicana Feminist Interpretation of the Farmworker Movement," *Aztlan: A Journal of Chicano Studies* 36, no. 2 (2011): 121–154.
32. On cosmopolitan solidarity, see Simon Derpmann, "Solidarity and Cosmopolitanism," *Ethical Theory and Moral Practice* 12, no. 3 (2009): 303–315. On solidarity and the welfare state, see Bayertz, "Four Uses of 'Solidarity,'" 21–25; and Jürgen Habermas, *The Postnational Constellation* (Cambridge, MA: MIT Press, 2001).
33. Andrea Sangiovanni also connects solidarity to the natural duty of justice, but doesn't consider fully how the requirements of the duty would be changed by non-ideal circumstances; instead he assumes the kind of robust reciprocity appropriate to ideal theory. See "Solidarity as Joint Action," *Journal of Applied Philosophy* 32, no. 4 (2015): 340–359, at 353–356. Aaron James similarly employs the natural duty of justice to specify duties of global justice, but unjustifiably assumes that only the territorially bound nation-state can address the assurance problem. Focusing on distributive justice, James constructs an ideal theory constrained by the assumption that we cannot know with any confidence what an alternative to a state-based international

order would look like. But this produces a status quo bias because, like Sangiovanni's account, it fails to heed the way our own practice of theorizing is affected by our habituation to injustice, as argued in chapter 4. See James, *Fairness in Practice: A Social Contract for a Global Economy* (New York: Oxford University Press, 2012), especially 103–127.

34. Mohanty, *Feminism Without Borders*, 3.

35. Roberto Mangabeira Unger, *False Necessity: Anti-Necessitarian Social Theory in the Service of Radical Democracy, Revised Edition* (New York: Verso, 2004), 267.

36. Allison Weir, *Identities and Freedom* (New York: Oxford University Press, 2011), 17.

37. Tommie Shelby, *We Who Are Dark: The Philosophical Foundations of Black Solidarity* (Cambridge, MA: Harvard University Press, 2005), 150.

38. Shelby, *We Who Are Dark*, 151.

39. Robert Gooding-Williams, *In the Shadow of Du Bois: Afro-Modern Political Thought in America* (Cambridge, MA: Harvard University Press, 2011), 231.

40. Avery Kolers's theory of solidarity also aspires to philosophically identify the object of solidarity apart from politics through "the construction of object groups in distinct circumstance zones," though he also acknowledges "it is impossible to completely solve this problem in theory." See Kolers, *A Moral Theory of Solidarity* (New York: Oxford University Press, 2016), 110.

41. "US and Chinese Labour Groups Collaborate Over Wal-Mart Strikes," *Reuters*, July 19, 2016; http://www.scmp.com/news/china/policies-politics/article/1991467/us-and-chinese-labour-groups-collaborate-over-wal-mart.

42. I thank an anonymous reviewer for drawing out this implication.

43. John Rawls, *Political Liberalism* (New York: Columbia University Press, 1996), xliv.

44. Kolers, *A Moral Theory of Solidarity*, 31–32.

45. Avery Kolers, "Dynamics of Solidarity," *Journal of Political Philosophy* 20, no. 4 (2012): 365–383, at 370.

46. Kolers, *A Moral Theory of Solidarity*, 47.

47. Kolers, *A Moral Theory of Solidarity*, 51.

48. Kolers, *A Moral Theory of Solidarity*, 149.

49. Scholz, *Political Solidarity*, 34.

50. Scholz, *Political Solidarity*, 254.

51. Scholz, *Political Solidarity*, 75.

52. Rawls, *Theory of Justice*, 336.

53. On the contemporary relation between ethical consumption and political action, see Margaret M. Willis and Juliet B. Schor, "Does Changing a Light Bulb Lead to Changing the World? Political Action and the Conscious Consumer," *Annals of the American Academy of Political and Social Science* 644, no. 1 (November 2012): 160–190.

54. Leif Wenar offers a dramatic description of the workers' meeting in *Blood Oil: Tyrants, Violence, and the Rules that Run the World* (New York: Oxford University Press, 2016): 333–334. For context on the Manchester Chamber of Commerce and Lancashire's cotton economy during the Civil War, see Sven Beckert, *Empire of Cotton: A Global History* (New York: Vintage Books, 2014): 242–273.

55. José Medina, *The Epistemology of Resistance: Gender and Raical Oppression, Epistemic Injustice, and Resistant Imaginations* (New York: Oxford University Press, 2013).

56. Clarissa Hayward, "Responsibility and Ignorance: On Dismantling Structural Injustice," *Journal of Politics* 79, no. 2 (2017): 396–408

57. Kolers, *A Moral Theory of Solidarity*, 39.

58. Kolers, "Dynamics of Solidarity," 371.

59. Kolers, "Dynamics of Solidarity," 373.

60. Kolers, *A Moral Theory of Solidarity*, 47.

61. Mark R. Warren, *Fire in the Heart: How White Activists Embrace Racial Justice* (New York: Oxford University Press, 2010), 42, 81.

62. For other views that do not ground duties of global justice in existing institutions but rather in the need for their reform, see Miriam Ronzoni, "The Global Order: A Case of Background Injustice? A Practice-Dependent Account," *Philosophy & Public Affairs* 37, no. 3 (2009): 229–256; Arash Abizadeh, "Cooperation, Pervasive Impact, and Coercion: On the Scope of Distributive Justice," *Philosophy & Public Affairs* 35, no. 4 (2007): 318–358.

63. Iris Marion Young, "Responsibility and Global Labor Justice," *The Journal of Political Philosophy* 12, no. 4 (2004): 365–388; Young, "Responsibility and Global Justice: A Social Connection Model," *Social Philosophy and Policy* 23, no. 1 (2006): 102–130; and Young, *Responsibility for Justice* (New York: Oxford University Press, 2011).

64. Young, *Responsibility for Justice*, 105.

65. Young, *Responsibility for Justice*, 44.

66. Young, *Responsibility for Justice*, 145. For arguments against the receipt of benefits being sufficient to generate political obligations, see Simmons, *Moral Principles and Political Obligations*.

67. See, for example, Martha Nussbaum's forward to *Responsibility for Justice*, ix–xxv.

68. See Michael Goodhart, "Interpreting Responsibility Politically," *Journal of Political Philosophy* 25, no. 2 (2017): 173–195, at 182.

69. On this point, see Carol C. Gould, "Varieties of Global Responsibility: Social Connection, Human Rights, and Transnational Solidarity," in *Dancing with Iris: The Philosophy of Iris Marion Young*, ed. Ann Ferguson and Mechthild Nagel (New York: Oxford University Press, 2009), 199–212; Christian Barry and Kate Macdonald, "How Should We Conceive of Individual Consumer Responsibility to Address Labour Injustices?," in *Global Justice and International Labour Rights*, ed. Yossi Dahan, Hanna Lerner, and Faina Milman-Sivan (New York: Cambridge University Press, 2016), 92–118.

70. Young, *Responsibility for Justice*, 159.

71. Young, *Responsibility for Justice*, 160.

72. Young draws on Onora O'Neill, *Towards Justice and Virtue: A Constructive Account of Practical Reasoning* (Cambridge: Cambridge University Press, 1996), 91–121.

73. George Black, "Your Clothes Were Made by a Bangladeshi Climate Refugee," *Mother Jones*, July 30, 2013, https://www.motherjones.com/environment/2013/07/bangladesh-garment-workers-climate-change/.

74. Daniel M. Zane, Julie R. Irwin, and Rebecca Walker Reczek, "Do Less Ethical Consumers Denigrate More Ethical Consumers? The Effect of Willful Ignorance on Judgments of Others," *Journal of Consumer Psychology* 26, no. 3 (July 2016): 337–349.

75. Young recognizes that blaming individuals for things they did not cause tends to generate resentment and so she takes pains to say that responsible individuals who fail to promote justice should not be blamed, but that "we can and should be criticized for not taking action, not taking enough action, taking ineffective action, or taking action that is counterproductive" (*Responsibility for Justice*, 144). But as critics like Martha Nussbaum have noted, this refusal of blame seems ad hoc. See *Responsibility for Justice*, xxii–xxiv. On neoliberal individual responsibility, see Adam Kotsko, "Neoliberalism's Demons," *Theory & Event* 20, no. 2 (2017): 493–509.

76. Goodhart, "Interpreting Responsibility Politically," 188.

77. Young, *Responsibility for Justice*, 145.

78. Ronen Shamir, "Capitalism, Governance, and Authority: The Case of Corporate Social Responsibility," *Annual Review of Law and Social Science* 6 (2010): 531–553.

79. Richard M. Locke, *The Promise and Limits of Private Power: Promoting Labor Standards in a Global Economy* (New York: Cambridge University Press, 2013); Tim Bartley, Sebastian Koos, Hiram Samel, Gustavo Setrini, and Nik Summers. *Looking Behind the Label: Global Industries and the Conscientious Consumer* (Bloomington: Indiana University Press, 2015).

80. Geneieve LeBaron, Jane Lister, and Peter Dauvergne, "The New Gatekeeper: Ethical Audits as a Mechanism of Global Value Chain Governance," in *The Politics of Private Transnational Governance by Contract*, ed. A. Claire Cutler and Thomas Dietz (New York: Routledge, 2017), 97–114.

81. As I noted in chapter 2, there are more effective forms of independent monitoring of supply chains that institutionalize meaningful worker participation and representation, such as the Accord on Building and Fire Safety in Bangladesh. But these depend for their effectiveness precisely on corporations ceding authority to other actors.

82. Julfikar Ali Manik and Nida Najar, "Bangladesh Police Charge 41 With Murder Over Rana Plaza Collapse," *New York Times*, June 2, 2015, https://www.nytimes.com/2015/06/02/world/asia/bangladesh-rana-plaza-murder-charges.html.

83. Office of the United States Trade Representative, "U.S. Trade Representative Michael Froman Comments on President's Decision to Suspend GSP Benefits for Bangladesh," June 27, 2013, https://ustr.gov/about-us/policy-offices/press-office/press-releases/2013/june/michael-froman-gsp-bangladesh.

84. Rachel Abrams, "Falling Short of Commitments to Overseas Factory Workers," *New York Times*, May 31, 2016, https://www.nytimes.com/2016/05/31/business/international/top-retailers-fall-short-of-commitments-to-overseas-workers.html.

85. As Sally Scholz notes, "Oppressors or architects of injustice will have a different relation to the solidary group and its members than those who, while not part of the resistance movement nor directly responsible for oppression and injustice, are privileged because of the unjust situation." See Scholz, *Political Solidarity*, 100–101.

86. Here I part ways with Thomas J. Donahue-Ochoa, who argues that "All systematic injustices harm *everyone* in the society that commits them," including perpetrators,

and consequently, suggests "we should not take too seriously the distinction between the victims and non-victims of injustice." See Donahue-Ochoa, *Unfreedom for All: How the World's Injustices Harm You* (New York: Oxford University Press, 2019), xii and xiv.

87. Rawls, *Theory of Justice*, 100.

88. Alison M. Jaggar, "Transnational Cycles of Gendered Vulnerability: A Prologue to a Theory of Global Gender Justice," *Philosophical Topics* 37, no. 2 (Fall 2009): 33–52.

89. Indeed, some theorists of solidarity give up the idea that the privileged party should expect any benefit in return. Carol C. Gould writes, "Although these new solidarities are implicitly reciprocal, this feature is not a salient aspect of its meaning when it pertains to better situated groups helping those worse off." See Gould, *Interactive Democracy: The Social Roots of Global Justice* (New York: Cambridge University Press, 2014), 113.

90. On the many political thinkers who endorse this line of thought, see Dana Villa, *Public Freedom* (Princeton, NJ: Princeton University Press, 2008).

91. Again, this idea is not limited to egalitarian liberals. Compare Bernard Williams's "critical theory principle," which says freedom is incompatible with social structures that manipulate people into accepting the status quo. See Williams, *In the Beginning Was the Deed: Realism and Moralism in Political Argument*, ed. Geoffrey Hawthorn (Princeton, NJ: Princeton University Press, 2005), 14.

92. Your Plan for Health, "Incentive Program for Faculty/Staff," https://yp4h.osu.edu/rewards/faculty-staff/, accessed July 19, 2018.

93. Paul Apostolidis similarly traces the interest in resisting neoliberalism shared by migrant day laborers and those with better employment in Apostolidis, *The Fight For Time: Migrant Day Laborers and the Politics of Precarity* (New York: Oxford University Press, 2019).

94. Alexis de Tocqueville, *Democracy in America*, trans. Arthur Goldhammer (New York: Library of America, 2004), 661.

95. Tocqueville, *Democracy in America*, 395. For a more thorough analysis, see Jack Turner, "American Individualism and Structural Injustice: Tocqueville, Gender, and Race," *Polity* 40, no. 2 (April 2008): 197–215.

96. W. E. B. Du Bois, *Black Reconstruction in America: 1860–1880* (New York: Free Press, 1998), 700–701.

97. W. E. B. Du Bois, "The Souls of White Folk," in *W. E. B. Du Bois: Writings*, ed. Nathan Higgins (New York: Library of America, 1986), 923–938.

98. See Du Bois, "Souls of White Folk," 926. For further analysis of this passage, see Ella Myers, "Beyond the Psychological Wage: Du Bois on White Dominion," *Political Theory* 47, no. 1 (2019): 6–31.

99. Du Bois, "Souls of White Folk," 926.

100. See Thuy Linh Tu and Nikhil Pal Singh, "Morbid Capitalism and Its Racial Symptoms," *n+1* 30 (Winter 2018): https://nplusonemag.com/issue-30/essays/morbid-capitalism/.

101. Raymond Arsenault, *Freedom Riders: 1961 and the Struggle for Racial Justice* (New York: Oxford University Press, 2006), 5.

102. Lydia Saad, "On King Holiday, a Split Review of Civil Rights Progress," *Gallup News*, January 21, 2008, https://news.gallup.com/poll/103828/civil-rights-progress-seen-more.aspx.

103. Liza Featherstone, *Students Against Sweatshops* (New York: Verso, 2002), 19–38.

104. Worker Rights Consortium, "Affiliate Colleges and Universities," December 1, 2017, https://www.workersrights.org/wp-content/uploads/2017/05/Affiliates12.1.17.pdf.

105. Clinton Yates, "Ohio State's Nike Deal Blows Away Michigan's," *Washington Post*, January 15, 2016, http://www.washingtonpost.com/news/early-lead/wp/2016/01/15/ohio-states-nike-deal-blows-away-michigans/.

106. Ashok Kumar and Jack Mahoney, "Stitching Together: How Workers Are Hemming Down Transnational Capital in the Hyper-Global Apparel Industry," *The Journal of Labor & Society* 17, no. 2 (June 2014): 187–210.

Chapter 6

1. Donald Trump, "Declaring America's Economic Independence," June 28, 2016, https://www.politico.com/story/2016/06/full-transcript-trump-job-plan-speech-224891.

2. Bernie Sanders, May 1, 2016, 8:01 p.m., https://twitter.com/berniesanders/status/726924424474042368

3. Tony Judt, "What Is Living and What Is Dead in Social Democracy?," *New York Review of Books* 56, no. 20, December 17, 2009, http://www.nybooks.com/articles/archives/2009/dec/17/what-is-living-and-what-is-dead-in-social-democrac/.

4. Samuel Moyn, *The Last Utopia: Human Rights in History* (Cambridge, MA: Harvard University Press, 2010), 42.

5. Richard Tuck, "For the British Left to Succeed, the UK Must Leave the European Union," *Vox*, July 12, 2016, https://www.vox.com/2016/7/12/12159936/brexit-british-left.

6. Joe Guinan and Thomas Hanna, "Forbidden Fruit: The Neglected Political Economy of Lexit," *IPPR Progressive Review* 24, no. 1 (Summer 2017): 14–24.

7. Richard Tuck, "The Left Case for Brexit," *Dissent Magazine*, June 6, 2016, https://www.dissentmagazine.org/online_articles/left-case-brexit.

8. Tuck, "Left Case for Brexit."

9. Quinn Slobodian, *Globalists: The End of Empire and the Birth of Neoliberalism* (Cambridge, MA: Harvard University Press, 2018), 87.

10. Notably, in other recent work, Tuck criticizes H. L. A. Hart for rejecting "the idea of a sovereign as the sole source of law." See Richard Tuck, *The Sleeping Sovereign: The Invention of Modern Democracy* (New York: Cambridge University Press, 2015), 271.

11. Christopher Bickerton and Richard Tuck, "A Brexit Proposal," November 2017, https://thecurrentmoment.files.wordpress.com/2017/11/brexit-proposal-20-nov-final1.pdf, 9.

12. Wendy Brown, *Undoing the Demos: Neoliberalism's Stealth Revolution* (Brooklyn, NY: Zone Books, 2015), 108.

13. Brown, *Undoing the Demos*, 221. Brown's call for mastery is especially striking because her earlier work diagnosed hyperbolic assertions of sovereignty as a neurotic

expression of declining state power. See Brown, *Walled States, Waning Sovereignty* (Brooklyn, NY: Zone Books, 2010).

14. Wolfgang Streeck, *Buying Time: The Delayed Crisis of Democratic Capitalism* (New York: Verso, 2014), 96.

15. Streeck, *Buying Time*, 189.

16. Wolfgang Streeck, "Between Charity and Justice: Remarks on the Social Construction of Immigration Policy in Rich Democracies," *Danish Centre for Welfare Studies Working Paper Series*, WP2017-5, 3.

17. Jürgen Habermas, "The Crisis of the European Union in the Light of a Constitutionalization of International Law," *European Journal of International Law* 23, no. 2 (May 2012): 335–348.

18. Of course, there are other critiques of Habermas's account to be made. For discussion of problems with the conception of political identity that accompanies his account of relational sovereignty, see Inés Valdez, *Transnational Cosmopolitanism: Kant, Du Bois, and Justice as a Political Craft* (New York: Cambridge University Press, 2019), 148–151.

19. Cf. Taiaiake Alfred, "Sovereignty," in *Sovereignty Matters: Locations of Contestation and Possibility in Indigenous Struggles for Self-Determination*, ed. Joanne Barker (Lincoln: University of Nebraska Press, 2005), 33–50; Kouslaa T. Kessler-Mata, *American Indians and the Trouble with Sovereignty: A Turn Toward Structural Self-Determination* (New York: Cambridge University Press, 2017).

20. Friedrich Hayek, *Law, Legislation and Liberty, Volume 2* (New York: Routledge, 1982), 61.

21. On neoliberal opposition to the EU and its predecessors, see Slobodian, *Globalists*, 184–193; Thomas Biebricher, *The Political Theory of Neoliberalism* (Stanford, CA: Stanford University Press, 2018), 181–184 and 188–192. On neoliberals favoring Brexit, see Quinn Slobodian and Dieter Plehwe, "The Neoliberals Who Opposed Europe," *Brave New Europe*, August 1, 2018, https://braveneweurope.com/quinn-slobodian-and-dieter-plehwe-the-neoliberals-who-opposed-europe; Ryan Bourne, "Hayek Would Have Been a Brexiteer," Institute of Economic Affairs Blog, March 18, 2016, https://iea.org.uk/blog/hayek-would-have-been-a-brexiteer.

22. On how penal power reinforces neoliberal economics, see Paul A. Passavant, "The Strong Neo-liberal State: Crime, Consumption, Governance," *Theory & Event* 8, no. 3 (2005) https://www.muse.jhu.edu/article/187839.

23. Carl Schmitt, *The Concept of the Political*, trans. George Schwab (Chicago: University of Chicago Press, 1995), 20 and 61. Neoliberals were also influenced by Schmitt's account of politics and economics as separate realms, though they reversed their priority. See Slobodian, *Globalists*, 10.

24. Carl Schmitt, *Political Theology: Four Chapters on the Concept of Sovereignty*, trans. George Schwab (Chicago: University of Chicago Press, 2005), 5.

25. Schmitt, *Concept of the Political*, 33.

26. Laura Valentini, *Justice in a Globalized World: A Normative Framework* (New York: Oxford University Press, 2011), 2.

27. Valentini, *Justice in a Globalized World*, 1. For an account of how "the global" be-
    came a hegemonic frame of reference in the 1990s, see Isaac Kamola, *Making the
    World Global: U.S. Universities and the Production of the Global Imaginary* (Durham,
    NC: Duke University Press, 2019).

28. William Scheuerman offers a similar criticism of Jürgen Habermas in "Global
    Governance without Global Government? Habermas on Postnational Democracy,"
    Political Theory 36, no. 1 (February 2008): 133–151. The suggestion that the fall of the
    USSR meant the end of deep political disagreement echoes Francis Fukuyama, *The
    End of History and the Last Man* (New York: Avon Books, 1992).

29. Works that do put the global justice literature in this context include Inés Valdez,
    "Association, Reciprocity, and Emancipation: A Transnational Account of the
    Politics of Global Justice," in *Empire, Race, and Global Justice*, ed. Duncan Bell
    (New York: Cambridge University Press, 2019), 120–144; Samuel Moyn, *Not
    Enough: Human Rights in an Unequal World* (Cambridge, MA: Harvard University
    Press, 2018), 146–172.

30. See Greg Grandin, *Empire of Necessity* (New York: Metropolitan Books, 2014),
    131–141.

31. Here I echo Lea Ypi's argument about the practical impossibility of disentangling
    domestic and international inequality in Ypi, *Global Justice & Avant-Garde Political
    Agency* (New York: Oxford University Press, 2012), 97–103.

32. In fact, a society that reliably protects its members from such rights violations might
    well require considerable efforts from individuals to contribute to the maintenance
    of viable police forces and similar public services necessary to ensure basic rights of
    noninterference. The distinction between burdens of noninterference and burdens
    of redistribution might thus be one of quantity rather than kind. See Henry Shue,
    Basic Rights: Subsistence, Affluence, and U.S. Foreign Policy, 2nd ed. (Princeton,
    NJ: Princeton University Press, 1996).

33. For this terminology, see Michael Blake, "Coercion and Egalitarian Justice," *The
    Monist* 94, no. 4 (2011): 555–570. Adherents to coercion theory include Blake,
    Valentini, Thomas Nagel, Mattias Risse, and Anna Stilz.

34. There is a significant literature seeking to define coercion, though not all its details
    are relevant here. This literature starts with Robert Nozick, "Coercion," in *Philosophy,
    Politics and Society: Fourth Series*, ed. Peter Laslett, W. G. Runciman, and Quentin
    Skinner (Oxford: Basil Blackwell, 1972): 101–135 and the essays, some in response
    to Nozick, collected in *Coercion: Nomos XIV*, ed. J. Roland Pennock and John W.
    Chapman (New York: Aldine Atherton, Inc., 1972). See also Joseph Raz's account in
    The Morality of Freedom (New York: Oxford University Press, 1986).

35. I say the domestic institutions of the state because there is an important related debate
    about the obligations of justice that derive from enforcing the state's borders. See, for
    example, Arash Abizadeh, "Democratic Theory and Border Coercion: No Right to
    Unilaterally Control Your Own Borders," *Political Theory* 36, no. 1 (2008): 37–65; and
    partly in response, David Miller, "Democracy's Domain," *Philosophy & Public Affairs*
    37, no. 3 (Summer 2009): 201–228.

36. Relevant defenders of discontinuity (though not necessarily of coercion theory) include David Miller, Jon Mandle, Stephen Macedo, Chandran Kukathas, Samuel Freeman, Thomas Nagel, and Michael Blake.

37. This recapitulates Kant's argument in *The Metaphysics of Morals*, largely found in §41–§49. See "The Metaphysics of Morals," in *Practical Philosophy (The Cambridge Edition of the Works of Immanuel Kant)*, trans. and ed. Mary J. Gregor (New York: Cambridge University Press, 1996), 353–603. I explicate and critique this argument at greater length in Benjamin McKean, "Kant, Coercion, and the Legitimation of Inequality," *Critical Review of International Social and Political Philosophy* (Published online August 24, 2019): 1–23, https://doi.org/10.1080/13698230.2019.1658481.

38. Thomas Nagel, "The Problem of Global Justice," *Philosophy & Public Affairs* 33, no. 2 (March 2005): 113–147, at 115.

39. Kant, "Metaphysics of Morals," 458–459.

40. Michael Blake, "Distributive Justice, State Coercion, and Autonomy," *Philosophy & Public Affairs* 30, no. 3 (Summer 2001): 257–296, at 258.

41. Michael Blake, "Agency, Coercion, and Global Justice: A Reply to My Critics," *Law and Philosophy* 35, no. 3 (2016): 313–335, at 322.

42. See Rawls, *Lectures on the History of Moral Philosophy*, ed. Barbara Herman (Cambridge, MA: Harvard University Press, 2000), 361.

43. Rawls's own justification for limiting global justice to the nation-state depends not on sovereignty but on the nature of peoples—group agents with a moral nature, made up of citizens bound by a culture of common sympathy. See John Rawls, *The Law of Peoples; with "The Idea of Public Reason Revisited."* (Cambridge, MA: Harvard University Press, 2001), 23.

44. John Rawls, "The Idea of Public Reason Revisited" in *Collected Papers*, ed. Samuel Freeman (Cambridge, MA: Harvard University Press, 199), 599. Describing egalitarian liberal accounts of justice as relational has wide currency in the global justice debate; see, for example, Andrea Sangiovanni, "Global Justice, Reciprocity, and the State," *Philosophy & Public Affairs* 35, no. 1 (Winter 2007): 3–39.

45. Blake, "Coercion and Egalitarian Justice," 557.

46. E.g., A. J. Julius, "Nagel's Atlas," *Philosophy & Public Affairs* 34, no. 2 (March 2006): 176–192.

47. Blake, "Distributive Justice, State Coercion, and Autonomy," 268 and Nagel, "The Problem of Global Justice," 129. Nagel somewhat mysteriously asserts that Blake's argument rests on "rather different" grounds (126), but whatever their differences, they do agree on what's relevant to the argument here.

48. Nagel, "The Problem of Global Justice," 128–129.

49. Blake, "Response to Critics," 320.

50. Blake, "Distributive Justice, State Coercion, and Autonomy," 269.

51. Blake, "Distributive Justice, State Coercion, and Autonomy," 272.

52. Valentini's account represents a possible exception here because she relies on a broader definition of coercion. Crucially, she counts *any* violation of freedom as a form of coercion, even when it is not intended to elicit compliance. This leads her to stand in an ambivalent relationship to sovereignty, as indicated by the odd parenthetical in

her claim that "The function of justice, that is, is to evaluate the moral legitimacy of (state) coercion" (124). See Valentini, *Justice in a Globalizing World,* 126–146, for her distinction between interactional and systemic conceptions of coercion.

53. Blake, "Distributive Justice, State Coercion, and Autonomy," 294.

54. Benjamin Powell and Matt Zwolinski, "The Ethical and Economic Case Against Sweatshop Labor: A Critical Assessment," *Journal of Business Ethics* 107, no. 4 (2012): 449–472, at 464. Emphasis in original.

55. For the argument that being forced to take a job is bad for the same reasons that coercion is bad, see Michael Kates, "Markets, Sweatshops, and Coercion," *Georgetown Journal of Law & Public Policy* 13 (2015): 367–383.

56. Powell and Zwolinski, "Case Against Sweatshop Labor," 465.

57. Matt Zwolinski, "Sweatshops, Choice, and Exploitation," *Business Ethics Quarterly* 17, no. 4 (2007): 689–727, at 701. Emphasis in original.

58. Blake, "Distributive Justice, State Coercion, and Autonomy," 265.

59. Nagel also makes this point, writing that "the only way to provide that assurance [that others will conform to desirable patterns of behavior] is through some form of law, with centralized authority to determine the rules and a centralized monopoly of the power of enforcement" (116). Similarly, Hayek says, "the task of the lawgiver is not to set up a particular order but merely to create conditions in which an orderly arrangement can establish and ever renew itself . . . This need for protection against unpredictable interference . . . is the essential condition of individual freedom, and to secure it is the main function of law." See Friedrich Hayek, *The Constitution of Liberty* (Chicago: University of Chicago, 1978), 161.

60. James C. Scott, *Against the Grain: A Deep History of the Earliest States* (New Haven, CT: Yale University Press, 2017): 219–256.

61. Friedrich Hayek, *Law, Legislation and Liberty, Volume 3* (New York: Routledge, 1982), 33. As I argued in chapter 1, neoliberals' recognition of the importance of social norms creates opportunities for reorientation in light of how they traverse the political and economic realms.

62. Richard A. Posner, "Social Norms and the Law: An Economic Approach," *American Economic Review* 87, no. 2 (May 1997): 365–369.

63. Brown, *Undoing the Demos,* 221.

64. On the political dangers of this appeal, see Elisabeth R. Anker, *Orgies of Feeling: Melodramatic Politics and the Pursuit of Freedom* (Durham, NC: Duke University Press, 2014).

65. Nagel, "Problem of Global Justice," 115.

66. Max Weber, "Politics as a Vocation," in *From Max Weber: Essays in Sociology,* trans. and ed. H. H. Gerth and C. Wright Mills (New York: Oxford University Press, 1958), 78. Emphasis in original.

67. Weber, "Politics as a Vocation," 78.

68. Weber, "Politics as a Vocation," 77–78. Emphasis in original.

69. Nagel, "Problem of Global Justice," 147.

70. Immanuel Kant, "Toward Perpetual Peace," in *Practical Philosophy (The Cambridge Edition of the Works of Immanuel Kant)*, trans. and ed. Mary J. Gregor (New York: Cambridge University Press, 1996), 343.

71. Blake, "Distributive Justice, State Coercion, and Autonomy," 281, footnote 31.

72. Eric Helleiner, "Filling a Hole in Global Financial Governance? The Politics of Regulating Sovereign Debt Restructuring," in *The Politics of Global Regulation*, ed. Walter Mattli and Ngaire Woods (Princeton, NJ: Princeton University Press, 2009), 89–120; Daniel W. Drezner, "Sovereignty for Sale," *Foreign Policy*, November 18, 2009, https://foreignpolicy.com/2009/11/18/sovereignty-for-sale/.

73. Nagel, "Problem of Global Justice," 141.

74. Nagel, "Problem of Global Justice," 143; Blake, "Distributive Justice, State Coercion, and Autonomy," 265.

75. Jean Cohen, "Whose Sovereignty? Empire Versus International Law," *Ethics and International Affairs* 18, no. 3 (December 2004): 1–24, at 24.

76. Cohen, "Whose Sovereignty?" 14.

77. Cohen, "Whose Sovereignty?" 15.

78. See Jean L. Cohen, *Globalization and Sovereignty: Rethinking Legality, Legitimacy, and Constitutionalism* (New York: Columbia University Press, 2012), 80–158.

79. Nagel, "The Problem of Global Justice," 128–129.

80. Nagel, "Problem of Global Justice," 129.

81. Nagel, "Problem of Global Justice," 128.

82. Tuck, "The Left Case for Brexit."

83. Arash Abizadeh, "On Demos and Its Kin: Nationalism, Democracy, and the Boundary Problem," *American Political Science Review* 106, no. 4 (November 2012): 867–882.

84. Amelia Gentleman, "The Week That Took Windrush from Low-Profile Investigation to National Scandal," *The Guardian*, April 20, 2018, https://www.theguardian.com/uk-news/2018/apr/20/the-week-that-took-windrush-from-low-profile-investigation-to-national-scandal.

85. On the importance of peers to the enforcement of norms, see Jon Elster, *The Cement of Society: A Study of Social Order* (New York: Cambridge University Press, 1989).

86. Deva R. Woodly, *The Politics of Common Sense: How Social Movements Use Public Discourse to Change Politics and Win Acceptance* (New York: Oxford University Press, 2015).

87. On the political construction of rape to justify coercive intervention, see Kristin Bumiller, *In An Abusive State: How Neoliberalism Appropriated the Feminist Movement Against Sexual Violence* (Durham, NC: Duke University Press, 2008). On the organizing that women of color are undertaking to reduce violence without relying on state action, see *The Color of Violence*, ed. INCITE! Women of Color Against Violence (Cambridge, MA: South End Press, 2006).

88. Monique Deveaux, "Beyond the Redistributive Paradigm: What Philosophers Can Learn from Poor-Led Politics," in *Ethical Issues in Poverty Alleviation*, ed. Helmut P. Gaisbauer, Gottfried Schweiger, and Clemens Sedmak (Basel: Springer International Publishing Switzerland, 2016), 225–245.

Conclusion

1. Quinn Slobodian, *The Globalists: The End of Empire and the Birth of Neoliberalism* (Cambridge, MA: Harvard University Press, 2018), 275–280.

2. Buck-Morss, *Hegel, Haiti, and Universal History* (Pittsburgh: University of Pittsburgh Press, 2009), 119.

3. Corey Robin, *The Reactionary Mind: Conservatism from Edmund Burke to Donald Trump, Second Edition* (New York: Oxford University Press, 2018), 239–272.

4. Adam Kotsko, "Trump as Neoliberal Heretic," *The Philosopher* 107, no. 2 (Spring 2019), https://www.thephilosopher1923.org/kotsko.

5. "Full Text: Donald Trump Announces a Presidential Bid," *Washington Post*, June 16, 2015, https://www.washingtonpost.com/news/post-politics/wp/2015/06/16/full-text-donald-trump-announces-a-presidential-bid/.

6. David J. Lynch, "Trump's China Deal Was Pitched as Boon for Working Class, but He Celebrated with Wall Street Titans," *Washington Post*, January 19, 2020, https://www.washingtonpost.com/business/economy/trumps-china-deal-was-pitched-as-boon-for-working-class-but-he-celebrated-with-wall-street-titans/2020/01/19/dfdf6296-3968-11ea-bf30-ad313e4ec754_story.html.

7. Melinda Cooper argues that naturalized gender hierarchies are internal to neoliberalism itself. See Cooper, *Family Values: Between Neoliberalism and the New Social Conservatism* (New York: Zone Books, 2017).

8. Key examples here include Thomas Nagel, "The Problem of Global Justice," *Philosophy & Public Affairs* 33, no. 2 (Spring 2005): 113–147; Saladin Meckled-Garcia, "On the Very Idea of Cosmopolitan Justice: Constructivism and International Agency," *Journal of Political Philosophy* 16, no. 3 (2008): 245–271; Richard W. Miller, "Cosmopolitan Respect and Patriotic Concern," *Philosophy & Public Affairs* 27, no. 3 (Summer 1998): 202–224.

9. See Richard Rorty, *Contingency, Irony, and Solidarity* (New York: Cambridge University Press, 1989); Stephen K. White, *The Ethos of a Late Modern Citizen* (Cambridge, MA: Harvard University Press, 2009); and Peter Singer, both his classic "Famine, Affluence, and Morality," *Philosophy and Public Affairs* 1, no. 3 (1972): 229–243, and more recently,*The Life You Can Save: Acting Now to End World Poverty* (New York: Random House, 2009). Notably, White has since argued that a concept of "political tack" must be added his proposed ethos of openness and vulnerability. See White, *A Democratic Bearing: Admirable Citizens, Uneven Injustice, and Critical Theory* (New York: Cambridge University Press, 2017).

10. For an introduction to the movement and its self-understanding, see William MacAskill, *Doing Good Better: How Effective Altruism Can Help You Help Others, Do Work that Matters, and Make Smarter Choices about Giving Back* (New York: Penguin Random House, 2016).

11. Rorty, *Contingency, Irony, Solidarity*, 198.

12. Jennifer Rubenstein, "The Lessons of Effective Altruism," *Ethics & International Affairs* 30, no. 4 (Winter 2016): 511–526.

13. See Michael N. Barnett, "International Paternalism and Humanitarian Governance," *Global Constitutionalism* 1, no. 3 (2012): 485–521.

14. Peter Singer, *The Most Good You Can Do: How Effective Altruism Is Changing Ideas About Living Ethically* (New Haven, CT: Yale University Press, 2015), 50.

15. MacAskill, *Doing Good Better*, 20.

16. On sweatshops, see MacAskill, *Doing Good Better*, 128–146; on "earning to give," see 76–78 and 147–178.

17. Joseph D'Urso, "Young, Smart and Want to Save Lives? Become a Banker, Says Philosopher," *Reuters*, July 27, 2015, https://www.reuters.com/article/us-global-charities-altruism-idUSKCN0Q10M220150727.

18. Singer, *The Life You Can Save*, 8.

19. Some of the most effective social movement organizations working on HIV/AIDS issues have pursued this linkage of demanding better policies to deal with the epidemic in Africa as well as better care in the US. See Darryl Fears, "Activists Decry D.C. AIDS Policy During Protest," *Washington Post*, December 2, 2009, http://www.washingtonpost.com/wp-dyn/content/article/2009/12/01/AR2009120103039.html.

20. For related critique of the practical inefficacy of Singer's view, see Andrew Kuper, "More Than Charity: Cosmopolitan Alternatives to the 'Singer Solution,'" *Ethics & International Affairs* 16, no. 2 (2002): 107–120.

21. Singer, *Life You Can Save*, 151. For criticism of the metaethical coherence of Singer's views on this point, see Thomas Nagel, "What Peter Singer Wants of You," *New York Review of Books*, March 25, 2010, https://www.nybooks.com/articles/2010/03/25/what-peter-singer-wants-of-you/.

22. David H. Autor, David Dorn, and Gordon H. Hanson, "The China Shock: Learning from Labor-Market Adjustment to Large Changes in Trade," *Annual Review of Economic* 8 (2016): 205–240.

23. Christoph Lakner and Branko Milanovic, "Global Income Distribution: From the Fall of the Berlin Wall to the Great Recession," *The World Bank Economic Review* 30, no. 2 (January 1, 2016): 203–232. Others dispute their interpretation of the data and argue that the lack of growth among the global 80th percentile does not capture the middle class in the US and EU, but rather reflects Japan's stagnant economy and the difficult circumstance of former Soviet countries over that period. See Caroline Freund, "Deconstructing Branko Milanovic's 'Elephant Chart': Does It Show What Everyone Thinks?," *Peterson Institute for International Economics Realtime Economic Issue Watch*, November 30, 2016, https://piie.com/blogs/realtime-economic-issues-watch/deconstructing-branko-milanovics-elephant-chart-does-it-show.

24. Branko Milanovic, *Global Inequality: A New Approach for the Age of Globalization* (Cambridge, MA: Harvard University Press, 2016), 3.

25. On inequality in China, see Shi Li and Haiyuan Wan, "Evolution of Wealth Inequality in China," *China Economic Journal* 8, no. 3 (2015): 264–287. On the number of billionaires in China compared to the United States, see *Hurun Global Rich List 2018*, February 28, 2018, http://www.hurun.net/EN/Article/Details?num=2B1B8F33F9C0.

26. Fan Shigang, *Striking to Survive: Workers' Resistance to Factory Relocations in China* (Chicago: Haymarket Books, 2018); China Labour Bulletin, "Wave of Nationwide

Worker Protests Highlights the Need for Effective Worker Representation," May 17, 2018, http://www.clb.org.hk/content/wave-nationwide-worker-protests-highlights-need-effective-worker-representation.

27. Milanovic, *Global Inequality*, 44–45.

28. Oxfam International, *Reward Work, Not Wealth*, Oxfam Briefing Paper January 2018, https://www.oxfam.org/en/research/reward-work-not-wealth, 19.

29. On the difficulty of perceiving some forms of political agency, see Sina Kramer, *Excluded Within: The Unintelligibility of Radical Political Actors* (New York: Oxford University Press, 2017).

30. James Tully, *Strange Multiplicity: Constitutionalism in an Age of Diversity* (New York: Cambridge University Press, 1995), 192.

31. Margaret E. Keck and Kathryn Sikkink, *Activists beyond Borders: Advocacy Networks in International Politics* (Ithaca, NY: Cornell University Press, 1998), 10–29.

32. Allison Weir, *Identities and Freedom* (New York: Oxford University Press, 2011), 78.

33. Richard H. King, *Civil Rights and the Idea of Freedom* (New York: Oxford University Press, 1992), 71.

34. Quoted in Mark R. Warren, *Fire in the Heart: How White Activists Embrace Racial Justice* (New York: Oxford University Press, 2010), 87.

35. On counterpublics, see Sharon Krause, *Freedom Beyond Sovereignty: Reconstructing Liberal Individualism* (University of Chicago Press, 2015), 107–124.

36. Warren, *Fire in the Heart*, 89.

37. Mark E. Warren offers a good discussion of the variety of skills one can acquire in *Democracy and Association* (Princeton, NJ: Princeton University Press, 2001), 70–77.

38. John Medearis, *Why Democracy is Oppositional* (Cambridge, MA: Harvard University Press, 2015), 146.

39. See Mark R. Warren, *Dry Bones Rattling: Community Building to Revitalize American Democracy* (Princeton, NJ: Princeton University Press, 2001), 57–61 and 216–226.

40. Charles Tilly and Lesley J. Wood, *Social Movements, 1768–2012, 3rd Edition* (New York: Routledge, 2016), 48. Note that Tilly and Wood's approach is in some respects still too tidy due to its overemphasis on the state as a target of social movements. See Elizabeth A. Armstrong and Mary Bernstein, "Culture, Power, and Institutions: A Multi-Institutional Politics Approach to Social Movements," *Sociological Theory* 26 (2008): 75–99.

41. Avery Kolers, "Social Movements," *Philosophy Compass* 11, no. 10 (October 2016): 580–590.

42. For example, Anna Stilz employs Michael Bratman's account of joint agency to bolster her view tying political obligation to the state in *Liberal Loyalty: Freedom, Obligation, and the State* (Princeton, NJ: Princeton University Press, 2009). Philip Pettit argues that Rawls's endorsement of such a view of joint agency undergirds his limited view of global justice in "Rawls's Peoples," in *Envisioning a New International Order: Essays on Rawls's "Law of Peoples,"* ed. Rex Martin and David Reidy (Oxford: Blackwell, 2004): 38–55.

43. Iris Marion Young, *Responsibility for Justice* (New York: Oxford University Press, 2011), 101–104. As I discuss in chapter 5, Young's own account of the institutional

connections between workers and consumers is flawed, though her account of groups provides solid ground for an account of social movements. On groups, see Young, *Justice and the Politics of Difference* (Princeton, NJ: Princeton University Press, 1990), 42–48 and Young, "Gender as Seriality: Thinking about Women as a Social Collective," *Signs: Journal of Women in Culture and Society* 19, no. 3 (Spring 1994): 713–738.

44. Ziad W. Munson, *The Making of Pro-Life Activists: How Social Movement Mobilization Works* (Chicago: University of Chicago Press, 2008), 4.

45. Munson, *Making of Pro-Life Activists*, 5.

46. Florence Passy, "Social Networks Matter. But How?," in *Social Movements and Networks: Relational Approaches to Collective Action*, ed. Mario Diani and Doug McAdam (New York: Oxford University Press, 2003), 21–48.

47. In this, my view of social movements for global justice differs from Lea Ypi's conception of an avant-garde, whom she sees as more self-conscious. See Ypi, *Global Justice & Avante-Garde Political Agency* (New York: Oxford University Press, 2012).

48. Hahrie Han, *How Organizations Develop Activists: Civic Associations and Leadership in the 21st Century* (New York: Oxford University Press, 2014), 91.

49. Judith Butler, *Notes Toward a Performative Theory of Assembly* (Cambridge, MA: Harvard University Press, 2015).

50. Michel Foucault, "The Subject and Power," in *The Essential Works of Foucault, 1954–1984, Volume 3: Power*, ed. James D. Faubion, trans. Robert Hurley (New York: New Press, 2001): 326–348, at 341.

51. See Michel Foucault, "The Ethics of the Concern for Self as a Practice of Freedom," in *The Essential Works of Foucault, Volume 1: Ethics, Subjectivity, and Truth*, ed. Paul Rabinow, trans. Robert Hurley (New York: New Press, 1997), 281–302, at 298.

52. Foucault, "Ethics of the Concern for Self," 283.

53. For useful case studies of such difficulties, see Clifford Bob, *The Marketing of Rebellion: Insurgents, Media, and International Activism* (New York: Cambridge University Press, 2005); Ronald J. Herring, "Why Did 'Operation Cremate Monsanto' Fail? Science and Class in India's Great Terminator-Technology Hoax," *Critical Asian Studies* 38, no. 4 (2006): 467–493; Aili Mari Tripp, "Challenges in Transnational Feminist Mobilization," in *Global Feminism: Transnational Women's Activism, Organizing, and Human Rights*, ed. Myra Marx Ferree and Aili Mari Tripp (New York: New York University Press, 2006), 296–312.

54. Kate MacDonald, *The Politics of Global Supply Chains* (Malden, MA: Polity Press, 2014), 62–64.

55. Here I differ from Avery Kolers, who suggests "mechanistic 'checklist' procedures" may be adequate for addressing this problem. See Kolers, *A Moral Theory of Solidarity* (New York: Oxford University Press, 2016), 113.

Index

Hegel, G. W. F., 7, 125
  Du Bois and, 116–17
  on individual self-awareness and
    state, 97–98
  institutional influences and, 17
  Kant and, 258n53
  outer limits of freedom and, 81
  on poverty, 257n70
  Rawls and, 16, 81–85, 88–89, 99,
    100–102, 106
  and rejection of coercion, 154–55
  on subjective/objective conditions of
    freedom, 92–96
  as unlikely theorist of freedom, 82–85
  and vindication of past injustice, 129–30
Hegelian expressivism, 89–92
Hobbes, Thomas, 53, 198
Honduras, union organizing in, 177
Hoppmann, Erich, 31
human capital theory, 42–43
  impacts on individuals, 41–43
humanitarianism
  versus disposition to solidarity, 215–19
  and neglect of political factors, 5–6
  as response to neoliberalism, 215–19

"I, Pencil," 52
ideal theory, Hegel's and Rawls's concepts
    of society in, 98–99, 114
immigrants, targeting of, 211
income inequality, in US, 26, 147–48
individual interest, for living in just
    society, 151–56
individual responsibility
  Friedman and, 41
  in global justice, 3, 6, 9–10
  orientation and, 11–12, 14
  Young's concept of, 19, 166–70
individualism, neoliberalism and, 33
Industrial Workers of the World
    (IWW), 156
inequality
  humanitarian reaction to, 215–19
  justifications of, 7
  Kant and, 191–92
  naturalization of, 202
  and outer limit of freedom, 108–11
  of wealth, increased, 147
  "winners-losers" response to, 213–14

injustice
  in disorienting world, 1–9
  freedom amid, 124–29
  habituation to, 130–32, 135–36, 220
  normalization of, 36
  outer limit of freedom and, 114–15
  reproducing, 130–31
*Inquiry into the Principles of the Good
    Society, An* (Lippmann), 23
institutions. *See also* neoliberal policies;
    unjust institutions
  in Hegel's concept of ethical life, 94–96
  oppressed *versus* privileged
    perceptions of, 12
  reconciliation with, 259n70
  and shaping of concept of freedom, 156
  and shaping of wants/desires, 101, 156
interdependence
  of objective/subjective elements of
    freedom, 91, 97, 99–100
  of individuals, 95
interest, individual, for living in just
    society, 151–56
International Labour Organization (ILO)
  wage recommendations of, 51
  work-related deaths and, 1
International Monetary Fund (IMF), 5, 187
  protests against, 212
International Organization for
    Standardization (ISO), 65
iPhone
  production of, 66
  tracking through supply chain, 48
  user tracking and, 60–61

James, Aaron, 270n33
Judt, Tony, 180
just society, interest and, 151–56
justice. *See also* distributive justice; natural
    duty of justice; racial justice
  actions in accord with, 108–9
  coercion and, 188–93
  Hayek and, 33–34
  Kantian premise and, 191–94
  and question of extension, 186
  Rawls and, 81–86, 151–56 (*see also
    Theory of Justice* [Rawls])
  stability of, political dispositions
    and, 96–100